Nietzsche's Free Spirit Philosophy

CW01432877

Nietzsche's Free Spirit Philosophy

Edited by Rebecca Bamford

ROWMAN & LITTLEFIELD
INTERNATIONAL

London • New York

Published by Rowman & Littlefield International, Ltd.
Unit A, Whitacre Mews, 26-34 Stannary Street, London SE11 4AB
www.rowmaninternational.com

Rowman & Littlefield International, Ltd. is an affiliate of Rowman & Littlefield
4501 Forbes Boulevard, Suite 200, Lanham, Maryland 20706, USA
With additional offices in Boulder, New York, Toronto (Canada), and London (UK)
www.rowman.com

Copyright © 2015 by Rebecca Bamford and contributors

All rights reserved. No part of this book may be reproduced in any form or by any
electronic or mechanical means, including information storage and retrieval systems,
without written permission from the publisher, except by a reviewer who may quote
passages in a review.

British Library Cataloguing in Publication Information Available
A catalogue record for this book is available from the British Library

ISBN: HB 978-1-78348-217-7
ISBN: PB 978-1-78348-218-4

Library of Congress Cataloging-in-Publication Data

Nietzsche's free spirit philosophy / edited by Rebecca Bamford.
pages cm
Includes bibliographical references and index.
ISBN 978-1-78348-217-7 (cloth : alk. paper) -- ISBN 978-1-78348-218-4 (pbk.) -- ISBN 978-1-
78348-219-1 (electronic)
1. Nietzsche, Friedrich Wilhelm, 1844-1900. I. Bamford, Rebecca, editor.
B3317.N5425 2015
193--dc23
2015024412

∞™ The paper used in this publication meets the minimum requirements of American
National Standard for Information Sciences Permanence of Paper for Printed Library
Materials, ANSI/NISO Z39.48-1992.

Printed in the United States of America

Contents

Notes on Abbreviations

Abbreviations of the titles of Nietzsche's works have been standardized throughout the essays in this volume, generally following the model of abbreviations used by the *Journal of Nietzsche Studies*. In the case of texts where a section number alone is not sufficient to identify relevant sections of these texts clearly, Roman numerals are used to indicate the volume number of the relevant text. Where necessary, a component text title abbreviation, or in some cases an abbreviation of a chapter title, is used to indicate from which part of a text material is drawn.

KSA: *Kritische Studienausgabe*
KSB: *Sämtliche Briefe. Kritische Studienausgabe*
KGB: *Briefwechsel: Kritische Studienausgabe*
eKGWB and BVN: *Digital Critical Edition of Nietzsche's Works and Letters*
PTAG: *Philosophy in the Tragic Age of the Greeks*
TL: "On Truth and Lying in an Extra-Moral Sense"
BT: *The Birth of Tragedy*
UM: *Untimely Meditations*
HH: *Human, All Too Human*
AOM: *Assorted Opinions and Maxims*
WS: *The Wanderer and His Shadow*
D: *Dawn*
GS: *The Gay Science*
Z: *Thus Spoke Zarathustra*
BGE: *Beyond Good and Evil*
GM: *On the Genealogy of Morals*
CW: *The Case of Wagner*
DD: *Dionysian-Dithyrambs*

TI: *Twilight of the Idols*
EH: *Ecce Homo*
AC: *The Antichrist*
NF: Notebook material and fragments
NL: *Nachlass*
WP: *The Will to Power*

Acknowledgements

Some words of thanks are owed to the many people who contributed to making this volume possible, and to organizations that facilitated this work. The volume authors, participants and members of the audiences at the Warwick Free Spirit workshops and conferences all deserve particular recognition for their enthusiastic and rigorous critical engagement with Nietzsche's free spirit writings.

The Warwick Free Spirit workshops and conferences at which many of the essays in this volume were developed were funded by a grant made to Keith Ansell-Pearson by the Small Research Grants programme of the British Academy. This funding has been crucial to the work of developing much of the scholarly work collected here, and the British Academy's generous support is gratefully acknowledged.

Thanks are owed to Walter de Gruyter for granting permission to publish Marcus Born's translation of his original essay 'Perspektiven auf eine Philosophie der Zukunft in *Jenseits von Gut und Böse*', in *Klassiker Auslegen: Friedrich Nietzsche, Jenseits von Gut und Böse*, ed. M. A. Born (Berlin: De Gruyter, 2014), 1–16, and to *Pli: The Warwick Journal of Philosophy* for granting permission to publish a revised version of Christa Davis Acampora's essay 'Senses of Freedom of the Free Spirit', *Pli: Warwick Journal of Philosophy* 25 (2014): 13–33. I am particularly grateful to Christoph Schirmer and Tanja Linhardt at de Gruyter, and to Matthew Dennis at *Pli: The Warwick Journal of Philosophy*, for their kind assistance with securing these permissions.

The College of Arts and Sciences at Quinnipiac University provided me with a research stipend during 2014–2015, which allowed me to dedicate much-needed time to complete my editorial work on this project. Séan Duffy, Chairperson of the Department of Philosophy and Political Science at

Quinnipiac University, helped me to structure my teaching responsibilities in a way that proved instrumental to project completion.

Thanks are owed to Sarah Campbell, Editorial Director (Philosophy) at Rowman & Littlefield International, and Editorial Assistant Sinéad Murphy, for acquiring the project and for their support of new scholarship in Nietzsche studies, and for their many efforts in facilitating the editorial process. A reviewer for Rowman & Littlefield International provided some helpful suggestions on how the structure of the volume might be productively envisioned in terms of the complex chronology of Nietzsche's writing on the free spirit; I hope that in implementing a chronological approach as suggested, the volume presents the contributors' work—and reflects the significance of Nietzsche's free spirit within his wider philosophy—more clearly and effectively than would otherwise have been the case.

Finally, two special words of appreciation: the first to Keith Ansell-Pearson, for his encouragement and his commitment to furthering scholarship on Nietzsche's free spirit writings; the second to Simon Stratford, for his wise counsel and support.

Introduction

Rebecca Bamford

On the back cover of the original 1882 edition of *The Gay Science*, Nietzsche remarks:

> This book marks the conclusion of a series of writings by FRIEDRICH
> NIETZSCHE whose common goal it is to erect a new image and ideal of the
> free spirit [des Freigeistes]. To this series belong:
> Human, all too human. With Appendix: Mixed Opinions and Aphorisms.
> The Wanderer and his Shadow.
> Dawn: Thoughts about the prejudices of morality.
> The Gay Science.[1]

This remark immediately opens up a number of questions about the free
spirit. Who or what exactly is the 'free spirit'? What would an ideal based
upon the free spirit be like? Is the free spirit solely an image or an ideal, or is
it also a psychological type? What characteristics particularly define free
spirits? Have there been any free spirits in the past, and could one become a
free spirit? Added to these questions about the nature and characteristics of
the free spirit are additional philosophical and textual questions, such as:
what is the kind of freedom that is practised by the free spirit? What would
the relationship of the free spirit be towards truth, religion, integrity and
morality? How does the free spirit emerge from Nietzsche's middle writings
into his later works? Does the free spirit change or develop, and if so, how?

These and other questions involved in developing a clear understanding
of Nietzsche's thinking on the nature and meaning of 'free spirit/s' are lent
further complexity by Nietzsche's critical engagement with his own writing.
It is not immediately clear whether or how Nietzsche's development of the
free spirit maps onto the precise chronology of his publications, which makes
the task of accounting for how the free spirit emerged in Nietzsche's thought

more challenging. We tend to think of Nietzsche's texts as we read them today, through the currently available published editions. Yet as Nietzsche's remark from the back cover of the original 1882 edition of GS illustrates, and as careful reading of Nietzsche's works shows, the free spirit texts of the original middle writings looked rather different to how we tend see them through the medium of print editions today. Nietzsche returned to write a series of prefaces to his works in 1886, which were appended to second editions of his writings. *Human, All Too Human* is an illustrative case in point. In this case, Nietzsche wrote two prefaces, appended one to the start of what had been the original HH (which we now think of as HH I) and appended the other to *Assorted Opinions and Maxims* and *The Wanderer and His Shadow*, now gathered together as HH II.[2] Thus, analysis of the free spirit needs to track the development of the free spirit with this complex chronological development in mind.

Added to this, Nietzsche found the question of his own philosophical development challenging, and some of his later textual interventions may tempt us to follow him too quickly in reframing his earlier work. As recent analysis has suggested, Nietzsche's letters from this period of his life indicate that he had begun to see his philosophical work in terms of a process of constant development, which—when combined with the opportunity to produce fresh editions of his work with a new publisher—enabled him to pursue what his letters indicate he thought of as the process of separating his work from himself.[3] A further layer of complexity is added to the issue of understanding the free spirit writings when we factor in the relationship between the prefaces and the original version of the middle writings in which the free spirit emerges on the one hand, and Nietzsche's further remarks reframing his own works in *Ecce Homo* on the other. This volume seeks to be sensitive towards the chronological complexity of the texts while also attending to the significance of Nietzsche's remarks on, and re-engagement with, his own writing and development.

Nietzsche's initial pursuit of the free spirit ideal results in his producing some of his most interesting books, including *Human, All Too Human, Dawn* and *The Gay Science*. The free spirit also crops up in Nietzsche's later writings, such as *Beyond Good and Evil*. However, despite this, the figure of the free spirit has been among the more neglected aspects of Nietzsche's corpus of late: only a few sustained analyses of these texts have been published since 2000.[4] The scholarly work collected together in this volume represents some of the most important threads of current and emerging scholarly debate on the free spirit and aims to address the complexity of locating and examining the free spirit within the body of Nietzsche's work. The contributions in this volume will, I hope, inspire scholars and readers of Nietzsche's philosophy to pay increased and detailed critical attention to the nature, meaning and purpose of the free spirit, and to the role of the free spirit in Nietzsche's broader philosophy, both in the context of Nietzsche's middle writings and in his later works. I also hope that readers will be inspired by the contributions of volume authors to continue to critically appraise the relevance of Nietzsche's free spirit to contemporary philosophical debates, for example on the nature of subjectivity, responsibility, the ethical life, moral psychology, the relationship between philosophy, science, and experimentation, art, style, education, our pursuit of knowledge and truth, and at the most fundamental level, debate on the methods in and through which we might conduct philosophical work most fruitfully.

The essays included in this volume do much helpful work to open up additional questions and issues for further scholarly investigation. More work on the multiplicity of research problems surrounding Nietzsche's free spirit certainly remains to be done. For instance, it would be interesting to explore additional possible ways to characterize the relationships between the free spirit writings and Nietzsche's work in *Thus Spoke Zarathustra*. Paying further attention to the complex chronology of the free spirit might prove helpful to understanding how Nietzsche understands and intervenes in his own thinking in relation to his development of Z. It would also be interesting to continue addressing questions of the influences of earlier philosophers and figures in the history of ideas on the language of, and the conceptual background to, Nietzsche's free spirit writings, as well as to Nietzsche's own critical engagement with the history of philosophy through the medium of his free spirit writings. And further consideration of the commitments involved in, and the ethical and social consequences of, Nietzsche's thinking on free spirits in greater depth may provide further useful assessment not only of Nietzsche's ethics, but also the continuing relevance of his ethics to contemporary work in ethics.

Essays in the volume are grouped into two main sections: 'Origins,' and 'Developments, Applications and Extensions.' The essays are organized with the chronology of Nietzsche's free spirit writings in mind. The practical purpose of using chronology as an organizing principle is to help readers to follow Nietzsche's thinking on the free spirit as it develops in his philosophy. Adopting a chronological approach also opens up opportunities for readers to reflect upon Nietzsche's own development as a philosopher during the periods in which he is writing on the idea of the free spirit. In different ways, contributors to the volume map the trajectory of Nietzsche's thinking on the free spirit, tracing out and critically examining connections and disjunctions between different texts and arguments by Nietzsche.

The initial group of contributions in the volume, 'Origins,' focuses on the emergence of the free spirit in Nietzsche's philosophy. These essays provide a clear sense of how Nietzsche presented his thinking on the free spirit within his middle writings, *Human, All Too Human*, *Dawn*, and *The Gay Science* and pay critical attention to the difference between the initial presentation of these texts and their later reframing and amendment by Nietzsche. Essays in this section also explore the influences of earlier works by Nietzsche on these origins of the free spirit and critically examine connections and disjunctions between these texts and works from the history of philosophy on which Nietzsche drew in the process of developing his free spirit writings.

Ruth Abbey's chapter provides a detailed critical examination of Nietzsche's engagement with La Rochefoucauld. Abbey challenges previous scholarship that has suggested La Rochefoucauld's influence on Nietzsche was at its height during the middle period writing, showing how Nietzsche's references to La Rochefoucauld are chronically ambivalent across his middle period writings. Abbey also explains that there is a greater degree of continuity between *Human, All Too Human* and *Dawn* than some previous scholarship has suggested, and encourages us to pay closer and more careful attention to connections between the texts comprising the free spirit series, so that we see Nietzsche's middle writings as essential to a clear understanding of the free spirit and indeed to understanding Nietzsche's wider philosophy.

Christine Daigle's contribution explores free spirit ethics and subjectivity, attending in particular to Nietzsche's development of the free spirit in *Human, All Too Human*. Daigle contends that the subject is constituted by the world as intentional consciousness and that it also constitutes itself through its encounter with the world. According to Daigle, free spirits are phenomenologists: they seek to uncover 'raw' experience of the world and to expose how we first encountered these experiences. Daigle uses this argument to develop an account of the free spirit as a subject who understands herself as an ambiguous multiplicity, on which basis she explores the ethical relationship between self, other and world as a part of the ethical ideal of the free spirit, including self-mastery and relationships of friendship.

In his chapter on Epicurean lessons of the free spirit writings, Keith Ansell-Pearson examines the character of the free-minded ethics that Nietzsche adopts in his middle writings. Ansell-Pearson's essay begins by laying out some key points of the work of Jean-Marie Guyau, a less well-known nineteenth-century philosopher with whose work Nietzsche was familiar. For Ansell-Pearson, the value of Guyau is that his work helpfully frames the way in which Nietzsche draws upon Epicureanism in his development of a free-minded ethics in his middle writings. Based on this analysis, Ansell-Pearson provides a detailed reading of D 449 in order to support his contention that while Nietzsche's 'morality of unselfing' in *Dawn* incorporates self-cultivation, the notion of self-cultivation is compatible with human relationships of care and openness to others.

Duncan Large's essay takes up the issue of the aesthetics of the free spirit, challenging the view that Nietzsche turns his back on art in *Human, All Too Human* and addressing the comparative neglect of aesthetics-focused aphorisms of HH II in the available scholarship. Large contends that Nietzsche's desire to reject Wagner involves a desire to liberate himself from his earlier aesthetic tastes and acquire new ones involves a process of aesthetic self-re-education on Nietzsche's part in the free spirit writings, which also serve as a self-educational model for others. To substantiate his account, Large first offers a detailed reading of the 1886 preface to the second volume of HH and then considers whether the evidence from HH II (and WS in particular) actually supports the claims that Nietzsche makes about HH II in that preface.

My own chapter considers how free spirits' engagement in a process of value countercalculation and healthy ethical growth in *Dawn* is logically possible, given that Nietzsche emphasizes diverse cultivation methods for emerging free spirited selves, yet also seems to deny that a unified self that might do the work of self-cultivation exists. In order to suggest a way to resolve this issue, I contend that lending renewed critical attention to Nietzsche's use of the imagery and language of cultivation—and, specifically, of gardens and gardening—in this text can shed some fresh light on how Nietzsche's claims concerning free spirit self-cultivation may be properly accounted for. I use work by Julien Offray de La Mettrie on the relationship between nature, morality and causality—with which work Nietzsche was acquainted—in order to further illuminate Nietzsche's thinking on how the free spirits of D may plausibly be considered self-cultivators.

In their contribution, Herman Siemens and Katia Hay explore the themes of probity, laughter and self-critique in Nietzsche's free spirit writings, calling attention to the difficulty of determining who, in fact, Nietzsche's free spirits are, or might be. As they find no clear answer to this issue, Siemens and Hay focus their attention upon the process that they find Nietzsche's free spirits to be constantly engaged in: namely what they refer to as an 'endless process of liberation'. With this in mind, they examine precisely what is needed for free spirits to undergo liberation and consider the kinds of difficulties or dangers that are involved in the liberation process. In so doing, they provide a clearer account of the functioning of laughter and tragedy in Nietzsche's free spirit writings, and develop a detailed analysis of the virtue they see as characteristic of the free spirit type: probity, or 'Redlichkeit'.

The essays gathered together in the second section of the volume, 'Developments, Applications and Extensions,' focus on how Nietzsche's free spirit re-emerges in his later writings, notably *Beyond Good and Evil* and *On the Genealogy of Morals*. These chapters explore some of the ways in which the free spirit impacts upon Nietzsche's rhetorical concerns in his later writings and give critical consideration to the implications of the free spirit for a number of philosophical issues, including the pursuit of truth and knowledge, the account of subjectivity to be found in Nietzsche's later works and the issue of freedom.

Katrina Mitcheson takes up the challenge that is presented by Nietzsche's question on the extent to which truth can stand to be incorporated, as discussed in aphorism 110 of *The Gay Science*, and connects this question to Nietzsche's later writings. Mitcheson contends that in order for us to fully appreciate the significance that the figure of the free spirit has in Nietzsche's wider thought, and to fully explain its development, it is necessary to address the issue of what the incorporation of truth actually involves. She suggests that the challenge faced by the free spirit is a distinctively experimental task of incorporating truth. According to Mitcheson, an important part of what constitutes a free spirit is the capacity to engage in the experimental incorporation of truth through appreciating possible boundaries to, and perspectives and limits on, inquiry while not needing to believe that the relevant boundaries, perspectives, and limits are immutable or permanent. Thus for Mitcheson, we may understand free spirits as pursuing sceptical projects of incorporating unbounded truth.

Marcus Born's contribution provides a critical assessment of how philosophical perspectives are presented in *Beyond Good and Evil*. Born discusses how evidence on pre-publication changes to the second part of BGE show that the relationship between the figures of the free spirits and of the philosophers of the future in this text work to produce a sustained reflection on how philosophical knowledge is developed and communicated. As Born shows, readers of BGE are not expected to passively absorb a philosophical teaching but are rather invited to generate their own perspectival truths through the act of struggling with the perspectives generated by the text of BGE.

Richard Schacht provides a detailed analysis of Nietzsche's thinking on the difference between free-spirited philosophers and philosophers of the future. Schacht's primary focus is on how Nietzsche's thinking on the free spirit in *Beyond Good and Evil* leads us to the distinction between free spirits and future philosophers in BGE 44. Schacht's analysis also works to connect the philosophers of the future with Nietzsche's writings completed after *Thus Spoke Zarathustra*. As Schacht contends, the philosopher of the future is particularly important to Nietzsche's wider philosophy and his critical engagement with values because it is this future philosopher who is best equipped to conduct the work of value creation.

In her contribution, Christa Acampora lays out the multiple senses of freedom that are at work within the broad sense of Nietzsche's free spirits as free, focusing in particular on Nietzsche's remarks in *Beyond Good and Evil*. Acampora differentiates between positive and negative senses of free-spirited freedom, and having surveyed some of these senses, examines their relevance to ongoing analysis of Nietzsche's views on agency and subjectivity. She shows that Nietzsche's free spirits incorporate a distinctive lack of attachment, which makes possible in them the enabling capacity of being free to form significant relations with others. The independence of the free spirit, so conceived, opens up the possibility of a different social or political structure.

Paul Bishop's chapter draws upon the work of Kant and of Jung in order to critically respond to the issue of what Nietzsche is attempting to express with his concept of the 'free spirit'. Bishop contends that the concept of 'der Freigeist' or 'der freie Geist' can be translated as 'free mind'. He proposes that Nietzsche's free mind may be read in the light of Kant, as a variation on Kant's concept of free beauty and hence as fundamentally an aesthetic concept, and that it may also be read in the wake of Jung along Idealist or perhaps even Neoplatonist lines. For Bishop, these interpretative possibilities open up fresh questions for Nietzsche scholarship, including whether Nietzsche's thinking on Plato was ultimately mistaken, whether it is possible to be a Nietzschean and an Idealist, and whether the free spirit may actually be seeking to become free from Nietzsche himself.

Daniel Conway draws on Nietzsche's retrospective prefaces of 1886–1887 to ground a critical engagement with the ideal of the free spirit. Conway's particular point of departure for commencing this analysis are Nietzsche's claims concerning the snares for his readers, as discussed in his preface to HH I. Having established reasons to be suspicious that we properly understand the fate of the free spirit in Nietzsche's later works, Conway develops an account of the fate of the free spirit through an analysis of the relationship between Nietzsche's free spirits and the 'last idealists' who are discussed in *On the Genealogy of Morals* (III 24). Conway argues that in GM III 24, Nietzsche is addressing a problem of mistaken belief among certain members of his readership: while those who identify as free spirits may genuinely believe themselves to be free spirits, they are in fact not as free as Nietzsche has encouraged them to believe themselves to be. According to Conway, these readers are the last idealists, who cannot themselves become the free spirits. However, as idealists, these mistaken readers still have substantial value to Nietzsche because their idealism forms the basis of a possible critical engagement with the ascetic ideal.

The concluding contribution of the volume is by Andreas Urs Sommer, who examines the figures of Nietzsche's free spirit and freed spirit in the writings of 1888. Sommer argues that Nietzsche's 1888 texts can be read as a form of self-empowerment of the free spirit. He traces out the transformations of free spirit and freed spirit in these later writings, arguing that the freed spirit is a legislator as well as an experimenter and a tempter. Sommer carefully differentiates between Nietzsche's tendency in these later writings to offer somewhat extreme retrospective claims about the free spirit as it is presented in his earlier works, and how Nietzsche's writing in *Ecce Homo* effectively projects the freed spirit's role of the legislator back onto the figure of Zarathustra. Sommer's analysis concludes with a question that remains pressing for all of us as readers of Nietzsche's free spirit writings: do the works of 1888 suggest that Nietzsche ultimately fails to demonstrate that the figure of the freed spirit succeeds in producing new and positive legislation—or is Nietzsche challenging us to become the philosophers of the future?

NOTES

1. Friedrich Nietzsche, *The Gay Science. With a Prelude in Rhymes and an Appendix of Songs*, trans. Walter Kaufmann (New York: Vintage Books, 1974).
2. On the interpretative importance of the 1886–1887 prefaces, see for example Claus-Artur Scheier, *Friedrich Nietzsche. Ecce Auctor: Die Vorreden von 1886*, ed. Claus-Artur Scheier (Hamburg: Felix Meiner Verlag, 1990); Keith Ansell-Pearson, 'Toward the *Übermensch*: Reflections on the Year of Nietzsche's *Daybreak*', *Nietzsche-Studien* 23 (1994): 123–45; Daniel W. Conway, 'Annunciation and Rebirth: The Prefaces of 1886', in *Nietzsche's Futures*, ed. John Lippitt (London: Macmillan, 1999), 30–47.
3. See for example Maria Cristina Fornari, "'And so I Will Tell Myself the Story of My Life". Nietzsche in His Last Letters (1885–1889)', in *As the Spider Spins: Essays on Nietzsche's Critique and Use of Language*, ed, João Constâncio and Maria João Mayer Branco (Berlin/Boston: Walter de Gruyter, 2012), 281–96.
4. Relevant scholarship includes Ruth Abbey, *Nietzsche's Middle Period* (Oxford: Oxford University Press, 2000); Amy Mullin, 'Nietzsche's Free Spirit', *Journal of the History of Philosophy* 38(3) (July 2000): 383–405; Matthew Meyer, 'The Three Metamorphoses of Nietzsche's Free Spirit,', *International Studies in Philosophy* 38(3) (2006): 49–63. Recently, Paul Franco has published a critical analysis of the free spirit 'trilogy', by which is understood *Human, All Too Human, Dawn* and the first four books of *The Gay Science*. See Franco, *Nietzsche's Enlightenment: The Free Spirit Trilogy of the Middle Period* (Chicago and London: University of Chicago Press, 2011).

BIBLIOGRAPHY

Abbey, Ruth. *Nietzsche's Middle Period*. Oxford: Oxford University Press, 2000.
Ansell-Pearson, Keith. 'Toward the Übermensch: Reflections on the Year of Nietzsche's Daybreak,' Nietzsche-Studien 23 (1994): 123–45.
Conway, Daniel W. 'Annunciation and Rebirth: The Prefaces of 1886'. In Nietzsche's Futures, edited by John Lippitt, 30–47. London: Macmillan, 1999.
Fornari, Maria Cristina. "'And so I Will Tell Myself the Story of my Life." Nietzsche in His Last Letters (1885–1889)'. In *As the Spider Spins: Essays on Nietzsche's Critique and Use of Language*, edited by João Constâncio and Maria João Mayer Branco, 281–96. Berlin/Boston: Walter de Gruyter, 2012.
Franco, Paul. *Nietzsche's Enlightenment: The Free Spirit Trilogy of the Middle Period*. Chicago and London: University of Chicago Press, 2011.
Meyer, Matthew. 'The Three Metamorphoses of Nietzsche's Free Spirit'. *International Studies in Philosophy* 38(3) (2006): 49–63.
Mullin, Amy. 'Nietzsche's Free Spirit'. *Journal of the History of Philosophy* 38(3) (July 2000): 383–405.
Nietzsche, Friedrich. *Beyond Good and Evil*. Translated by Marion Faber. Oxford: Oxford University Press, 1998.
Nietzsche, Friedrich. *Dawn: Thoughts on the Presumptions of Morality*. Translated by Brittain Smith. Stanford: Stanford University Press, 2011.
Nietzsche, Friedrich. *Ecce Homo: How to Become What You Are*. Translated by Duncan Large. Oxford and New York: Oxford University Press, 2007.
Nietzsche, Friedrich. *The Gay Science. With a Prelude in Rhymes and an Appendix of Songs*. Translated by Walter Kaufmann. New York: Vintage Books, 1974.

Nietzsche, Friedrich. *Thus Spoke Zarathustra: A Book for Everyone and Nobody*. Translated by Graham Parkes. Oxford: Oxford University Press, 2005.

Scheier, Claus-Artur. *Friedrich Nietzsche. Ecce Auctor: Die Vorreden von 1886*. Edited and introduced by Claus-Artur Scheier. Hamburg: Felix Meiner Verlag, 1990.

I

Origins

Chapter One

Skilled Marksman and Strict Self-Examination

Nietzsche on La Rochefoucauld

Ruth Abbey

Nietzsche's writings, both published and unpublished, contain thirty-nine references to the seventeenth-century French moralist, La Rochefoucauld (1613–1680).[1] Twenty of these occur during the years he was composing and publishing his middle period works (1876–1882). Twelve of those twenty middle-period mentions appear in published writings, with nine of the dozen being clustered in HH.[2] After the middle period, the vast bulk of the references to La Rochefoucauld appear in unpublished manuscripts. Based on the published works, it is easy to see why Brendan Donnellan finds that 'La Rochefoucauld's influence upon the German . . . was at its height, in the middle or aphoristic period'.[3] Robert Pippin, however, argues that the impact of the French moralist tradition, which includes Montaigne and Pascal along with La Rochefoucauld and others, persists beyond the middle period through its effect on Nietzsche's conception of himself as a psychologist.[4] Pippin even argues that the best way to understand Nietzsche is 'as one of the great "French moralists" . . . that is how he sees himself . . . [and] what he is trying "to do" with his work'.[5]

This chapter is based on an exhaustive survey of Nietzsche's remarks about La Rochefoucauld across his corpus. There are, of course, influences and engagements that such name counting cannot capture: Nietzsche could easily have La Rochefoucauld in mind without mentioning him,[6] just as he could have been affected by the moralist in ways that he himself was unaware of. So we must exercise caution in inferring too much from explicit references. However, these numbers do usefully suggest two things: first,

13

that although Nietzsche had, according to Donnellan, been familiar with the moralist's work since his student days,[7] his direct invocation of La Rochefoucauld is one of the things that separates the middle-period writings from the earlier works. Secondly, even though he continued to think with, about, and against La Rochefoucauld, Nietzsche grew less willing to make this engagement as explicit as he had in the middle period.

On the basis of this survey, I question Donnellan's claim that the middle period marks the high point of La Rochefoucauld's influence on Nietzsche: it is simply then that it was most visible. And within the published works, Nietzsche's overt engagement was concentrated in, without being confined to, HH. But even during the middle period, he was ambivalent about the Duc de La Rochefoucauld, and remained so for most of his oeuvre. While Nietzsche admires the moralist's psychological perspicacity, he worries that La Rochefoucauld's approach is reductionist, that it sees only the bad in humans, and that it colludes with Christianity. For all his skepticism about human motivation then, La Rochefoucauld is ultimately insufficiently skeptical about how he evaluates that motivation. This concern is encapsulated in a notebook entry from the time between the publication of D and GS, which says that La Rochefoucauld

> denies humans' good qualities but should also have been suspicious of the supposedly evil ones. When the skeptical moralist mistrusts morality, it still remains to him to be skeptical about his mistrust [leugnete die 'guten' Eigenschaften des Menschen—er hätte auch die „bösen' leugnen sollen. Wenn der moralische Skeptiker beim Mißtrauen gegen die Moral angelangt ist,so bleibt ihm noch ein Schritt zu thun—die Skepsis gegen sein Mißtrauen]. (NF-1882, 3[1])

Such persistent reservations give us pause before Pippin's claim, too: although Nietzsche strove to emulate this French moralist in some respects, there are others in which he did not model himself after La Rochefoucauld and, indeed, sought to avoid some of the pitfalls he sees the moralist as prey to.

It seems reasonable to infer that Nietzsche's relationship to Paul Rée is a major factor explaining his shifting willingness to cite La Rochefoucauld in his published writings. Nietzsche and Rée met in 1873 and went on to become firm friends and close collaborators.[8] Rée is said to have carried a copy of La Rochefoucauld's major work, the *Maxims,* with him at all times and strove to emulate the duke's pithy writing style.[9] It cannot be a coincidence that only after encountering Rée does Nietzsche begin to cite La Rochefoucauld, despite his longer standing knowledge of and admiration for the duke's work.[10] With the close of the middle period, Nietzsche and Rée's friendship was in disarray, never to be repaired and, from this time onward, references to La Rochefoucauld are largely consigned to the notebooks. There is no obvious reason why Nietzsche should minimize his presence in his published works other than that citing the duke is a reminder of his former close connection to Rée.[11] A good illustration of the link between these two figures in Nietzsche's mind comes from the notebooks of 1883, right around the time of the rupture with Rée. Praising French writers such as Montaigne, Chamfort, Pascal and Stendahl, in addition to the duke, Nietzsche slides into a seemingly unrelated observation about Rée's personality (NF-1883, 7[17]). The Rée variable suggests that Nietzsche's references to La Rochefoucauld are rarely simply that, for in thinking with the duke, Nietzsche is also thinking with, about, and against Rée.[12] This further implies that in praising or criticizing the moralist, Nietzsche may be also covertly praising or criticizing Rée.

CHRISTIAN SCIENCE

The first reference to La Rochefoucauld in Nietzsche's published works appears at the outset of book 2 of HH. HH 35 is an important passage within the middle period for a number of reasons. It contains the first direct reference to HH's title, opening with remarks about the effects of reflecting on the 'human, all too human'.[13] Second, Nietzsche equates such reflection with 'psychological observation' [die psychologische Beobachtung] and in so doing echoes the title of Rée's collection of aphorisms, *Psychological Observations* [Psychologische Beobachtungen], published in 1875. Third, the passage testifies in other ways to the impact of Rée on Nietzsche's thinking at this stage of his intellectual career. Book 2's title, 'On the History of the Moral Sensations' ['Zur Geschichte der moralischen Empfindungen'], alludes to a work published by Rée in the previous year, *On the Origins of the Moral Sensations* [Der Ursprung der moralischen Empfindungen] (Nietzsche cites this in HH 37 and HH 133). Finally, in addition to alluding to the aphorism via the reference to Rée's 1875 collection, this passage makes first explicit mention of the aphorism as a genre. Nietzsche points out that although short, sharp sentences that penetrate the heart and puncture the pride provide ideal vehicles for truths about human psychology, they are very difficult to compose. Those who have never attempted this craft—and that is the vast majority—fail to appreciate the challenge it poses. Although the passage ends by talking about readers of maxims, Nietzsche could have Rée in mind here, tacitly either applauding his success at the difficult task of composing aphorisms or excusing his failure at the same.

This important passage also enumerates the benefits of psychological observation. Its practice affords relief from the burdens of living because when one is on the hunt for insights into the human psyche, any situation, no matter how awkward or dull, can turn a profit. The rewards that such observations bring have, however, been forgotten as Nietzsche laments that he lives in an age inept and inexperienced at generating psychological insights. Not only do his contemporaries fail to engage in psychological observation, they do not even know earlier experts in this art, such as La Rochefoucauld. Rare is it to find anyone who has read this 'great master of the psychological maxim' (HH 35), and even rarer to find someone who reads without reviling him. This is, of course, indirect praise for Rée as a rare individual. Like Rée, but unlike most of their contemporaries, Nietzsche also appreciates the maxim as a medium of psychological aperçus. In this way, he is continuing to present himself as an untimely thinker, but in the middle period, his influences and interests differ from those in the essays that comprise the *Untimely Meditations*.

But Nietzsche also insists on the timeliness of such untimely reflections, urging that close psychological observation is now necessary. It represents the way forward by freeing people of the errors and misjudgements of previous doctrines, based as they were on false psychological premises, such as the belief in unegoistic action (HH 37). Rée is 'one of the boldest and coldest of thinkers' [einer der kühnsten und kältesten Denker] (HH 37), and their age needs such cold intellects (HH 38). So although La Rochefoucauld's legacy is largely dormant in contemporary Europe, Nietzsche believes that he and Rée are in the process of reviving it, firm in the conviction that the present and the future need these unfashionable insights into the realities and complexities of human motivation.

La Rochefoucauld reappears in HH 36 as Nietzsche, in the interests of balance, weighs the disadvantages of psychological observation. The major disadvantage is that psychological insight corrodes belief in human goodness. Disabusing humans of their faith in benign human nature can diminish their happiness and can even reduce the amount of goodness in the world by making people mutually mistrustful. A suspicious approach to human motivation can, in this way, become a self-fulfilling prophecy. So there is a definite trade-off between illusion, happiness, trust in one's fellows, and 'philanthropy' [Menschenfreundlichkeit] on the one hand, versus truth and 'the spirit of science' [Geiste der Wissenschaft] on the other. The gain in truth was not listed in HH 35 as one of the advantages of psychological observation, where the focus fell instead on the comforts and consolations it provides in even 'the thorniest and most disagreeable stretches of one's own life' (HH 35). But now that such an increase has been introduced as a further benefit of psychological observation, La Rochefoucauld belongs on its side, with his tendency to deflate people's confidence in their own and others' virtuous motives. And Rée stands alongside La Rochefoucauld 'like skillful marksmen who again and again hit the bullseye . . . of human nature' [zielenden Schützen, welche immer und immer wieder in's Schwarze treffen . . . der menschlichen Natur] (HH 36).

Even though the marksmen's 'skill evokes amazement' (HH 36), Nietzsche worries that these 'masters of psychical examination' implant 'a sense of suspicion and reductionism into the souls of men' [den Sinn der Verkleinerung und Verdächtigung in die Seelen der Menschen]. This reference to La Rochefoucauld thus ends with a view of the archery team as seen from the concerned perspective of the philanthropist. In this regard, HH 36 effectively reproduces a section from the notebooks from the end of 1876 to summer 1877 where Nietzsche had coupled La Rochefoucauld and Rée as skillful marksmen, while also expressing doubts about the harmful effects of their arrows. He worries that human welfare might be damaged by the way they diminish human motives and engender suspicion about them. The italicized sections in this passage from the notebooks show the terminology they share with HH 36:

> This is the effect of *La Rochefoucauld* and *of the author of Psychological Observations*: these *sharply aimed shots always hit the bullseye*, but in the interests of human welfare one might wish that they didn't have *this effect of reductionism and suspicion*. [Dies ist die Wirkung von *La Rochefoucauld* und vom *Verfasser der psychologischen Beobachtungen*: diese *scharfzielenden Schützen treffen immer ins Schwarze*, aber im Interesse der menschlichen Wohlfahrt möchte man wünschen, daß sie nicht *diesen Sinn der Verkleinerung und Verdächtigung* hätten]. (NF-1876, 23[41])

In notebook fragments after HH, Nietzsche cycles back to this concern that the moralist's hermeneutic of suspicion entails a worrisome belittling of humans. La Rochefoucauld seems to cast a misanthropic gaze upon his species, finding only a hateful sight [den Anblick des Menschen hässlich]. Nietzsche suggests that his own approach is different and, we are left to infer, more scientific, for it does not adopt such a judgemental stance. 'We however regard man as belonging to nature which is neither evil nor good' [Wir rechnen ihn zur Natur, die weder böse noch gut ist und finden ihn dort nicht immer häßlich] (NF-1880, 6[382]).[14] A note from the following year likewise suggests that La Rochefoucauld errs by seeing only the lowest part of the human psyche and taking its measure from there (NF-1881, 11[4]). The perspicacious moralist and skilled marksman is now shown to have blinkered vision.

Nietzsche's earliest reference to La Rochefoucauld, in a different notebook entry from 1876, paired him with Christianity, for both are useful when you want to suspect humans' motives (NF-1876, 18[21]). This again betrays significant reservations about the value of La Rochefoucauld's approach, for throughout HH Nietzsche argues that Christian psychology 'served the end, not only of casting suspicion on everything human, but of oppressing, scourging and crucifying it' (141). Christianity 'crushed and shattered man completely and buried him as though in mud: into a feeling of total depravity' (HH 114). Nietzsche explains that 'It is easy to see how designating the ineluctably natural as bad, and then invariably finding it so, makes men worse then they need be' (HH 141). So once again, the danger is that this jaundiced perspective becomes self-fulfilling—it helps to shape what it claims to find.

This accusation that La Rochefoucauld is, perhaps unwittingly, perform-ing psychology in the service of Christianity persists into the notebooks from the later period as well. One passage finds that the moralist's 'consciousness of the true motive springs of nobility of mind' has been 'darkened by Chris-tianity' [christlich verdüsterte Beurtheilung] (NF-1884, 25[178]).[15] This is echoed two years later with the reference to 'the Christian darkening in La Rochefoucauld' (Die christliche Verdüsterung in Larochefoucauld) (NF-1886, 7[65]). A notebook entry from 1887 suggests that Christianity has, on the one hand, advanced psychological insight—presumably by fostering strict self-examination. But by presupposing the sinful, fallen nature of hu-man motivation, it has become an impediment to future psychological dis-coveries. La Rochefoucauld and Pascal are representatives of this double movement. [Das Christenthum bezeichnet damit einen Fortschritt in der psychologischen Verschärfung des Blicks: La Rochefoucauld und Pascal.] (NF-1887, 10[57]).[16]

So when it comes to his legacy as a psychologist, Nietzsche offered a mixed assessment of La Rochefoucauld. On the one hand, the duke is a perspicacious penetrator of the psyche and, as such, a harbinger of a more scientific attitude towards human motivation. But on the other, he exagger-ates the dark side of the psyche, and in doing so, holds himself hostage to a Christian evaluation of humans' sinful and fallen nature. Such ruminations on the risks and rewards of La Rochefoucauld's example pose pertinent questions for Nietzsche's own approach in the middle period and beyond. Why assume that psychological observation will find hearts of darkness as it scrutinizes human behavior? Or the primacy of self-love, self-interest or any other motive? A genuinely scientific approach would remain open-minded about what the close scrutiny of moral action and moral motivation will yield. Here it is worth noting that by the term *science*, Nietzsche simply means the careful, dispassionate quest for knowledge and the possibility of seeing the world as it really is, without wishful thinking or need imputing or imposing meaning and without religious and metaphysical beliefs dictating findings. Being genuinely suspicious in a scientific manner about the well-springs of human action and the gaps and contradictions between professed and actual motivations should not presuppose that all motivations will prove to be problematic.

'TIS A PITY HE'S SO NAÏVE

La Rochefoucauld is also invoked in the middle period's first sustained dis-cussion of pity. The value of pity is, of course, a topic that assumes great importance in the middle period as in Nietzsche's subsequent writings. HH 50 begins by endorsing La Rochefoucauld's views on this topic as expressed in his 'Self-Portrait'. The moralist distinguishes between those who are capable of reason and others, recommending that pity be the province of the latter. Not driven by reason, this group needs emotions like pity to spur them to help others. For the rational, pity is not only redundant but risky because it 'enfeebles the soul' [die Seele enkräfte] (HH 50). Although those who are protective of their soul's welfare should take care not to experience pity, they should nonetheless feign it when appropriate, because inferior types will be consoled by shows of pity in their direction. 'One should, to be sure, manifest pity, but take care not to possess it' (HH 50). The accuracy of Nietzsche's account of La Rochefoucauld's view here contrasts with one of the references to him in the published writings after the middle period. There La Rochefoucauld is again invoked as a critic of pity (GM Preface 5) but is said to hold pity in contempt or disdain [der Geringschätzung des Mitleidens]. This is, however, an exaggeration on Nietzsche's part. As we have just seen, the duke deems that pity can be a useful emotion for some people, either to motivate them to help others or to take consolation in expressions of sympathy from others.

But what both of Nietzsche's appeals to La Rochefoucauld as a critic of pity obscure is how little attention the moralist actually pays to pity. His most extended discussion occurs in his 'Self-Portrait' where it occupies only one paragraph among four pages. In his *Maxims*, pity is exposed as a form of self-concern, rather than genuine concern for the other. In the suffering of another, we anticipate the possibility of ourselves afflicted in that way and help them in the expectation that if we suffer misfortune, they will reciprocate at that later date.[17] Good deeds motivated by pity are, therefore, a type of self-interested insurance scheme—we pay now in case we need help later. The cognate concept, compassion, is mentioned on one other occasion, and in a way that Nietzsche would endorse. In maxim 463, La Rochefoucauld declares that expressions of compassion for our enemies' suffering are often motivated more by pride than by goodness. Showing compassion reminds them that we are superior to them.[18] But given his penchant for unmasking apparently charitable acts as self-interested, one might expect La Rochefoucauld to target pity more frequently than he actually does.[19]

While HH 50 basically endorses the view expressed in La Rochefoucauld's 'Self-Portrait', Nietzsche also accuses the moralist of being insufficiently suspicious of pity seekers' motives. He suggests that what spurs people to seek pity is not their being sufficiently stupid to be consoled by this so much as their thirst for power. They want to hurt those who have not been similarly disadvantaged or made wretched by inciting them to feel sorry for the sufferer. Such power to cause distress in unafflicted people affirms that the pitied are not wholly devoid of strength and power. Making oneself an object of pity becomes a (minor) triumph rather than a further diminution of the self. Hence Nietzsche's conclusion that 'the thirst for pity is thus a thirst for self-enjoyment, and that at the expense of one's fellow men; it displays man in the whole ruthlessness of his own dear self: but not precisely in his "stupidity" as Larochefoucauld thinks' (HH 50). So in the space of just fourteen passages within book 2 of HH, Nietzsche has gone from voicing concern about the harm that La Rochefoucauldian suspicion might do to human welfare, happiness, and what we would today call social capital, to chiding the moralist for being too sanguine about the motives of pity seekers. It is interesting to note that on three separate occasions in the notebooks, Nietzsche accuses La Rochefoucauld of being naïve (NF-1882, 4[54]; NF-1887, 9[67]; NF-1888, 12[1]). The subject matter is not pity in these instances—it varies with each entry—but nonetheless, the moralist's dearth of suspicion is a recurring theme in Nietzsche's assessment of him, as is his excess of suspicion.

PSYCHOLOGICAL EGOISM

HH's final invocation of La Rochefoucauld comes in one of its broadsides against what Nietzsche insists is the oxymoron of unegoistic action [unegoistischen Handlungen].[20] He cites the moralist's maxim that any belief that one loves one's mistress for love of her is mistaken (HH 133).[21] So in this instance, Nietzsche recruits the moralist as an ally in his campaign against the Christian-inspired fallacy that humans can act without regard to themselves. Illustrating again the close connection between Rée and La Rochefoucauld for Nietzsche at this time, the passage also directs readers to Rée's *On the Origins of the Moral Sensations*. Citing this passage, Maudemarie Clark and Brian Leiter contend that in HH, Nietzsche endorses La Rochefoucauld's 'thoroughgoing psychological egoism'.[22] As they reconstruct it, Nietzsche reasons that if morality requires unegoistical actions, but La Rochefoucauld is correct that all actions are at base egoistical, then morality is impossible. Nietzsche still follows Schopenhauer uncritically in holding unegoistical action in high esteem, while at the same time demonstrating its impossibility.[23]

Citing this same passage from HH, Paul Franco contests part of Clark and Leiter's interpretation. As I understand it, Franco agrees that in HH Nietzsche fails to question the moral premium traditionally placed on unegoistical actions but rejects Clark and Leiter's other claim that Nietzsche adheres to psychological egoism.[24] Franco argues instead that HH strives to subvert any neat distinction between the egoistical and the unegoistical. This is, in turn, part and parcel of that work's larger challenge to oppositional thinking.[25] I agree with Franco that Nietzsche was not a fully signed-up psychological egoist in HH, and that his real interest lay in destabilizing any strong separation between the egoistic and the unegoistic. And as Donnellan points out, insofar as Nietzsche exposes the egoism that underlies action, it is not in order to condemn it. He aspires towards a more neutral analysis of egoism's role in moral life, which is in keeping with the middle period's ambition to provide a scientific account of morality.[26] But Nietzsche does not reduce everything to egoism: his position is much too subtle to be described in that way. Although space precludes a detailed elaboration of this claim,[27] a sample of passages from HH serves to illuminate it. Returning to HH 133, we find him saying that 'no man has ever done anything that was done only for others and without any personal motivation' [Nie hat ein Mensch Etwas gethan, das allein für Andere und ohne jeden persönlichen Beweggrund gethan wäre] (HH 133). To assert that egoism is, or even must be, among the motives for action, and that humans cannot act without reference to themselves, is not to say that egoism is the exclusive, or even the major, motive behind all actions. Consider HH 46 which outlines a 'Sympathy more painful than suffering' [Mitleider stärker als Leiden], according to which a person suffers badly from their friend doing something shameful. One of the reasons for this suffering is that 'our love for him is stronger than his own love for himself' [sodann ist unsere Liebe zu ihm . . . stärker, als seine Liebe zu sich selbst]. Nietzsche concludes that 'the unegoistic in us . . . is affected more strongly by his guilt than is the unegoistic in him' [so wird das Unegoistische in uns . . . doch stärker durch seine Schuld betroffen, als die Unegoistische in ihm]. This passage conveys a genuine faith in not just the possibility but the reality of unegoistical love and concern. This passage, HH 46, also suggests that the breakthrough Clark and Leiter impute to D was already present in HH, for they argue that it is only with D that Nietzsche admits that 'actions can be in some sense unegoistic'.[28] Further evidence of the highly nuanced analysis of egoism offered in HH comes from considering 'the political value of fatherhood', for HH 455 outlines one way in which egoism can be broadened through paternity.

Conversely, when HH 95 gestures towards 'The Morality of the Mature Individual' [Moral des reifen Individuums], Nietzsche laments that moral action has not been sufficiently egoistic, for in the past people have paid too little attention to what really benefits them because of morality's valorizing of the impersonal. We 'suffer from the all-too-little regard paid to the personal in us, it has been badly cultivated' [leiden . . . an der allzugeringen Beachtung des Persönlichen an uns, es ist schlecht ausgebildet]. This handful of passages suggests a supple, multifaceted approach to egoism in HH. It can coexist with unegoistic motivations, and is sometimes overpowered by them. It can be expanded and modified; it has not yet reached its full potential. To hold that in HH Nietzsche is a psychological egoist (in the manner of someone like Hobbes) is to flatten out the much more variegated and fascinating psychological terrain of that work.

My claim that Nietzsche does not adhere to a monochromatic psychological egoism in HH could, however, be challenged by a section from the later notebooks. Ruminating on 'Egoism and its problem!' (NF-1886, 7[65]),[29] he suggests that, sunk in Christian gloominess, La Rochefoucauld 'extracted egoism from everything and thereby reduced the value of things and of virtues'.[30] Nietzsche presents himself as countering that by trying to prove 'that there could not be anything other than egoism'. This suggests prima facie that while he does adhere to a doctrine of psychological egoism, he sees himself as rebutting rather than following La Rochefoucauld by contending that exposing the egoism of all actions need not devalue them. However, Nietzsche's subsequent remarks in this passage support my claim, and Franco's, that rather than simply unveiling egoism as the inevitable basis of all action, Nietzsche is questioning the standard division between egoistic and non-egoistic. As he goes on to say, at that time he sought to show 'that in those whose ego is weak and thin the power of great love also grows weak—that the greatest lovers are so from the strength of their ego—that love is an expression of egoism, etc.' [den Menschen, bei denen das ego schwach und dünn wird, auch die Kraft der großen Liebe schwach wird,—daß die Liebendsten vor allem es aus Stärke ihres ego sind,—daß Liebe ein Ausdruck von Egoismus ist usw]. This does not need to be read as 'what looks like love is always egoism', but rather as showing egoism as a necessary, but not exclusive, component in great love.

SUSPICION AND REDUCTION[31]

In reading Nietzsche as subscribing to La Rochefoucauld's psychological egoism in HA, Clark and Leiter presuppose that the moralist is, in fact, a proponent of psychological egoism. In this same vein, Donnellan writes of 'the Frenchman's analysis of the ubiquitous selfishness of human nature,' while according to Pippin, the 'petty egoism' La Rochefoucauld finds 'everywhere finally belittles man (sic) unfairly'.[32] Franco insists that 'Nietzsche was never a psychological egoist in the sense that La Rochefoucauld was'.[33] In conjunction with challenging the idea that Nietzsche was a psychological egoist in HH, I dispute the view that La Rochefoucauld propounds a doctrine of psychological egoism in any straightforward way. Rather than looking at the moral world, seeing only egoism everywhere, and purveying a misanthropic belittling of humans, La Rochefoucauld is better understood as drawing attention to the mystery and complexity of the psyche.

Rather than reductively flattening out all motivation to egoism or self-love, the moralist depicts most things as pluri-causal. This, in turn makes inferences about motivation, and that which is morally praise- or blame-worthy on the basis of observed actions, highly dubious. As he says, 'Vanity, shame, and especially temperament, often form the worth of men and the virtue of women' [La vanité, la honte, et surtout le tempérament, font **souvent** la valuer des hommes, et la vertu des femmes].[34] The way that different, and sometimes radically different, impulses can contribute to a single out-come is clear in Maxim 213. 'The love of glory, the fear of shame, the idea of making one's fortune, the desire to make life comfortable and agreeable, and the intent to lower others, are often the causes of that worth which is so celebrated among humans' [L'amour de la gloire, la crainte de la honte, le dessein de faire fortune, le désir de rendre notre vie commode et agréable, et l'envie d'abaisser les autres, sont **souvent** les causes de cette valeur si célèbre parmi les homes]. Conversely, what is notionally the same drive can produce very diverse effects in different individuals: 'Avarice often produces contrary effects; there is an infinite number of humans who sacrifice their whole good for dubious and distant hopes, others scorn great future gains in favor of small current interests' [L'avarice produit souvent des effets contra-ires: il y a un nombre infini de gens qui sacrificent tout leur bien à des espérances douteuses et eloginées, d'autres méprisent de grands avantages à venir pour de pétits intérêts presents].[35] In this same vein, Maxim 233 offers a long rumination on the different sorts of hypocrisy involved in affliction.

Within each individual, action can be produced by a set of competing urges and interests, making a pure drive or motive rare indeed. Even disen-tangling the various impulses that operate on any occasion is difficult, either in oneself or in others. As a consequence of the psyche's mystery and com-plexity, La Rochefoucauld cautions against placing too much faith in appear-ances: 'The world more often rewards the appearance of merit than merit itself' [Le monde récompense **plus souvent** les apparences du mérite que le mérite même].[36] He repeatedly reveals that moral action can be much more than, much less than, quite different from, or the exact opposite of, what it is taken to be. But to tell of the difficulty of locating 'le mérite même' is not to deny its existence. It might be difficult to judge 'whether clean, sincere and noble behavior is an effect of probity or of cleverness' [Il est difficile de juger si un procédé net, sincère et honnête est un effet de probité ou d'habilité], but probity can still be a motive.[37] It is worth noting too that perhaps in order to compound awareness of the complexity of moral life, La Rochefoucauld usually refrains from definitive pronouncements about the causes and consequences of moral action. Precisely because 'it is difficult to judge', he typically softens his claims with modifiers like 'often' [souvent] as the bolded sections of the quotations above indicate.[38]

The moralist neither demonstrates the impossibility of virtuous action nor sets out to destroy or discredit all values and ideals. In addition to underlining the dangers inherent in quick and clean assessments of action and motivation, La Rochefoucauld's work harbours a positive ideal—that of l'honnête homme. Recognition of this ideal reinforces the claim that his project is not simply to reduce and flatten out our understanding of psychological motiva-tion, for there is also something positive to be aspired to. Nietzsche himself evinces some awareness of this in a notebook passage from just after GS, where he observes that 'From La Rochefoucauld glimmers through a very noble mode of thinking of society at that time: he himself is a disappointed idealist' [Aus La Rochefoucauld schimmert eine sehr noble Denkart der damaligen Gesellschaft hindurch: er selber ist ein enttäuschter Idealist] (NF-1883, 7[40]).

Although space precludes a detailed exposition, the noble ideal of the honnête homme, or gentleperson, embodies an aesthetic approach to ethics, with such individuals cultivating their taste and their reason, working on themselves to become better, pursuing self-knowledge and treating others with respect and consideration. In this positive ethos that the duke adduces, terms like delicacy, subtlety, grace, the art of pleasing and gentleness are pivotal. Thus maxim 99 recommends that 'Politeness of spirit consists of thinking of things that are noble and refined' [La politesse de l'esprit consiste à penser des choses honnêtes et délicates].[39] La Rochefoucauld's writings can be read, moreover, as not only sketching a profile of the honnête homme but also helping his readers to shape themselves in its direction by distinguishing between 'the true' [les vrais] and 'the fake' [les faux] 'honnêtes gens'.[40] L'honnêteté is a rare achievement, to be sure, but it is not impossible and certainly worth striving for. An idealist disappointed is still an idealist.

IN DENIAL

As noted above, nine of the twelve published references to La Rochefoucauld from the middle-period years appear in HH. In D's sole reference to La Rochefoucauld, Nietzsche distances himself from the moralist by distinguishing two types of deniers of morality. The duke is classed among those who expose the hypocrisy and deception involved in moral life: people think, and like to think, of themselves as operating out of one set of motives when really they are driven by another. Nietzsche classes himself (and only himself, for no others are nominated), as a different kind of denier. His brand of morality denial rejects the idea 'that moral judgments are based on truths' [dass die sittlichen Urtheile auf Wahrheiten beruhen] (D 103). Although he does not elaborate the difference here, it can be inferred that La Rochefoucauld thinks that amour-propre really is a common human motivation, irrespective of how it is dressed up, concealed, or foresworn by those so motivated. In exposing self-love as among the grounds for much supposedly moral action, La Rochefoucauld sees himself to be advancing true knowledge about morality and the psyche.

But Nietzsche moves beyond this first position to suggest that judgements about morality or immorality are not based in truth, whatever the phenomenology of moral experience might be [Ich leugne . . . dass es einen Grund in der Wahrheit giebt, sich so zu fühlen].[41] He seems to be aspiring to a more radical critique of morality than that which he associates with La Rochefoucauld, without at the same time denying the value of some of the actions typically dubbed *moral* nor the danger of some of those typically deemed immoral. Although I find this passage opaque and puzzling, my guess that what Nietzsche means when he says that 'moral judgments are not based on truth' is the rejection of any sort of moral realism, indicating instead that all moral judgements are social constructions and conventions. If this is what they are, then decisions about what is moral and immoral are still important and in some ways valid, but they cannot claim the seal of eternity nor any grounding in nature or reality. So if we continue to hold some actions to be moral or immoral, it will be on the basis of a different understanding of the relationship between human action and metaphysics than heretofore.[42]

Yet Nietzsche does not repudiate this first form of morality denial entirely: indeed, he sees its type of suspicion to be correct in very many cases and of the highest use overall [in sehr vielen Fällen ein feines Misstrauen nach Art des ersten Gesichtpunctes . . . auch im Rechte und jedenfalls vom höchsten allgemeinen Nutzen ist] (D 103). In fact, his commendation of those who think in the spirit of La Rochefoucauld [im Geiste des La Rochefoucauld] suggests that the difference between morality deniers is more of one degree than kind. In referring to those who think in the spirit of La Rochefoucauld, he no doubt has Rée in mind, and as they are still friends at this point, Nietzsche might want to mute any critique of this position. Or he might really see his own position on denying morality as a modification of this other one.

In their discussion of this passage, Clark and Leiter measure a greater distance between the two types of morality denial than I do, and for them D 103 is both an 'important passage . . . of great value in understanding the argument of *Daybreak*' and part and parcel of the wider shift they detect in Nietzsche's analysis of morality between HH and D.[43] In the move from HH to D, Clark and Leiter contend, as we have seen, that Nietzsche renounces the psychological egoism of La Rochefoucauld.[44] He also questions why unegoistical actions should be more highly prized than others.[45] For Clark and Leiter, the critique of morality begun in D instigates the more searching and more original analysis ultimately developed in Nietzsche's later works.[46] This makes it a more important book in his corpus than is typically appreciated.

Julian Young also contends that an important shift occurs from HH to D, with the latter losing HH's malice. The notebooks from this time reveal that Nietzsche 'finally realizes what is fundamentally wrong with Rée's and La Rochefoucauld's taste for the dark side'.[47] Young offers a translation of NF-1880, 6[382] which, as noted above, observes that both Christians and La Rochefoucauld see humans as ugly, whereas Nietzsche's preferred position is less judgemental, deeming them neither good nor evil. The problem with Young's inference that this marks a departure from Nietzsche's earlier assessment is that a passage from the notebooks before HH makes a similar

point: that while La Rochefoucauld focuses on the non-noble human motivations, a position that goes beyond judgements about sins and virtues is more
appropriate. As Nietzsche says there, the Christian view that there are no
virtues, only sins, could just as easily be transformed into the claim that there
are no sins, only virtues. He proposes instead that no actions are good or evil
in themselves [es an sich weder gute noch böse Handlungen giebt] (NF-1876,
23[152]). The notebook passage from 1880 that Young takes to signal an
important shift cannot encapsulate a new insight on Nietzsche's part if it
effectively echoes sentiment already expressed some years earlier.

In contrast to these commentators, I position Nietzsche differently vis-à-
vis La Rochefoucauld, and also suggest greater continuity between HH and
D. One reason, as suggested above, is that I don't think that Nietzsche ever
cleaved so closely to La Rochefoucauld in HH as other commentators do.
Instead, he expressed ambivalence about La Rochefoucauld's approach to
moral life in HH and in the contemporaneous notebooks. Praise of the moralist was often accompanied by reservations, such as that his suspicious stance
corrodes humans' trust in one another, or he mistakes the worst parts of the
psyche for the whole, or he is in collusion with Christianity. Second, I do not
gauge the gap that Nietzsche puts between himself and La Rochefocauld in
the 'Two Deniers' passage to be as great as Clark and Leiter do. Nietzsche
makes it clear that he still finds much to value in La Rochefoucauld's kind of
morality denial. Third, the closing remarks of the 'Two Deniers' passage,
that some traditional moral values will continue to be valued, albeit for
different reasons than in the past, closely echoes a point from WS that certain
traditional virtues like 'moderation, justice, repose of soul' [Mässigkeit,
Gerechtigkeit, Seelenruhe] will be recognized as useful even by those who
have cast off traditional approaches to morality (WS 212). This suggests that
D is not quite the break point that Clark and Leiter take it to be.

Of course Clark and Leiter could reply that WS is close in time to D: the
former was published in 1880 and the latter in 1881. But interpreters who
underscore the differences between HH and D should acknowledge that what
became HH was originally three separate publications. When tracing subtle
shifts in Nietzsche's thinking over what is a very short, and highly experimental phase, there is something anachronistic in talking about HH as a
single entity, rather than a post hoc amalgam of three initially separate
works.[48] Moreover, the problem with saying that WS is sufficiently close in
time to share D's critique of La Rochefoucauld is that, as discussed below,
WS 214 also contains an encomium to La Rochefoucauld and his fellow
French moralists. This illustrates my thesis about Nietzsche's chronic ambivalence about the duke.

Other passages from D echo closely passages in HH, which further casts
doubt on any robust separation between these books. D 145, for example, is
subtitled 'Unegoistisch', and with its questioning of the idea that love is

unegoistic, basically rehearses the passage from HH discussed above where Nietzsche cites La Rochefoucauld's maxim that any belief that one loves one's mistress for love of her is mistaken (HH 133). Entitled 'Apparent Egoism' [Der Schein-Egoismus], D 105 reiterates the point of HH 95 'The Morality of the Mature Individual', discussed above. Again Nietzsche laments that moral action has not been sufficiently egoistic, for people have paid too little attention to what is really good for them because morality has championed the impersonal. Thus we read that 'the great majority . . . do nothing for their ego their whole life long; what they do is done for the phantom of their ego which has been formed in the heads of those around them and has been communicated to them' [Die Allermeisten . . . thun . . . ihr Lebenlang Nichts für ihr ego, sondern nur für das Phantom von ego, welches sich in den Köpfen ihrer Umgebung über sie gebildet und sich inhen mitgethelit hat] (D 105). Franco describes this as a 'change of tack' from HH, for 'instead of pointing to the egoistic basis of our putatively nonegoistic actions, Nietzsche shows that our putatively egoistic actions are not egoistic at all'.[49] Yet this is precisely the point Nietzsche makes in HA 95, so there is no straightforward change of tack.

CONCLUSION

Notwithstanding the ambivalence that pervades Nietzsche's references to La Rochefoucauld across his oeuvre, some expressions of unalloyed praise do exist. The first comes, as we might predict from Donnellan's remarks quoted above, in a middle-period text. WS groups the duke with other French writers about whom Nietzsche waxes lyrical (WS 214). So great is his admiration for this school of thought that its members not only warrant favorable comparison with the Greeks, but on measures such as wit and style, are held to surpass them.[50] Although all these writers were French, Nietzsche dubs the passage that sings their praises 'European Books', and the ability to transcend national boundaries and any related chauvinism, becomes, from the middle period onward, a trait he very much appreciates. But what is perhaps most remarkable about this passage's paean to the moralists is that on two occasions Nietzsche admits to finding himself lost for words [ich bin in Verlegenheit zu Ende zu definiren . . . ich bin wieder in Verlegenheit, meine Liste zu schliessen]. Were this a passage from the notebooks, such admissions of speechlessness would be less remarkable, but to publish a passage that twice interrupts itself by saying that it cannot utter sufficient praise for these writers is certainly noteworthy.

Three of the writers celebrated in the 'European Books' paean—Montaigne and Chamfort as well as La Rochefoucauld—are also praised in a notebook entry from 1883 which lauds France as a 'much purer nation of *Geist*' [eine viel reinlichere Nation des Geistes] (NF-1883, 7[17]) than Germany. A notebook entry from the following year again sees La Rochefoucauld paired with Montaigne, but this time they are joined by non-French figures and forces such as Machiavelli and Jesuitism. All are praised as 'the high point of honesty' [Redlichkeit] and contrasted favorably with the Germans (NF-1884, 25[74]). Nietzsche's final reference to La Rochefoucauld is also wholly positive. *Ecce Homo*'s section 'The Wagner Case' speaks admiringly of France's 'seventeenth century of strict self-examination' [härter Selbstprüfung], which passed the Germans by. La Rochefoucauld is emblematic of this invaluable psychological tradition. Not only did the Germans fail to produce thinkers of this caliber but, as we saw in the early passages of HH, barely any of Nietzsche's contemporaries read, and fewer admired, the French masters of psychological dissection. It is fascinating to see in this passage from EH that Descartes is the only other seventeenth-century figure to join La Rochefoucauld by being nominated as part of that seminal tradition. This serves as a reminder of the role Descartes played in the very first edition of HH, which, in lieu of a preface, included a passage from part 3 of the *Discourse on Method*.[51] Nietzsche expunged the passage from the book's subsequent edition, along with its dedication to Voltaire. How poorly we know Nietzsche if we don't read the original middle-period writings.

NOTES

1. Based on Friedrich Nietzsche, *Digitale Kritische Gesamtausgabe Werke und Briefe* http://www.nietzschesource.org/#eKGWB. Robert Pippin puts the number at twenty-seven in his *Nietzsche, Psychology, and First Philosophy* (Chicago: University of Chicago Press, 2010), 8, note 14.
2. The work currently known as *Human, All Too Human* amalgamates three writings. What is now its first volume was published separately in 1878 under the title eventually given to the work as a whole. What is now Volume 2 comprises two shorter writings, also originally published separately from one another. 'Assorted Opinions and Maxims', was first published in 1879, and 'The Wanderer and His Shadow' in 1880. These three writings were fused into a single, two-volume work under the title HH in 1886. Nietzsche also then composed a preface for each volume. References to HH, AOM, WS and the 1886 prefaces will not be preceded by volume number in this chapter, in order to emphasize the developmental focus of the reading that I provide.
3. Brendan Donnellan, 'Nietzsche and La Rochefoucauld', *The German Quarterly* 52(3) (1979): 303.
4. Pippin, *Nietzsche, Psychology, and First Philosophy*, 8–10.
5. Pippin, *Nietzsche, Psychology, and First Philosophy*, 9, cf. 23. Montaigne is the major model for Nietzsche in Pippin's analysis (10–12, 14). Indeed, having asserted La Rochefoucauld's importance, Pippin says very little about how Nietzsche appropriated his ideas or even what they were.
6. As seems to be the case in HH 37 where Nietzsche confesses some discomfort with the unscientific origins of psychological observation. Born in the salon, and engaged in for motives other than pure intellectual probity, the maxim nonetheless captured 'countless individual observations regarding the human and all too human'.
7. Donnellan, 'Nietzsche and La Rochefoucauld', 303.
8. Robin Small offers a detailed and informative account of their friendship in *Nietzsche and Rée: A Star Friendship* (Oxford: Clarendon Press, 2005), 3.

9. Small, *Nietzsche and Rée*, 3.

10. Cf. Jonathan Cohen's remarks on Rée's influence on Nietzsche in *Science, Culture, and Free Spirits: A Study of Nietzsche's Human, All-Too-Human* (New York: Prometheus, 2010), 52–53. It is not so much that Rée introduced new ideas or concerns but that their friendship was a force for galvanizing some of Nietzsche's existing interests. See also Thomas Brobjer, *Nietzsche's Philosophical Context: An Intellectual Biography* (Urbana: University of Illinois Press, 2008), 41, 62.

11. On Nietzsche's tendency to rewrite, or un-write, his history with Rée, see my *Nietzsche's Middle Period* (Oxford: Oxford University Press, 2000), 145–46, Julian Young, *Friedrich Nietzsche: A Philosophical Biography* (New York: Cambridge University Press, 2010), 522, and Cohen, *Science, Culture, and Free Spirits*, 124.

12. It is striking how large Rée looms in Brobjer's account of his philosophical influences and how negligible a role La Rochefoucauld occupies. Brobjer, *Nietzsche's Philosophical Context*, 42, 71, 145 n. 6 and passim.

13. I use the Hollingdale translations of Nietzsche's work, with occasional modifications. I am grateful to Branden Kosch for translating the notebook passages after the middle period. Any other translations are my own.

14. I am quoting Young's translation of this passage in *Friedrich Nietzsche*, 298 n*.

15. This passage appears in WP as #94. NF-1884, 25[84] also pairs La Rochefoucauld with Christianity: both are to be defended against [Man wehrt sich gegen La Rochefoucauld und das Christenthum].

16. NF-1883, 7[40], discussed below, also connects La Rochefoucauld with Christianity. Donnellan, 'Nietzsche and La Rochefoucauld', 313–14, also discusses Nietzsche's assimilation of La Rochefoucauld to the Christian tradition.

17. Maxim 264. I use Stuart Warner and Stéphane Douard's bilingual edition of the *Maxims* with several modifications of their translations. See Warner and Douard, translation, introduction and notes. *Maxims* by La Rochefoucauld. South Bend, IN: St. Augustine's Press, 2001.

18. Cf. Donnellan, 'Nietzsche and La Rochefoucauld', 317, n. 18.

19. It is also mentioned in, but not the subject of, maxim 503.

20. HH 37 also attacks the idea of unegoistic action. Although it does not specify La Rochefoucauld, Nietzsche probably has him in mind. For other critiques, see HH 57, 92, 132.

21. Nietzsche cites HH 374.

22. Maudemarie Clark and Brian Leiter, Introduction, in *Daybreak: Thoughts on the Prejudices of Morality*, ed. Maudemarie Clark and Brian Leiter (Cambridge: Cambridge University Press, 1997), xxii–xxiv.

23. Clark and Leiter, Introduction, xxiv–xxv.

24. Paul Franco, *Nietzsche's Enlightenment: The Free-Spirit Trilogy of the Middle Period* (Chicago: University of Chicago Press, 2011), 60.

25. Franco, *Nietzsche's Enlightenment*, 26–27, 60.

26. Donnellan, 'Nietzsche and La Rochefoucauld', 306. Cf. Franco, *Nietzsche's Enlightenment*, 241 n. 17. Nietzsche gestures toward this at the end of HH 133. See my discussion of his belief in the original innocence of all action in Abbey, *Nietzsche's Middle Period*, 26–33.

27. I also discuss this in Abbey, *Nietzsche's Middle Period*, 20–21 and chapter 3.

28. Clark and Leiter, Introduction, xxv.

29. I cite Kaufmann and Hollingdale's translation from WP 362, although they date the passage at 1885.

30. La Rochefoucauld is also cast as a critic of egoism in (NF-1885, 2[165]).

31. As we saw above, HH 36 worries that psychology after the style of La Rochefoucauld may implant 'a sense of suspicion and reductionism into the souls of men'.

32. Donnellan, 'Nietzsche and La Rochefoucauld', 305. Pippin, *Nietzsche, Psychology, and First Philosophy*, 10.

33. Franco, *Nietzsche's Enlightenment*, 237, n42.

34. Warner and Douard, *Maxims*, 220.

35. Warner and Douard, *Maxims*, 492, cf. 173.

36. Warner and Douard, *Maxims*, 166.

37. Warner and Douard, *Maxims*, 170.

38. Warner and Douard, *Maxims*, 170.
39. Warner and Douard, *Maxims*, 99.
40. Warner and Douard, *Maxims*, 202, cf. 203, 206.
41. Cf. HH 39 where feeling free does not guarantee that one is free.
42. See HH 96, 97 and 99 where Nietzsche argues that morality is grounded in custom and convention, and further back, force. On morality as grounded in custom and convention, see also AOM 89, WS 40, D 9, 19, 101, GS 29. For a discussion of his views on this, see Abbey, *Nietzsche's Middle Period*, 10–14.
43. Clark and Leiter, Introduction, xiv, xxiv–xxvi.
44. Bernard Reginster, by contrast, detects psychological egoism in both HH and D. See Reginster, 'Nietzsche on Selflessness and the Value of Altruism', *History of Philosophy Quarterly* 17(2) (2000): 184.
45. Clark and Leiter, Introduction, xxiv–v.
46. Clark and Leiter, Introduction, xxv, xxxiv.
47. Young, *Friedrich Nietzsche*, 298, n*.
48. See Abbey, 'Lumping It and Liking It', 131–54.
49. Franco, *Nietzsche's Enlightenment*, 71.
50. Here Nietzsche suggests that the Greeks would have enjoyed the French moralists, but a notebook entry from 1883 retracts that, for Nietzsche claims that La Rochefoucauld or Pascal 'has the whole Greek taste against him' [hat den ganzen griechischen Geschmack gegen sich] (NF-1883, 8[15]).
51. The passage is included in Gary Handwerk's translation of Friedrich Nietzsche, *Human, All Too Human I*, Stanford, CA: Stanford University Press, 1997.

BIBLIOGRAPHY

Abbey, Ruth. '*Human, All Too Human*: A Book for Free Spirits'. In *A Companion to Friedrich Nietzsche: Life and Works*, edited by Paul C. Bishop, 114–34. New York: Camden House, 2012.
Abbey, Ruth. 'Lumping It and Liking It: On Reading the Works of Nietzsche's Middle Period'. In 'Nietzsche's Free Spirit Trilogy', *Pli: The Warwick Journal of Philosophy* 25 (2014): 131–54.
Abbey, Ruth. *Nietzsche's Middle Period*. Oxford: Oxford University Press, 2000.
Brobjer, Thomas. *Nietzsche's Philosophical Context: An Intellectual Biography*. Urbana, IL: University of Illinois Press, 2008.
Clark, Maudemarie and Brian Leiter. Introduction. In *Daybreak: Thoughts on the Prejudices of Morality*, edited by Maudemarie Clark and Brian Leiter, vii–xxxv. Cambridge: Cambridge University Press, 1997.
Cohen, Jonathan. *Science, Culture, and Free Spirits: A Study of Nietzsche's Human, All-Too-Human*. New York: Prometheus, 2010.
Donnellan, Brendan. 'Nietzsche and La Rochefoucauld', *The German Quarterly* 52(3) (1979): 303–18.
Franco, Paul. *Nietzsche's Enlightenment: The Free-Spirit Trilogy of the Middle Period*. Chicago: University of Chicago Press, 2011.
Nietzsche, Friedrich. *Daybreak: Thoughts on the Prejudices of Morality*. Translated by R. J. Hollingdale. Introduction by Maudemarie Clark and Brian Leiter. Cambridge: Cambridge University Press, 1997.
Nietzsche, Friedrich. *Digital Critical Edition of the Complete Works and Letters*. Based on the critical text by G. Colli and M. Montinari, edited by Paolo D'Iorio. Berlin/New York, de Gruyter, 1967–.
Nietzsche, Friedrich. *Human, All Too Human*, Translated by R. J. Hollingdale. Introduction by Richard Schacht. Cambridge: Cambridge University Press, 1996.
Nietzsche, Friedrich. *Human, All Too Human I*. Translated by Gary Handwerk. *The Complete Works of Friedrich Nietzsche*. Stanford, CA: Stanford University Press, 1997.

Nietzsche, Friedrich. *The Will to Power*. Translated by Walter Kaufmann and R. J. Hollingdale. New York: Vintage Books, 1968.

Pippin, Robert. *Nietzsche, Psychology, and First Philosophy*. Chicago: University of Chicago Press, 2010.

Reginster, Bernard. 'Nietzsche on Selflessness and the Value of Altruism', *History of Philosophy Quarterly* 17(2) (2000): 177–200.

Small, Robin. *Nietzsche and Rée: A Star Friendship*. Oxford: Clarendon Press, 2005.

Warner, Stuart, and Douard Stéphane, translation, introduction and notes. *Maxims* by La Rochefoucauld. South Bend, IN: St. Augustine's Press, 2001.

Young, Julian. *Friedrich Nietzsche: A Philosophical Biography*. New York: Cambridge University Press, 2010.

Table 1.1. Distribution of References to La Rochefoucauld across Nietzsche's Corpus

	Year	Work		Year	Work
1	1876	NF-1876, 18[21]	21	1883	NF-1883, 7[17]
2		NF-1876, 23[41]	22		NF-1883, 7[40]
3		NF-1876, 23[152]	23		NF-1883, 8[15]
4	1878	HH 35	24	1884	NF-1884, 25[74]
5		HH 36	25		NF-1884, 25[84]
6		HH 36	26		NF-1884, 25[178]
7		HH 36	27		NF-1884, 25[348]
8		HH 36	28		NF-1884, 25[419]
9		HH 50	29		NF-1884, 26[404]
10		HH 50	30	1885	NF-1885, 2[165]
11		HH 50	31		NF-1885, 34[80]
12		HH 133	32		NF-1885, 38[5]
13	1879	WS 214	33	1886	NF-1886, 7[6]
14	1880	NF-1880, 6[175]	34		NF-1886, 7[65]
15		NF-1880, 6[382]	35	1887	NF-1887, 9[67]
16	1881	NF-1881, 11[4]	36		NF-1887, 10[57]
17		D 103	37		GM Pref.5
18	1882	NF-1882, 3[1]	38	1888	NF-1888, 12[1]
19		GS 122	39	1889	EH
20		NF-1882, 4[54]			

Chapter Two

The Ethical Ideal of the Free Spirit in *Human, All Too Human*

Christine Daigle

Nietzsche referred to his middle period works as his 'whole free spiritedness [meine ganze Freigeisterei]'.[1] In these works, he parts ways from earlier influences and builds the foundation for his mature philosophy. His concern with the individual qua individual leads him to consider how one, the human being, experiences oneself, how one experiences the presence of others, and how one encounters the world, that is, how the world and the objects therein appear to one. His inquiries into these questions anticipate traditional phenomenology. In addressing them, he formulates an understanding of the human being as an embodied intentional consciousness that is an ambiguous multiplicity. However, his fundamental concern is ethical since his goal is to identify the ways in which one may flourish as an individual.

This ethical concern permeates the entire Nietzschean corpus, although it finds different expressions over time. Nietzsche's views change, modulate, and may even be said to radicalize themselves in his later writings. In this chapter, I wish to focus on the ethical ideal of the free spirit as it is articulated in *Human, All Too Human*.[2] This is the work in which the figure first emerges in full bloom and is construed as the ethical ideal towards which one should strive. This ethical ideal is primordially an epistemological one. Indeed, to be a free spirit, one must embrace the Enlightenment stance and reject any received opinion that does not sustain the test of one's own experiencing. As we will see, the free spirit is conceived as one who is animated by the spirit of inquiry and is not content with received opinions or faith. The free spirit's search for truth entails inquiring into oneself as seeker and potential knower as well as inquiring into the world. The first step in the search for truth requires dismantling metaphysics, morality, religion and art as discourses that convey alienating false views about the human being and the world. Through historical philosophizing, the free spirit will be able to move beyond those false views and undertake his own search for truth. This will lead the free spirit to uncover that truths have been invented by human beings.

This proposal, first introduced in 'Truth and Lies in a Nonmoral Sense' and revisited in HH, follows from Nietzsche's understanding of the constitutive activity of consciousness, which amounts to a phenomenological concept of intentionality. Conceiving of oneself as such an intentional consciousness allows the free spirit to take up his experiences and the things closest to him in a new way. As we will see, however, the free spirit's search for truth will only be successful if he engages with others who can be his friends. I will explain that agonistic friendship, the free spirit's association with the right individuals, namely those that are deemed equals, will lead to his flourishing and self-knowledge. At the time of HH, Nietzsche is confident that such relations are possible and may lead one to authentic flourishing. Admittedly, his confidence wanes afterwards as he recognizes the limitations of this ideal of the free spirit. Indeed, the free spirit may be the one who can uncover the truth about untruth and perhaps even uncover the truth of one's own being as this dynamic being that constantly makes itself and its world. However, it may be that he lacks the strength necessary to accept it, to truly incorporate it, and this could explain why Nietzsche ends up turning to other iterations of his ethical ideal such as the *Übermensch*.

To understand how Nietzsche construes his ethical ideal of the free spirit, we must first grasp his view of the human subject. In the opening chapter of HH, Nietzsche begins to set the stage for his view of the subject as an intentional embodied consciousness. The view he develops there, and holds to thereafter, is phenomenological.[3] For example, Nietzsche explains that, 'We behold all things through the human head and cannot cut off this head' (HH I 9). And in another aphorism of 'Of First and Last Things' he says, 'we have been the colourists [of the world]: it is the human intellect that has made appearance appear and transported its erroneous basic conceptions into things' (HH I 16). This amounts to saying that consciousness perceives and shapes the world as soon as it encounters it. The world is a phenomenon for consciousness. That is, the real world for consciousness and whatever world in itself or realm of being there might be is without effect on it. It is, in fact, worthy of 'Homeric laughter' as he puts it (HH I 16). This view of intentional consciousness that constitutes the world is also present in the writings that follow HH.[4] This passage of *The Gay Science* is an example where Nietzsche exclaims: 'How should explanations be at all possible when we first turn everything into an *image*, our image! It will do to consider science as an attempt to humanize things as faithfully as possible; as we describe things and their one-after-another, we learn how to describe ourselves more and more precisely (GS 112). In *Dawn*, Nietzsche explains, 'Only when he has attained a final knowledge of all things will man have come to know himself. For things are only the boundaries of man' (D 48). Here, Nietzsche is dealing with the understanding of things as things in themselves and as phenomena. Things in themselves are indeed the limits of human consciousness: when it encounters the thing in-itself, the phenomenon arises as consciousness constitutes it as a thing for itself, as an object for consciousness. Consciousness is also constituted through this process: its framing of the phenomenon in turn establishes itself as it perceives and shapes the object and the world. Being a consciousness of and in the world, it is modified and generated by what it constitutes. Consciousness is instituted by this movement out of itself that it is as intentionality. Intentional consciousness generates a co-constitutive process whereby the world and itself are concomitantly constituted. Poetically put: 'there is absolutely no escape, no backway or bypath into the *real world*! We sit within our net, we spiders, and whatever we may catch in it, we can catch nothing at all except that which allows itself to be caught in precisely *our* net' (D 117).[5] I take these passages as indicative of a Nietzschean notion of intentional embodied consciousness that constitutes its world and itself.[6]

Conceiving of the subject as such leads Nietzsche to consider the subject to be a multiplicity. The view he further elaborates in *Thus Spoke Zarathustra* with regard to the body as grand reason complicates the notion of intentionality by taking into consideration the embodiment of consciousness and magnifies the inner multiplicity of the subject. The phrase he uses in *Beyond Good and Evil* encompasses various elements of intentionality. In BGE 12, discussing one of the prejudices of philosophers, he explains that it is not necessary to dismiss the notion of soul.[7] Rather, he is interested in revising our understanding of such a concept. He says that 'the way is open for new versions and refinements of the soul-hypothesis; and such conceptions as 'mortal soul,' and 'soul as subjective multiplicity', and 'soul as social structure of the drives and affects', want henceforth to have citizens' rights in science' (BGE 12). The subject is thus a manifold that experiences itself as multiple. The Nietzschean subject is an 'ambiguous multiplicity'.[8] Nietzsche speaks of an inner multiplicity of the 'social structure of the drives and affects'. We are ambiguous multiplicities that individuate ourselves in a dynamic and continuous process. This process is the embodiment of a struggle between individual will and the force of situation as the individual wishes to determine him- or herself and yet is determined by its being (physiology) and its being-in-the-world (its historical and cultural location) as well as its being-with-others. Richard Cohen explains:

> Starting with the body, Nietzsche uncovers a philosophy of fragmentation, of various forces each pulling in its own direction to establish provisional moments of stasis, reflected as symptoms—ideas, images, or desires—in con-

sciousness. . . . The Nietzschean self is thus constantly reinventing itself, releasing new energy configurations. Its 'overcoming' is a constant shattering of the 'idols' of pretended unity.[9]

The multiple and ambiguous subject is constantly seeking its own unity while continuously shattering it in a process of self-overcoming, which incorporates responses to its being-in-the-world and being-with-others. As Kristen Brown puts it, the Nietzschean subject is 'a field of swarming, cross-pollinating forces constituting these co-constructs'.[10]

In order to better understand this notion of ambiguous multiplicity, it is useful to consider Nietzsche's perspectivism and how it relates to his phenomenological understanding of human beings. As I have explained above, human consciousness generates the phenomenal world through its beholding. Once our human head encounters being, the world emerges; the world and its various phenomena are generated and 'coloured' by us. We are truly creators in that the process of constitution ensues from our beholding the world. Nietzsche explains that the self emerges from this dual-act of perception/creation of the phenomenon that is the being of intentional consciousness. I constitute the world, the world constitutes me. I am weaved with the world I have constituted, and there is a flow of (self-)constitution that occurs with my being conscious.[11] This is the fabric of the ambiguous multiplicity that we are.

This consciousness exists as embodied. This is, as I have said, another facet of our ambiguous multiplicity. Nietzsche speaks of the body as a great intelligence—the equivalent of an intentional consciousness, since it is the body that 'thinks'—and it undergoes a process of individuation wherein conscious thought emerges and the body acts in the world, consequently generating its ego—a tool for itself. Conscious thought is thus generated by the interaction between the great intelligence of the body—Nietzsche calls it 'the grand reason'[12]—and the world. This grand reason constitutes the world as it acts within it and encounters it. It is conscious of it—as raw consciousness—and constitutes itself by the same token. That is the bidirectional process of intentionality to which I referred earlier. The end result is that we have a multi-layered subjectivity that is both a grand reason—intentional consciousness—and a little reason—rational consciousness—which Nietzsche refers to as 'thinking'. Eric Blondel explains this section while emphasizing the multiplicity of the subject that this view entails. He says, 'The body, as a plurality-unity, is the locus of the interpretation which constitutes the chaos of the world in plural unities, in signs'.[13] The interpreting body is an ambiguous multiplicity, in movement, the play of affects and drives which constitutes for itself the world and the tools to interpret it and act upon it. Subjectivity is this embodied consciousness as manifold.

There is not only a multiplicity of conscious processes that are experienced as an embodied intentionality. Just as there are a good number of conscious mental states, there is also a host of unconscious mental states.[14] Nietzsche indicated so much in the very beginning of *Schopenhauer as Educator*. There he asks: 'How can the human being get to know himself? He is a dark and veiled thing; and if the hare has seven skins, the human being can shed seven times seventy skins and still not be able to say: "This is really you, this is no longer outer shell"' (SE 1). Analyzing GS 354 of *The Gay Science*, Paul Katsafanas offers an interesting perspective on this issue. He argues that there is a clear distinction between conscious and unconscious mental states in Nietzsche and that consciousness is presented as the sum total of conscious mental states.[15] In GS 354, Nietzsche is clear that

> we could think, feel, will, and remember, and we could also 'act' in every sense of that word, and yet none of all this would have to 'enter our consciousness'

and again he claims,

> Man, like every living being, thinks continually without knowing it; the thinking that rises to consciousness is only the smallest part of all this—the most superficial and worst part—for only this conscious thinking takes the form of words, which is to say signs of communication, and this fact uncovers the origin of consciousness.

These quotations indicate very clearly that there is an inner multiplicity that has to do with a separation between the unconscious and the conscious part of our selves. What complicates matters a great deal is the fact that Nietzsche locates more than affects and drives in the unconscious; thinking happens there, too, as does willing. Thus, there is a rationality of the body, the grand reason, indeed, as Zarathustra would have it, 'There is more reason in your body than in your best wisdom' (Z I Despisers of the Body).

To sum up: The Nietzschean subject constitutes itself through its encounter with the world, and, as intentional consciousness, it is constituted by the world. It is a worldly being: the world is filled with objects, and the subject's being conscious of these objects allows for consciousness to become what it is. The world and its objects are thus the conditions of possibility for consciousness: if there was nothing external to consciousness, it could not be. But there is no fixity of objects, of the world, and therefore of the subject. Everything happens in a dynamic process of flux.[16] Prior to the part I quoted earlier from HH, about the human being as the colourist of the world, Nietzsche specifies: 'this painting—that which we humans call life and experience—has gradually *become*, is indeed still fully in course of becoming' (HH I 16). The phenomenal realm becomes, the subject becomes. In the twofold bidirectional process of constitution, a subject emerges, albeit a fluctuating and fragmented one: this subject is itself a manifold. In D, Nietzsche explains that 'with every moment of our lives some of the polyp-arms of our being grow and others dry up, depending on the nourishment that the moment does or does not supply. As stated earlier, all our experiences are, in this sense, types of nourishment' (D 119).

The subject is constituted by a manifold of experiences. It is clear that the human being thus conceived is a being-in-the-world; this world, however, is not only populated by objects that allow consciousness to constitute itself but also by other subjects. Therefore, Nietzsche's subject is both a being-in-the-world and a being-with-others. In the same way that it is constituted by the objects it encounters through the intentional process, it is also constituted by the others it meets. In fact, in GS 354, Nietzsche explains that '*consciousness has developed only under the pressure of the need for communication*; . . . Consciousness is really only a net of communication between human beings' (GS 354). Nietzsche is not a careful phenomenologist, and he equivocates on the term 'consciousness' in his writings. The 'consciousness' he is referring to here is none other than the little reason, the tool of the body. According to him, then, the little reason emerges with the development of language, and language develops because we interact with other human beings. The desire to communicate generates that layer of consciousness. Nietzsche says that 'consciousness does not really belong to man's individual existence but rather to his social or herd nature' (GS 354). Again, this is not to say that if we were removed from a social setting, we would not be conscious beings. However, there would be no need for the development of the little reason. Clearly then, the existence of others and their presence in the world are constitutive of what an individual is, as an ambiguous multiplicity. The intersubjective realm of language and communication further shapes the consciousness of every individual. In proposing this view of the origin of that part of consciousness, the little reason, Nietzsche is making the human subject ontologically dependent on the other. The being of others is part of our own being. This is another facet of the ambiguous multiplicity that we embody, and it has important ethical implications. As we will see next, the free spirit is the being who understands herself as such an ambiguous multiplicity and also knows that she is the creator of the world through its constitutive activity as intentional consciousness.

This conception of the human subject as a fluctuating ambiguous multiplicity entails interesting views about ethical becoming. Indeed, how is one to conceive of the ethical ideal that one should aim for? Is the ethical ideal some kind of reification of one's being, a becoming one and unified? Nietzsche's view is more complicated than that and aims to not only maintain the ambiguous multiplicity of becoming but to foster it.[17] Exploring the issue of individuality in Nietzsche, Nuno Nabais has suggested that 'since individuality is not a primary datum to be found by each individual within himself, it has to be reconceived as a task to be accomplished'.[18] This reaches back to the ideas explored in the first section of the fourth of the *Untimely Meditations*, 'Schopenhauer as Educator', where Nietzsche says:

We are accountable to ourselves for our own existence [the German has 'Dasein' which is important in terms of the interpretation I am offering here, namely to understand the human being as a being-in-the-world and a being-with-others. One sees the connection with Heidegger.]; consequently, we also want to be the real helmsmen of our existence and keep it from resembling a mindless coincidence. (UM IV 1)

And further,

> your true being does not lie deeply hidden within you, but rather immeasurably high above you, or at least above what you commonly take to be your ego. (UM IV 1)

That self [das eigentliche Selbst] that one must become is identified as our ethical goal. But the key to authenticity is to know oneself as this ambiguous multiplicity that I have described. To understand what one is is the key to one's authentic ethical becoming. And, as Nietzsche says, 'No one can build for you the bridge upon which you alone must cross the stream of life, no one but you alone. . . . There is one single path in this world on which no one but you can travel' (UM IV 1). Knowing thyself is the key to becoming oneself, which is identified as the ethical imperative in GS 270. In order to know oneself, however, one must be freed from traditional understandings of morality and the moral self. This is the point at which the free spirit comes into play.

The concept of the free spirit emerges in HH, and my analysis will focus on the concept as it appears in this book. Aphorism 225 of chapter 5, 'Tokens of Higher and Lower Culture' explores the free spirit as a relative concept.[19] Nietzsche says, 'He is called a free spirit who thinks differently from what, on the basis of his origin, environment, his class and profession, or on the basis of the dominant views of the age, would have been expected of him' (HH I 225).[20] He is an exception as opposed to the rule, which is to be a fettered spirit, a creature of habits who has faith in institutions and supports them. His intellect is of a superior quality and sharpness. However, this does not entail that the free spirit possesses the truth. Thus, Nietzsche says: 'What characterizes the free spirit is not that his opinions are the more correct but that he has liberated himself from tradition, whether the outcome has been successful or a failure. As a rule though, he will nonetheless have truth on his side, or at least the spirit of inquiry after truth: he demands reasons, the rest demand faith' (HH I 225). Because of this, the free spirit is perceived as evil and to be a threat by the fettered spirits because he defies their own commonly held beliefs. His spirit of inquiry, which remains lighthearted against the age of seriousness (HH I 240), leads him to question things and embody a skeptical outlook, to pursue the goals of the Enlightenment in himself (HH II WS 221), which is to say to dare think on his own and for himself without

recourse to authority. In aphorism 292, Nietzsche appeals to the reader so
that she tries to make of herself a free spirit. He indicates how to achieve this:
by not looking down on experience (indicating that any soil bears fruits) and
by making oneself an instrument of knowledge since knowledge frees the
spirit (HH I 288). In section 252, the acquisition of knowledge is described as
a form of overcoming. Therefore, every pursuit of truth is considered worthwhile. Knowledge makes one 'conscious of one's strength', and allows one
to go 'beyond former conceptions' (HH I 252). Indeed, what matters is for
the free spirits to avoid any inertia of their spirit, which may lead to a
stiffening of their thoughts. Exercising skepticism, the free spirit will be the
enemy of convictions and will be on the path of truth, a special path, one
which will entail error. Indeed, as Nietzsche would have it, the free spirit is
an ever-evolving concept, and error is an integral part of its progress (HH II
AOM 4).

The concluding two chapters of book 1 of HH provide us with a portrait
of the free spirit and his philosophy of the morning. It follows a series of
aphorisms on truth and convictions. In aphorism 637, Nietzsche says of the
free spirit that 'even if he should be altogether a thinking snowball, he will
have in his head, not opinions, but only certainties and precisely calculated
probabilities'. Further, he says that the way of the free spirits is to 'advance
from opinion to opinion, through one party after another, as noble *traitors* to
all things that can in any way be betrayed' (HH I 637). Free spirits seek
'spiritual nomadism' (HH II AOM 211). This is part of the obligation, for
free spirits, to become masters of themselves. To be such, one must have
freed oneself from alienating beliefs and convictions. This means adopting
the critical skeptical stance that Nietzsche champions. One must free oneself
from 'conceptions of morality, religion and metaphysics. Only when this
sickness *from one's chains* has also been overcome will the first great goal
have truly been attained: the separation of man from the animals' (HH II WS
350).[21] The noble freed spirit's motto shall be: 'Peace all around me and
good will to all things closest to me' (HH II WS 350).

Nietzsche explains that the free spirit will be a mindful spirit, one who will
suspend her own internal eye every now and then in order to better experiment
and, therefore, better know herself (HH II WS 236). He indicates that it is crucial
to focus on experiences before analyzing them. He says: 'Do not want to see
prematurely.—For as long as one is experiencing something one must give
oneself up to the experience and close one's eyes: that is to say, not be an
observer of it while still *in the midst* of it. For that would disturb the absorption
of the experience: instead of a piece of wisdom one would acquire from it
indigestion' (HH II WS 297). This is really illuminating with regard to my
reading. Indeed, Nietzsche wants us to focus on the experience, to 'bracket off'
the analyzing activity of little reason and to focus on how consciousness experiences things. The free spirit is to pay attention to the experience itself and to the

experience of things closest to her. In the last section of the book, the Shadow expresses his satisfaction to the Wanderer saying, 'Of all you have said nothing has pleased me more than a promise you have made: you want again to become a good neighbour to the things closest to you' (HH II WS 350). Being a good neighbour means to be fully attentive to the experience rather than letting the little reason take over with its analytical skills and discursive explanations— metaphysical, religious, moral, artistic and otherwise traditional—those very explanations that pass as authoritative discourse but that are really only our own 'colouring' of the world and objects therein. The free spirit philosophizes historically, conducts a phenomenological reduction, and goes back to things themselves in the process of seeking self-knowledge. This entails uncovering the genealogy of the discourses that, taken together, are supposed to constitute our body of knowledge and certainties. Such genealogical analysis shows that these discourses are human creations. They amount to a phenomenological reduction in that they seek to uncover the raw experience of the world and how we first encountered it. The free spirit is thus a phenomenologist.

One of the most important obligations to fulfill for the free spirit is to be master of oneself. Self-mastery entails self-knowledge. Learning about things is important but it is of most importance to learn about ourselves (HH II WS 266)—perhaps through knowing things as suggested earlier. In WS, Nietzsche emphasizes the importance of the Other who can assist one in knowing oneself. He has already indicated that it is important to have friends who will give us access to our own fortress (HH II WS 491), that we need others as railings for our own development (HH II WS 600), and that we must be open to the voice of others and the situation. We are not rigid single individuums (HH II WS 618). Everyone needs a complement, a shadow (HH II WS 258).

One must be one's own lawgiver, be a free spirit who embodies all the characteristics and virtues mentioned. But it remains that the very being of the human, the fact that we are ontologically dependent on others and always in their presence requires that this becoming happens in relation to others.[22] For self-overcoming to be possible, interaction with the other is required. But not just any other. If it is true that the subject is ontologically dependent on others—if it is constituted by the others with whom it is in relation as a being-with-others—it becomes imperative that the individual be in the company of the 'right' individuals. In a way, a member of the herd cannot help but share in the herd mentality: the herd permeates him as he permeates it. Likewise, a noble soul will be noble in virtue of being permeated by the noble mentality if he associates with likewise noble individuals.[23] Who one associates with is crucial for the being-with-others we are. Nietzsche understands so much when he says: 'Are you a slave? If so, you cannot be a friend. Are you a tyrant? If so, you cannot have friends' (Z I Friend). As Robert C.

Miner explains, 'there are human types with whom it is *unhealthy* to be friends'.[24]

This is why free spirits need to find other free spirits to keep company and why Nietzsche's views of friendship imply an agonistic relation. Simply put: one must engage in relations with others that will bring the best out of oneself.[25] Explaining the writing and thinking process at work in HH, Nietzsche writes:

> —Thus when I needed to I once also invented for myself the 'free spirits' . . . 'free spirits' of this kind do not exist, did not exist—but, as I have said, I had need of them at that time if I was to keep in good spirits while surrounded by ills . . . as brave companions and familiars with whom one can laugh and chatter when one feels like laughing and chattering, and whom one can send to the Devil when they become tedious—as compensation for the friends I lacked. (HH I Preface 2)

However, those free spirits *qua* friends have to serve an important ethical function beyond keeping one's good company. Nietzsche speaks of a 'refined concept of friendship' belonging to noble morality.[26] Others with whom we engage will serve as role models if they are higher types, in Nietzsche's case, free spirits/friends. But, more deeply, being in the presence of such individuals should entice us to overcome ourselves, which is the Nietzschean ethical imperative. As he puts it in GS: '"You shall become the person you are"'. (GS 270) Nietzsche explains, 'In your friend you should possess your best enemy. Your heart should feel closest to him when you oppose him. . . . You cannot adorn yourself too well for your friend: for you should be to him an arrow and a longing for the [Overhuman]' (Z I Friend; translation modified). The friend should pull us upwards, should serve as that stepladder towards our highest self.

This agonistic relation affects our very being. The ontological relation to the other that I have described earlier implies that, in such relations, our being-in-the-world is modified ontologically but that also, as a result, our ethical being is shaped and modified by these relations. In his article on the Nietzschean notion of friendship, Miner emphasizes the ethical role of friendship if it is established on an agonistic relation with the other.[27] Miner further suggests that friendship, for Nietzsche, rests upon a search for truth. When it aims at such, it must be construed in agonistic terms, otherwise 'If friendship becomes content with the mere tolerance of difference or otherwise loses its oppositional character, it becomes a counterfeit of itself'.[28] Relations with others need to be nurtured so that they can put the individual on the path of self-overcoming. Only agonistic relations will serve that purpose for oneself and for the friend. Ontologically, my relation to the other is fundamentally constitutive of myself. Ethically, it determines whether I will engage on the path of self-overcoming. Politically, it will be the determining factor of whether social groups flourish and bring humanity closer to Over-humanity. As Rosalyn Diprose puts it, in Nietzsche, 'the political is ontological, but only insofar as it is always intersubjective'.[29] The ontological grounds the ethical and the political. We are being-with-others ontologically, ethically and politically.

Because of the interplay of the various constitutions of the subject that I have talked about, I qualify the Nietzschean subject as an ambiguous multiplicity, one that is the embodiment of its own fragmentation that is in a constant process of self-individuation, aiming upwards towards its authentic, fragmented and multiple ambiguous self. The Nietzschean subject, as will to power and in a constant process of self-overcoming, is the perpetual making of itself through these multiple constitutive acts that involve connecting and disconnecting its various parts as it exists in the world. It is thus an ambiguous multiplicity: a fluctuating multiplicity that cannot be grasped or defined because it is in constant flux. It is an embodied and living dividuum that individuates—and dividuates—itself as it goes through life.

Conceiving of the subject in this way has important ethical consequences. In a context where my subjectivity and my ethical being is deeply dependent on my being-with-others, one understands Nietzsche's admonitions to associate oneself with the right individuals. Since we are embodied beings-in-the-world that are beings-with-others, our individual flourishing is largely determined by our relations with others. We need others to push us on the path of self-overcoming. Friendship is thus essential to one's flourishing. However, genuine friendship is possible only among equals[30] who are willing to engage in agonistic relations.

It is important to emphasize that the highest self one can become is still an ambiguous multiplicity. Part of becoming authentic, Nietzsche's ethical worry, is to know oneself as this ambiguous multiplicity that one is and to will to be this ambiguous multiplicity. The free spirit is the one who has the strength to do this. Coming to the realization that one is this ambiguous multiplicity, the free spirit will resist the reification of itself in a unity and will nurture herself as the embodied dividuum she is. Actually, the relation to the Other also provides that challenge to reification. Being-with-others entails being divided and multiple. But one must be authentic about it. One must will to be what one is. The free spirit, as authentic, will opt for embodying the dividuum and will thus be on the path of Ubermenschlichkeit. The free spirit is none other than this embrace of oneself as ambiguous multiplicity: a dynamic state of being qua becoming, not the end-goal to a linear progress of being, rather the process of individuation itself, if and only if it is embraced authentically.

As Nietzsche continues to deal with the concept of the free spirit in the writings that follow HH, he gradually feels the limitations of this concept. He claims that the concept may have put morality on its head but is itself moral in the end. Saying that the free spirit is 'accomplished', he claims that it is not his ideal.[31] While the concept morphs and evolves and is eventually replaced by the Übermensch as the ethical ideal we must strive for, Nietzsche retains the concept of the free spirit and discusses it again in BGE. There are some significant differences between the free spirit of HH and the later iteration, not so much as to the nature of the concept itself as to the role Nietzsche attributes it.[32] In part 2 of BGE, Nietzsche still advocates adopting a critical stance towards knowledge, one of the key features of the free spirit. He also revisits the idea that the world is erroneous and has been created by us and anticipates the sections of *Twilight of the Idols* where he rejects both the real and the apparent world.[33] The free spirit is again considered to be the one who sees clearly into what is, that is, '*voir clair dans ce qui est*'.[34] But Nietzsche also indicates that 'a new species of philosophers is coming up' (BGE 42). These philosophers of the future, as he calls them, will be experimenters [Versuchers]. He conceives of them as related to the free spirits and yet different. He says: 'they, too, will be free, *very* free spirits, these philosophers of the future—though just as certainly they will not be merely free spirits but something more, higher, greater, and thoroughly different that does not want to be misunderstood and mistaken for something else' (BGE 44).

Whether the philosopher of the future, as *very* free spirit, is an improvement over the ideal of the free spirit as conceived in HH is a question I do not wish to settle.[35] It is clear that the free spirit has paved the way for the later figures of the Übermensch and philosopher of the future. And, as I hope to have shown in this chapter, within the economy of HH and the principles advanced in it regarding the human being and notions of flourishing, the free spirit, as conceived in this book, is a viable ethical ideal. It may provide us with a tamed vision of Nietzsche, one that does not cohere easily with the later more radical Nietzsche, but as far as HH is concerned the free spirit *is* the phenomenological ethical ideal of authenticity and search for truth that we should all aim for.

NOTES

1. On the back cover of the first edition of *The Gay Science*, Nietzsche indicates that 'with this book, the series of writings by Friedrich Nietzsche, of which the overall goal is the erection of the image of the Free Spirit, comes to completion. *Human, All Too Human* with appendices 'Assorted Opinions and Maxims' and 'The Wanderer and His Shadow', *Daybreak* and *The Gay Science* belong to this series' [Mit diesem Buche kommt eine Reihe von Schriften Friedrich Nietzsche's zum Abschluss, deren gemeinsames Ziel ist, ein neues Bild und Ideal des Freigeistes aufzustellen. In diese Reihe gehören: *Menschliches, Allzumenschliches* mit Anhang: *Vermischte Meinungen und Sprüche*; *Der Wanderer und sein Schatten*; *Morgenröthe. Gedanken über die moralischen Vorurtheile*; *Die fröhliche Wissenschaft*]. Nietzsche attests to the same idea about this body of work in a letter to Lou Salomé referring to: 'The work of 6 years

(1876–1882), my whole "free-spiritedness"!' [das Werk von 6 Jahren (1876–1882), meine ganze 'Freigeisterei'!] (BVN-1882, 256—Brief an Lou von Salomé: 03/07/1882).

2. In this chapter, I have used the following translations: 'On Truth and Lies in a Nonmoral Sense', in *Epistemology: the Classic Readings*, ed. David E. Cooper (Oxford: Blackwell, 1999); 'Schopenhauer as Educator,' trans. Richard T. Gray, in *The Nietzsche Reader*, ed. Keith Ansell-Pearson and Duncan Large (Oxford: Wiley-Blackwell, 2006), 142–60; *Human, All Too Human. A Book for Free Spirits*, trans. R. J. Hollingdale (Cambridge: Cambridge University Press, 1996); *Daybreak: Thoughts on the Prejudices of Morality*, trans. R. J. Hollingdale (Cambridge: Cambridge University Press, 1997); *The Gay Science. With a Prelude in Rhymes and an Appendix of Songs*, trans. Walter Kaufmann (New York: Vintage Books, 1974). *Thus Spoke Zarathustra. A Book for Everyone and No One*, trans. R. J. Hollingdale (London: Penguin Books, 1969); *Beyond Good and Evil. Prelude to a Philosophy of the Future*, trans. Walter Kaufmann (New York: Vintage, 1989).

3. What follows revisits and borrows arguments I have developed in more detail in 'The Intentional Encounter with 'the World', in *Nietzsche and Phenomenology. Power, Life, Subjectivity*, ed. Élodie Boublil and Christine Daigle (Bloomington: Indiana University Press, 2013), 28–43.

4. While this view emerges as part of the free-spiritedness [Freigeisterei], it endures well beyond it. In many sections of his later writings, Nietzsche refers to and uses implicitly this same phenomenological view of intentional consciousness. The critique of the realm of the thing in itself, for example, is first explored in details in HH I but is maintained throughout the corpus and reiterated in shorter form in TI Reason 6 and the famous TI Fable.

5. It is to be noted that Nietzsche uses the same image of the spider in 'On Truth and Lies in a Nonmoral Sense' towards the end of the first section. There, he is talking about our way of constructing the world, using representations of time and space and says: 'But we produce these representations in and from ourselves with the same necessity with which the spider spins'. (Nietzsche, 'Truth and Lies in a Nonmoral Sense', 190). This discussion of representations of time and space brings Nietzsche close to Kantian epistemology. I have discussed the proximity of some of their views and how it unfolds into Nietzsche's own phenomenological views in my 'The Intentional Encounter with "the World"'.

6. This phenomenological concept is present in seeds in Nietzsche's philosophy. The understanding of consciousness as intentionality entails that consciousness only exists as conscious of something. Being conscious of the world it constitutes both itself and the world.

7. It should be stressed that Nietzsche sometimes equivocates on the terms he uses and uses some terms to refer to other notions. In this case, I don't think Nietzsche refers to the traditional notion of soul as the spiritual eternal part of human beings but rather to the more mundane and very human consciousness.

8. For an extensive discussion of this notion, see my 'The Subject as Ambiguous Multiplicity: Embodying the Dividuum', in *Ohnmacht des Subjekts—Macht der Persönlichkeit*, ed. Christian Benne and Enrico Mueller (Schwabe Verlag, 2014), 153–166. What follows here is a summary of some of the ideas explored in more depth in this previous essay.

9. Richard A. Cohen, 'Levinas, Spinozism, Nietzsche, and the Body', in *Nietzsche and Levinas: after the death of a certain God*, ed. Jill Stauffer and Bettina Bergo (New York: Columbia University Press, 2009), 179.

10. Kristen Brown, *Nietzsche and Embodiment. Discerning Bodies and Non-Dualism* (Albany, NY: State University of New York Press, 2006), 41.

11. There is a lot of agreement between Husserl and Nietzsche on these questions as I have shown in my 'The Intentional Encounter with "the World"'.

12. Hollingdale translates 'große Vernunft' as 'great intelligence', but that is not quite right; it should be 'reason.' Translating as 'intellect' rather than 'reason' has an unfortunate effect that the implicit critique of Kant is lost.

13. My translations of: 'l'esprit-intellect conscient devient l'*instrument* d'un corps interprétant inconscient'. (282) 'Si le corps est premier, c'est comme modèle de *mixte*. Si la multiplicité est première, le corps comme jeu des affects sera premier (comme multiplicité) *par rapport à l'intellect* conçu comme unifiant-simplifiant, alors qu'il sera second par *rapport au chaos du monde*'. (284) 'le corps, comme unité-pluralité, est le lieu de l'interprétation qui constitue le

chaos du monde en unités plurielles, en signes'. (Éric Blondel, *Nietzsche, le corps et la culture* (Presses universitaires de France, 1986), 292).

14. It has been objected against my view that the use of 'mental states' brings Nietzsche closer to analytic philosophy of mind than he should be. However, I am not sure what other phrase to use to refer to what states of the mind are.

15. He explains that part of 'what Nietzsche means when he says that consciousness is a multiplicity is that there is no faculty named Consciousness, which stands apart from our conscious mental states; rather, there is only a host of conscious mental states'. Paul Katsafanas, 'Nietzsche's Theory of Mind: Consciousness and Conceptualization', *European Journal of Philosophy* 13(1), 2005: 12–13.

16. Joseph Hillis Miller says in 'The Disarticulation of the Self in Nietzsche', *The Monist* 64(2) (1981): 252, that 'There is no solid object to cause subject but only one single 'phenomenal realm' within which all these fictitious entities and the lines between them are constructed.' Miller makes this statement specifically in relation to Nietzsche's note 'Toward a psychology of epistemology [Zur Psychologie und Erkenntnisslehre]' (NF-1887-11[113], Nov. 1887-März 1888).

17. In what follows I revisit and borrow arguments from my essay 'The Nietzschean Virtue of Authenticity—"Wie man wird, was man ist"', *Journal of Value Inquiry* 49(3) (2015, forthcoming). In that piece, I focus on ethical becoming and in what way Nietzsche values authenticity as a virtue. I argue that he can be conceived as a virtue ethicist who focuses on the development of the moral agent, a view to be contrasted however with that of Aristotle.

18. Nuno Nabais, 'The Individual and Individuality in Nietzsche', in *A Companion to Nietzsche*, ed. Keith Ansell-Pearson (Oxford: Blackwell, 2009), 82. As Keith Ansell-Pearson puts it, 'There is a kind of 'core' for Nietzsche, but this is simply the potential for a self. Nietzsche's self is the product of both nature (*physis*) and culture'. (Keith Ansell-Pearson, 'In Search of Authenticity and Personality: Nietzsche on the Purification of Philosophy', *American Catholic Philosophical Quarterly* 84(2) (2010): 285).

19. It is interesting to note that the concept emerges in the context of a discussion of progress and socio-cultural evolution. The figure is presented not only as an ethical ideal but also as the needed trigger for major socio-cultural changes. In this chapter, he proposes that progress is the result of the dialectical relation between the free spirit and the fettered spirit.

20. This statement alone is an indication that we have a mixture of structuralism and existentialism in Nietzsche. The structuralist in him understands that one is shaped by one's location in culture but the existentialist in him also believes it is possible to assess those and critically understand how they alienate and subdue us, thus freeing ourselves from their power. Only a being with great strength will be able to do so. The free spirits possess such strengths. Nietzsche says: 'Talent.— In as highly developed a humanity as ours now is everyone acquires from nature access to many talents. Everyone *possesses inborn talent*, but few possess the degree of inborn and acquired toughness, endurance and energy actually to become a talent, that is to say to become what he *is*: which means to discharge it in works and actions'. (HH I 263) I note the use of the phrase 'becoming what one is' in this quote.

21. It ought to be noted that the first four chapters of HH I which precede the emergence of the free spirit consist in this endeavour. These chapters dismiss as illusory and alienating human-made discourses metaphysics, morality, religion and art, thus paving the way for the emergence of the figure of the free spirit, the one who sees these discourses for what they are.

22. Rosalyn Diprose has pointed this out from a different angle. She explains that Nietzsche's philosophy comprises an often disregarded openness to the other. She claims that 'the distance necessary to self-overcoming is given in proximity to others'. (Rosalyn Diprose, *Corporeal Generosity. On Giving with Nietzsche, Merleau-Ponty, and Levinas*, [Albany, NY: State University of New York Press, 2002], 27). Her point is that if one was caught in a solipsistic trap, there would be nothing pushing one to overcome oneself.

23. In this context, Zarathustra's ten-year retreat in a cave in the company of his animals (each representing higher virtues) may be read as a way to ensure that he is not 'infected' by the lower men and last men. Interestingly, when he emerges of his retreat and goes back to men, he does become sick! But he does feel the urge to go back to men and come down from his cave.

24. Robert C. Miner, 'Nietzsche on Friendship', *Journal of Nietzsche Studies* 40(2) (2010): 49.
25. See Daniel I. Harris, 'Friendship as Shared Joy in Nietzsche', *Symposium: The Canadian Journal of Continental Philosophy* 19(1): 199–221.
26. See Miner, 'Nietzsche on Friendship', 69. In this passage, he is referring to what Nietzsche proposes in BGE 260.
27. Miner, 'Nietzsche on Friendship'.
28. Miner, 'Nietzsche on Friendship', 49. Miner further explains that friendship among higher types requires a balancing of qualities and that 'The highest friendships are difficult to maintain. This is true, I have shown, because they require their participants to hold at least three pairs of opposed qualities in a delicate balance. These are love of self, along with dissatisfaction with self; candor toward the friend, along with appropriate reserve and perhaps even the occasional deception; and solitude and companionship'. (56)
29. Diprose, *Corporeal Generosity*, 176.
30. Needless to say and following what was said above, 'equals' here does not entail a strict equality. Indeed, if two individuals were the same, they could not engage in this dynamic agonistic relation.
31. Nietzsche says that 'Morality is vanquished and overcome through free-spiritedness [Die Moral ist durch die Freigeisterei auf ihre Spitze getrieben und überwunden.]' (NF-1882-4[16]—Nachgelassene Fragmente November 1882–Februar 1883) But despite this important role, the free spirit is itself moral: 'However now do we recognize that free-spiritedness is itself moral.[Aber jetzt erkennen wir die Freigeisterei selber als Moral.]' (NF-1882-6[4]—Nachgelassene Fragmente Winter 1882–83) In a letter to Lou Salomé from that same period, he says: 'Do not let yourself be fooled and do not believe that the Free Spirit is my ideal. [Lassen Sie sich nicht über mich täuschen—Sie glauben doch nicht, daß, der Freigeist mein Ideal ist?]' (BVN-1882-335—Brief an Lou van Salomé: verm. 24. November 1882) and again in a letter to Köselitz, discussing the publication of Z, he says: 'What is certain is that with it, I have stepped over into another world—the "Free Spirit" is *fulfilled*. [Gewiß ist, daß ich damit in eine andere Welt hinübergetreten bin—der "Freigeist" ist *erfüllt.*]' (BVN-1883-397—Brief an Heinrich Köselitz: 02/04/1883) This is the period of writing Z.
32. Concerning the free spirit in BGE and HH, see also essays by Christa Acampora, Katrina Mitcheson, and Richard Schacht in this volume.
33. See in particular the series of aphorisms 34, 35 and 36 in BGE.
34. Nietzsche quotes Stendhal's description of a good philosopher as a definition of 'A final trait of the free-spirited philosopher'. To see clearly into the being of things, into what is, is an important trait and one that has been indicated in HH.
35. Here I only want to gesture toward the distinctions that Nietzsche envisions and not dwell in a detailed analysis of them. The reader will refer to the essay by Jacob Golomb, who has explored the subtle differences between the concepts of 'we free spirits' and 'free spirit *par excellence*' in his 'Can One Really Become a "Free Spirit Par Excellence" or an *Übermensch*', *Journal of Nietzsche Studies* 32(2) (2006): 22–40. See also essays by Acampora, Mitcheson, and Schacht in this volume.

BIBLIOGRAPHY

Ansell-Pearson, Keith. 'In Search of Authenticity and Personality: Nietzsche on the Purification of Philosophy'. *American Catholic Philosophical Quarterly* 84(2) (2010): 283–312.
Blondel, Éric. *Nietzsche, le corps et la culture*. Presses universitaires de France, 1986.
Brown, Kristen. *Nietzsche and Embodiment. Discerning Bodies and Non-Dualism*. Albany, NY: State University of New York Press, 2006.
Cohen, Richard A. 'Levinas, Spinozism, Nietzsche, and the Body'. In *Nietzsche and Levinas: after the Death of a Certain God*, edited by Jill Stauffer and Bettina Bergo, 165–84. New York: Columbia University Press, 2009.

Daigle, Christine. 'The Intentional Encounter with "the World"'. In *Nietzsche and Phenomenology. Power, Life, Subjectivity*, edited by Élodie Boublil and Christine Daigle, 28–43. Bloomington: Indiana University Press, 2013.

Daigle, Christine. 'The Subject as Ambiguous Multiplicity: Embodying the Dividuum'. In *Ohnmacht des Subjekts—Macht der Persönlichkeit*, edited by Christian Benne and Enrico Mueller, 153–66. Schwabe Verlag, 2014.

Daigle, Christine. 'The Nietzschean Virtue of Authenticity—"Wie man wird, was man ist"', *Journal of Value Inquiry* 49(3) (2015).

Diprose, Rosalyn. *Corporeal Generosity. On Giving with Nietzsche, Merleau-Ponty, and Levinas*. Albany, NY: State University of New York Press, 2002.

Golomb, Jacob. 'Can One Really Become a "Free Spirit Par Excellence" or an *Übermensch*'. *Journal of Nietzsche Studies* 32(2) (2006): 22–40.

Harris, Daniel I. 'Friendship as Shared Joy in Nietzsche'. *Symposium: The Canadian Journal of Continental Philosophy* 19(1) (2015): 199–221.

Katsafanas, Paul. 'Nietzsche's Theory of Mind: Consciousness and Conceptualization'. *European Journal of Philosophy* 13(1) (2005): 1–31.

Miller, Joseph Hillis. 'The Disarticulation of the Self in Nietzsche'. *The Monist* 64(2) (1981): 247–61.

Miner, Robert C. 'Nietzsche on Friendship'. *Journal of Nietzsche Studies* 40(2) (2010): 47–69.

Nabais, Nuno. 'The Individual and Individuality in Nietzsche'. In *A Companion to Nietzsche*, edited by Keith Ansell-Pearson, 76–94. Oxford: Blackwell, 2006.

Nietzsche, Friedrich. *Beyond Good and Evil. Prelude to a Philosophy of the Future*. Translated by Walter Kaufmann. New York: Vintage, 1989.

Nietzsche, Friedrich. *Digital Critical Edition of the Complete Works and Letters*. Based on the critical text by G. Colli and M. Montinari, edited by Paolo D'Iorio. Berlin/New York, de Gruyter 1967–.

Nietzsche, Friedrich. *Daybreak. Thoughts on the Prejudices of Morality*. Translated by R. J. Hollingdale. Cambridge: Cambridge University Press, 1997.

Nietzsche, Friedrich. *The Gay Science. With a Prelude in Rhymes and an Appendix of Songs*. Translated by Walter Kaufmann. New York: Vintage Books, 1974.

Nietzsche, Friedrich. *Human, All Too Human. A Book for Free Spirits*. Translated by R. J. Hollingdale. Cambridge: Cambridge University Press, 1996.

Nietzsche, Friedrich. 'On Truth and Lies in a Nonmoral Sense'. In *Epistemology: The Classic Readings*, edited by David E. Cooper, 180-95. Oxford: Blackwell, 1999.

Nietzsche, Friedrich. 'Schopenhauer as Educator'. Translated by Richard T. Gray. In *The Nietzsche Reader*, edited by Keith Ansell-Pearson and Duncan Large, 142–60. Oxford: Wiley-Blackwell, 2006.

Nietzsche, Friedrich. *Thus Spoke Zarathustra. A Book for Everyone and No One*. Translated by R. J. Hollingdale. London: Penguin Books, 1969.

Nietzsche, Friedrich. *Twilight of the Idols/The Anti-Christ*. Translated by R. J. Hollingdale. Harmondsworth: Penguin, 1968.

Chapter Three

Beyond Selfishness

Epicurean Ethics in Nietzsche and Guyau

Keith Ansell-Pearson

It is so ungenerous to always play the giver and the presenter and to show one's face in the process. But to give and to present and to conceal one's name and favour! Or to have no name, like nature in which what refreshes most of all is precisely that, finally and for once, we no longer encounter there a giver or a presenter, no longer a 'gracious countenance'!—To be sure, you foolishly forfeit this refreshment as well, for you have stuck a God into nature—and now everything is once more unfree and uneasy! —Nietzsche, *Dawn* 464[1]

One of the earliest references to Epicureanism in Nietzsche's corpus is an incidental remark in *Schopenhauer as Educator* where he says that to write today in favour of an education that sets goals beyond money and acquisition, that takes a great deal of time, and also encourages solitude, is likely to de disparaged as 'refined egoism' and 'immoral cultural Epicureanism' (UM IV 6). Epicurus does not become an important component in Nietzsche's published philosophy until around 1878–1879 when he draws on him again and becomes inspired by certain Epicurean notions and ideals. In the texts of the free spirit period, Nietzsche is ploughing his own field and he knows well the charge that will be levelled against him: indulging precisely in immoral Epicureanism. Indeed, at this time he was inspired by Epicurus's conception of friendship and the ideal of withdrawing from society and cultivating one's own garden. He liked to refer to his philosophy as 'my Epicurean garden' (KSB 5, 460). If philosophical therapeutics is centred on a concern with the healing of our own lives so as to return us to the joy of existing,[2] then in the texts of his middle period Nietzsche can be seen to be an heir to this ancient Epicurean tradition. The difference is that he is developing a therapy for the sicknesses of the soul under modern conditions of social control and discipline. In a note from 1881, he states that he considers the various moral schools of antiquity to be 'experimental laboratories' containing a number of recipes for the art of living and holds that these experiments now belong to us as our legitimate property: 'we shall not hesitate to adopt a Stoic recipe just because we have profited in the past from Epicurean recipes' (KSA 9, 15 [59]). Indeed, it is the case that in D Nietzsche draws on both Epicurus and Epictetus as a way of attacking the morality of living for others and promoting an ethics centred on self-cultivation.[3]

In this chapter I want to examine the character of this ethics as it centres on an Epicurean legacy and consider in particular critical concerns one might have about such an ethics. To illuminate some of the problems at hand, I shall begin by referring to the work of Jean-Marie Guyau, a neglected philosopher from the second half of the nineteenth century, with whose writings Nietzsche was familiar, and whose work I find especially fruitful for getting a critical handle on the legacy of an Epicurean ethics. The aim of the chapter is to illuminate the character of the free-minded ethics Nietzsche is espousing in his middle-period texts.[4]

GUYAU ON EPICURUS

Guyau (1854–1888) is an impressive philosopher of the second half of the nineteenth century and the author of path-breaking books on ethics and the philosophy of life. Known at the time as 'the Spinoza of France', he was read as an inspiring 'immoralist' in America by the likes of Josiah Royce and William James.[5] Nietzsche tremendously admired his work, even though he ultimately regarded him as a free thinker and not a genuine free spirit. Guyau's major work on ethics was published in 1885 (Nietzsche read it at this time) and is entitled in English as *Sketch of Morality Independent of Obligation or Sanction* [*Esquisse d'une morale sans obligation, ni sanction*].[6] Prior to this work, Guyau had published studies of ancient and modern ethics (especially English utilitarianism), being especially concerned with Epictetus and Epicurus with regard to the ancients, and with Darwin and Spencer with regard to the moderns. He also published an essay on 'problems in contemporary aesthetics' in 1884, and in 1887, a fascinating tome entitled *The Non Religion (or Irreligion) of the Future,* which Nietzsche also read and admired.[7]

Guyau's text on Epicurus was published in 1878 and is entitled *The Morality of Epicurus and Its Relation to Contemporary Doctrines.* We know Nietzsche read and was familiar with Guyau's major texts on morality and religion, but it is not known if he read this text. For Guyau, no other doctrine has been the object of more attacks and criticism than ancient and modern

Epicureanism, and this is largely because it goes so strongly against received opinion on those things that are most dear to the human heart, notably morality and religion—the two topics we may note that become the centre of Nietzsche's critical inquiries from 1878 onwards. Guyau praises Friedrich Albert Lange for showing the important role Epicurus's ideas have played in the development of modern ideas and for placing Epicurus among the most seminal materialist thinkers. Moreover, 'the moment seems to have arrived when we can more fairly appreciate the Epicurean doctrine and seek the portion of truth it contains'.[8]

Guyau sees Epicureanism as representing several innovations in the critique of religion. He notes that the system of Hobbes is essentially irreligious: miracles are attacked, and the 'natural seed' of religion is held to be in fear, ignorance, and man's innate penchant for hasty conclusions. The Epicureans of the eighteenth century, such as La Mettrie, Helvetius, and d'Holbach, openly attack religion. Guyau cautions us to exercise philosophical restraint on this matter, however, since these thinkers failed to see 'that the religious sentiment, existing in fact, had to be taken into account; that it represented a tendency, legitimate or not, of human nature, and that philosophy had to seek to satisfy it to a certain extent'.[9] Finally, Guyau notes the successes of Epicureanism in his own time, with the cosmological systems of Democritus and Epicurus triumphing again in the natural sciences, and in the moral and social sciences the doctrines that derive from Epicureanism have received a vital renewal in the English school, and this represents for him an advance over the Stoicism restored by Kant: 'How many old ideas and rooted customs Epicureanism has contributed to ridding the moral domain of!'[10] In the religious sphere, Epicurus's labours to liberate human thought from belief in the marvellous, the miraculous, and the providential will continue to live on and have an influence. Nietzsche, we can note, shares this preference for Epicureanism in relation to making advances in the scientific study of morality (see HH II WS 216).

For Guyau, the chief idea of the Epicurean doctrine is the ethical one: pleasure and pain are the sole forces that set being in motion and the sole levers by whose aid action is produced. Once this principle is posed, it is held that the most appropriate morality for each individual is the act of securing for oneself the greatest amount of personal pleasure, or what a certain utilitarianism might call 'the regularization of egoism'.[11] As Guyau notes, before Spinoza Hobbes attempted to construct a geometry of morals, Helvetius constructed a physic of morals, and d'Holbach a physiology of morals'.[12] Guyau regards Epicurean morality as resting on a confusion of fact and duty and sees the contemporary English school—Bentham, Stuart Mill, and Spencer—as providing the necessary corrective, so that instead of personal pleasure being the sole legitimate end of our moral being, it is also the pleasure of others that needs to concern us. This was to become a key component in

Guyau's subsequent efforts to construe the future of morality. Here he expresses his position as follows, which is worth citing at length:

> When in thought we descend the scale of beings, we see that the sphere in which each of them moves is narrow and virtually closed. When on the contrary, we climb towards superior beings we see their sphere of action open up, expand, and increasingly mix with the sphere of action of other beings. The *self* is less and less distinguished from other *selves*; or rather, it has greater need of them in order to constitute itself and to survive. This scale that thought has just travelled, humankind has already travelled in part in its evolution. Its departure point was egoism, but egoism by virtue of the very fecundity of each life was led to grow, to create outside itself new centres for its own action. At the same time, sentiments correlative to this centrifugal tendency were slowly born and covered over the egoist principles that served as their principle. We are moving towards an era where egoism will retreat further and further within us, will be less and less recognizable. When that ideal era arrives, beings will no longer, so to speak, be able to enjoy in solitude: their pleasure will be like a concert where the pleasure of others will enter in as a necessary element. . . . The predominant part played by sociable sentiments must be taken note of by every doctrine and in whatever we may conceive the principles of morality. No doctrine can close the human heart. We cannot mutilate ourselves, and pure egoism would be meaningless, an impossibility. In the same way that the ego is considered an illusion by contemporary psychology, that there is no personality, that we are composed of an infinite number of beings and tiny consciousnesses, in the same way we might say that egoist pleasure is an illusion: my pleasure does not exist without the pleasure of others. . . . My pleasure, in order to lose nothing of its intensity, must maintain all of its extension. [13]

Guyau regards 'evolutionist morality' as both a development of Epicureanism and also its best criticism. What is demonstrated by it is the insufficiency of the principle of pure egoism. It is this 'egoism', of course, and the appeal to the necessity of solitude, that Nietzsche will endeavour to revitalise in the texts of his free spirit period. He notes in *Ecce Homo* with respect to *Dawn*, simplifying in fact what he has actually done in the text, that it is with this work that his campaign against morality begins and that it centres on the claim that the morality of modern decadence, altruistic morality, takes itself to be morality itself, and he adds that he is the enemy of the morality of unselfing' (EH Destiny 3).

The problem of pure egoism that Guyau is identifying is to be located for him in Epicurus's original teaching. Although not lacking in 'grandeur', the teaching amounts to locking the self in upon itself. Given the definition of pleasure as a state of repose for both body and soul, a state of physical equilibrium and intellectual ataraxia, Epicurus deduces from it the ideal that for every human being the highest pleasure consists in retreating into the self and seeking everything within oneself without any external aid or repose. Guyau prefers Hobbes's correction on this point, in which he maintains that pleasure 'is in its essence movement, action, energy, consequently, progress' or forward movement: 'To enjoy means to act, and acting means advancing'.[14] Guyau insists that although pleasure is accompanied by an internal equilibrium and harmony of all our faculties, this is only a condition of pleasure that in fact allows for a more expansive action in all directions. Moreover, pleasure is not anything immobile but subject to the laws of universal evolution. Let me now look in some detail at how Guyau wishes to move beyond so-called Epicurean hedonism. I say *so-called* since it is a moot point to associate Epicurus's teaching with hedonism. One commentator has incisively argued, for example, that Epicurus is mostly concerned with securing inner tranquillity, or ataraxia, and his philosophy of pleasure has to be seen as part of this overarching and overriding goal.[15] Having noted this, let me stick with Epicureanism as a philosophy of pleasure and follow for now Guyau's arguments against it.

LIFE AND PLEASURE: BEYOND HEDONISM

For Guyau, the cause operating within us before any attraction of pleasure is life.[16] Pleasure is but the consequence of an instinctive effort to maintain and enlarge life, and nature is to be regarded as self-moving and self-governing. Guyau writes:

> One does not always act with the view of seeking a *particular pleasure*—limited and exterior to the act itself. Sometimes we act for the pleasure of acting . . . . There is in us an accumulated force which demands to be used. If its expenditure is impeded, this force becomes desire or aversion; if the desire is satisfied, there is pleasure; if it is opposed, there is pain. But it does not follow from this that the stored-up activity unfolds itself solely *for the sake* of pleasure—with pleasure as motive. Life unfolds and expresses itself in activity because it is life. In all creatures pleasure accompanies, much more than it provokes, the search after life.[17]

For Guyau, Epicurus, along with his faulty thinking about evolution, in which pleasure is said to create an organ's function, needs correcting on this point. In addition, he argues contra Bentham that 'to live is not to calculate, it is to act'.[18] An essentially Spinozist position—the tendency to persist in life is the necessary law of life—is deduced: 'The tendency of the creature to continue in existence is at the root of all desire, without forming in itself a determinate desire'.[19] Guyau takes this tendency to be one that goes beyond and envelops conscious life, so it is 'both the most radical of realities and the inevitable ideal'.[20] Therefore, Guyau reaches the conclusion that the part of morality that can be founded on positive facts can be defined as, 'the science which has for object all the means of *preserving* and *enlarging* material and

intellectual life'.[21] His ethics centre, then, on a desire to increase 'the intensity of life' which consists in enlarging the range of activity under all its
forms and that is compatible with the renewal of force.[22] A superior being is
one that practices a variety of action; thought itself is nothing other than
condensed action and life at its maximum development. He defines this
superior being as one which 'unites the most delicate sensibility with the
strongest will'.[23]

Although the evolved human being possesses a source of varied enjoyment in its own activity, this does not mean that such a human being will
decide to shut itself up in itself, establishing an autarchic realm of self-
sufficiency, like some Stoic sage. For Guyau, intellectual pleasures are both
the most inward pleasures and also the most communicative, being both
individual and social. The bonds that the sharing of the higher pleasures can
generate create a particular kind of obligation: 'an emotional bond—a union
produced by the complete, or partial, harmony of sentiments or thoughts'.[24]
Guyau does not, of course, deny that there is often conflict and disagreement
over values and ideals, but at the same time he insists new bonds between
individuals arise from the sharing of the higher pleasures. Indeed, he maintains that the higher we rise in the scale of evolution, the more we see the
highly social and sociable character of the pleasures of humankind.

We moderns are becoming more intellectual in our enjoyments and tastes,
and with this arises a 'universal consciousness'. in which consciousness becomes easier of penetration.[25] It is on this point that Guyau thinks we are
going beyond the life of pleasures envisaged by Epicurean philosophy. In
modern conditions of human social evolution, we find that the self distinguishes itself less and less from other selves and, in fact, has more in need of
them so as to form itself and flourish. Here Guyau locates an important
principle of human evolution: although the point of departure is selfishness,
it is such 'by virtue of the very fecundity of all life', and it is 'obliged to
enlarge itself, to create outside of itself new centres of its own action'.[26] For
Guyau, then, human evolution is on the way to an epoch in which primitive
selfishness will more and more recede. Compared to the selfish component
of our existence, the sphere of altruism is becoming considerably larger, and
even the so-called purely physical pleasures, such as eating and drinking,
only acquire their full charm when one shares them with others. The social
sentiments are, then, of crucial importance for understanding the character of
our enjoyments *and* pains: 'Neither my sufferings nor my pleasures are absolutely my own'.[27]

There is for Guyau an abundance of life that motivates us to care and
work not only for ourselves but for others. This is, in large part, what he
means when he seeks to locate 'morality'—the sphere of the social expansion
of the human animal and of other-regarding actions—within life itself. Life
has two main aspects: nutrition and assimilation, on the one hand, and pro-

duction and fecundity on the other. The more a life form takes in, the more it needs to give out. Even in the life of the cell we can locate a principle of expansion and one that prevents any individual being sufficient unto itself. Moreover, the 'richest life' is to be found in the life that lavishly spends itself, sacrificing itself within certain limits, and sharing itself with others. The most perfect organism will also be the most sociable being: not simply because this carries with it certain evolutionary advantages but also because it is part of the higher moral development of life itself. It is on this point that Guyau sharply distinguishes himself from the likes of Bentham and the school of utilitarianism. It is within the very depths of our being that the instincts of sympathy and sociability emerge and that the English school has shown us to be more or less artificially acquired in the course of human evolution, so being little more than adventitious in consequence.

For Guyau, the higher life is that which expands beyond the narrow horizon of the individual self. We have, he thinks, a need to go out of ourselves to others: 'we want to multiply ourselves by communion of thoughts and sentiments'.[28] We enjoy others knowing that we exist, feel, suffer, and love. In this respect, then, 'we tear the veil of individuality', and this is not simple vanity but a fecund desire to 'burst the narrow shell of the self'.[29] Guyau, however, is not naïve in his appreciation of 'life': he draws our attention to the phenomenon of 'altruistic debauchery' in which one lives too much for others and neglects a healthy care of self.[30] So, although he is keen to attack what he sees as the dogmatism of egoism,[31] he also appreciates the need for a healthy form of egoism consisting in the cultivation of a care of self.

MIDDLE PERIOD NIETZSCHE

In turning to Nietzsche, I want to focus largely on his middle period, especially the text *Dawn*. At this point in his intellectual development, Nietzsche has no philosophy of life, such as might be encapsulated in the doctrine of the will to power, and he does not express the concerns about Epicurus that characterize his late writings, such as the criticism of decadence (see AC 30, 58). So, we find Nietzsche at a definite point in his development, the point as he puts it in D of a 'moral interregnum' (D 453), and he is happy to cultivate his Epicurean garden. For Nietzsche, Epicurus experiences a oneness with nature and attains serenity in the face of the tumultuous character of existence. Moreover, although Epicurus suffers from existence, it is the suffering that gives his achievement of happiness a profound meaning (GS 45). Nietzsche appears to be inspired by Epicurus's cultivation of a voluptuous, but modest, appreciation of existence, as well as by the attainment of serenity through a practice of psychic tranquillity: Nietzsche has a special take on Epicurean *ataraxia*. Nietzsche's Epicurean-inspired doctrine at this time is clearly stated in aphorism 338 of *The Gay Science*, and I quote from it:

> Live in seclusion so that you *can* live for yourself. Live in *ignorance* about what seems most important to your age . . . the clamor of today, the noise of wars and revolutions should be a mere murmur for you. You will also wish to help—but only those whose distress you *understand* entirely because they share with you one suffering and one hope—your friends—and only in the manner in which you help yourself. (GS 338)

We need to be careful in thinking how best to interpret such a doctrine, and in my view it would be too hasty to level criticisms at Nietzsche for neglecting the critical observations on Epicurean teaching we find, for example, in Guyau. This is because Nietzsche at this time is undertaking a specific project of ethical reformation and has specific reasons for wanting to promote an ethics of self-cultivation. Of course, we can question whether these reasons are well founded and whether they belie even a misanthropic or sociopathic set of sentiments on his part. My view is that this is going too far, though it is clear that his free-thinking project does at times give the appearance of bordering on these tendencies, but this we might say is part of the risks undertaken by a free-spirited project of ethical reformation, if decidedly not one of revolution: Nietzsche's project is one of what he calls 'small doses' (D 534) and 'slow cures' (D 462). Unlike Guyau, Nietzsche does not and cannot appeal to the interests of a broadened humanity as a whole, though he clearly favours an Enlightenment project, and hence his suspicions about love and the philanthropic sentiment that he regards as informing a great deal of the modern moral sensibility and that he has little time for. Let me now explore this set of issues in a little more detail.

What are the concerns we might have over Nietzsche's project, and how might a close reading of the texts yield a subtler Nietzsche on ethical matters? It is widely thought that Nietzsche invokes a notion of subjectivity as self-absorbed, as something whole to itself fully represented and self-contained.[32] In his consideration of the 'self and other in Nietzsche', Elliot Jurist notes that Nietzsche's concern is with self-gratification—with such things as narcissism, instinctual satisfaction, and the will to power—and argues that this concern 'interferes with the way he characterizes the relationship between self and others' and, moreover, that he leaves the issue of our relation to others unresolved: 'Nietzsche himself acknowledges the social constitution of agency; yet he opts not to pursue this and not to concentrate fully on coming to terms with the experience of being-for-another'.[33] Jurist notes the complexity and intricacy, if not the delicacy, of Nietzsche's actual position or set of positions when he comments on the fact that 'competing tendencies' characterize Nietzsche's attitude towards others. So, on the one hand, Jurist contends, we encounter him seemingly countenancing cruelty and exploitation, and repeatedly stressing the need for solitude. And yet, on the other hand, we see him approaching the study of human relationships 'with a subtlety and a psychological astuteness that should not be overlooked'.[34]

As Ruth Abbey notes, Nietzsche's purpose in attacking the presumptions and prejudices of morality, for example, through conducting a genealogy of morality, is practical. He wants to discredit and demote values that promote the common interest and so as to clear the ground for the creation and resurgence of those that foster and ethics of individual self-care and self-fashioning. This extends to his re-appraisal of the value of self-love, in which, as Nietzsche writes, we are to forgive ourselves for our own ego and love ourselves as an act of clemency.[35] Only individuals who experience this love of self are capable of generous and beautiful actions. It becomes necessary, then, for Nietzsche to strip egoism and self-love of their usual adverse connotations, as when he states 'egoism is not evil' (HH I 101).[36] This does not mean for him, of course, that all is vanity or that, while all action might derive from egoism, all egoism is the same.[37] We need to distinguish between types of egoism and distinguish between crude and immature egoism and egoism that is mature and refined.

I think it prudent to bear in mind a point astutely made by Abbey, namely, that Nietzsche's supposedly scientific analyses of morality have a therapeutic intent, so that when he praises egoism, rather just describing it, he is 'deliberately compensating for the calumny it has suffered and continues to suffer in moral frameworks'.[38] Still, it is important that Nietzsche provide his readers with models of the relation between the self and its others. As we shall see, it is far-fetched to claim, as Jurist does, that Nietzsche is more concerned with narcissism than he is with relatedness.[39] Again, the context of Nietzsche's 'campaign' against morality, as he calls it, is of crucial importance: he is advancing an ethics of self-cultivation as an ethics of resistance and in the context of his worries over the moral tendencies of commercial society. Let me turn to this.

DAWN'S CAMPAIGN AGAINST MORALITY

The 'campaign' centres largely on a critique of what Nietzsche sees as the modern tendency, the tendency of his own century, to identify morality with the sympathetic affects and compassion [Mitleid], so as to give us a 'definition' of morality. Throughout D, Nietzsche operates with several critical conceptions of morality. He is keen to attack the view that everything that exists has a connection with morality, and thus a moral significance can be projected onto the world (D 3, 90, 100, 197, 563). He voices an opposition to both 'picturesque morality' (D 141) and 'petty bourgeois morality' (D 146) and speaks of his own 'audacious morality' [verwegenen Moralität] (D 432).

With regard to the modern prejudice, which is one of the main foci of his polemic in the book, here there is the presumption that we know 'what actually constitutes morality': 'It seems *to do* every single person *good* these days to hear that society is on the road to *adapting* the individual to fit the needs of the throng and that the *individual's happiness as well as his sacrifice* consist in feeling himself to be a useful member of the whole . . .' (D 132). As Nietzsche sees it, then, the modern emphasis is on defining the moral in terms of the sympathetic affects and compassion [Mitleid]. We can, he thinks, explain the modern in terms of a movement towards managing more cheaply, safely, and uniformly individuals in terms of *'large bodies and their limbs'*. This, he says, is *'the basic moral current of our age'*: 'Everything that in some way supports both this drive to form bodies and limbs and its abetting drives is felt to be *good . . .'* (D 132).

For Nietzsche, then, the principal presumption that holds sway in the Europe of his day is that the sympathetic affects define the essence of the moral, such as actions deemed to be congenial, disinterested, of general utility, and so on. He also thinks we are busy building a society of 'security' in which the chief goal is to protect individuals from various hazards of life and so reduce human suffering and conflict. In *Dawn* Nietzsche's focus is not, as is widely supposed, on Christianity as the religion of pity or compassion—he maintains that until the eighteenth century such a virtue was a subsidiary and nonessential aspect of this religion. The view that morality means nothing other than disinterested, useful, and congenial actions is the residuum of Christian sentiments, once the strictly egotistical, foundational belief in the importance of eternal personal salvation and the dogmas on which this belief rested, receded, and there then came into the foreground ancillary beliefs in love and love thy neighbour which harmonized with ecclesiastical charity. There emerges in modernity a cult of love for humanity and the idea of surpassing the Christian ideal became, 'a secret spur of all French freethinkers from Voltaire through to August Comte', for example, the latter's moral formula of '*vivre pour autrui* [live for others]' (D 132).

Nietzsche's main target in the book, then, is what he sees as the fundamental tendency of modern commercial society and its attempt at a 'collectivity-building project that aims at disciplining bodies and selves and integrating them into a uniform whole'.[40] Here 'morality' denotes the means of adapting the individual to the needs of the whole, making him a useful member of society. This requires that every individual is made to feel, as its primary emotion, a connectedness or bondedness with the whole, with society, in which anything truly 'individual' is regarded as prodigal, costly, inimical, extravagant, and so on. Nietzsche's great worry is that genuine individuality and a healthy concern with self-fashioning will be sacrificed and this, in large part, informs his critique of what he sees as the cult of sympathetic affects within modernity.

In the book, Nietzsche devotes a significant number of sections to the topic of the affect of compassion [Mitleid], largely concentrated in book 2 of the text. His aim is to outline some of the perspectives by which we can gain some genuinely reflective insight into the affect of compassion and to encourage us to pursue critical lines of inquiry, so compassion [Mitleid] will be shown to be not a pure other-regarding affection, to be an injurious affect, to have value for specific cultures, and so on (D 132–38).[41] His criticism rests on a number of concerns. Let me mention two.

(a) A concern that in extolling compassion as the panacea to our moral anxieties we are in danger of existing as fantasists. Nietzsche wonders whether people speak with such idolatry about love—the 'food of the gods'—simply because they have had so little of it. But would not a utopia of universal love be something ludicrous?—'each person flocked around, pestered, longed for not by one love . . . but by thousands, indeed by each and everyone'. (D 147) Instead, Nietzsche wants us to favour a future of solitude, quietude, and even being unpopular. The imperatives of philosophies of universal love and compassion will serve only to destroy us. If they tempt us we should put them to the test and stop all our fantasizing (D 137).

(b) A concern that in its cult of the sympathetic affects, modern society is in danger of providing the image of a single moral-making morality that amounts to a tyrannical encroachment on the requirements of individual self-cultivation. In an essay on pity and mercy in Nietzsche, Martha Nussbaum argues that Nietzsche's project is one that aims to bring about a revival of Stoic values—self-command and self-formation—within a post-Christian and post-Romantic context (she criticizes him for this Stoicism).[42] The picture frequently presented is one of Nietzsche advocating, in place of an ethics of sympathy or compassion, one of idiosyncratic self-assertion or the value of unbridled egoism. This is, clearly, a caricature, and fails to capture what we might call the Stoic demands Nietzsche places on the self and its cultivation: harshness toward oneself, self-discipline, self-control, honesty, and a profound love of fate.[43] An important aphorism in this regard is 139, which runs:

> You say that the morality of being compassionate is a higher morality [Moral] than that of Stoicism? Prove it! But remember that what is 'higher' and 'lower' in morality is not, in turn to be measured by a moral yardstick: for there is no absolute morality [Moral]. So take your rule from somewhere else—and now beware! (D 139)

Here we see Nietzsche contesting the idea that there is a *single* moral-making morality—he never contests the idea that morality is necessary, only that

there is a single, absolute conception of it. However, other models of the self
and its relation to others are offered in D, as we shall see, and these serve to
complicate the sage model of complete self-sufficiency and isolated aloof-
ness that we might attribute to Nietzsche.

It is clear that Nietzsche is not in D advocating the overcoming of all
possible forms of morality. Where morality centres on 'continual self-command and self-overcoming . . . in great things and in the smallest', he champions it (HH II WS 45). His concern is that 'morality' in the forms it has
assumed in the greater part of human history, right up to Kant's moral law,
has opened up an abundance of sources of displeasure and to the point that
one can say that with every 'refinement in morality' [Sittlichkeit] human
beings have grown '*more and more dissatisfied* with themselves, their neighbour, and their lot' (D 106). The individual in search of happiness, and who
wishes to become its own lawgiver, cannot be treated with prescriptions to
the path to happiness simply because individual happiness springs from one's
own unknown laws, and external prescriptions only serve to obstruct and
hinder it: 'The so-called "moral" precepts are, in truth, directed against individuals and are in no way aimed at promoting their happiness' (D 108).
Indeed, Nietzsche himself does not intend to lay down precepts for everyone.
As he writes, 'One should seek out limited circles and seek and promote the
morality appropriate to them' (D 194). Up to now, Nietzsche notes, the moral
law has been supposed to stand above our personal likes and dislikes; we did
not want to impose this law upon ourselves but preferred to take it from
somewhere or have it commanded to us. If we examine what is often taken to
be the summit of the moral in philosophy—the mastery of the affects—we
find that there is pleasure to be taken in this mastery. I can impress myself by
what I can deny, defer, resist, and so on. It is through this mastery that I grow
and develop. And yet morality, as we moderns have come to understand it,
would have to give this ethical self-mastery a bad conscience. If we take as
our criterion of the moral to be self-sacrificing resolution and self-denial, we
would have to say, if being honest, that such acts are not performed strictly
for the sake of others; my own fulfilment and pride are at work, and the other
provides the self with an opportunity to relieve itself through self-denial.

The morality that humanity has cultivated and dedicated itself to is one of
'enthusiastic devotion' and 'living for others' in which it looks down from
certain exalted heights on the more sober morality of self-control (which is
regarded as egotistical). Nietzsche suggests the reason why morality has been
developed in this way is owing to the enjoyment of the state of intoxication
which has stemmed from the thought that the person is at one with the
powerful being to whom it consecrates itself; in this way 'the feeling of
power' is enjoyed and is confirmed by a sacrifice of the self. For Nietzsche,
such an overcoming of the self is impossible: 'In truth you only *seem* to
sacrifice yourselves; instead, in your thoughts you transform yourselves into

gods and take pleasure in yourselves as such' (D 215). In examining the inflated character of moral thinking and language, Nietzsche is dealing with a problem that preoccupies him in his middle period: the problem of fanaticism. As he notes at one point in the text, such 'enthusiasts' will seek to implant the faith in intoxication 'as *the* life within life: a terrible faith!' (D 50). Such is the extent of Nietzsche's anxiety that he wonders whether humanity as a whole will one day perish by its spiritual fire-waters and by those who keep alive the desire for them. The 'strange madness of moral judgements' is bound up with states of exaltation and 'the most exalted language' (D 189).

Nietzsche appeals to the Stoic Epictetus for an example of a non-fanatical mode of living and as a counterweight to modern idealists who are greedy for expansion. Epictetus's ideal human being, lacking all fear of God and believing strictly in reason, 'is not a preacher of penitence' (D 546). Although this ancient thinker was a slave, the exemplar he invokes is without class and is possible in every class. Nietzsche also admires Epictetus on account of his dedication to his own ego and for resisting the glorification of thinking and living for others (D 131). Of course, this is a partial and selective appropriation of Epictetus on Nietzsche's part. Although his chief concerns are with integrity and self-command, Epictetus is also known for his Stoic cosmopolitanism in which individuals have an obligation to care for their fellow human beings, and Nietzsche is silent about this aspect of Stoic teaching.[44] Nevertheless, it is true that the ethical outlook of Epictetus does invite people 'to value their individual selves over everything else',[45] and for Nietzsche, he serves as a useful contrast to Christian thinkers, such as Pascal, who considered the ego to be something hateful:

If, as Pascal and Christianity claim, our ego [Ich] is always *hateful*, how might we possibly ever allow or assume that someone else could love it—be it God or a human being! It would go against all decency to let oneself be loved knowing full well that one only *deserves* hate—not to mention other feelings of repulsion.—'But this is precisely the kingdom of mercy'.—So is your love-thy-neighbour mercy? Your compassion mercy? Well, if these things are possible for you, go still one step further: love yourselves out of mercy—then you won't need your God any more at all, and the whole drama of original sin and redemption will play itself out to the end in you yourselves. (D 79)

We are to look askance at impatient political invalids who seek change through the bloody quackery of revolution and instead carry out small, personal experiments, establishing ourselves as our own *reges* (D 453). In the future, Nietzsche hopes, the inventive and fructifying person shall no longer be sacrificed and 'numerous novel experiments shall be made in ways of life and modes of society' (D 164). When this takes place, we will find that an enormous load of guilty conscience has been purged from the world. Humanity has suffered for too long from teachers of morality who wanted too much all at once and sought to lay down precepts for everyone (D 194). In the future, care will need to be given to the most personal questions and create time for them (D 196). Small individual questions and experiments are no longer to be viewed with contempt and impatience (D 547). Contra the presumptions of morality, then, he holds that we ourselves are experiments and our task should be to want to be such (D 543). In place of the ruling ethic of sympathy and self-sacrifice, which can assume the form of a 'tyrannical encroachment', Nietzsche invites individuals to engage in self-fashioning, cultivating a self that others can behold with pleasure, a 'lovely, peaceful, self-enclosed garden . . . with high walls to protect against the dangers and dust of the roadway, but with a hospitable gate as well' (D 174).[46]

Nietzsche acknowledges, then, that there is a need for the self to express, albeit in a subtle manner, its altruistic drive. However, the question remains: in all of this concern with finding and inventing one's self, through modes of self-cultivation, what of the relation of the self to others? To negotiate this question I now want to turn in the final part of the chapter to a reading of one particular aphorism in D, an especially intriguing one.

A READING OF *DAWN* 449

Ah! How it nauseates me to *impose* my thoughts on another! How I take pleasure in every mood and secret conversion within myself by which the thoughts *of others* prevail over my own! From time to time there occurs an even higher celebration, when for a change one is *allowed to give away* one's spiritual house and possessions like the father confessor who sits in the corner, eager for *one in need* to come and recount the travail of his thoughts in order that he, the father confessor, might once again fill his hand and heart and *lighten* his burdened soul. Not only does he eschew all praise for what he does: he would also like to avoid any gratitude, for gratitude is invasive and has no respect for solitude and silence. He seeks to live nameless or lightly ridiculed, too humble to awaken envy or enmity, armed with a head free of fever, a handful of knowledge and a bag full of experiences, to be, as it were, a doctor of the spirit to the indigent and to aid people here and there whose head is *disturbed by opinions* without their really noticing who has helped him! Not to be right vis-à-vis this person and to celebrate a victory, but to speak with him in such a way that, after a tiny unobserved hint or objections, he himself says what is right and, proud of the fact, walks away! Like a modest hostel that turns away no one in need, that is, however, forgotten about afterward or laughed at! To have no advantage, neither better food, nor purer air, nor a more joyful spirit—but to share, to give back, to communicate, to grow poorer! To be able to be humble so as to be accessible to many and humiliating to none! To have experienced much injustice and have crawled through the worm-tunnels of every kind of error in order to be able to reach many hidden souls along their secret paths! Always in a type of love and a type of self-interest and self-enjoyment! To be in possession of a dominion and at the same time inconspicuous and renouncing! To lie constantly in the sun and the kindness of grace and yet to know that the paths rising to the sublime [zum Erhabenen] are right at hand!—That would be a life! That would be a reason to live, to live a long time. (D 449)

This aphorism poses a number of interpretive challenges, and it is clearly central to any interpretation of Nietzsche on the relation between the self and others. The way Nietzsche envisages this relation is extraordinarily complicated. In this aphorism, Nietzsche is envisaging a modest existence for the self, moving from matters of the body (not indulging oneself with better food) to matters of the soul (not even having a more joyful spirit), and entailing a mode of existence that shares, returns, and communicates, freely making oneself poor in this manner of being and dwelling. Indeed, he refers to it as a 'humble' mode of living, one that is accessible to many and does not entail humiliating anyone. One suffers from existence, such is the vulnerability of the self, and yet still profits from one's experiences of life and to the point where one can aid and instruct others. One can love and one can attend to the needs and cares of the self. One constructs one's dominion, but in a way that is not self-centred, but in fact 'self-renouncing'. Living in this manner, one can wish to live well and live a long time: one is ascending paths to the sublime, that is, peaks of elevated existence in which, from the vantage point of the heights one has climbed, one can look down upon the experiences of life that have been conquered and overcome. The portrait depicted seems to be that of some new sage, a person who has tempered emotional and mental excess, so is 'armed with a head free of fever, a handful of knowledge and a bag full of experiences', and can be a 'doctor of the spirit to the indigent', aiding people whose heads are subject to the reign of doxa. One lives without praise or gratitude, silently and even namelessly. The aid offered to the other is, therefore, of a delicate kind: one seeks to preserve one's own space in the process and to ensure that the integrity of the other person is respected. 'Love' is perhaps a strong word for Nietzsche to use in this example, but he is clearly hinting at a special mode of care of others, and one that is not at all free of self-interest and self-enjoyment.

Such an aphorism clearly shows that Nietzsche's campaign against morality, by which he means the 'morality of unselfing', possesses a complicated character, at least as it is articulated in *Dawn*. Nietzsche's focus on the self and on egoism is of a highly ethical character, and in two senses: (a) it has a concern with self-cultivation; (b) this cultivation is not without care for others, including the duties and responsibilities that come with such care. Here we can agree with Foucault's insight into the paradox of a precept of care of self that signifies for us today either egoism or withdrawal, but which for centuries was a positive principle, serving as the matrix for dedicated moralities. Christianity and the modern world have based the codes of moral strictness on a morality of non-egoism to the point where we forget that such codes originated in an environment marked by the obligation to take care of oneself.[47] Martha Nussbaum claims that in his cult of Stoic strength Nietzsche depicts 'a fearful person, a person who is determined to seal himself off from risk, even at the cost of loss of love and value'.[48] Like the otherworldliness he abhors, the Stoicism he endorses is a form of self-protection, expressing 'a fear of this world and its contingencies'.[49] However, *Dawn* 449 clearly shows that Nietzsche is open to a doctrine of love, albeit of an unconventional kind, and that he is not advocating an ethic of a retreat into the self, one that would be independent of specifically human relations of care and openness to the other.

NOTES

My thanks to Rebecca Bamford for helpful feedback on the chapter that has helped me to finesse my reading of Nietzsche.

1. I have referred to the following translations of Nietzsche: *Unfashionable Observations,* trans. Richard T. Gray (Stanford: Stanford University Press, 1995); *Human, All Too Human,* trans. R. J. Hollingdale (Cambridge: Cambridge University Press, 1986); *Dawn: Thoughts on the Presumptions of Morality,* trans. Brittain Smith (Stanford: Stanford University Press, 2011); *The Gay Science,* trans. Walter Kaufmann (New York: Random House, 1974); *Ecce Homo,* trans. Duncan Large (Oxford: Oxford University Press, 2007).
    2. Pierre Hadot, *Philosophy as a Way of Life,* trans. Michael Chase (Oxford: Basil Blackwell, 1995), 87.
    3. Epicurus is a significant and inspiring figure for Nietzsche at the time of his free spirit texts (1878–1882); by the time of the late writings (1886–1888), he is a more ambivalent figure for Nietzsche, still the 'soul-soother' of later antiquity but also said to be a typical decadent. With the return of the Dionysian in his thinking, which disappears in his middle-period writings, we get the fundamental contrast between 'Epicurean delight' [Vergnügen] and 'Dionysian joy' [Lust]: 'I have presented such terrible images to knowledge that any "Epicurean delight" is out of the question, Only Dionysian joy is sufficient: *I have been the first to discover the tragic'* (KSA 11, 25 [95]; WP 1029).
    4. See also Paul Bishop's discussion of translating '*der Freigeist* or *der freie Geist'* as 'free mind' in this volume.
    5. See William James, 'The Moral Philosophy and the Moral Life', in *The Will to Believe* (New York: Dover, 1956), 184–216; Josiah Royce, *Studies of Good and Evil: A Series of Essays upon Problems of Philosophy and of Life* (New York: Appleton & Co., 1899), chapter 12, 349–84. On the reception of Guyau as an immoralist, see Geoffrey C. Fidler, 'On Jean-Marie Guyau, Immoraliste', *Journal of the History of Ideas* 55 (1994): 75–98.
    6. Thomas Brobjer notes that Nietzsche's reading of the text 'is likely to have been of major importance for his views on ethics', *Nietzsche's Philosophical Context* (Urbana: University of Illinois Press, 2008, 91). For the purposes of this chapter, I have been able to consult the fourth edition of the French from 1896 and the English translation of 1898 based on the second edition. The differences between the different editions are slight.
    7. For some details, see Brobjer, *Nietzsche's Philosophical Context*, 102 and 235, note 32.
    8. J. M. Guyau, *La Morale D'Epicure et les rapports avec les doctrines contemporaines* (Paris: Librairie Germer Baillière, 1878), 280.
    9. Guyau, *La Morale D'Epicure,* 288.
    10. Guyau, *La Morale D'Epicure,* 288.
    11. Guyau, *La Morale D'Epicure,* 281.

12. Guyau, *La Morale D'Epicure*, 281.
13. Guyau, *La Morale D'Epicure*, 282–83.
14. Guyau, *La Morale D'Epicure*, 284.
15. See Malte Hossenfelder, 'Epicurus—hedonist malgré lui', in *The Norms of Nature: Studies in Hellenistic Ethics*, ed. Malcolm Schofield and Gisela Striker (Cambridge: Cambridge University Press, 1986), 245–65.
16. J. M. Guyau, *A Sketch of Morality Independent of Obligation or Sanction*, trans. Gertrude Kapteyn (London: Watts & Co., 1898), 210.
17. Guyau, *A Sketch of Morality*, 77.
18. Guyau, *A Sketch of Morality*, 211.
19. Guyau, *A Sketch of Morality*, 79.
20. Guyau, *A Sketch of Morality*, 75.
21. Guyau, *A Sketch of Morality*, 75.
22. Guyau, *A Sketch of Morality*, 76.
23. Guyau, *A Sketch of Morality*, 35.
24. Guyau, *A Sketch of Morality*, 94–95.
25. Guyau, *A Sketch of Morality*, 95.
26. Guyau, *A Sketch of Morality*, 95.
27. Guyau, *A Sketch of Morality*, 96.
28. Guyau, *A Sketch of Morality*, 84.
29. Guyau, *A Sketch of Morality*, 84.
30. Guyau, *A Sketch of Morality*, 85.
31. Guyau, *A Sketch of Morality*, 65.
32. Alison Ainley, '"Ideal Selfishness": Nietzsche's Metaphor of Maternity', in *Exceedingly Nietzsche: Aspects of Contemporary Nietzsche-Interpretation*, ed. David Farrell Krell and David Wood (London: Routledge, 1988), 116–31, 124.
33. Elliot L. Jurist, *Beyond Hegel and Nietzsche. Philosophy, Culture, and Agency* (Cambridge, MA.: MIT Press, 2000), 258.
34. Jurist, *Beyond Hegel and Nietzsche*, 246.
35. Ruth Abbey, *Nietzsche's Middle Period* (Oxford: Oxford University Press), 35.
36. Cited in Abbey, *Nietzsche's Middle Period*, 36.
37. Abbey, *Nietzsche's Middle Period*, 36.
38. Abbey, *Nietzsche's Middle Period*, 38.
39. Jurist, *Beyond Hegel and Nietzsche*, 261.
40. Michael Ure, 'The Irony of Pity: Nietzsche contra Schopenhauer and Rousseau', *Journal of Nietzsche Studies* 32 (2006): 68–92, 88 note 45.
41. It is perhaps important to bear in mind that in taking to task *Mitleid* in the ways that he does in these sections of D, Nietzsche is working with Schopenhauer's conception of it where it involves the complete identification with the suffering of another. See A. Schopenhauer, *On the Basis of Morality*, trans. E. F. J. Payne (Providence: Berghahn Books, 1995), 144.
42. Martha C. Nussbaum, 'Pity and Mercy: Nietzsche's Stoicism', in Richard Schacht (ed.), *Nietzsche, Genealogy, Morality*, ed. Richard Schacht. Berkeley: University of California Press, 1994), 139–67. (1994, p. 140). The figure Nussbaum esteems over Nietzsche is Rousseau, who is prized for his 'eloquent writings on pity' ('Pity and Mercy', 140) and whose thinking lies at the basis of 'democratic-socialist thinking' (1994, p. 159). For an intelligent response to some of Nussbaum's concerns over Nietzsche on *Mitleid*, see Gudrun von Tevenar, 'Nietzsche's Objections to Pity and Compassion', in von Tevenar (ed.), *Nietzsche and Ethics* (Bern: Peter Lang, 2007), 263–81; for a critique of Rousseau on pity, see Ure, 'The Irony of Pity'. .
43. See R. M. Elveton, 'Nietzsche's Stoicism: The Depths are Inside', in Paul Bishop (ed.), *Nietzsche and Antiquity: His Reaction and Response to the Classical Tradition* (New York: Camden House, 2004), 192–203, 193.
44. Thomas Brobjer suggests that Nietzsche did not read the extended 'Discourses' and was only familiar with Epictetus's short 'Manual' or *Enchiridion*, and this might account for the somewhat one-sided portrait of him we get from Nietzsche's appraisal. See Brobjer, 'Nietzsche's Reading of Epictetus', *Nietzsche-Studien* 32 (2003): 429–35, 430. For a full picture of Epictetus see A. A. Long, *Epictetus: A Stoic and Socratic Guide to Life* (Oxford: Oxford University Press, 2002).

45. See Long, *Epictetus*, 3. Long also notes that Epictetus devotes more thought to the care of the self than he does to what is incumbent on human beings as members of society (30).
46. See also my discussion in 'Care of Self in Dawn: On Nietzsche's Resistance to Bio-Political Modernity', in *Nietzsche As Political Philosopher*, ed. Barry Stocker and Manuel Knoll (Berlin and New York: de Gruyter, 2014), 269–86.
47. For Foucault's insights see 'Technologies of the Self', in *Technologies of the Self: A Seminar with Michel Foucault*, ed. Luther H. Martin et al. (London: Tavistock, 1988), 16–50; and *The Hermeneutics of the Self: Lectures at the College de France 1981–2*, trans. Graham Burchell (New York: Palgrave Macmillan, 2005).
48. Nussbaum, 'Pity and Mercy: Nietzsche's Stoicism', 140.
49. Ibid.

BIBLIOGRAPHY

Abbey, Ruth. *Nietzsche's Middle Period*. Oxford: Oxford University Press, 2000.
Ainley, Alison. '"Ideal Selfishness": Nietzsche's Metaphor of Maternity'. In *Exceedingly Nietzsche: Aspects of Contemporary Nietzsche-Interpretation*, edited by David Farrell Krell and David Wood, 116–31. London: Routledge, 1988.
Ansell-Pearson, Keith. 'Care of Self in Dawn: On Nietzsche's Resistance to Bio-Political Modernity'. In *Nietzsche As Political Philosopher*, edited by Barry Stocker and Manuel Knoll, 269–286. Berlin and New York: de Gruyter, 2014.
Brobjer, Thomas H. *Nietzsche's Philosophical Context: An Intellectual Biography*. Urbana: University of Illinois Press, 2008.
Brobjer, Thomas H. 'Nietzsche's Reading of Epictetus'. *Nietzsche-Studien* 32 (2003): 429–34.
Elveton, R. M. 'Nietzsche's Stoicism: The Depths Are Inside'. In *Nietzsche and Antiquity: His Reaction and Response to the Classical Tradition*, edited by Paul Bishop, 192–203. New York: Camden House, 2004.
Fidler, Geoffrey C. 'On Jean-Marie Guyau, Immoraliste', *Journal of the History of Ideas* 55 (1994): 75–98.
Foucault, Michel. *The Hermeneutics of the Self: Lectures at the College de France 1981–2*. Translated by Graham Burchell. New York: Palgrave Macmillan, 2005.
Guyau, J. M. *La Morale D'Epicure et les rapports avec les doctrines contemporaines*. Paris: Librairie Germer Baillière, 1878.
Guyau, J. M. *A Sketch of Morality Independent of Obligation or Sanction*. Translated by Gertrude Kapteyn. London: Watts & Co., 1898.
Hadot, Pierre. *Philosophy as a Way of Life*. Translated by Michael Chase. Oxford: Basil Blackwell, 1995.
Hossenfelder, Malte. 'Epicurus—hedonist malgré lui'. In *The Norms of Nature: Studies in Hellenistic Ethics*, edited by Malcolm Schofield and Gisela Striker, 245–65. Cambridge: Cambridge University Press, 1986.
James, William. 'The Moral Philosophy and the Moral Life'. In *The Will to Believe*, 184–216. New York: Dover, 1956.
Jurist, Elliot L. *Beyond Hegel and Nietzsche. Philosophy, Culture, and Agency*. Cambridge, MA: The MIT Press, 2000.
Long, A. A. *Epictetus: A Stoic and Socratic Guide to Life*. Oxford: Oxford University Press, 2002.
Martin, Luther H., Huck Gutman and Patrick H. Hutton, eds. *Technologies of the Self: A Seminar with Michel Foucault*. London: Tavistock, 1988.
Nietzsche, Friedrich. *Dawn: Thoughts on the Presumptions of Morality*. Translated by Brittain Smith. Stanford: Stanford University Press, 2011.
Nietzsche, Friedrich. *Ecce Homo*. Translated by Duncan Large. Oxford: Oxford University Press, 2007.
Nietzsche, Friedrich. *Friedrich Nietzsche: Sämtliche Briefe. Kritische Studienausgabe*. 8 Volumes. Edited by Giorgio Colli and Mazzino Montinari. Berlin and New York: de Gruyter, 1986.

Nietzsche, Friedrich. *The Gay Science*. Translated by Walter Kaufmann. New York: Random House, 1974.

Nietzsche, Friedrich. *Human, All Too Human*. Translated by R. J. Hollingdale. Cambridge: Cambridge University Press, 1986.

Nietzsche, Friedrich. *Unfashionable Observations*. Translated by Richard T. Gray. Stanford: Stanford University Press, 1995.

Nussbaum, Martha C. 'Pity and Mercy: Nietzsche's Stoicism'. In *Nietzsche, Genealogy, Morality*, edited by Richard Schacht, 139–67. Berkeley: University of California Press, 1994.

Royce, Josiah. *Studies of Good and Evil: A Series of Essays upon Problems of Philosophy and of Life*. New York: Appleton & Co., 1899.

Schopenhauer, Arthur. *On the Basis of Morality*. Translated by E. F. J. Payne. Providence: Berghahn Books, 1995.

Ure, Michael. 'The Irony of Pity: Nietzsche contra Schopenhauer and Rousseau'. *Journal of Nietzsche Studies* 32 (2006): 68–92.

Von Tevenar, Gudrun. 'Nietzsche's Objections to Pity and Compassion'. In *Nietzsche and Ethics*, edited by Gudrun von Tevenar, 263–81. Bern: Peter Lang, 2007.

Chapter Four

The Free Spirit
and Aesthetic Self-Re-Education

Duncan Large

The standard view of the aesthetics of the free spirit trilogy is that, effectively, it doesn't have one, or at least not much of one. The story goes that by the time of *Human, All Too Human*, Nietzsche is embarrassed by *The Birth of Tragedy*'s 'aesthetic justification of the world', its pro-Wagnerian 'artist's metaphysics', and abandons them. His discomfort with Wagner is already apparent from the labouredness of his work on the fourth *Untimely Meditation, Richard Wagner in Bayreuth*, which took him far longer than the other three to compose, and it was brought to a head in a very concrete manner by Nietzsche's psychosomatic histrionics during the first Bayreuth Festival in August 1876, when he took himself off to the Bohemian Forest and began making notes under the heading 'The Ploughshare' in a notebook which would eventually turn into HH.[1]

In Nietzsche's own personal case, then, it would appear that the free spirit becomes so (becomes what he is) by freeing himself from the shackles of his earlier artistic preference and indeed his preference for art *tout court*. The private rejection of his mentor-cum-father figure produces in turn a seismic *volte-face* in his public thought (insofar as he still had a public, a readership, by this stage). In the 1878 text HH, in addition to explicitly rejecting his other early mentor, Schopenhauer, Nietzsche implicitly rejects Wagner and all he stands for, leading to a root-and-branch re-evaluation—in the sense of devaluation, *Abwertung*—of art and aesthetics in favour of a new scientistic, Enlightenment paradigm, the practice of what he calls the 'Chemistry of Concepts and Sensations' (HH 1),[2] an 'Estimation of Unpretentious Truths' (HH 3), and so on. Statements such as: 'The scientific man is the further evolution of the artistic' (HH 222) or 'One must have loved religion and art like mother and nurse. . . . But one must be able to see beyond them; outgrow them' (HH 292) suggest that there is not much for the aesthetician to find here, except perhaps a kind of 'negative aesthetics'. It would appear that HH conceives of art as something you outgrow, that Nietzsche here is speaking with the Paul of I Corinthians—'when I became a man of science, I put away childish artistic things'—and that his break with Wagner, which he figures as the archetypal self-overcoming, represents at the same time a kind of 'over-coming of art'—for the duration of the 'free spirit period', at least, until the re-assertion of the aesthetic paradigm with the work of art that is *Thus Spoke Zarathustra*, and a rebirth of interest in the Dionysian aesthetic (now very differently conceived from BT) in Nietzsche's late work.

I am calling this the standard, consensual view of the matter because general studies on Nietzsche's aesthetics by scholars such as Matthew Ram-pley, Philip Pothen, and Aaron Ridley[3]—insofar as they discuss the fate of Nietzsche's aesthetic theory in the free spirit trilogy at all—tend merely to emphasise that Nietzsche turns his back on art in favour of science at this juncture. Pothen reads HH in conjunction with Hegel on the 'death of art',[4] while Aaron Ridley's study segues from a first chapter on *The Birth of Tragedy* as 'redemption through art' to a second on 'redemption through science' in HH. Allan Megill, considering 'Nietzsche and the aesthetic' in his book *Prophets of Extremity*, goes so far as to jump from BT and the 1873 essay 'On Truth and Lies in an Extramoral Sense' straight to Z, bypassing the free spirit trilogy altogether.[5] The standard view of the occlusion of aesthet-ics in the free spirit trilogy has also been effectively adopted by four of the more recent English-language studies focusing on the trilogy itself, namely Ruth Abbey's *Nietzsche's Middle Period*, Michael Ure's *Nietzsche's Thera-py*, Jonathan R. Cohen's *Science, Culture and Free Spirits*, and, most recent-ly, Paul Franco's *Nietzsche's Enlightenment*.[6] Abbey's study analyses a number of philosophical themes and forms in the trilogy, but not Nietzsche's reorientation of aesthetics; Ure follows Nehamas in focussing on the 'artful shaping of the soul', on self-cultivation as an 'aesthetic game',[7] but precisely not on the cultivation of the aesthetic sense in these works; Cohen focuses on the reorientation towards scientific culture in volume I of HH. Franco is closest to my concerns here, and he at least devotes six pages of *Nietzsche's Enlightenment* to 'Overcoming Romantic Art' in HH, but his analysis is still largely confined to volume I.[8]

Even those who reject or nuance the standard overgeneralisation, then, gener-ally do so by dwelling on the fourth chapter of volume I of HH, 'From the Souls of Artists and Writers'. This is Nietzsche's set-piece engagement with matters aesthetic in the aftermath of the break with Wagner, and it focuses on general questions concerning the status of art. The chapter title is a clue here: in German, 'Aus der Seele [singular] der Künstler und Schriftsteller [plural]' implies that there is a collective soul, a single common mentality shared by all artists and writers, which this chapter takes as it mission to analyze, rather than differentiating between individuals. Implicitly, of course (since he is not mentioned by name anywhere in the text), pluralising the figure of the artist is already intended as a slap in the face to Wagner, who has hitherto served as Nietzsche's highly singular instantiation of the artist figure and his soul. As Franco notes of this chapter, 'Most of the aphorisms in the original, 1878 HH deal with art in general and not with specific historical styles or aesthetic attitudes'.[9] For this reason, I think, 'From the Souls of Artists and Writers' has been privileged in any discussion of the aesthetics of the free spirit period, and the aesthetic sections of the second volume of HH—which, rather than tarring all artists and writers with the same brush, are often specific (*ad hominem*) discussions of individual writers, artists, composers—have been neglected, especially by scholars outside of the German-speaking world.

In this chapter, I want to attempt something of a corrective to this situation. My overarching question is simply: what is the aesthetic attitude of the free spirit? Or to adapt Aaron Ridley's felicitous formulation: What is the meaning of the free spirit's aesthetic ideals?[10] Does the free spirit even have an aesthetic attitude, or is art one of the things on which he turns his back? Is the free spirit . . . free of art? Such a rhetorical question is perhaps always going to be knocked down, and indeed I want to argue that the standard view I have just been sketching is an oversimplification. I will focus on a close reading of Nietzsche's narrative about the birth of the free spirit in the 1886 preface to the second volume of HH, where it seems to me that he is making it clear that—especially in *Assorted Opinions and Maxims* (1879) and *The Wanderer and his Shadow* (1880)—it was essential to him to consider the project of the free spirit in aesthetic terms as well as in terms of religion, morality, and so on. In this respect, I want to make a distinction between the two volumes of HH—following an insight of Julian Young's, when he argues that 'whereas art, in *Human [All Too Human]*, is consigned to the realm of glorious memory, in *[Mixed] Opinions [and Maxims]*, Nietzsche recovers his sense of its indispensability'.[11] By focusing in on sections from WS, in particular, I aim to draw attention to the development in Nietzsche's aesthetic attitudes over the course of the free spirit trilogy itself, rather than considering it as a single undifferentiated period.

In the preface to the second volume of HH, Nietzsche argues that the education of the free spirit starts with aesthetics, in that he writes of the birth of the free spirit out of the demise of Wagnerian aesthetics, but this precisely does not represent the demise of aesthetics *per se*. Instead, the conscious desire to reject Wagner amounts to a desire also to liberate himself from his previous aesthetic tastes and is accompanied by a desire to acquire some new ones. But how do you do that? How do you acquire a new taste, how do you educate a taste? I am interested in how Nietzsche (claims he) goes about doing that and then how he presents it to others, to his readers (in that he sees himself as educator and his texts as manuals). It is for this reason that my title foregrounds the task of education and self-education in the free spirit trilogy. The chapter is divided in two parts: first, I will give a reading of the preface to HH volume II as an aesthetic programme; then I will focus on HH volume II in the light of it, asking whether it actually lives up to the retrospective rationalisation which the posthumous preface represents.

THE PREFACE TO *HUMAN, ALL TOO HUMAN* VOLUME II AS AN AESTHETIC PROGRAMME

Fundamental to Nietzsche's conception of the free spirit is his narrative of his own personal self-emancipation from bondage to the master of Bayreuth, and he is intensely proud of having achieved this for himself. The story of what he calls his 'great emancipation' begins in HH I Preface 3, but he returns to the theme in the preface to volume II, which was written for the reissuing of AOM and WS as, precisely, 'volume two' of HH. The new preface was written (and dated) September 1886, that is, after his intellectual career had already moved on in numerous ways, with the completion of the free spirit trilogy, the work on Z, and the inception of the (ultimately abortive) *Will to Power* project occupying the intervening years. Since Nietzsche claims at the outset of this preface that 'my writings speak *only* of my overcomings' (HH II Preface 1), though, he effectively casts these reflections as doubly retrospective, in that he is looking back from 1886 to works of 1879-1880, while claiming that they are already monuments to his (self-)overcoming. In this preface, he is looking back at the decisive break in his intellectual career of the mid-1870s, then, and figuring the transition from the world of BT in a number of interesting ways which I would like to look into in more detail now. Here is section 2 of the preface to Volume II, in its entirety:

> The 'Assorted Opinions and Maxims' were, like 'The Wanderer and his Shadow', first published *singly* as continuations and appendices of the above-named human-all-too-human 'Book for free spirits': at the same time as a continuation and redoubling of a spiritual cure [geistigen Kur], namely of the *anti-romantic* self-treatment [Selbstbehandlung] that my still healthy instinct had itself discovered and prescribed for me against a temporary attack of the most dangerous form of romanticism. May these same writings now, after six years of convalescence, prove acceptable *united* as the second volume of *Human, All Too Human*: perhaps taken together they will teach their precepts more powerfully and clearly—they are *precepts of health* [Gesundheitslehre] that may be recommended to the more spiritual natures of the generation just coming up as a *disciplina voluntatis*. There speaks out of them a pessimist whose insights have often made him jump out of his skin but who has always known how to get back into it again, a pessimist, that is to say, well disposed *towards* pessimism—and thus in any event no longer a romantic: what? should a spirit who understands the serpent's prudent art [Schlangenklugheit] of

changing his skin not be permitted to read a lecture [Lektion] to our pessimists of today, who are one and all still in danger of romanticism? And at the very least to demonstrate to them how it is—*done*? . . .(HH II Preface 2)

From the outset of this discussion, then, the path to Nietzsche's true self is presented as an overcoming of Romanticism. [12] Specifically, Romanticism is presented as a spiritual illness from which he needs to recover. That is the master trope here, but there are a number of others competing: first, there is the medical image of the (self-administered) cure, which Nietzsche claims is arrived at instinctively, without any exertion of will, and which Michael Ure calls 'indisputably an homage to Stoic and Cynic practices of the self'. [13] Second, and closely related: he naturalises the process with the image of a snake sloughing off its skin (cf. D 573). Third, though: whereas Nietzsche claims to have cured himself 'naturally' and 'instinctively' (i.e., without conscious effort), for anyone else this kind of cure is going to require a supreme effort of will. This is what one might call the perspectival truth of self-overcoming: he presents it to others as a *disciplina voluntatis*. Fourth (again, closely related): presenting his experiences to others in this way is explicitly labelled an educational model—a *Gesundheitslehre*, a *Lektion*—presented specifically to the coming generation. This echoes the preface to HH I on the rising generation of the free spirits: for the moment it is still a model of education for others, rather than of self-education, but that is set to change.

In the next section of this preface Nietzsche continues by naming Wagner and explaining that it was high time for him to move on. But with the loss of Wagner (and of certainty in the Wagnerian cause) he also lost his sense of a task:

> My *task* [*Aufgabe*]—where had it gone? [wohin war sie?] What? Was it now not as if my task had withdrawn from me, as though I would for a long time to come cease to have any right to it? How was I going to be able to endure this *greatest* of privations? (HH II Preface 3)

The sense of disorientation expressed here, encapsulated in the anguished question 'Wohin?', is reminiscent of the words of the madman in *The Gay Science* 125, the famous passage where Nietzsche first writes of the death of God:

> 'Whither is God?' [Wohin ist Gott?] he cried; 'I will tell you. We have killed him—you and I. All of us are his murderers. But how did we do this? How could we drink up the sea? Who gave us the sponge to wipe away the entire horizon? What were we doing when we unchained this earth from its sun? Whither is it moving now? [Wohin bewegt sie sich nun?] Whither are we moving? [Wohin bewegen wir uns?]' (GS 125)

The parallel between the abandonment of Wagner and the death of God, as Nietzsche will later formulate it, is instructive here, for just as humanity as a whole is obliged by the death of God to confront the spectre of nihilism and create new values, so the symbolic patricide which the break from Wagner represents confronts Nietzsche with the need to create new aesthetic values (including, of course, a new value for aesthetics in the first place). A reorientation is required in the wake of the break with Wagner, then—he needs to find some new bearings. And whereas the madman's questions in GS 125 are left hanging, here Nietzsche answers his own question thus:

> I began by *forbidding* myself, totally and on principle, all romantic music, that ambiguous, inflated, oppressive art that deprives the spirit of its severity and cheerfulness and lets rampant every kind of vague longing and greedy, spongy desire. '*Cave musicam*' is to this day my advice to all who are man enough to insist on cleanliness in things of the spirit; such music unnerves, softens, feminises, its 'eternal womanly' draws *us*—downwards! (HH II Preface 3)

Nietzsche is still enough of a Schopenhauerian to appreciate that it is music that speaks most directly and powerfully of and to the will (which he is now calling instinct) and therefore that it is most important to tackle music first. Naturally enough, his anti-Romanticism expresses itself in the first instance negatively, and he forbids himself Romantic music: like the Old Testament God, the self-legislator tells himself 'thou shalt not listen to Wagner' for fear of being (re-)infected, unmanned by the music's lubricious sensuality. At this point, then, the free spirit sounds rather like Odysseus stopping the ears of his crew and having himself lashed to the mast so as to resist the sensuous wiles of Romantic art. Ironically, of course, there are also more pertinent parallels with the magician Klingsor's magic garden in Wagner's *Parsifal*: Nietzsche simply cannot help himself figuring his rejection of Wagner in (unconsciously?) Wagnerian terms. The fate of the self-castrated Klingsor awaits him if he is not very careful, it would seem, but his chosen cure—cutting Romanticism out of his life—sounds dangerously Christian, too, if we are to believe the later analysis in *Twilight of the Idols*, where he writes: 'The church fights against passion with every kind of excision: its method, its 'cure', is *castratism*' (TI Morality 1).

At this stage, he shies away from such inflammatory rhetoric, though: the anti-Romantic Dr Nietzsche is not proposing to wield the scalpel and be a self-vivisectionist—instead he has a much less radical and more benign(-sounding) cure for himself:

> Just as a physician places his patient in a wholly strange environment so that he may be removed from his entire 'hitherto,' from his cares, friends, letters, duties, stupidities and torments of memory and learn to reach out his hands and senses to new nourishment, a new sun, a new future, so I, as physician and

patient in one, compelled myself to an opposite and unexplored *clime of the soul*, and especially to a curative journey into strange parts, into *strangeness* itself, to an inquisitiveness regarding every kind of strange thing. . . . (HH II Preface 5)

Physician and patient in one, he prescribes himself the cure of self-distantiation, self-alienation, deliberately turning his back on what has gone before and heading off into unfamiliar territory, sailing off onto uncharted new seas (and this Columbus-inspired rhetoric is particularly pronounced in Nietzsche's writing when he is living in the 'Kolumbus-Stadt' of Genoa, where he wrote much of the free spirit trilogy).[14] The theme of turning away, 'being removed from one's entire "hitherto"', is reminiscent of the opening of book 4 of GS, the section 'Sanctus Januarius': '*Looking away* shall be my only negation' (GS 276), or for that matter the description of HH in EH where Nietzsche recalls that: 'One error after another is calmly put on ice' (EH Books HH 1). This procedure is far from idyllic, though, and still represents an act of coercion ('compelled myself'), of self-violence, a willed (wilful) perversity in order to destroy the self he had hitherto been.

What particularly interests me about this section is that the education motif is now (finally) self-applied. In other words, this is where the theme of what I am calling 'aesthetic self-re-education' emerges, as, precisely, an ascetic ideal. The administering of a cure begins with an act of renunciation ('so that he may be removed'), then becomes an exercise in educating the senses ('so that he may . . . learn'). The process now begins to sound like a physiotherapist training the body to recover from a trauma (or for that matter a horticulturist training a plant to climb a trellis). The instinctual rejection of Romanticism needs to be followed, in other words, by the work of (conscious) self-cultivation or *Selbstzucht*. This is how Nietzsche remembers the text when he describes it in EH: '*Human, All Too Human*, that monument to a rigorous self-discipline [Selbstzucht], with which I swiftly despatched all the "higher swindle", "idealism", "fine feeling" and other femininities I had brought in' (EH Books HH 5).

Nietzsche's notion of *Selbstzucht* blurs the distinction between instinctuality and free will which we saw earlier; specifically, it establishes a feedback loop whereby the apparently unconscious work of the instinct (set against the conscious work of the *disciplina voluntatis*) is analysed as a construct, the product of conscious, methodical action. The key passage here is in TI, where Nietzsche describes instinct formation as the result of a process of (willed, disciplined) internalisation:

Now let there be no mistake here about the methodology: a disciplining [Zucht] of feelings and thoughts alone counts for almost nothing (—here lies the great misunderstanding in German education, which is a complete illusion): you have to win over the *body* first. The strict maintenance of significant and select gestures, a commitment to live only with people who do not 'let themselves go,' is perfectly sufficient to make you significant and select: within two or three generations everything has already been *internalised*. It is decisive for the fate of a nation and of humanity that culture is begun in the *right* place—*not* in the 'soul' (which was the disastrous superstition of the priests and semi-priests): the right place is the body, gesture, diet, physiology—the *rest* follows on from this. (TI Maxims 47)

This, then, is what I mean by my title term 'aesthetic self-re-education': training an instinct, training a taste; recognizing in the first place that taste is a physiological phenomenon. With this, Nietzsche has of course come a long way from classical (post-Kantian) aesthetics, and the Schillerian echo in my title is intended ironically. In his comparative study of the two writers, Nick Martin points out the parallels between Schiller's *Aesthetic Letters* and the Nietzsche of the earlier 1870s—of BT and the contemporary notes, including one where he sets himself the explicitly Schillerian task of 'education through art' (KSA 7: 115, 5[82]).[15] What happens to this aesthetic programme after BT, though? For one thing, that kind of imported notion drops away from Nietzsche's philosophical vocabulary: terms from the broad semantic field of 'aesthetic education' such as *Kunstunterricht, Kunstbildung, Kunsterziehung, Aesthetische Bildung*, or *Kunstpädagogik* simply do not appear in his work. In the free spirit trilogy, I want to argue, Nietzsche understands the notion of aesthetic education very differently to Schiller, who uses it to describe aesthetics (beauty) as a means of moral education, rather than the process of educating taste itself. Let us not ignore the irony, though, that the very notion of aesthetic education is a German Romantic project, which Nietzsche is seeking to turn against itself by weaning himself off Romanticism.

NIETZSCHE'S AESTHETIC EXERCISE PROGRAMME

So far, largely through an analysis of the preface to HH volume II, I have derived a model of aesthetic self-re-education which involves not so much spiritual exercises (à la Loyola) as bodily ones, insofar as tastes are conceived (like drives, and the two are connected—tastes simply are drives in Nietzsche's later philosophy) as aspects of human physiology. We have been jumping far ahead of the free spirit trilogy, though, by focusing on the 1886 preface and its retrospective rationalisations. In the remainder of this chapter, then, I want to turn to HH itself, and look at what it actually achieves in this light. What happens when Nietzsche alienates himself from his self hitherto? The preface to HH volume II leaves the story at the point where he abandons Wagner and adopts anti-Romanticism as his new watchword, so I want now to consider what the (here unspoken) implications are for the rest of the free spirit's aesthetic programme, focusing on the group of aphorisms that is sections 87–170 of WS.

First, a word about formal matters. The break between the early and middle periods in Nietzsche's output is most apparent in formal terms because he abandons the form of the essay or treatise and, spurred on by his reading of the French *moralistes* in particular, adopts instead an aphoristic style which is one of the hallmarks of the free spirit trilogy. Nietzsche won't return to essayistic form till much later on, with *On the Genealogy of Morals* and *The Antichrist*: it is almost as if what Adorno will call 'the essay as form' becomes tainted in Nietzsche's eyes by association with Wagner, and he needs to liberate himself from it, too, from the 'grand narrative' sweep of BT with Wagner as its crucially redemptive figure. Instead, aphoristic form lends itself to the new atmosphere of respect for *petits faits* and resistance to metaphysics, what Ricoeur will call the hermeneutics of suspicion.

Turning to thematic considerations: in the first instance, as we have seen, Nietzsche seeks to wean himself off Wagner's music and simply tells himself not to listen to it. One might perhaps say that his initial aesthetic response is, rather, to self-administer an anaesthetic, and he does indeed go cold turkey. He doesn't see Wagner again after 1876 and denies himself occasions to listen to Wagner's music. For example he doesn't allow himself to hear the Prelude to Wagner's *Parsifal* till as late as January 1887—at which point, though, he asks Köselitz whether 'in purely aesthetic terms' Wagner has ever written anything better (KSB 8: 12), for he knows full well the strength of his residual attachment to Wagner's music, however much he is genuinely repelled by the ideology and the psychology of the man. I would argue that he actually remains fascinated by Wagner even *in absentia*, and that this is apparent from the extent to which moving on from Wagner is (initially, at least) encapsulated in a simple inversion of his previous aesthetic judgements.

Nietzsche's view of the history of music had hitherto always been skewed by Wagner, so in WS he takes the opportunity to revisit the history of music on his own terms. Nietzsche works chronologically through the Austro-German musical tradition, with a series of appreciations of individual composers, starting with J. S. Bach (WS 149), Handel (WS 150), Haydn (WS 151), Beethoven and Mozart (WS 152), Schubert (WS 155), Mendelssohn (WS 157) and Schumann (WS 161). The only non-German composer mentioned is 'the inimitable Pole, Chopin' (WS 159–60), who already occupies the special place in his affections which will be particularly evident in EH. Nietzsche's evaluations are often now at variance with Wagner's, and at times he is clearly trying to be deliberately provocative. For example, he seeks to rub Wagner's nose in his newly expressed liking for the music of Mendelssohn, say, or a disparagement of Wagner's musical god, Beethoven. The main standard-bearer of the anti-Wagnerian tendency in music at this period was of course Brahms (championed in opposition to Wagner by Han-slick), and indeed before Nietzsche left Wagner's house, Wahnfried, for good in August 1874, he clumsily attempted to provoke Wagner and signal his increasing distance from him by repeatedly placing the score of Brahms's *Triumphlied* on the piano.[16] Nietzsche flirts with Brahms, then, but amusing-ly he cannot ultimately bring himself to espouse Brahms's music, later dis-missing him as a 'master copier' in the second epilogue to *The Case of Wagner*. Instead of Brahms, of course, in that text, Nietzsche will take up the cudgels in the name of Bizet, and the description in WS 152 of Mozart's taking his inspiration from what Nietzsche describes as 'the liveliest life of the *south*' is already indicative of the kinds of musical opposition to Wagner Nietzsche will develop over the decade to come. For the moment, though, he is still concerned to try and salvage the Austro-German tradition in music, and the break with Wagner by no means amounts to a break with cultural nationalism as such.

Beyond music, the rejection of Wagner leads directly to an interest in (and in some cases clearly the development of a taste for) many other cultural features which he had hitherto been denied, or had denied himself. Ironically, then, what is presented in the preface to HH volume II negatively, as anti-Romanticism, also correlatively opens up a great many new possibilities for Nietzsche, who realises that he had allowed too much of his taste to be dictated by Wagner hitherto and now programmatically takes himself out of his own comfort zone. In particular, by contrast with BT and the UM, in WS he shows a willingness (for the first time in any sustained way) to comment on a plethora of more contemporary figures and trends in literature and music, rather than just exponents from the classical world or Wagner. Yes, many individual figures with whom he had previously associated Wagner (such as Shakespeare) become tainted now and unavailable to him, but by way of compensation, Nietzsche allows himself to opine on many figures (such as the dramatist Kotzebue at AOM 170) on whom he would previously have been prevented from writing by his allegiance to Wagner. Following on from the section devoted to Laurence Sterne in AOM 113,[17] WS represents the first time in Nietzsche's published output that he shows any kind of sustained preoccupation with prose literature rather than drama or poetry. General remarks on the 'ugliness' of German prose writing (WS 90, 91, 95) are followed by more detailed appreciations of individual German prose writers: Jean Paul (WS 99), Lessing (WS 103), Wieland (WS 107), Herder (WS 118), Schiller the essayist (WS 123). The literary writers with whom we more generally associate Nietzsche—Stendhal, Heine, Dostoevsky—are at this point still to be discovered and appreciated, and their praises will be sung in later works (especially EH). With these sections in WS, though, Nietzsche soberly enters through the gates of horn into the age of prose and finally turns his back on the poetic excesses of BT.

More generally, as well, one can speak of a retreat from the avant-garde in WS. In aesthetic terms, Nietzsche's Wagnerianism had previously allied him with all that was most self-consciously culturally 'progressive' (the 'music of the future' and so on). Now he cultivates a taste for the classical in many respects and permits himself a relatively conservative interest in canonicity and the production of cultural masterpieces. Once again, the break with Wagner proves to be no break with cultural nationalism as such, for when Nietzsche turns to discuss German prose writing, he goes so far as to claim that it is the most German of all the literary genres, 'an original product of German taste', a signpost to an 'original German culture' (WS 91). Moreover, he is still prepared to be personally identified with this German literary tradition, too (what he calls in WS 95 'Our Prose'), and doesn't disown it.

On rejecting Wagner, does Nietzsche achieve an autonomy of taste, though? I think the simple answer to that is 'no', or at least 'not yet', not in the free spirit trilogy. Apart from anything else, for all his talk of autonomy, pride in the diagnostic flair of his nostrils, and so forth, in matters of taste, Nietzsche is often surprisingly willing to be led by others. In this free spirit period, many of his aesthetic judgements remain warped by (and thus indirectly, dialectically dependent on) Wagner, even when Wagner is no longer in a position to perform the role of arbiter of taste for him directly. Nor is Wagner Nietzsche's only aesthetic prism, and Goethe remains an enduring reference point (in AOM 113 on Sterne, for example). It is amusing to think that in one sense Nietzsche's emerging Francophilia merely reflects the influence on his taste, not of Richard Wagner but of Cosima Wagner, and in EH he will reflect, precisely, on how she provides him with an education in taste (EH Clever 3). Nietzsche was never ashamed to make use of the judgements of others in arriving at his own opinions—hence the relatively frequent presence in his personal library of manuals and secondary reference works on areas such as literary history in which he didn't take a professional interest. To cite a few other instances: his copy of Jacob Burckhardt's *Der Cicerone* is quite heavily annotated;[18] he frequently acts on the recommendations of his friends; he claims not to read newspapers, but the one periodical to which he admits a subscription is the *Journal des débats*, where he reads reviews of new works and then promptly asks his publisher to 'arrange' the books for him. None of this will change during the free spirit period, and for all the heroic isolation of the pose, it's crucial that we don't believe the hype.

CONCLUSION

Heroic isolation is a quintessentially Romantic posture: not for nothing have publishers reached so readily for those iconic Caspar David Friedrich images to decorate the covers of Nietzsche's works. In conclusion, then, let us return to the question of Nietzsche's purported anti-Romanticism.

On one level 'Romanticism' is simply the stick with which he chooses to beat Wagner, but abandoning Wagner is not the same thing as abandoning Romanticism, and composers whom he begins to praise in this period—Chopin and Mendelssohn, Schubert and Schumann—are certainly 'Romantic' in orientation. As Paul Franco puts it: 'It seems that romantic, Wagnerian art has its uses for the free spirit'.[19] In literature, the story is somewhat different, for in WS Nietzsche explicitly rejects the great Romantic novelist Jean Paul while ignoring Schlegel, Tieck, Hoffmann and other greats of the Romantic period. Yet one might have expected a literary anti-Romantic to prefer literary Realism, or indeed Naturalism, but Nietzsche prefers the writing of so-called Poetic Realism (he champions Adalbert Stifter and Gottfried Keller here: WS 109); he doesn't read the two novelists now acknowledged as the two greatest German masters of Realism, Theodor Fontane or Wilhelm Raabe, and Gustav Freytag—author of the best-selling *Debit and Credit* [*Soll und Haben*] (1855)—is represented in Nietzsche's library only by his work on dramatic theory *Die Technik des Dramas*.[20] In literature as in music, then, Nietzsche's supposed 'anti-Romanticism' in the middle period doesn't really amount to much—he remains surprisingly Romantic in his tastes (and after all, he loves Wagner's music till the end).[21]

In the context of aesthetics, Nietzsche's break with Wagner clearly inaugurates a transitional period. As Ruth Abbey remarks of HH: 'Nietzsche's twists and turns make it appropriate to consider the role of art in a more scientific or enlightened age as another of those issues that churns throughout this work'.[22] The abandonment of the 'grand narrative' of BT leaves him to some extent bereft, but it is to Nietzsche's credit that he fights shy of simply adopting another mentor figure, and instead he aims to find—and then self-inculcate—a set of tastes which will be compatible with the new chastened (more prosaic, more modest) aesthetic of the free spirit trilogy and its allegiance to a science-based culture. The more experimental aesthetics of self-alienation is bound to lead to some failures, some wrong turnings, but it also allows him to spread his wings and become much more confident in commenting (as a non-specialist, of course) on subjects such as contemporary literature and music. As in the second chapter of EH, the parade of (newfound) tastes and preferences allows the reader to understand better who Nietzsche is and serves in turn as a means of educating the reader into discovering their own tastes and becoming themselves. The fact that a number of the exponents Nietzsche now adopts happen to be Romantics is ultimately rather incidental, for what is important is the mechanism by which he seeks to retrain or re-engineer his taste. The programme of aesthetic self-re-education is formulated in the preface to volume II of HH in 1886, a crucial text which bridges between the modest assertions of Volume II of HH and the much better worked-through physiological aesthetics of the later philosophy. By the model outlined in TI, changes in taste result from the exertion of self-discipline over time in order to internalize what begins as a self-alienation and make it instinctual, and during the free spirit trilogy Nietzsche simply hasn't had enough time to get there yet.

NOTES

1. Cf. Duncan Large, 'Nietzsche's *Helmbrecht*; or, How to Philosophise with a Plough-share', *Journal of Nietzsche Studies* 13 (1997): 3–22; Duncan Large, '*Untimely Meditations*', in *A Companion to Friedrich Nietzsche: Life and Works*, ed. Paul Bishop (Rochester, NY, and Woodbridge: Camden House, 2012), 87–107.

2. Nietzsche quotations are taken from the following translations: *Human, All Too Human*, trans. R. J. Hollingdale (Cambridge: Cambridge University Press, 1996); *Daybreak*, trans. R. J. Hollingdale (Cambridge: Cambridge University Press, 1982); *The Gay Science*, trans. Walter Kaufmann (New York: Random House, 1974); *Twilight of the Idols*, trans. Duncan Large (Oxford and New York: Oxford University Press, 1998); *Ecce Homo: How To Become What You Are*, trans. Duncan Large (Oxford and New York: Oxford University Press, 2007).

3. Matthew Rampley, *Nietzsche, Aesthetics and Modernity* (Cambridge: Cambridge University Press, 2000); Philip Pothen, *Nietzsche and the Fate of Art* (Aldershot: Ashgate, 2002); Aaron Ridley, *Nietzsche on Art* (London and New York: Routledge, 2007).

4. Pothen, *Nietzsche and the Fate of Art*, 45–71.

5. Allan Megill, *Prophets of Extremity: Nietzsche, Heidegger, Foucault, Derrida* (Berkeley, Los Angeles and London: University of California Press, 1985), 60–61.

6. Ruth Abbey, *Nietzsche's Middle Period* (Oxford and New York: Oxford University Press, 2000); Michael Ure, *Nietzsche's Therapy: Self-Cultivation in the Middle Works* (Lanham, MD: Lexington Books, 2008); Jonathan R. Cohen, *Science, Culture, and Free Spirits: A Study of Nietzsche's* Human, All Too Human (New York: Prometheus, 2010); Paul Franco, *Nietzsche's Enlightenment: The Free-Spirit Trilogy of the Middle Period* (Chicago and London: University of Chicago Press, 2011).

7. Ure, *Nietzsche's Therapy*, 7, 25 53.

8. Franco, *Nietzsche's Enlightenment*, 38–44. Cf. Rampley, *Nietzsche, Aesthetics and Modernity*, 121–34 ('Towards a New Evaluation').

9. Franco, *Nietzsche's Enlightenment*, 41.

10. Cf. Aaron Ridley, 'What Is the Meaning of Aesthetic Ideals?', in Salim Kemal, Ivan Gaskell and Daniel W. Conway (eds), *Nietzsche, Philosophy and the Arts* (Cambridge: Cambridge University Press, 1998), 128–47.

11. Julian Young, *Nietzsche's Philosophy of Art* (Cambridge: Cambridge University Press, 1992), 73. Cf. Ridley, *Nietzsche on Art*, 46: 'even in its alleged dotage, art may have its uses'.

12. On Nietzsche's Anti-Romanticism, cf. Adrian Del Caro, *Nietzsche Contra Nietzsche: Creativity and the Anti-Romantic* (Baton Rouge: Louisiana State University Press, 1989).

13. Ure, *Nietzsche's Therapy*, 70.

14. Cf. Duncan Large, 'Nietzsche and the Figure of Columbus', *Nietzsche Studien* 24 (1995): 162-83.

15. Cf. Nicholas Martin, *Nietzsche and Schiller: Untimely Aesthetics* (Oxford and New York: Oxford University Press, 1996), 152.

16. Cf. R. J. Hollingdale, *Nietzsche: The Man and his Philosophy*, 2nd edition (Cambridge and New York: Cambridge University Press, 1999), 92–93; cf. also David S. Thatcher, 'Nietzsche and Brahms: A Forgotten Relationship', *Music and Letters* 54/3 (1973): 261–80.

17. Cf. Duncan Large, '"The Freest Writer": Nietzsche on Sterne', *The Shandean* 7 (1995): 9–29.

18. Cf. Giulio Campioni et al., eds, *Nietzsches persönliche Bibliothek* (Berlin and New York: De Gruyter, 2003), 161–62.

19. Franco, *Nietzsche's Enlightenment*, 42.

20. Campioni et al., eds, *Nietzsches persönliche Bibliothek*, 233.

21. On Nietzsche's relation to Romantic philosophy, cf. Judith Norman, 'Nietzsche and Early Romanticism,' *Journal of the History of Ideas* 63(3) (2002): 501–19; Klaus Vieweg, ed., *Friedrich Schlegel und Friedrich Nietzsche: Transzendentalpoesie oder Dichtkunst mit Begriffen* (Paderborn: Schöningh, 2009).
22. Ruth Abbey, *'Human, All Too Human: A Book for Free Spirits'*, in *A Companion to Friedrich Nietzsche*, ed. Paul Bishop (Rochester, NY, and Woodbridge: Camden House, 2012), 128.

BIBLIOGRAPHY

Abbey, Ruth. *'Human, All Too Human: A Book for Free Spirits'*. In *A Companion to Friedrich Nietzsche: Life and Works*, edited by Paul Bishop, 114–34. Rochester, NY, and Woodbridge: Camden House, 2012.
Abbey, Ruth. *Nietzsche's Middle Period*. Oxford and New York: Oxford University Press, 2000.
Campioni, Giulio et al. (eds). *Nietzsches persönliche Bibliothek*. Berlin and New York: De Gruyter, 2003.
Cohen, Jonathan R. *Science, Culture, and Free Spirits: A Study of Nietzsche's* Human, All Too Human. New York: Prometheus, 2010.
Del Caro, Adrian. *Nietzsche Contra Nietzsche: Creativity and the Anti-Romantic*. Baton Rouge: Louisiana State University Press, 1989.
Franco, Paul. *Nietzsche's Enlightenment: The Free-Spirit Trilogy of the Middle Period*. Chicago and London: University of Chicago Press, 2011.
Hollingdale, R. J. *Nietzsche: The Man and His Philosophy*. 2nd edition. Cambridge and New York: Cambridge University Press, 1999.
Large, Duncan. '"The Freest Writer": Nietzsche on Sterne'. *The Shandean* 7 (1995): 9–29.
Large, Duncan. 'Nietzsche and the Figure of Columbus'. *Nietzsche Studien* 24 (1995): 162–83.
Large, Duncan. 'Nietzsche's *Helmbrecht*; or, How to Philosophise with a Ploughshare'. *Journal of Nietzsche Studies* 13 (1997): 3–22.
Large, Duncan. *'Untimely Meditations'*. In *A Companion to Friedrich Nietzsche: Life and Works*, edited by Paul Bishop, 86–107. Rochester, NY, and Woodbridge: Camden House, 2012.
Martin, Nicholas. *Nietzsche and Schiller: Untimely Aesthetics*. Oxford and New York: Oxford University Press, 1996.
Megill, Allan. *Prophets of Extremity: Nietzsche, Heidegger, Foucault, Derrida*. Berkeley, Los Angeles and London: University of California Press, 1985.
Nietzsche, Friedrich. *Daybreak*. Translated by R. J. Hollingdale. Cambridge: Cambridge University Press, 1982.
Nietzsche, Friedrich. *Ecce Homo: How to Become What You Are*. Translated by Duncan Large. Oxford and New York: Oxford University Press, 2007.
Nietzsche, Friedrich. *The Gay Science*. Translated by Walter Kaufmann. New York: Random House, 1974.
Nietzsche, Friedrich. *Human, All Too Human*. Translated by R. J. Hollingdale. Cambridge: Cambridge University Press, 1996.
Nietzsche, Friedrich. *Twilight of the Idols*. Translated by Duncan Large. Oxford and New York: Oxford University Press, 1998.
Norman, Judith. 'Nietzsche and Early Romanticism'. *Journal of the History of Ideas* 63(3) (2002): 501–19.
Pothen, Philip. *Nietzsche and the Fate of Art*. Aldershot: Ashgate, 2002.
Rampley, Matthew. *Nietzsche, Aesthetics and Modernity*. Cambridge: Cambridge University Press, 2000.
Ridley, Aaron. *Nietzsche on Art*. London and New York: Routledge, 2007.
Ridley, Aaron. 'What Is the Meaning of Aesthetic Ideals?' In *Nietzsche, Philosophy and the Arts*, edited by Salim Kemal, Ivan Gaskell and Daniel W. Conway, 128–47. Cambridge: Cambridge University Press, 1998.

Thatcher, David S. 'Nietzsche and Brahms: A Forgotten Relationship'. *Music and Letters* 54/3 (1973): 261–80.

Ure, Michael. *Nietzsche's Therapy: Self-Cultivation in the Middle Works*. Lanham, MD: Lexington Books, 2008.

Vieweg, Klaus, ed. *Friedrich Schlegel und Friedrich Nietzsche: Transzendentalpoesie oder Dichtkunst mit Begriffen*. Paderborn: Schöningh, 2009.

Young, Julian. *Nietzsche's Philosophy of Art*. Cambridge: Cambridge University Press, 1992.

Chapter Five

Health and Self-Cultivation in *Dawn*

Rebecca Bamford

The medical and therapeutic dimensions of Nietzsche's philosophy have been receiving increased attention. Jessica Berry has directed our attention to the relationship between health—as this theme figures in Nietzsche's philosophical psychology—and the history of medical empiricism.[1] She argues that the promotion of mental and physical health is an important feature of how Skeptics lived their philosophy, and this informed the connection between health and philosophical writing in Nietzsche's own case.[2] Berry explicitly connects Nietzsche's concept of 'great health' with the Pyrrhonians' suspension of judgement, *epochē*, and the healthy product of *epochē*: tranquillity, or *ataraxia*.[3] On her account, Nietzsche understands *ataraxia*, not as a bovine state of calm or as a state that is somehow opposed to suffering, but as a wholly positive state of 'psychophysical balance' and 'as an indication of strength, life, health'—and in fact, *as a state of cheerfulness*'.[4] Thus she claims that Nietzsche adopts a distinctively Pyrrhonian attitude in holding that 'to philosophize out of health and to philosophize out of cheerfulness are one and the same thing'.[5] Michael Ure has argued that Nietzsche's 'artful shaping of the soul' through the philosophy of the middle works involves real therapeutic and psychological work—the act of shaping the soul into a 'healthy psychological configuration'.[6]

Keith Ansell-Pearson has also drawn attention to the connection between health and cheerfulness and to the role of these concepts within the specific context of Nietzsche's ethics of self-cultivation in *Dawn*.[7] Reinforcing Berry's point on Nietzsche's sceptical synthesis of cheerfulness and health, Ansell-Pearson directs our attention to D 148, in which Nietzsche raises the '[*d*]*istant prospect*' of re-imagining morality:

—And so what, then, are these things one *calls* moral actions and that at any rate exist and need to be explained? They are the effects of several intellectual slipups.—And supposing one were able to free oneself of these errors, what would happen to 'moral actions'? —Owing to these errors we have heretofore ascribed to certain actions a higher value than they possess: we severed them from 'egotistical' and 'unfree' actions. If, as we are constrained to do, we now reclassify them with the latter, we no doubt *lower* their value (value-feeling, the value we feel they have) [Werthgefühl], and indeed by more than is fair, because, owing to their alleged, profound, and intrinsic difference, the 'egotistical' and 'unfree' actions in this case were heretofore appraised too low.— Accordingly, will these very actions be performed less frequently from this day forward because from now on they will be less appreciated?—Inescapably! For a good long while, at least as long as the balance of value-feelings remains under the reaction of past mistakes! (D 148)[8]

Nietzsche claims that by returning 'healthy courage for, and the good cheer of, those actions decried as egoistical' we are restoring '*value*' to these actions and depriving the of the '*evil conscience!*' they acquired through customary morality (D 148). He admits that the 'countercalculation' of values that he is proposing in this aphorism will take some time to come to fruition (D 148). But it is clear that Nietzsche thinks this countercalculation is one in which free spirits participate.

Nietzsche makes several claims about the free spirits engaging with value critique and value development in D. He says that what 'moves and determines the free spirit [was den freien Geist bewegt und bestimmt]' is the 'rare and preeminent distinction of *being able* to alter his opinions' (D 56).[9] As Nietzsche suggests, 'And it is his ambition (*not* his faint heart) that even reaches up for the forbidden fruits of the *spernere se sperne* and the *spernere se ipsum*: let alone that he would experience before them the fear of the vain and complacent!' (D 56). The free spirit is contrasted with the figure of the apostate of the free spirit, whom we react to, Nietzsche says, with deep disgust—not for moral reasons, but because of the repellent dishonesty of the apostate's character, which strikes us in the way that the sight of a 'repulsively diseased person' affects a doctor (D 56). Further considering how free spirits will contribute to cultural change, Nietzsche describes how the happiness of refined (aristocratic) culture is based on a sense of superiority, and then points out that nowadays, 'thanks to all the free spirits [Dank allen freien Geistern]' who have made it possible to aspire to an ideal of '*victorious wisdom* [*siegreichen Weisheit*]', this happiness is beginning 'to climb to an even higher level' (D 201).

Experience plays a key role in the process of countercalculating values, and more broadly, re-imagining morality. Discussing the difference between theory and experience in moral behaviour, Nietzsche suggests that while many moral weaknesses in a person are overlooked, providing that the person always professes allegiance to the '*strictest theory of morality* [*strengsten Theorie der Moral*]', the life of the 'free-spirited moralist [der freigeistischen Moralisten]' is always placed under the microscope because, 'a false step in life is the surest argument against an unwelcome insight' (D 209). The importance of experience to '[e]ven great spirits [Auch grosse Geister]' is underscored in D 564, where Nietzsche points out that just to the other side of experience, contemplation ceases, even in their cases, and 'infinite empty space and stupidity' begin. Finally, Nietzsche discusses the tragedy that the free spirits [die freien Geister] make by breaking of the hearts of the 'settled' in turning their backs on 'their opinion, their faith' (D 562).[10]

Yet even while it is clear that Nietzsche sees free spirits as participating in a process of developing value countercalculation and ethical growth in D, several things about the free spirits' involvement in such a process are unclear. More remains to be done to account for the precise nature of the process of self-cultivation.[11] And while Nietzsche discusses a range of cultivation methods, for instance through the drives (D 105, 109, 202, 203), through avoidance of rule following with regard to one's health (D 322), through environmental changes (D 435, 462) and through adopting and embodying particular virtues, such as moderation [Mässigkeit] (D 536) and probity [Redlichkeit] (D 456), he also displays substantial doubt that a unified self capable of free action exists (D 109, 128, 148)—so the question of how free spirits act at all, let alone act to cultivate selves, needs resolution.[12]

My main claim in this essay is that paying renewed attention to Nietzsche's use of the imagery and language of cultivation and, specifically, of gardens and gardening in *Dawn* can shed some fresh light on these issues, in particular the issue of how free spirits might meaningfully be cultivators.[13] I will lay out some of the main pieces of textual evidence concerning Nietzsche's commitment to a broad ethics of *cultivation* (rather than specifically *self*-cultivation) in D. Having established that there is a cultivation process under discussion, I shall then move on in later parts of this chapter to consider *self*-cultivation, Broadly, I aim to show how free spirits as a type fit into the ethical work undertaken by Nietzsche in this text.

NIETZSCHE ON GARDENS IN *DAWN*

Cultivation is recognized as important to Nietzsche's middle writings. Nietzsche's original plan for a title for D was *The Ploughshare: Thoughts on the Prejudices of Morality*, and as Duncan Large points out, as late as July–August of 1882, Nietzsche was still considering a two-volume edition of the free spirit 'trilogy' with the title, *The Ploughshare: A Tool for Liberating the Spirit*.[14] My focus here is on Nietzsche's discussion of cultivation in a specific context: the case of gardens and gardening.

In the first of four important aphorisms discussing humans as types of garden in D, Nietzsche takes critical issue with a 'contemporary moral fashion' in which the principle that 'moral actions are actions generated by sympathy [Sympathie] for others' is commonly accepted (D 174).[15] Nietzsche explains that his objection to sympathy-based morality is about the negative and unhealthy effects that moral behaviour based on sympathy has upon human beings (D 174).[16] As he explains, the effect of this behaviour is to 'grate off' the rough edges of humanity, to such an extent that 'heralds of sympathetic affects' are, Nietzsche complains, 'well on the way to turning humanity into *sand*' —'[t]iny, soft, round, endless grains of sand!' (D 174). With this concern in mind, at the end of the aphorism, Nietzsche raises a question concerning the utility of two different forms of moral behaviour. Specifically, he asks whether a person:

> is *more useful* to another by immediately and constantly leaping to his side and *helping* him—which can, in any case, only transpire very superficially, provided the help doesn't turn into a tyrannical encroachment and transformation—or by *fashioning* out of oneself something the other will behold with pleasure, a lovely, peaceful, self-enclosed garden, for instance, with high walls to protect against the dangers and dust of the roadway, but with a hospitable gate as well. (D 174)

Here, Nietzsche is critically engaging with morality that is based on sympathetic affect. His concern is based on the negative effect that this sort of morality has on our relationships with others. Moral behaviour based on sympathetic affect may involve that a self problematically excludes or encroaches upon others, even including in the *expression* of sympathetic affects such as compassion to others.[17] He imagines an alternative ethics that is based on (aesthetically pleasing) self-fashioning, in which such encroachment or exclusion is absent. The aphorism is constructed in such a way as to present us with a choice to make between morality based on sympathetic affect, on the one hand, and an ethic of self-fashioning, or self-cultivation, on the other. Notice that Nietzsche doesn't tell us the answer to his utility question in D 174 directly. Certainly, he indicates that the effects of moral behaviour based on sympathetic affect—superficial help at best, and tyrannical encroachment at worst—make it highly questionable, and he makes the peaceful garden-self alternative sound distinctly attractive by comparison. Yet he still leaves us to reflect on the merits of an ethics of cultivation for ourselves; in so doing, our choosing to help others is by no means *prohibited*.

In a subsequent aphorism, Nietzsche again uses the metaphor of a garden to introduce how dissimulation [Verstellung] has been involved in our moral behaviour:

Dissimulation as duty.—For the most part, goodness [die Güte] has been developed by extended dissimulation [lange Verstellung] that sought to appear as goodness: wherever great power has taken hold one has recognized the necessity of precisely this type of dissimulation—it exudes certainty and confidence and increases hundredfold the sum of real physical power [physischen Macht]. The lie is, if not the mother, then the wet nurse of goodness. Honesty [Ehrlichkeit] too has, for the most part, been reared to maturity on the requirement that one seem honest and upright: within the hereditary aristocracies. The long-standing practice of dissimulation turns into, at last, *nature*: in the end dissimulation cancels itself out, and organs and instincts are the hardly anticipated fruits in the garden of hypocrisy [und Organe und Instincte sind die kaum erwarteten Früchte im Garten der Heuchelei]. (D 248)

Unlike the peaceful garden of D 174, this garden is described as a hypocritical one, in which cultivation of social behaviours that increase power is based on a *pretence* of honesty. But interestingly, what eventually emerges from this garden of hypocrisy are the organs and instincts for a 'natural' honesty. As Nietzsche puts it, what begins as dissimulation turns into '*nature* [*Natur*]': what we initially pretend to be (being honest) is ultimately what we *become*.

Attending to Nietzsche's use of the word *Ehrlichkeit* or 'honesty' can help us to appreciate his goal concerning critical engagement with morality here. As Melissa Lane has pointed out, D is distinctive among Nietzsche's free spirit 'trilogy' (by which is meant HH, D, and books 1–4 of *The Gay Science*) because D marks a point where Nietzsche's earlier and consistent use of *Ehrlichkeit* ceases—and instead, Nietzsche begins to use the term *Redlichkeit* (probity, integrity).[18] According to Lane's analysis of a related aphorism, D 456, *Ehrlichkeit* is an old and conventional virtue, while *Redlichkeit* is a young and still developing virtue; on this latter point, she directs our attention to a later aphorism in which Nietzsche remarks that probity—*Redlichkeit*—is 'something in the making [etwas Werdendes]' that we can 'advance or retard, as we see fit [das wir fördern oder hemmen können, je nachdem unser Sinn steht]' (D 456).[19]

Mapping *Ehrlichkeit* and *Redlichkeit* onto Nietzsche's critical engagement with morality in D, we can see that even while conventional honesty or *Ehrlichkeit* is associated with the kind of customary morality that Nietzsche criticizes, a *new* form of the virtue of probity in the shape of *Redlichkeit* is open to cultivation.[20] The difference between these two concepts illustrates why Nietzsche's garden and cultivation imagery and talk in D is more broadly relevant to his critical engagement with customary morality and his re-imagination of the ethical in the text, and also highlights that in D 248 the garden under discussion in the aphorism really is that of *humans*, whose organs and instincts—including those for virtuous behaviour—are open to cultivation, like plants.

This leads on to a third aphorism in which Nietzsche likens humans to gardens. This example involves a more specific analogy between gardening and thinking.[21] Nietzsche discusses conclusions that will spring forth in any event without cultivation of the 'earth' of the thinker: '*Gardener and garden.*—Out of damp dreary days, solitude, and loveless [lieblosen] words directed at us, *conclusions* spring up like mushrooms: one morning they are there, we know not where they came from, and stare at us, peevish and grey. Woe [Wehe] to the thinker [Denker] who is not the gardener but only the earth for the plants [Gewächse] that grow in him!' (D 382).[22] Thinking is explicitly identified as a form of cultivation activity in D 382. The warning in this aphorism is thus concerned with what happens if a thinker does not engage in cultivation: conclusions will sprout anyway, regardless of whether the thinker wants them to or not. The fungal imagery in this aphorism recalls the imagery of the repulsive apostate of the free spirit mentioned earlier, who has given up on their free spiritedness and has become 'a "believer"' (D 56). The apostate of the free spirit is described by Nietzsche as repellent and diseased, because the apostate's *dishonesty* represents 'something fungal, edematous, overgrown, festering' (D 56).

Nietzsche's claim in D 382 is more broadly indicative of his concern with connecting humans, thinking, and life in D. The unhealthy mushroom conclusions of D 382 result from a renunciation of the world that is too extreme, which, as Nietzsche warns elsewhere, leads to an 'infertile' and 'melancholic' solitude (D 440). The activity of thinking is already a direct part of life and the world; our difficulty lies with coming to appreciate this. Paying attention to the use of 'solitude' is helpful to grasping Nietzsche's point. The negative kind of renuciatory solitude of which Nietzsche warns is nothing like the positive conception of a free-minded 'thinker's *vita contemplativa*' (D 440). Such a *vita contemplativa* specifically involves relinquishing the *vita practica* that the thinker knows already, for the sake of the 'water' and '*serenity*' that nourish thinking (D 440). Those thinkers who dwell in great streams of thought and feeling quite understandably desire rest and silence; as Nietzsche further explains, the philosophy of such thinkers is still a part of life, unlike the work of thinkers who decide to take a rest from life when they 'give themselves over to meditation' (D 572).[23]

In a fourth garden aphorism, D 560, Nietzsche connects his remarks on drives in earlier parts of D (e.g., D 119, 132, 331, 422, 553) with the issue of freedom. He makes a claim about what we are free to do, which bears heavily upon how we might understand cultivation in a moral sense:

> *What we are free to do.*—One can handle one's drives like a gardener [Man kann wie ein Gärtner mit seinen Trieben schalten] and, though few know it, cultivate the seeds [die Keime] of one's anger, pity, musing, vanity [des Zornes, des Mitleidens, des Nachgrübelns, der Eitelkeit] as fruitfully and

advantageously as beautiful fruit on espaliers [wie ein schönes Obst an Spalieren]; one can do so with a gardener's good or bad taste and, as it were, in the French or English or Dutch or Chinese style; one can also let nature have her sway and only attend to a little decoration and cleaning up here and there; finally, one can, without giving them any thought whatsoever, let the plants, in keeping with the natural advantages and disadvantages of their habitat, grow up and fight it out amongst themselves—indeed, one can take pleasure in such wildness, and want to enjoy just this pleasure, even if one has one's difficulties with it. We are free to do all this: but how many actually know they are free to do this? Don't most people *believe* in *themselves* as completed, *fully grown facts*? Haven't great philosophers, with their doctrine of immutability of character [der Lehre von der Unveränderlichkeit des Charakters], pressed their seal of approval on this presumption [Vorurtheil]? (D 560)[24]

Nietzsche is claiming that we are free to engage in *cultivating drives*, and he suggests that the drives we are to cultivate are *our own* drives. He is also clear that *knowing* about our freedom to cultivate really does matter significantly to being able to exercise our drive-cultivation freedom. I shall return to the issue of knowing of one's freedom to cultivate later. Meantime, notice that the characterization of these drives as different 'seeds' [Keime] in this aphorism helps to clarify Nietzsche's view of freedom as developmental. Two important Stoic influences are at work in Nietzsche's thinking here; following work by Maryanne Cline Horowitz, these may be summarized as follows: (i) Diogenes Laertius's conception of 'Nature as a force moving of itself' whereby Nature gives rise to offspring produced and organized through Nature's own seminal principles [*spermatikoi logoi*], (ii) widespread Stoic use of the metaphor of seeds to account for knowledge and of virtue as developmental, for example by Seneca in his *Epistles*.[25]

With these four examples in place, it should be clear that Nietzsche is committed in D to examination of human beings as gardens, and to considering better and worse approaches to the cultivation of these gardens. But these aphorisms also include some challenging philosophical puzzles. Nietzsche hints at an account of ethical subject relationships in which one cultivates oneself for *others* as well as for *oneself* in these aphorisms, but does not provide a complete explanation of this. It is also unclear as to how much sense Nietzsche's claim that we are free to cultivate drives really makes (D 560). Specifically, as several other scholars have pointed out, when we consider this claim in the context of Nietzsche's account of drives [Triebe] in D, it is unclear from which subjective point of unity the practice of self-cultivation—handling 'one's drives like a gardener'—could be organized and managed.[26] Added to this, if we did truly believe ourselves to be 'completed, *fully grown facts* [vollendete *ausgewachsene Thatsachen*]', then it is unclear how we could *stop* believing this of ourselves, in any way that would make a meaningful difference to our lives (D 560). Attending to sources of Nietzsche's talk of cultivation may help to address these puzzles.

GARDENS, POLYPS AND MOLES

Nietzsche's re-evaluation of morality has been explicitly associated with metaphors of gardens and gardening by Ruth Abbey, who discusses this association in the particular contexts of Nietzsche's critique of pity and of his thinking on friendship in the middle writings.[27] Following Abbey's work, Michael Ure also describes Nietzsche's use of a garden metaphor in D 174 as 'the metaphor of the self's cultivation of itself' in Nietzsche's middle works and draws out a connection (via Foucault) between Nietzsche's use of the garden metaphor and the Stoic concept of *epimeleia heautou* understood as active work on the self.[28] And this same connection between cultivation, health and ancient philosophy was readily apparent to Nietzsche, who in 1879 described his own philosophy as 'my Epicurean garden! [mein Garten Epikurs!]'.[29]

However, we should note that ancient philosophy is not the *only* set of influences on Nietzsche's praise of gardens and his broad affirmation of the philosophical significance of cultivation: modern philosophy also exerts an influence upon Nietzsche's cultivation talk. For instance, Graham Parkes has provided a detailed analysis of themes of cultivation, vegetal propagation and fruition in Nietzsche's writing on ethics and psychology, which explores the connections between Montaigne's and Nietzsche's views on propagation.[30] Gary Shapiro has renewed our attention to cultivation in Nietzsche's philosophy, focusing in particular on cultivation in *Thus Spoke Zarathustra*.[31] Shapiro acknowledges the influence of Epicurus's garden philosophy upon Nietzsche's work, suggesting that for Nietzsche, the garden signifies a place of refuge and solitude in which the philosopher may do their work, and that the garden offers us a model for self-care.[32] But he also directs our attention to the particular influence of Voltaire upon Nietzsche's talk of gardens and cultivation, and in particular to the imperative that 'we should cultivate our garden' as spoken by the eponymous main character at the end of Voltaire's *Candide*.[33]

George J. Stack and Brian Domino have suggested that a third modern philosopher, Julien Offray de La Mettrie, informs Nietzsche's use of cultivation imagery in his free spirit writings and D in particular.[34] Friedrich Albert Lange provided extensive discussion of La Mettrie's materialist philosophy—along with Abraham Tremblay's famous and influential discovery of the self-regenerating polyp—in his *History of Materialism*, which Nietzsche read, and upon which he commented favourably.[35] As Stack and Domino both note, it is not clear that Nietzsche ever read La Mettrie's philosophy other than through the medium of Lange's book. However, comparing Nietzsche with La Mettrie is worthwhile. As Stack shows, there is an interesting range of similarities between Nietzsche and La Mettrie, and it is clear that through his reading of Lange, Nietzsche had learned from La Mettrie; Brian Domino also affirms that Nietzsche was well aware of La Mettrie's discussion of the polyp in *L'Homme Machine* [Man–Machine] (1748) through his reading of Lange.[36] To these accounts, I would add that reading La Mettrie's *L'Homme Machine* in company with Nietzsche's D is instructive, because La Mettrie's developmentally focused materialism provides a framework that may be used to help advance our understanding of free spirits as developmental cultivators. As we will see, by attending to the polyp, plant man and mole analogies included in La Mettrie's materialist philosophy, we may pursue a clearer explanation of development as a key feature of Nietzsche's thinking on free spirits and ethics in D. I shall review relevant examples from La Mettrie before turning to evidence from D that supports this proposal.

In *L'Homme Machine*, La Mettrie's discussion of Tremblay's auto-regenerative polyp appears first in a discussion of health, which La Mettrie suggests is required for unbelief as well as for inquiry growing out of unbelief; the polyp as auto-regenerator is used as an example of how causality, if understood as a part of Nature, need depend neither on chance nor on God, and how natural causality can thus be separated out from these two mistaken factors in explaining phenomena.[37] The polyp is also used in a broader sense here, as an illustration of how coming to know the 'weight of the Universe', as La Mettrie puts it, 'will not affect' a true atheist negatively, rather than this weight of knowledge 'crushing' the atheist as some might expect.[38] La Mettrie's polyp subsequently appears as part of a comment on the existence of the soul, in which La Mettrie criticizes the view that the soul 'is generally spread throughout the body' and attributes this view (which as he notes the polyp seems to initially support—though ultimately he says the polyp does not support it) to unwise use of an 'obscure and meaningless' term.[39]

Perhaps most strikingly, La Mettrie also uses the polyp as part of his discussion of human reproduction and embryonic development. Describing a human embryo, La Mettrie writes,

> Let us look at man inside and outside his shell, and examine under a microscope the youngest embryos, four, six, eight or fifteen days old; after this stage we can do it with the naked eye. What can we see? Only the head: a little round egg with two black dots which indicate the eyes. Before that, as everything is more formless, we can see only a medullary pulp, which is the brain, in which are formed first of all the origin of nerves or the source of feeling and the heart which already, in this pulp, possesses by itself the capacity to beat: this is Malphigi's *punctum saliens*, which perhaps owes part of its liveliness to the influence of the nerves. Then we gradually see the head lengthening its

neck, which dilates to form first the thorax, into which the heart has already dropped down and settled, and then the belly which is separated off by a dividing wall (the diaphragm). Dilations create, here the arms, hands, fingers and hairs, there the thighs, legs, feet, etc., the only difference being their position which makes them act to support or balance the body. It constitutes a striking vegetative growth: the hair which covers the tops of our heads corresponds to leaves and flowers elsewhere. In all quarters nature is equally luxuriant. Finally the rector spirit in plants is situated in the place where we have our soul, which is man's quintessence.

Such is nature's uniformity that we can begin to feel the analogy between animal and vegetable kingdoms, between man and plant. Perhaps there are even animal plants; in other word plants that, while vegetating, either fight like polyps or perform other functions specific to animals.[40]

La Mettrie's analogy between 'man and plant' and his image of the 'animal plants' here, along with the notion of contest between animals and polyps, have strong Nietzschean resonances both in D and in other free spirit writings, such as BGE.[41] The key point of using the polyp analogy here, in a description of the human embryo, is to emphasize the importance of ongoing natural development. The idea that luxuriant vegetative growth and struggle are common to living things, and that we can observe and analyze behaviour in terms of this vegetative growth and struggle, are clearly developmental.[42] This includes development in moral behaviour; as La Mettrie also remarks in *L'Homme Machine*, speaking of dispositions, all of our 'estimable qualities' come from nature and it is to her that 'we owe all that we are;' he asserts that the 'moral sphere' is dependent on the 'physical sphere'.[43] La Mettrie's mention of the uniformity of nature also supports this view; he conceives of nature's variety as infinite, and by 'uniformity of nature' he means, not just infinite variety, but also the luxuriance and striking growth described in this passage.[44]

Following immediately on from his 'man and plant' analogy, La Mettrie provides another analogy that is helpful to the task of understanding D. Speaking of human reproduction, La Mettrie speculates that while it seems hard to see how 'the phenomena of reproduction' could be explained without the 'convenient relationship of the parts' involved, that while it seems to him that 'the male does everything, whether the woman is asleep or is most lascivious', and that while he could suppose the organisation of body parts to be 'fixed for eternity in the man's very seed or worm', he claims that he refuses to judge these matters because they cannot be determined through sensory observation, likening humans to moles in terms of our powers of observation:

> But all this is far beyond the reach of even the most excellent observers. As they are no able to see any of this, they can no more judge the mechanism by

which bodies are created and develop than a mole can judge the distance that can be covered by a deer.

We are veritable moles in the field of nature; we hardly cover more ground than that animal and it is only our pride that places limits on things that have none. We are like a watch saying (a storyteller would make it an important character in a frivolous work): 'What! Was I made by that stupid workman, I who can divide up time, who can indicate so precisely the sun's course, who can tell out loud the hours which I indicate! No, that is impossible.' In the same way, ungrateful wretches that we are, we despise the common mother of all the kingdoms, to use the language of the chemists. We imagine, or rather assume, a cause higher than the one to which we owe everything and which has truly created everything in an inconceivable way. [45]

There is an obvious connection to D to observe in light of La Mettrie's mole analogy. Nietzsche used the image of the mole [Maulwurf] in the first section of his 1886 preface to D in order to suggest that what he had been doing in the 575 aphorisms comprising the original edition of D was working to undermine the psychological foundations of morality. He subsequently explains that in D, he was investigating and digging away at our 'ancient *trust*' in morality (D Preface 2). [46] But there is also a less obvious, and I think more fruitful, point to observe in La Mettrie's mole analogy concerning our understanding of *causality*, which connects La Mettrie's mole analogy directly with the aphorisms of the first edition of D, rather than with Nietzsche's reframing of the content of these original aphorisms in his preface to D— which as we know was added to the second edition of the text in 1887.

While he does not identify La Mettrie as an influence upon Nietzsche's development of D as a 'free spirit' text, Paul Franco does draw attention to how initial aphorisms of D explore the relationship between mistaken understanding of causality and customary morality in his recent analysis of Nietzsche's free spirit texts. [47] In particular, Franco discusses the possibility of desolation as the 'only possible' result of 'the disenchantment of the world by science' (i.e., a turn towards science and away from morality and metaphysics by society). For Franco, the desolation possibility is something that Nietzsche considered but ultimately rejected in D. Franco takes part of his evidence for this claim from Nietzsche's allusion to Raphael's *Transfiguration* in D 8. In this aphorism, Nietzsche divides humanity, as conceived of by Raphael in his painting, into three groups—'the helplessly suffering, the bewilderedly dreaming, the celestially transported'—and suggests that as we now no longer view the world in this way, Raphael would today be able to see a new transfiguration. For Franco, the nature of this proposed new transfiguration should be understood as the morally transformative work of D, which Nietzsche commences in the next aphorism with an analysis of the morality of custom [Sittlichkeit der Sitte] (D 9). Franco suggests that the moral transfiguration in D is made possible by a scientific turn, supporting this claim with evidence from D 24, which discusses difficulties with refutation of the proposed goodness of a precept and meagre scientific worth of moral precepts, and D 33.

Examination of this latter aphorism in particular supports a linking of La Mettrie's remarks on causality with Nietzsche's developmental (rather than transfigurative) analysis of causality and morality in D. Nietzsche suggests that 'the man of science' must learn to distrust misleading *'higher feelings'* in order to cast off the 'spell' with which customary morality has bewitched us:

> Under the oppression of superstitious fear, one suspects that there must be a great deal more than meets the eye to this washing off of cleanliness, one concocts secondary and tertiary meanings, one ruins any sense of, and pleasure in, reality and ends up valuing it only *insofar as it can be a symbol.* Thus under the spell of the morality of custom [Sittlichkeit der Sitte], human beings disdain first the causes, second the effects, and third reality, and they concoct all their higher sentiments (reverence, sublime exaltation, pride, gratitude, love) *from an imaginary world* [*eine eingebildete Welt an*]: the so-called higher world [die sogenannte höhere Welt]. And even today we still witness the consequences: wherever human feeling is *exalted*, you will find there, in some form or other, that imaginary world at work. (D 33)

Nietzsche is not suggesting that we should have no higher feelings at all but rather that our cultivation of such feelings has cultivated according to a paradigm of an imaginary higher world, home to supernatural powers—he speaks explicitly of a 'new demonic [dämonische] power and caprice'— whose wrath we believe we must 'appease'. This cultivation paradigm has resulted in unfortunate consequential fruit: we are held captive by the form of morality on which our current conception of higher feelings is based, namely the morality of custom. Because the focus of such morality lies with our following custom in order to appease supernatural malevolence, as Nietzsche points out here, customary morality stands in the way of our investigation of 'true natural causes': superstitious fear of the consequences of transgression discourage us from violating moral, or investigative, customs.[48] As an alternative, Nietzsche suggests, the 'man of science [dem wissenschaftlichen Menschen]' should suspect higher feelings for the meantime, and should focus on natural, rather than supernatural, explanations for phenomena (D 33).

This helps to clarify why it is that our mistaken understanding of causality is one of the folk confusions Nietzsche is working so hard to clear away in D: our mistaken view of causality leads to problematic inferences about morality. As we saw, La Mettrie uses his mole analogy to (i) illustrate our confusion and error when we try to go beyond the evidence of sensory observation, (ii) propose that our limited understanding prompts a mistaken conception of causality, and (iii) highlight the effect of this error about causality on our efforts to investigate and understand ourselves and the world, such as mistaken attribution of the working of God or of chance instead of materialist explanations for phenomena. And La Mettrie ties this directly to moral thinking and behaviour, which he thinks explicable in natural developmental terms. Notice that Nietzsche makes the same claim in D as part of his critical engagement with customary morality.

Nietzsche discusses how the morality of custom [Sittlichkeit der Sitte] holds us in thrall through superstitious fear:[49] 'It is that fear of a higher intellect that commands through tradition, fear in the face of an inexplicable, indeterminate power, of something beyond the personal—there is superstition in this fear' (D 9). Nietzsche thinks that obedience to tradition involves thinking of oneself as living in accordance with terms of customs that are embedded in society, yet without thinking of oneself as an individual. His explanation as to why this is necessary prioritizes the role of custom: 'Originally, then, everything was a matter of custom, and anyone wishing to elevate himself above custom had to become lawgiver and medicine man and a demigod of sorts: that is, he had to create customs—a terrifying, life-threatening, thing!' (D 9). To develop new customs by thinking of oneself in individual terms invites the possible wrath of the unknown power, on top of possible exclusion from the customary moral community. Customary morality depends on being embedded within and supported by the obedient behaviour of a cultural community; offenses against this form of morality result in negative consequences for that community; as such, individual actions against morality cannot be tolerated. Under customary morality conditions, individual thinking and action provokes horror; originality is considered, and considers itself, 'evil and dangerous' (D 9). Our fear of performing some anti-traditional action and of the negative consequences for society reinforces a pervasive mood of superstitious fear.

Given this, Nietzsche claims that our 'sense of customary morality [Sinn der Sittlichkeit]' and our 'sense of causality [Sinn der Causalität]' are in 'counteraction [Gegenbewegung]' (D 10). As our sense of causality increases, he claims, the moral realm diminishes; 'fantastic causalities' previously believed to ground old customs [Sitten] are destroyed, and respect for the authority of custom is eroded along with the anxiety and constraint characterizing customary morality (D 10). In D 11, Nietzsche provides further support for his claim about causality and for an additional claim about the unhealthy effect of customary morality, by pointing to the connection between morality and folk medicine. Both morality and folk medicine, he claims, are 'the most dangerous pseudosciences [die gefährlichsten Scheinwissenschaften]':

The morality that reigns in a community is being worked upon by everyone at every moment; most people serve up example after example for the purported *relationship between cause and effect* and, by extension, between guilt and punishment; confirm this relationship as well-founded; and strengthen their faith in it. (D 11)

Even in cases where people form new observations or even in rare cases allow their faith to weaken, Nietzsche contends, just like folk medicine, folk morality is unscientific and, like folk medicine, is something we need to move away from (D 11).

Nietzsche does not propose a *single* new morality in D as an alternative to customary or folk morality: as he writes, 'remember that what is "higher" and "lower" in morality is not, in turn to be measured by a moral yardstick: for there is no absolute morality [es giebt keine absolut Moral]. So take your rule from somewhere else—and now beware!' (D 139).[50] Paying close attention to Nietzsche's point that mistakes about causality form a core part of customary morality returns us to the issue that is fundamentally at stake in D: the issue of how to go about re-imagining morality in a way that does not perpetuate confusion about causality and in a way that promotes health. The raw materials available for free spirits to do this work, as discussed in examination of four important garden aphorisms in D, are natural materials: drives. The specific tools available are those techniques of drive cultivation that are available to free spirited cultivators. But as the drives in question belong, as Nietzsche claims in D 560, to *individuals*, this returns us to the issue of whether and how *self*-cultivation is meaningfully possible in D.

CULTIVATING FREE SPIRITS

Nietzsche makes several claims about the weak degree of self-knowledge of those in the grip of customary morality, namely that their self-knowledge is much less extensive than we often imagine, that it is based on drives and not purely on rational self-awareness, and that language further confuses their understanding (e.g. D 115, 119 and 120). He uses the polyp in D 119 as part of a detailed analysis of how our self-knowledge is necessarily incomplete because of our partial knowledge of drives:

With every moment of our lives some of the polyp-arms [Polypenarme] of our being grow and others dry up, depending on the nourishment that the moment does or does not supply. As stated earlier, all our experiences are, in this sense, types of nourishment [der Nahrung]—seeds sown, however, with a blind hand devoid of any knowledge as to who hungers and who already has abundance. And as a consequence of this contingent alimentation of the parts, the whole, fully grown polyp [Polyp] turns out to be a creature no less contingent [Zufälliges] than is its maturation.

As we saw through comparing La Mettrie's materialism with Nietzsche's thinking, Nietzsche is interested in providing a natural explanation for subjectivity and human development. His two key points in this part of the aphorism are (i) that cultivation is a matter of experience and nourishment and (ii) that experience and nourishment, along with maturation, are naturally contingent. In light of this point on contingency, notice that any 'gardener' we might be tempted to infer within the aphorism is 'blind' and 'devoid of knowledge' about the needs that the plants have with regard to their nourishment. Nietzsche's disabling and eliding of a causally effective 'gardener' seems to capture a problem of 'self'-cultivation: it seems initially unlikely that we could talk meaningfully about cultivating ourselves, or of free spirits as cultivating themselves, or even talk in a weaker sense about cultivation of *de-individuated* drives, especially if our self-knowledge is as limited as Nietzsche suggests is the case.

Two previous discussions of this problem of subjectivity in Nietzsche's free spirit texts are worth noting here. In a detailed account of subjectivity and freedom in D, Carl B. Sachs frames the problem of subjectivity for Nietzsche in D by asking how a multiplicity of drives and affects could constitute a feeling and thinking subject.[51] Christa Acampora has raised the same issue: she claims that, (i) as drive nourishment is unknowable and the work of chance, therefore (ii) drive-orchestration would be the work of whichever drive happens to be dominant, not of a unified self.[52]

In responding to the problem of subjectivity, Sachs contends that previous accounts have failed to appreciate that in indicating drives as the components of selves, we are never *merely* a bundle of drives and affects; we are interpreted and interpreting drives and affects.[53] He differentiates between two forms of subjectivity operating in D: heteronomous subjectivity, where the subject is organized through procedures and techniques external to it, such as authority and tradition, and autonomous subjectivity, a continual work in progress.[54] Mapping this distinction onto free spirits in D, he suggests that the question of the free spirit thus becomes how problematically heteronomous subjects can engage in becoming autonomous; his response is that developing autonomy requires free spirits to engage in overcoming morality and pursuing an ethics of self-fashioning.[55]

Acampora is more skeptical than Sachs about self-cultivation as a solution to the subjectivity problem, because she thinks that it is unclear that Nietzsche provides us with a sufficiently robust account of unification for responsible self-cultivation, and because she doubts that Nietzsche presents a normative ideal for full personhood with which we can be satisfied.[56] Instead, she favours an account of free spirits as freeing themselves from addictive attachments, including from any overwhelming sense of themselves as detached, to loosen the soul for attachments that have developmental value.[57] As she notes, this process is experimental and risky for free spirits.[58]

While I agree with Acampora that experimentation plays an important role in free spirit subjectivity, that Nietzsche's talk of the self can seem incoherent, and that free spirits work to free themselves from addictive attachments, I think Sachs's differentiation between heteronomous and autonomous subjectivity is important to explaining why Nietzsche still seems to be committed to talk of *self*-cultivation as meaningful, even given his apparent rejection of a unified self in D 119. Looking at Sachs's distinction between forms of subjectivity in light of Nietzsche's cultivation talk, itself understood in light of La Mettrie's 'man as plant' analogy, may help to make this aspect of Nietzsche's thinking on subjectivity in D clearer.

The apparent conflict between unified self and self as a mere composite of drives is also evident within D 560. There, Nietzsche emphasizes that we have the freedom to cultivate drives, and specifically *our* drives; this does seem to be a firm claim on his part.[59] Nietzsche also acknowledges that there is a significant barrier to our freedom as self-cultivators: namely, 'presumption [Vorurtheil]'.[60] The particularly insidious presumption Nietzsche identifies in D 560 is the mistaken belief that our characters are complete, fully-grown, and immutable 'facts'. Like D 119, this claim seems to undermine his self-cultivation claim in the same aphorism. However, Nietzsche further suggests that mistaken belief in character fixity has been further reinforced by the work of presumptuous, so-called great philosophers and that the presumption is problematic specifically because it prevents people from *knowing* they have the freedom to cultivate their drives. If we believe our characters are fixed, then we remain unaware of needs, of problems that may be blighting our lives, or even that there is a possibility of pursuing meaningful change and development. Attending to the reason why Nietzsche thinks not knowing is a problem is helpful in resolving this apparent confusion.

To this end, note that D 560 is not the first instance in the text where Nietzsche discusses *not knowing* as a problem. In D 83, discussing what seem to be two competing explanations for humanity (natural and supernatural), he writes:

> *Poor humanity!*—One drop of blood too much or two little in the brain can make our life unspeakably miserable and hard, such that we suffer more from this one drop of blood than Prometheus from his vulture. But the most horrible thing of all is not even *knowing* that this drop of blood is the cause. 'The devil!' Or 'sin!' instead.—

George Stack points out that while discussing how temperament rests on a physiological basis that determines human character in *L'Homme Machine*, La Mettrie observes something very close to Nietzsche's claim in D 83 concerning the physiological basis for cognitive diversity: 'A mere nothing, a tiny fibre, some trifling thing that the most subtle anatomy cannot discover, would have made two idiots out of Erasmus and Fontanelle'.[61] If we follow this materialist view, then two things become clearer about Nietzsche's claim in D 83: (i) physiological diversity provides a natural, material, explanation for diverse responses to experience (in contrast to the supernatural/customary morality explanations Nietzsche argues *against* in D); (ii) our not knowing is *not* a problem because of our being unaware—it is a problem because *not knowing reinforces problematically unhealthy supernatural/customary morality explanations*. Nietzsche isn't providing an account of drives and self-knowledge in the absence of an agenda in D; his broader concern in D is with tackling customary morality and its negative impact on human flourishing, and this needs to be included in explanations of subjectivity in D.

If we now apply this insight to D 560, notice that instead of adopting a sense of subjects as victims of chance or some supernatural entity, we can consider subjects to be products of what Sachs terms the 'material conditions of subjectivity'.[62] Combining this with La Mettrie's analogy of 'man as plant' enables us to separate out two components of Nietzsche's position in D more clearly: his account of drives as a multiplicity of which our self-knowledge is always incomplete (as described in, for example, D 119) and self-driven cultivation of drives (as discussed in D 560). Notice that this illustrates a *process* of cultivating *healthier* humans than customary morality allows, rather than affirming the existence of a unified, fixed, self existing independently of nature and time.

Seed-drives include *emotions* such as anger, pity and vanity, and they include *musing* or *thought* [Nachgrübeln] (D 560).[63] Nietzsche mentions six specific methods of cultivating drives in D: (i) avoiding drive-gratification opportunities; (ii) 'planting regularity into the drive; (iii) generating super-satiation and disgust;' (iv) using an association of an agonizing thought; (v) redirecting one's energy resources to a distracting end; (vi) and general exhaustion (D 109). These methods may be applied to conscious thought and to feeling directly (in the manner of the gardener in D 560), and they may also involve only the minimal gardener from D 119 who cultivates 'with a blind hand devoid of any knowledge as to who hungers and who already has abundance'—namely, *experience*. The seed-drives of D 560 are present in us naturally (in the sense that the drives are there anyway), but they may also be *cultivated* in the same way that (for instance as Nietzsche discusses in a compelling visual analogy that chimes with La Mettrie's 'animal-plant') apple trees may be cultivated on espaliers. By virtue of being what they are, apple trees tend to grow and produce apples anyway. But if we want to cultivate more fruitful, healthier, apple trees—and cultivate them more easily—then it may help to prune each tree and tie it to a frame to control growth and to promote greater fruit yield.

With this, let us return to Sachs's heteronomous/autonomous subjectivity distinction. We have tended to think of Nietzsche presenting us with a choice of selves in D: *either* a 'self'-less composite of drives *or* self as a unity of consciousness. However, Nietzsche's cultivation talk shows that thinking in terms of a strict binary is unhelpful. It may be more *fruitful* for the purpose of developing *autonomous* free spirits to think of our selves in *both* senses, instead of seeing an incommensurable choice between multiplicity and unity of self. If we did so, we could cultivate drives through nourishment and experience of conscious thought and feeling, while acknowledging that we can also still be worked *on*—be *done*—without necessarily always knowing it (D 120).[64] Free-spirited subjects can count as the emerging products of the conditions of natural (or material) subjectivity, and explicitly as a subjective product *in motion*—albeit often slow motion, which Nietzsche clearly acknowledges (D 148).[65] So, free-spirited subjects begin as purely heteronomous, unfree, subjects that are cultivated by authority and tradition and which cultivate themselves as heteronomous through thoughts and feelings derived from such tradition (though *not knowing* they do such work). But free-spirited subjects distinctively acquire knowledge and use of self-cultivatory power and may begin to develop as autonomous subjects, continuing to do so even as they struggle with the effects of heteronomy.

To summarize my thinking on what is happening in D concerning subjectivity and cultivation: (i) unfree spirits are heteronomous cultivated and cultivating subjects; (ii) free spirits are (or at least have the potential to become) autonomously cultivated and cultivating subjects; (iii) whether heteronomous or autonomous, subjects are cultivated *and* cultivators. Free spirits may need to know of their heteronomous origin and of their potentially fully autonomous cultivator subjectivity in order to begin to pursue autonomy, given the prevalence of customary morality and its toxic, de-individualising, effects.

Taking our cue from La Mettrie's 'man as plant' and 'animal-plant' analogies, we might usefully think of this emerging autonomous self in terms of plant movement: *tropisms*. Moving to understand the free spirited subject as a developmental organism that is cultivated by its experiences, including past heteronomous subjective experiences, and which also cultivates itself autonomously, is a key point that I think Nietzsche has to commit to as a part of addressing the problem of customary morality in D. This fits with the notion of self-fashioning of D 506, but underlines the *biological* basis of self-cultivation: Nietzsche notes that we can take pleasure in different approaches towards cultivation of seed-drives—for example we might pleasurably adopt a particular style of gardening such as the French or English or Dutch or Chinese style, we might engage in more minimal garden maintenance, or we might simply let the plants [die Pflanzen] run wild, growing or withering depending on the local conditions that obtain (D 560).

These cultivation options also fit with the individualism that Nietzsche suggests we must nurture in order to counter customary morality and its explicitly de-individualising effects (D 493). For instance, in discussing consumption of one's own philosophical fruit, Nietzsche says that in the past he had denigrated the fruit growing on his own tree but now realizes he would be a fool to do so (D 493). Indeed, an organism meeting the conditions for minimally sufficient health and strength to undergo the process of becoming a more autonomous, free-spirited subject might, plausibly, start to find their own 'most delicious' fruit nourishing and start to benefit from this nourishment (D 493).[66] Nietzsche's call to nurture individualism does not fit with his remarks on drives in D 119 or D 109—*unless* we suppose him to envisage more than one form of subjectivity (heteronomous and autonomous) in D. Thinking of subjectivity as developmental in the terms of Nietzsche's cultivation talk also helps us imagine one way in which free spirits might (constantly) develop out of the state of superstitious fear that Nietzsche diagnoses as caused by customary morality, towards the possibility of a new or 'great health' that one 'does not merely have but acquires continually' (GS 382).[67]

CONCLUSION

Several scholars have suggested that we do not need to think of free spirits as particular people or as specific individuals, but rather that we may think of free spirits as an intermediary ideal, or as a type.[68] Given the legacy of La Mettrian materialism along with Nietzsche's extensive horticultural imagery and talk in D that I have presented in this chapter, I would like to suggest a different term according to which we may characterize free spirits in D (and which may ultimately prove worth adopting in broader analysis of the concept of 'free spirits'). This term is a horticultural one: *cultivar.*

As David Gledhill notes, the term 'cultivar' includes all varieties or derivatives of wild plants that are raised under cultivation; cultivars are maintained by unnatural treatment, and selection pressures by humans, and have one or more distinctive attribute separating them from their relatives.[69] The free spirits of D fit this description of a cultivar: abandoning customary morality and adopting a natural understanding of causality, those who begin the process of becoming free spirits develop the distinctive attribute of the setting aside of the superstitious fear that characterises customary morality.[70] In so doing, they may become healthy enough to engage in the wide-ranging experimentation necessarily for further (and ongoing) moral and value development.[71] The key advantage of identifying free spirits as cultivars is that it reinforces the sense that while the free spirit is not Nietzsche's ultimate philosophical ideal, it is an important part of a developmental process for humanity, the seeds of which are already clearly present in Nietzsche's cultivation talk in D.[72]

Identifying free spirits as cultivars also provides at least a partial explanation for the ancestry and philosophical function of the odd figure of the 'plant "human being" [die Pflanze 'Mensch']' who appears in the final section of part 2 of *Beyond Good and Evil* on 'The Free Spirit' and who is there described as having grown vigorously tall (BGE 44). Nietzsche suggests that the vigorous growth of the plant-human has depended on a substantial increase in the precariousness of the plant's situation (BGE 44). The height of the plant-human fulfils the promise that Nietzsche imagines in a hypothetical domain of 'grander and taller beings' mentioned in D 201. The 'long periods of pressure and discipline' that contribute to the life will of the plant-human becoming intensified into an 'unconditional power-will', as Nietzsche claims in BGE 44, may be likened to the horticultural treatment of non-human cultivars as described by Gledhill. The developmental function of the free spirit in Nietzsche's middle writings is thus reinforced in the figure of the plant-human from BGE: as Nietzsche indicates there, the 'plant-human' free spirit is what makes possible a new figure: the '*very* free spirit' or 'philosopher of the future' (BGE 44).[73]

NOTES

1. Jessica N. Berry, *Nietzsche and the Ancient Skeptical Tradition* (New York: Oxford University Press, 2011), 6.
2. Berry, *Nietzsche and the Ancient Skeptical Tradition*, 99–101.
3. Berry, *Nietzsche and the Ancient Skeptical Tradition*, 136–42.
4. Berry, *Nietzsche and the Ancient Skeptical Tradition*, 141.
5. Berry, *Nietzsche and the Ancient Skeptical Tradition*, 141. Berry suggests that we should think of health as a 'framing question' for Nietzsche's work on diagnosing value systems in his *On the Genealogy of Morals* (*Nietzsche and the Ancient Skeptical Tradition*, 135–36).
6. Michael Ure, *Nietzsche's Therapy: Self-Cultivation in the Middle Works* (Lanham: Lexington Books, 2008), 7–8.
7. Keith Ansell-Pearson, 'Beyond Compassion: On Nietzsche's Moral Therapy in *Dawn*', *Continental Philosophy Review* 44(2) (2011): 179–204.
8. I have referred to the following translations (occasionally modified, as noted throughout): *Dawn: Thoughts on the Presumptions of Morality*, trans. Brittain Smith (Stanford: Stanford University Press, 2011); *The Gay Science. With a Prelude in Rhymes and an Appendix of Songs*, trans. Walter Kaufmann (New York: Vintage Books, 1974). *Beyond Good and Evil*, trans. Marion Faber (Oxford: Oxford University Press, 1998).
9. Amy Mullin has previously drawn attention to the opinion-changing capacity of the free spirit. See Mullin, 'Nietzsche's Free Spirit', *Journal of the History of Philosophy* 38:3 (July 2000): 393.
10. As Nietzsche acknowledges, this is stressful for the free spirits, who, like Odysseus, 'at some point have to descend to the dead to alleviate their grief and soothe their tenderness' (D 562).
11. Chapters by Katrina Mitcheson and by Herman Siemens and Katia Hay in this volume also address this problem.
12. Carl B. Sachs has discussed this issue in the context of D extensively and proposes a helpful solution in 'Nietzsche's *Daybreak*: Toward a Naturalized Theory of Autonomy', *Epoché* 13(1) (2008): 95. Acampora raises the same issue in 'Senses of Freedom of the Free Spirit', *Pli: Warwick Journal of Philosophy* 25 (2014): 27–32, and also in her chapter in this volume, which expands on her earlier work. I shall return to this issue later.
13. Graham Parkes has already drawn attention to the importance of Nietzsche's language of cultivation, though his account does not explore free spirits or their role/s in Nietzsche's middle

works in depth. Parkes, *Composing the Soul: Reaches of Nietzsche's Psychology* (London: University of Chicago Press, 1994), especially chapter 5. Michael Marder has also provided a helpful discussion of Nietzsche and plants as part of a broader account of plant-thinking, though his account does not focus substantially on *Dawn* and is based substantially on discussion of aphorisms from notebook material. See Marder, *Plant-Thinking: A Philosophy of Vegetal Life* (New York: Columbia University Press, 2013), 38–47.

14. Large, 'Nietzsche's Helmbrecht. Or: How To Philosophise With A Ploughshare', *Studia Nietzscheana* (2014): http://www.nietzschesource.org/SN/d-large-2014.

15. Ure, *Nietzsche's Therapy: Self-Cultivation in the Middle Works*, 202–3.

16. Ansell-Pearson claims that Nietzsche is promoting an ethic of self-fashioning in this aphorism, in response to concern about 'market-driven atomization and de-individuation' as well as to the tyranny of a morality of sympathetic affect ('Beyond Compassion', 188–90).

17. As Ruth Abbey has shown, Nietzsche's critical engagement with pity is not absolute but nuanced, making allowances for differences of individual type and context in assessing whether or not pity is defensible or appropriate ethical behaviour. See Abbey, *Nietzsche's Middle Period* (Oxford: Oxford University Press, 2000), 71.

18. For a more detailed analysis of Nietzsche's use of 'Ehrlichkeit' and 'Redlichkeit', see Melissa Lane, 'Honesty as the Best Policy?: Nietzsche on Redlichkeit and the Contrast between Stoic and Epicurean Strategies of the Self,' in *Histories of Postmodernism: The Precursors, The Heyday, The Legacy*, ed. Mark Bevir, Jill Hargis and Sara Rushing, 28–29 (New York: Routledge, 2007).

19. Lane, 'Honesty as the Best Policy?' 28.

20. On 'Redlichkeit', see the essay by Herman Siemens and Katia Hay in this volume.

21. I discussed the significance of this analogy in D 382 for Nietzsche's overall project in D in my '*Daybreak*,' in *A Companion to the Works of Friedrich Nietzsche*, ed. Paul Bishop, (Rochester, NY: Boydell & Brewer [Camden House], 2012), 139–57.

22. Translation modified.

23. On Nietzsche's use of water imagery in this text, see my '*Daybreak*', 150–51.

24. Translation modified from 'shoots' to 'seeds'. Smith renders 'die Keime' as 'shoots' in his translation, which I think obscures the Stoic imagery here. I am grateful to Stefan Heßbrüggen for pointing out this Stoic influence upon D 560 to me. Graham Parkes has pointed out that seed imagery also occurs in Plato, for example in the *Timaeus*, and provides a detailed analysis connecting this aspect of Plato's work to Nietzsche's thinking on ethics and psychology in *Composing the Soul*, 186–93.

25. Horowitz, 'The Stoic Synthesis of the Idea of Natural Law in Man: Four Themes', *Journal of the History of Ideas* 35(1) (1974): 3–16.

26. Sachs, 'Nietzsche's *Daybreak*', 85. Acampora, 'Senses of Freedom', 27–32, and also in this volume.

27. Abbey, *Nietzsche's Middle Period*, 69–70, 83.

28. According to Ure, Nietzsche provides an 'overdetermined allusion' to 'Old Testament, classical, Christian and medieval romance images of the paradise garden' in D 174, and uses the garden metaphor in a way that draws upon both the classical and Christian intellectual traditions, but which distinguishes itself from the Christian tradition. Ure, *Nietzsche's Therapy: Self-Cultivation in the Middle Works*, 68, 202.

29. Nietzsche writes this in a letter to Paul Rée dated 31 October 1879 (BVN-1879-899). On this point, see also Keith Ansell-Pearson's chapter in this volume.

30. Parkes, *Composing the Soul*, especially chapter 5.

31. Gary Shapiro, 'Earth's Garden-Happiness: Nietzsche's Geoaesthetics of the Anthropocene,' *Nietzsche-Studien* 42(1) (2013): 67–84.

32. Shapiro, 'Earth's Garden-Happiness', 83.

33. Shapiro, 'Earth's Garden-Happiness', 75. Ure does not devote significant attention to the influence of Voltaire upon Nietzsche's use of this theme (*Nietzsche's Therapy: Self-Cultivation in the Middle Works*, 68, 202–5). Thomas Brobjer notes that Nietzsche visited Voltaire's estate at Ferney and spent substantial time reading Voltaire with Paul Rée and Malwida von Meysenbug in 1876, then dedicated the original volume of *Human, All Too Human* to Voltaire in 1878, *Nietzsche's Philosophical Context: An Intellectual Biography* (Urbana and Chicago:

University of Illinois Press, 2008), 63. However, we should also note with Ruth Abbey (this volume) that Nietzsche removed the dedication to Voltaire in the second, two-volume, edition of HH comprising HH, AOM and WS along with its two prefaces.

34. Brian Domino, 'Polyp Man', in *A Nietzschean Bestiary: Becoming Animal beyond Docile and Brutal*, ed. Christa Davis Acampora and Ralph R. Acampora (Lanham, MD: Rowman & Littlefield, 2004), 43. On Lange's discussion of La Mettrie and the influence of this on Nietzsche's composition of HH and D, particularly with regard to La Mettrie's thinking on language and physiology, see also George J. Stack, *Lange and Nietzsche* (Berlin and New York: de Gruyter, 1983), 138–40.

35. Domino, 'Polyp Man', 43. Today, biologists refer to Tremblay's 'polyp', discovered in 1741, as a 'hydra'—though I shall retain use of 'polyp' in what follows, in order to illustrate relevance to Nietzsche's writings as this is also the term Nietzsche used. Tremblay's experiments were important at the time because they seemed to provide evidence opposing preformation and supporting epigenesis, the theory that life acquires form through some active organizing process unique to living things. On the hydra, see Ted Everson, *The Gene: A Historical Perspective* (Westport, CT: Greenwood Publishing Group, 2007), 23–24.

36. Stack, *Lange and Nietzsche*, 140–41; Domino, 'Polyp Man', 43–44.

37. Julien Offray de La Mettrie, 'Machine Man', in *Machine Man and Other Writings*, ed. Ann Thomson (Cambridge: Cambridge University Press, 1996), 24.

38. La Mettrie, 'Machine Man', 24. Compare La Mettrie's ambiguous image of the (non)crushing weight of atheism with Nietzsche's notion of the greatest weight, namely eternal recurrence (GS 341).

39. La Mettrie, 'Machine Man', 32.

40. La Mettrie, 'Machine Man', 36–37.

41. See, for example, BGE 44, in which Nietzsche discusses the development of 'plant man'; I will return to this point. On contest in Nietzsche's philosophy, see Christa Davis Acampora, *Contesting Nietzsche* (Chicago: University of Chicago Press, 2013).

42. La Mettrie expanded on the plant man notion in another 1748 essay, 'Man as Plant', in which the polyp appears once again: 'After the vegetables and minerals—bodies without a soul—come beings which begin to be animate, such as the polyp and all the animal-plants still unknown today, which other favoured Tremblays will discover in time'. See La Mettrie, 'Man as Plant', in *Machine Man and Other Writings*, ed. Ann Thomson (Cambridge: Cambridge University Press, 1996), 85.

43. La Mettrie, 'Machine Man', 16, 26.

44. On nature's infinite variety and resources see La Mettrie, 'Machine Man', 10, 12. The celebratory quality of La Mettrie's descriptions is in keeping with Nietzsche's affirmation of aesthetic pleasure to be found in contemplating a garden self, for example, in D 174.

45. La Mettrie, 'Machine Man', 37. Note once again the Stoic influence in La Mettrie's discussion of 'seed' or semen as incorporating an organizing principle for reproduction and development of the human organism.

46. On Nietzsche's mole, see David Farrell Krell, 'The Mole: Philosophic Burrowings in Kant, Hegel, and Nietzsche', *boundary 2*, 9(3)–10(1), Why Nietzsche Now? A Boundary 2 Symposium (1981): 169–85; Debra B. Bergoffen, 'On Nietzsche's Moles', in *A Nietzschean Bestiary: Becoming Animal beyond Docile and Brutal*, ed. Christa Davis Acampora and Ralph R. Acampora (Lanham, MD: Rowman & Littlefield, 2004), 243–50. See also my '*Daybreak*', 141.

47. Franco, *Nietzsche's Enlightenment: The Free Spirit Trilogy of the Middle Period* (Chicago and London: University of Chicago Press, 2011), 62–64.

48. See my 'Mood and Aphorism in Nietzsche's Campaign against Morality', *Pli: Warwick Journal of Philosophy* 25 (2014): 55–76.

49. Remarks from this paragraph are drawn from my previous discussion of superstitious fear and customary morality in D in Bamford, 'Mood and Aphorism', 55–76.

50. Keith Ansell-Pearson points this out in 'Beyond Compassion', 186.

51. Sachs, 'Nietzsche's *Daybreak*', 85.

52. Acampora, 'Senses of Freedom', 27–32. See also Acampora, this volume.

53. Sachs, 'Nietzsche's *Daybreak*', 85.

54. Sachs, 'Nietzsche's *Daybreak*', 94–95.
55. Sachs, 'Nietzsche's *Daybreak*', 94–95. Mitcheson also points out that only latent health and strength are required to undertake the move from fettered to free (heteronomous to autonomous) spirit. See Mitcheson, *Nietzsche, Truth and Transformation* (Basingstoke: Palgrave Macmillan, 2013), 152.
56. Acampora, 'Senses of Freedom', 29. See also Acampora, this volume. Poellner, 'Nietzschean Freedom', in *Nietzsche on Freedom and Autonomy*, edited by Ken Gemes and Simon May (Oxford: Oxford University Press, 2009), 154.
57. Acampora, 'Senses of Freedom', 27–32. See also Acampora, this volume.
58. Acampora, 'Senses of Freedom', 27–32. See also Acampora, this volume.
59. On material conditions, see Sachs, 'Nietzsche's *Daybreak*', 82. As Parkes discusses, the cultivation options discussed in D 560 are a form of sublimation of drives. See Parkes, *Composing the Soul*, 169. See also Ansell-Pearson, 'Beyond Compassion', 196.
60. The subtitle of D reinforces the connection between Nietzsche's critical engagement with morality of custom, his re-imagination of the ethical, and his thinking here on presumption as a barrier to cultivation of drives: 'thoughts on the presumptions of morality [Gedanken über die moralischen Vorurtheile]'.
61. Stack, *Lange and Nietzsche*, 140; La Mettrie, 'Machine Man', 10.
62. Sachs, 'Nietzsche's *Daybreak*', 93.
63. I do not claim here that Nietzsche differentiates between emotion and thought wholesale.
64. On conscious versus unconscious mental states in Nietzsche, see Paul Katsafanas, 'Nietzsche's Theory of Mind: Consciousness and Conceptualization', *European Journal of Philosophy* 13(1) (2005): 1–31. See also Christine Daigle (this volume).
65. Sachs, 'Nietzsche's *Daybreak*', 93. On the Nietzschean self as an achievement, see R. Lanier Anderson, 'What is a Nietzschean Self?' In *Nietzsche, Naturalism, and Normativity*, ed. Christopher Janaway and Simon Robertson (Oxford: Oxford University Press, 2009). On subject multiplicity as a prerequisite for change, see Mitcheson, *Nietzsche, Truth and Transformation*, 135.
66. On minimal conditions see Mitcheson, *Nietzsche, Truth and Transformation*, 152.
67. On this constant development of free spirits, see also Siemens and Hay (this volume).
68. Mullin describes developmental stages of free spirithood, from the least to the more mature. See Mullin, 'Nietzsche's Free Spirit', 396–400. Acampora suggests thinking of the free spirit as the spirit of an age or a spiritual capacity in her 'Senses of Freedom', 31. Bishop (this volume) suggests thinking of the free spirit as an attitude or outlook. Christine Daigle (this volume) discusses the free spirit as an intermediary ideal in which Nietzsche loses confidence in his later writings.
69. For example, characteristics may include clones derived through asexual reproduction, plants retaining relevant characteristics that are grown from seed resulting from open pollination, or inbred lines from self-fertilization. Gledhill, *The Names of Plants* (Cambridge: Cambridge University Press, 2008), 26–27.
70. On superstitious fear in Nietzsche's critique of morality in D, see Bamford, 'Mood and Aphorism'.
71. On experimentalism see my '*Daybreak*', 144–48.
72. See the chapters by Christine Daigle and Andreas Urs Sommer (this volume).
73. For a more detailed analysis of free spirits versus freed spirits as creators of something new, see Andreas Urs Sommer (this volume). For a connection between Nietzsche's plant-philosophy and the concept of will to power see Marder, *Plant-Thinking*, 38–47.

BIBLIOGRAPHY

Abbey, Ruth. *Nietzsche's Middle Period*. Oxford: Oxford University Press, 2000.
Acampora, Christa Davis. *Contesting Nietzsche*. Chicago: University of Chicago Press, 2013.
Acampora, Christa Davis. 'Senses of Freedom of the Free Spirit'. *Pli: Warwick Journal of Philosophy* 25 (2014): 13–33.

Anderson, R. Lanier. 'What Is a Nietzschean Self?' In *Nietzsche, Naturalism, and Normativity*, edited by Christopher Janaway and Simon Robertson, 201–35. Oxford: Oxford University Press, 2009.

Ansell-Pearson, Keith. 'Beyond Compassion: On Nietzsche's Moral Therapy in *Dawn*'. *Continental Philosophy Review* 44(2) (2011): 179–204.

Ansell-Pearson, Keith. 'On the Sublime in Dawn'. *The Agonist* 2(1) (2009): 5–30.

Bamford, Rebecca. '*Daybreak*'. In *A Companion to the Works of Friedrich Nietzsche*, edited by Paul Bishop, 139–57. Rochester, NY: Boydell & Brewer (Camden House), 2012.

Bamford, Rebecca. 'Mood and Aphorism in Nietzsche's Campaign against Morality'. *Pli: Warwick Journal of Philosophy* 25 (2014): 55–76.

Bergoffen, Debra B. 'On Nietzsche's Moles'. In *A Nietzschean Bestiary: Becoming Animal beyond Docile and Brutal*, edited by Christa Davis Acampora and Ralph R. Acampora, 243–50. Lanham, MD: Rowman & Littlefield, 2004.

Berry, Jessica N. *Nietzsche and the Ancient Skeptical Tradition*. New York: Oxford University Press, 2011.

Brobjer, Thomas. *Nietzsche's Philosophical Context: An Intellectual Biography*. Urbana and Chicago: University of Illinois Press, 2008.

Domino, Brian. 'Polyp Man'. In *A Nietzschean Bestiary: Becoming Animal beyond Docile and Brutal*, edited by Christa Davis Acampora and Ralph R. Acampora, 42–49. Lanham, MD: Rowman & Littlefield, 2004.

Franco, Paul. *Nietzsche's Enlightenment: The Free Spirit Trilogy of the Middle Period*. Chicago and London: University of Chicago Press, 2011.

Everson, Ted. *The Gene: A Historical Perspective*. Westport, CT: Greenwood Publishing Group, 2007.

Gledhill, David. *The Names of Plants*. Cambridge: Cambridge University Press, 2008.

Horowitz, Maryanne Cline. 'The Stoic Synthesis of the Idea of Natural Law in Man: Four Themes'. *Journal of the History of Ideas* 35(1) (1974): 3–16.

Katsafanas, Paul. 'Nietzsche's Theory of Mind: Consciousness and Conceptualization'. *European Journal of Philosophy* 13(1) (2005): 1–31.

La Mettrie, Julien Offray de. 'Machine Man' and 'Man as Plant'. In *Machine Man and Other Writings*, edited by Ann Thomson, 1–39. Cambridge: Cambridge University Press, 1996.

Lane, Melissa. 'Honesty as the Best Policy?: Nietzsche on Redlichkeit and the Contrast between Stoic and Epicurean Strategies of the Self'. In *Histories of Postmodernism: The Precursors, The Heyday, The Legacy*, edited by Mark Bevir, Jill Hargis and Sara Rushing, 25–51. New York: Routledge, 2007.

Large, Duncan. 'Nietzsche's Helmbrecht. Or: How to Philosophise with a Ploughshare'. *Studia Nietzscheana* (2014): http://www.nietzschesource.org/SN/d-large-2014.

Marder, Michael. *Plant-Thinking: A Philosophy of Vegetal Life*. New York: Columbia University Press, 2013.

Mitcheson, Katrina. *Nietzsche, Truth and Transformation*. Basingstoke: Palgrave Macmillan, 2013.

Mullin, Amy. 'Nietzsche's Free Spirit'. *Journal of the History of Philosophy* 38(3) (July 2000): 383–405.

Nietzsche, Friedrich. *Beyond Good and Evil*. Translated by Marion Faber. Oxford: Oxford University Press, 1998.

Nietzsche, Friedrich. *Dawn: Thoughts on the Presumptions of Morality*. Translated by Brittain Smith. Stanford: Stanford University Press, 2011.

Nietzsche, Friedrich. *Digital Critical Edition of the Complete Works and Letters*. Based on the critical text by G. Colli and M. Montinari, edited by Paolo D'Iorio. Berlin/New York, de Gruyter 1967–.

Nietzsche, Friedrich. *The Gay Science. With a Prelude in Rhymes and an Appendix of Songs*. Translated by Walter Kaufmann. New York: Vintage Books, 1974.

Parkes, Graham. *Composing the Soul: Reaches of Nietzsche's Psychology*. London: University of Chicago Press, 1994.

Poellner, Peter. 'Nietzschean Freedom'. In *Nietzsche on Freedom and Autonomy*, edited by Ken Gemes and Simon May, 151–79. Oxford: Oxford University Press, 2009.

Sachs, Carl B. 'Nietzsche's *Daybreak*: Toward a Naturalized Theory of Autonomy'. *Epoché* 13(1) (2008): 81–100.

Shapiro, Gary. 'Earth's Garden-Happiness: Nietzsche's Geoaesthetics of the Anthropocene'. *Nietzsche-Studien* 42(1) (2013): 67–84.

Stack, George J. *Lange and Nietzsche*. Berlin and New York: de Gruyter, 1983.

Ure, Michael. *Nietzsche's Therapy: Self-Cultivation in the Middle Works*. Lanham: Lexington Books, 2008.

Chapter Six

Ridendo Dicere Severum

On Probity, Laughter and Self-Critique
in Nietzsche's Figure of the Free Spirit

Herman Siemens and Katia Hay

I. WHO ARE THE FREE SPIRITS IN *THE GAY SCIENCE*?

In *Beyond Good and Evil* 44, Nietzsche seems to distinguish between 'fake' and 'real' *free spirits*; between 'libres-penseurs' and 'free thinkers [Freidenk-er]' on the one hand and 'free, *very* free spirits', on the other. While the former only *seem* to be free with their very 'modern ideas', but in fact are quite unfree and superficial, the latter are the true philosophers of the future, the ones that not only aim to be 'free spirits', but aspire to something 'higher, bigger' (KSA 5.60f.). In *Gay Science*, we find a similar distinction or ambiguity: in GS 23 (*'The Signs of Corruption'*), when Nietzsche talks about the 'freest spirits [freieste Geister]', he seems to be referring to 'free thinkers' whom he identifies as the followers and products of the Enlightenment. But at the same time, he says that *until now* these have still been influenced by the 'devotees of the old religion' in as much as they are prejudiced against prejudice, prejudiced against superstition (KSA 3.395).[1] On other occasions, however, Nietzsche writes as a free spirit in the first person plural (e.g., GS 343; KSA 3.574f.). But, then, when he talks about the free spirit *par excellence*, he suggests that this type of free spirit has not yet been; that he or she is yet to come:

[O]ne could conceive of a delight and power of self-determination, a *freedom of the will*, in which the spirit takes leave of all faith and every wish for certainty, practiced as it is in maintaining itself on light ropes and possibilities and dancing even beside abysses. Such a spirit would be the *free spirit* par excellence. (GS 347; KSA 3.583)

In effect, we cannot find a straightforward answer to the question, *who are the free spirits?*—what is clear, though, is that they are not like the *Übermensch*, in the sense that the *Übermensch* tends to be depicted as an ultimate goal, an almost unanimous, collective *Ziel*: 'Well then! Well now! You higher men! The mountain of the human future is now ready to give birth. God died: now *we* want—the *Übermensch* to live' (Z IV Higher Man; KSA 4.357); whereas the free spirit, be it past or future, is constantly engaged in a very specific process: an endless process of liberation or *Befreiung*. It is for this reason that in this chapter, we will be focusing primarily on the process itself, rather than on the subject undergoing the process. What is at stake for us is *how* that process is realized: What is needed for the free spirit to undergo liberation? What kinds of difficulty or dangers does it involve, and how does Nietzsche's gay science negotiate them?

Der Grosse Befreier (or the Great Liberator)

Nietzsche's late preface to GS is well-known for its retrospective, perhaps also somewhat contrived, description of the genesis of the thoughts that are embodied in his book. It is here that Nietzsche introduces his philosophico-psychological experimental enquiry into the relation between illness and thought, body and soul, which he then describes as a fundamental tool for philosophical (self-)awareness and (self-)critique:

> [O]ne is better than before at guessing the involuntary detours, alleyways, resting places, and *sunning* places of thought to which suffering thinkers are led and misled on account of their suffering; one now knows where the sick *body* and its needs unconsciously urge, push and lure the mind—towards sun, stillness, mildness, patience, medicine. (GS Preface 2; KSA 3.348)

Once we begin to think of our own interpretations and views of the world as a response to the body and its human, all too human needs, we develop a special sense, a suspicion that enables us to see through all those mental constructions and realize that they only serve to support and comfort our sick and weak bodies. Not surprisingly, Nietzsche's auto-diagnosis includes the recognition that he, too, like so many other thinkers before him, was sick, and he presents GS as the result of his recovery.

Nietzsche describes this process of convalescence and recovery (i.e., the process that takes one through different forms of health and through different philosophies) as the process by which our bodily and mental dispositions are translated, interpreted and misinterpreted into thoughts. 'Precisely this art of transfiguration *is* philosophy' (GS Preface 3; KSA 3.349), says Nietzsche.

Moreover, he describes his recovery and his newly acquired philosophical standpoint as one that is characterized by having undergone a certain form of liberation or *Befreiung*. 'Great pain is the ultimate liberator of the spirit' (GS Preface 3; KSA 3.350), Nietzsche writes. But this leaves us with at least three questions: What exactly is Nietzsche's philosophy freeing itself [sich befreien] from? Why is this process painful? And, of course: where does this freedom take us?[2]

If we think of the examples Nietzsche gives us, we can say that the liberation he is referring to is a liberation from certain thoughts and beliefs that had never been questioned before. Indeed, the liberator of the spirit is also 'the teacher of the great suspicion' who shows us that there are no ultimate truths (there is always the possibility of questioning our 'truths') and makes us 'descend into our ultimate depths and put aside all trust, everything good-natured, veiling, mild, average—things in which formerly we may have found our humanity' (GS Preface 3). In the process, our most cherished ideals and 'truths' are exposed as the products of the sick body they have served to veil and its needs for consolation, redemption and escape. It is therefore not surprising that this process should be also painful. On the contrary, what might seem surprising is that Nietzsche finds it liberating. In GS 297, Nietzsche describes the 'liberated spirit' [befreiter Geist] as the one who is able not only to endure being contradicted [Widerspruch-Vertragen-können], but most importantly as the one who has acquired the ability to contradict with '*good* conscience' (KSA 3.537).[3] 'Good conscience' accompanies his 'hostility towards what is familiar, traditional, sacred' (KSA 3.537). So perhaps one could say that this process of *Befreiung* is painful because it is radical, and because it is destabilizing, it changes everything and turns all our assumptions upside down; because it redefines everything, sees through everything—it even sees through the pain itself. But it is liberating because it also releases us from all those acquired self-deceiving strategies and constructs, beliefs and superstitions that we have elaborated for centuries in order to *avoid* the pain. In other words, pain is finally what cuts through all those intricate forms of escape and confronts us with what we were trying so hard to avoid, so that we no longer need and are liberated from this constant self-deluding effort. And what is most important, the result of this painful process is that we gain the ability, in Nietzsche's terms, to *dance*, that is, to affirm that painful process and enjoy the absence of false sources of security, stability and constancy.

Somewhat paradoxically, though, this 'liberation' does not come without a series of constraints:

> We philosophers are not free to separate soul from body as the common people do; we are even less free to separate soul from spirit. We are no thinking frogs, no objectifying and registering devices with frozen innards—we must con-

stantly give birth to our thoughts out of our pain and maternally endow them
with all that we have of blood, heart, fire, pleasure, passion, agony, conscience, fate, and disaster. Life—to us, that means constantly transforming all
that we are into light and flame, and also all that wounds us; we simply *can* do
no other. And as for illness: are we not almost tempted to ask whether we can
do without it at all? (GS Preface 3; KSA 3.350)

'We' liberated philosophers or *freie Geister* are no longer free to misinterpret
ourselves in the same way as others have done before us. There are certain
'liberties' we can no longer afford to take. There is, so to say, no going back
to 'false' ideas about the possibility of separating, as Descartes did, knowledge, mind or thought, on one side, from life, embodied experience and
practice on the other—'Sum, ergo cogito: cogito, ergo sum' (GS 276). For,
as we have already seen above: thought is nothing but an 'interpretation and
misunderstanding of the body' (GS Preface 2; KSA 3.348). However, this
liberating and transformative insight itself raises further and deeper questions, questions that touch on further and deeper sources of 'pain'.[4] Indeed,
far from 'resolving' the problem of the relation between mind and body or
knowledge and life, it lays bare the problem in a way that can no longer be
avoided or 'resolved'. For it is not just a matter of understanding the ways in
which knowledge-claims are unconscious (mis-)interpretations of the body
and its needs. The problem, in the end, is much more serious and has to do
with the realization that error, illusion or untruth are necessary conditions *for*
life. At stake here is a figure of thought bound up with the figure of the free
spirit from the very start in HH, where Nietzsche launches the notion of
critical reason that will characterize his philosophy throughout the middle
period. The philosophy of the free spirit takes off from the recognition of the
unconditional value of truth or truthfulness [Wahrhaftigkeit, Redlichkeit][5]
for the pursuit of knowledge, and the recognition that knowledge is of irreducible and irreversible value in modernity. As Nietzsche puts it in D 429: 'we
would all prefer the demise of humanity to the regression of knowledge'
(KSA 3.265). What this knowledge reveals, however, is the pervasiveness of
error, illusion or untruth, indeed their necessity as conditions for life, so that
the passion for knowledge stands in irreconcilable conflict with life. Characteristic of GS is the *existential turn* it gives to this problem: Because knowledge itself is situated within embodied existence, the question of knowledge
is posed within the question of an existence that can actually be lived: How
to live in the face of the truth that our truth-seeking as free spirits is condi-
tioned by the untruth we need as living beings? In this regard, 'the great pain'
has its source in what we might call the *existential impossibility of reconcil-*
ing life and knowledge. Nietzsche's 'gay science' is conceived as a way to
make the life of knowledge possible in the light of this existential contradiction and to turn this bitter truth into something light and joyful.

It is perhaps in this light that we can understand Nietzsche's claim in GS 324—*In media vita*—that the 'great liberator' is not pain itself, but rather a thought that can liberate us from our existential pain as knowers: the thought that 'life could be an experiment for the knower—not a duty, not a disaster, not a deception!', but '*a means to knowledge*' (KSA 3.552f.). This thought, Nietzsche claims, unlocks a new 'world of dangers and victories' (KSA 3.552f.). It is by *living dangerously for the sake of knowledge* that we can embody the real unity between life and knowledge without succumbing to their contradiction. Indeed, according to Nietzsche, this thought leads us, not only to a new form of knowledge, but also to a new form of life in which we can learn '*to live gaily and laugh gaily*' (KSA 3.553). In what follows, we will attempt to explicate Nietzsche's gay science as a life-experiment of the knower, beginning with an examination of the existential contradiction between life and knowledge as it is developed in GS and the accompanying *Nachlass*.

II. THE CONTRADICTION BETWEEN KNOWLEDGE AND LIFE AND 'GAY SCIENCE' AS *ALTERNATION*

In GS 110, on the *Origin of knowledge*, Nietzsche describes the history of human intellect as a history of errors. Among these errors, Nietzsche considers, for instance, the idea of 'substance' (i.e., 'that there are enduring things') or the idea of 'freedom' (i.e., 'that our will is free') (KSA 3.469). The main problem, however, and what is most significant about Nietzsche's analysis in this aphorism, is the thought that these errors are not merely intellectual: we cannot simply correct these errors by realizing that our beliefs (in substance, identity, freedom, etc.) are wrong, because they have become part of us, part of what constitutes us as living beings, so that our whole life depends or is based upon these errors. These errors have been *incorporated* [*einverleibt*] by us, lived by us. And yet, as Nietzsche points out, 'we' are now able to identify them as errors. The reason for this, according to Nietzsche, has been 'a subtler development of probity [Redlichkeit] and skepticism' (KSA 3.470). Through a strict sense of probity or honesty, we 'thinkers' have become aware of the fact that our knowledge is founded upon life-preserving errors.

Until this point of the aphorism, it might seem that Nietzsche is giving us an optimistic account of the history of knowledge. The figure of the thinker is described as 'the being in whom the drive to truth and those life-preserving errors are fighting their first battle' (KSA 3.471), so that one gets the feeling that there are many battles to come and that the hero-thinker will always, in some way or other, succeed in his or her quest for truth. But in the course of the text, it becomes clearer that this first battle might well be the one and only real battle, the one that we always need to fight again and again, because once we realize that errors are necessary for life, it is not just a matter of recognizing our errors as such; rather, the only way to confront and correct them will be to radically change our way of life, so that the question we need to address and the life 'experiment' we need to engage in as knowers is: To what extent can we do without lies and errors? Or '[t]o what extent can truth stand to be incorporated? [Inwieweit verträgt die Wahrheit die Einverleibung?]' (GS 110).

What Nietzsche means by this question is spelled out in a posthumous note from the period of GS, a note in which the philosophical basis of the conflict between life and knowledge is laid bare. In this note, the problem is also driven to an extreme by the existential turn Nietzsche gives it:

> [A.] For there to be any degree of consciousness in the world, an unreal world of error had to—come into existence: beings with the belief in that which endures in individuals etc. Only after an imaginary world in contradiction with absolute flux had come into existence *could* something *be known on this basis*—indeed in the end the fundamental error upon which all others rest can be seen (because oppositions can be *thought*)—[B.] yet this error can only be destroyed by destroying life: the ultimate truth of the flux of things does not allow for *incorporation*, our **organs** (for *life*) are oriented to error. This is how in the wise man the *contradiction between life* and his ultimate decisions arises; his *drive* to knowledge has the belief in error and life in this belief as its presupposition. (NL 11[162] 9.503f.)

We see here the question of GS 110—'[t]o what extent can truth stand to be incorporated?'—reformulated as the thesis that 'the ultimate truth of the flux of things does not allow for *incorporation*'. The truth of absolute flux or Becoming cannot be lived with: On the one hand, the presuppositions of human thought and knowledge (identity and opposition) necessarily falsify the reality we want to know; on the other, overcoming these errors would destroy human life. But what exactly is the argument?

In the first part [A.], Nietzsche argues that there is an irresolvable conflict between reality and the presuppositions for conscious thought, because conscious thought is only possible on the basis of certain presuppositions, such as identity, stability over time and individuation. These categories form the necessary basis for knowledge [Erkenntnis], yet they are all errors [Irrthümer] because they falsify the truth of things: the reality of absolute flux or Becoming. In other words, conscious thought and knowledge are only possible through the opposition of (an unreal world of) Being to (the real world of) Becoming, so that the originary category or error on the ground of knowledge is that of opposition [Gegensatz]. From this we could conclude that as knowers, we may want to know the truth of things or reality, but we are condemned to falsify it by the necessary presuppositions of thought.

However, in the second part of the argument [B.], Nietzsche takes the conflict between reality (or truth) and thought one step further by arguing that those foundational errors are not just necessary conditions for conscious thought but also necessary conditions for life. The underlying thesis is that consciousness is but an organ of the organism, and our organs, being life-enabling, can only incorporate reality in a way that opposes the absolute flux of Becoming with a counter-world of durable beings. Thus, the conflict between reality or truth and thought ([A.]), now becomes a conflict between truth and life. The errors of thought (Being, opposition) are not just thought-enabling, but also life-enabling, so that to negate or eliminate them would be to eliminate or destroy life—*our* life. This is what Nietzsche means when he says that 'the ultimate truth of the flux of things' does not allow for incorporation [Einverleibung] by the organic living beings that we are.

There is only knowledge as embodied in life, that is, embodied in the life of the knower. But the *existential* conditions for knowledge (i.e., the conditions for life) contradict truth, which at the same time is the only real goal of knowledge. In other words: untruth is *both* the counter-pole to the passion for knowledge *and* the necessary condition for the passion for knowledge as a form of life. This formulation drives the contradiction to an extreme and forces the questions: Under what conditions is knowledge as a form of life possible? Under what conditions can knowledge be lived with? What are the limits to the devotion to truth? Or (with reference to GS 110, 11 and 57): how much truth can a living being take or 'incorporate'?

Nietzsche addresses these questions in the final part of the same *Nachlass* note, where he takes issue with the bitter pain caused by our insight into the existential conditions for knowledge:

> Life is the condition for knowing. *Erring* is the condition for life, indeed erring in the most fundamental sense. Knowing about the errors does not cancel them! That is nothing bitter!
>
> We must love and cultivate erring, it is the womb of knowing. Art as the cultivation of delusion—our cult.
>
> To love and advance life for the sake of knowing, to love and advance erring deluding for the sake of life. To give life an aesthetic significance, *to develop our taste for it*, is the fundamental condition for the passion for knowledge.
>
> In this way we discover here as well a night and day as a condition of life for *us*: Wanting-to-know and wanting-to-err are ebb and flow. If *one* rules absolutely, the human being goes to ground; and *with it the capacity* [for knowledge]. (NL 11[162] KSA 9.504)

As free spirits, we need to find a way to confront the necessary error or untruth that is our existential condition as knowers. But we need to confront it in a way that enables us to love it, to enjoy it, to celebrate it as the condition for our devotion to truth as knowers. Nietzsche's response is to give it an aesthetic significance, to view the necessary untruth of existence from a perspective in which untruth is not negative, bitter or tragic. But this can only mean: to view it from a perspective in which error or untruth do not derive their meaning and value from their opposition to truth as the highest value, as its negative counter-pole; that is, to view it from a perspective *other* than that of knowledge. But in that case, we must be able to switch perspectives between knowing or the will to knowledge, devoted to truth as the highest value, and art or the good will to untruth or error. In effect, this requires that we alternate between two perspectives, as between day and night, as our *ebb and flow*. This ideal of alternation is described more fully in another *Nachlass* note, where Nietzsche writes:

> We have need of blindness intermittently and must leave certain articles of faith and errors in us untouched—as long as they *preserve* us in life.
>   We must be *conscience-free* with regard to truth and error as long as it concerns living—precisely *so that* we can then make use of life once again in the service of truth and intellectual conscience. This is our ebb and flow, the energy of our contraction and expansion. (NL 11[217] KSA 9.526)

In the first movement of our ebb and flow, we must suspend our conscience, our intellectual demand for truth, for the sake of life, so that, in the second movement, we can suspend the demands of life for the sake of truth and knowledge. Each perspective excludes the other, yet each perspective on its own, taken as a fixed or absolute, is impossible. In the first, truth is subordinated to life as the highest value. We are forced to consciously will untruth— yet, as moderns 'we would all prefer the demise of humanity to the regression of knowledge' (D 429). In the second perspective, life is subordinated to truth as the highest value, and we are forced to will the destruction of life, of our life or existence as knowers. Thus, the life of knowledge can only be lived if we find a way to balance the demands of knowledge—our intellectual conscience—and the demands of life (qua condition for knowledge)— semblance [Schein] or untruth [das Unwahre], to balance them as counter-powers [Gegenmächte], giving each its full weight or autonomy, but using the other to limit it in a life-enabling dynamic of alternation, ebb and flow, contraction–expansion.

   This solution to the problem of life and knowledge receives its most sophisticated formulation in GS 107—*Our ultimate gratitude to art*—where the problem is focused on the concepts of probity [Redlichkeit] and laughter. In this aphorism, as in GS 110, *Redlichkeit*, or the unconditional pursuit of truth, reveals the pervasiveness of untruth and, specifically: that error is the condition for all sensate, knowing existence. From the perspective of knowledge, this insight is unbearable and cannot be lived with: on its own, '*[p]robity* [*Redlichkeit*] would lead to nausea [Ekel] and suicide' (GS 107; KSA 3.464). We therefore need a counterweight or counterforce [Gegenmacht] to *Redlichkeit*: to be able to break from the perspective of knowledge and truth so as to view this irreducible untruth from an affirmative perspective: 'But now our probity [Redlichkeit] has a counterforce [Gegenmacht] that helps us avoid such consequences: art, as the *good* will to semblance [dem *guten* Willen zum Scheine]' (GS 107; KSA 3.464). With the good will to untruth, we can then interpret our lives as knowers, our existential contradiction, in a different light, in a way that we can affirm.

It is art that offers us this perspective, but a specific art: one whose qualities are radically Other to the qualities of knowledge or *Redlichkeit*: It is light and light-footed—where *Redlichkeit* is grave and ponderous; it is supple—where *Redlichkeit* in unbending and stringent; and it is playful, and ever ready to laugh and make fun—where *Redlichkeit* is serious. The key to Nietzsche's 'aesthetic justification' in GS is, then, to cultivate *the art of laughter* in dynamic alternation with the seriousness of *Redlichkeit*. And while the term 'aesthetic justification' does not occur again after GS, this thought recurs implicitly and performatively throughout Nietzsche's oeuvre, as when he writes in BGE: 'How could even Plato have endured life—a Greek life to which he says No—without an Aristophanes!' (BGE 28; KSA 5.47). We may think also of the ways in which Nietzsche weaves jokes and laughter into the seriousness and gravity of his insights,[6] so that in the end he makes us cry and laugh,[7] just as he himself claims to cry and laugh when writing his 'songs'.[8]

This alternation model can be seen as describing a form of life as an 'experiment for the knower' (GS 324), one that enables the free spirit to pursue knowledge under the sign of *Redlichkeit* without succumbing to the devastating insights it affords into the errors that we must incorporate and embody as living beings. On this model, we risk everything, living dangerously for the sake of knowledge: all our cherished 'truths' and values are exposed as self-serving delusions under the unbending discipline of *Redlichkeit*, while the art of laughter saves us from the unbearable insight into delusion and error as the condition for our existence as knowers. And yet, the alternation model raises as many questions as it answers. How are we to understand the art of laughter and its life-saving qualities? And how exactly does the passage from *Redlichkeit* to laughter occur? If laughter and art are a 'counterforce' to knowledge, does this mean that we need laughter in order to break (from) the perspective of knowledge, or can the perspective of knowledge somehow break its own spell and lead to us to laughter? In order to address these questions, we need to examine the concept of *Redlichkeit* more closely.

III. FROM *REDLICHKEIT* TO LAUGHTER

As one would expect, *Redlichkeit* is an important and recurrent theme in the *Nachlass* in the period from GS to BGE. In these notes, much that is discussed does not come to light in the published works, and that holds also for the alternation model. In them, Nietzsche develops a naturalistic, (partly) physiological account of *Redlichkeit*, as a drive [Trieb] or fusion of several drives,[9] but one that distances us from direct 'inspiration' by our animal drives, enabling us to resist them (NL 6[234] KSA 9.259). One of the key problems in these notes is the conflict between knowledge and life—how to account for this drive for truthfulness in naturalistic terms, given that deception and error [Verstellung, Irrthum] are natural conditions for life. In his reflections, Nietzsche distinguishes an *outward Redlichkeit*—towards others, towards things—from an *inner Redlichkeit gegen sich*—towards oneself, and argues that the capacity for deception and disguise [Verstellung], so important for animal life, presupposes truthfulness or *Redlichkeit gegen sich*: the capacity to see a lie as a lie, to distinguish deception from reality, error from truth (NL 6[236] KSA 9.260). But in the course of the notes, this *Redlichkeit gegen sich* takes on a dynamic character of its own and becomes the key to another problem that runs through the notes: how to effect the (self-)overcoming of morality? In effect, the expression 'Redlichkeit gegen sich' crosses the semantic range of the term 'gegen' from: (1.) probity *towards* [*gegen*] oneself, to: (2.) probity *against* [*gegen*] oneself or even (3.) probity *against itself*. There is, Nietzsche contends, an unavoidable self-destructive dynamic intrinsic to *Redlichkeit,* and through this dynamic, morality kills itself [bringt sich um] and dies: *Redlichkeit* is 'the last consequence of morality hitherto [die letzte Consequenz der bisherigen Moralität]' (NL 1[42] KSA 10.20), the final, conclusive movement. In this line of thought, Nietzsche situates the perspective of knowledge *within* the perspective of morality; *Redlichkeit* is treated as a moral value and a moral problem. These two points in the *Nachlass*—that *Redlichkeit* is a moral value, and that morality comes to an end through the self-destructive dynamic of *Redlichkeit*—are not clearly present in Nietzsche's published account of the alternation model in GS 107. As we will try to show, they offer a key for understanding the transition from *Redlichkeit* to laughter.

In broad terms, Nietzsche's line of thought in the *Nachlass* can be reconstructed as follows:

1. The perspective of knowledge is actually a moral perspective.
2. As a moral perspective, it is subject to the same critique as all moral values.
3. The consequence of this critique is the self-destruction of morality: morality kills itself [bringt sich um] in *Redlichkeit.*

1. The moral character of *Redlichkeit* is first explicitly thematized in a retrospective note from 1882–1883, where Nietzsche reflects on his activity as a *freie Geist*:

> [I]n this whole business I discovered *living morality, driving* force. I had only *imagined* to be beyond good and evil.
> Free spiritedness *itself* was a *moral activity*
> 1) as probity [*Redlichkeit*]
> 2) as courage (6[1] KSA 10.232)

The free spirit's *Redlichkeit*, Nietzsche concedes, does not go beyond good and evil, but remains bound to morality. Yet it is described in dynamic terms—it is a '*living morality*', a '*driving* force' behind our agency, even if it is inescapably moral in character. A 'refined' *Redlichkeit*, he writes elsewhere, is the capacity to engage a 'lack' (the confines of morality) as a 'force'.[10] But what does Nietzsche mean by 'morality' and why is *Redlichkeit* a moral force? Indeed, why should *Redlichkeit* breathe new 'life' into morality, making it a '*driving* force'?

In note 35[5] from 1885, Nietzsche characterises morality in pluralistic, historical terms. A morality is a normative order of human evaluations or human types that asserts itself as absolute and unconditional. As such, morality conflicts with knowledge: it is 'antiwissenschaftlich', for genuine knowledge of morality—a comparative, critical treatment of morality—would have to be beyond good and evil. But then, Nietzsche asks:

> Is knowledge [Wissenschaft] still possible? What is searching for truth, truthfulness, probity [Redlichkeit] if not something moral? And without these evaluations and their corresponding actions: how would knowledge be *possible*? Take conscientiousness [Gewissenshaftigkeit] out of knowing—and where is knowledge? Is scepticism in morality not a contradiction insofar as the highest refinement of moral claims is active here: as soon as the sceptic no longer feels these finer value-discriminations in matters of truth as binding [maaßgebend] he no longer has a reason to doubt or investigate: for that, *the will to know would have to have an entirely different root from truthfulness.* (NL 35[5] KSA 11.510)

As an activity, knowledge is 'moral' in the sense that it takes the value of truth, truthfulness or *Redlichkeit* as unconditionally binding [maaßgebend]. It is this unconditional value of truth, as we have seen, that characterises the perspective of knowledge from HH on, but here its problematic nature is set out in detail. On the one hand, morality conflicts with knowledge or science [Wissen/Wissenschaft], and it does so for two reasons. By definition, a morality posits its norms or values as absolute and unconditional, and what science shows is precisely the diversity of moralities and their historical conditions. More than that, however, knowledge is driven by the critical demand to limit knowledge and to question all absolute and unconditional claims and cannot therefore be pursued from a moral perspective. On the other hand, the pursuit of knowledge *without* the unconditional value of truth as motivating force would be impossible, making moral scepticism as a practice self-contradictory, since it presupposes the unconditional value of truth and 'the highest refinement of moral claims'. Science of morality is, it seems, neither possible (practicable) from within a moral perspective, nor from without. The inevitable consequence of this line of thought is the cognitive resignation and complete demotivation of knowledge described at the end of the above note. But Nietzsche also suggests the possibility of an alternative: that the will to know could have a source radically other than *Redlichkeit*. We will return to this alternative form of knowledge under the sign of laughter. At present a more pressing question is raised by Nietzsche's argumentation. It concerns the status of *Redlichkeit*, not just as morality, but as the activity of the 'highest refinement of moral demands'. In what sense does morality culminate in truthfulness?

The status of *Redlichkeit* at the limits of morality is specified in several notes—as 'the most stringent standpoint of morality' (NL 1[28] KSA 10.15), 'the last consequence of morality hitherto' (NL 1[42] KSA 10.20) or the 'consequence of enduring moral habits' (NL 25[447] KSA 11.132); it is 'our current form of morality itself' (NL 2[191] KSA 12.161) or the 'last virtue' (NL 1[145] KSA 12.44). The key to these claims is given in GS 357 (KSA 3.599f.), where, for the first time, Nietzsche describes the advent of modern Nihilism under the sign of Schopenhauer's *Redlichkeit*, or *Rechtschaffenheit*. In a passage he will later quote in GM III 27 (KSA 5.409) when discussing the genealogy of the will to truth, Nietzsche ascribes a self-destructive logic to Christian beliefs and values that culminates in Schopenhauer's 'unconditional, honest atheism [unbedingte redliche Atheismus]':

> The ungodliness of existence counted for him as something given, palpable, indisputable; he always lost his philosopher's composure and became indignant when he saw anyone hesitate or beat about the bush on this point. This is the locus of his whole integrity; unconditional, honest atheism is simply the *presupposition* of his way of putting the problem, as a victory of the European conscience won finally and with great difficulty; as the most fateful act of two thousand years of discipline for truth that in the end forbids itself the lie of faith in God. . . . One can see what it was that actually triumphed over the Christian God: Christian morality itself, the concept of truthfulness that was taken ever more rigorously; the father confessor's refinement of the Christian conscience, translated and sublimated into a scientific conscience, into intellectual cleanliness at any price. (GS 357; KSA 3.600)

Our two-thousand-year discipline towards truth begins when Christian dog-ma gives rise to the supreme value of the Christian confession, truthfulness, which then forbids faith in God and Christian dogma; it then develops through the refinement of truthfulness into scientific or intellectual con-science, the will to truth, which in the end forbids the lie of a moral world-order. This narrative clarifies and specifies Nietzsche's claim in the *Nachlass* that morality culminates in truthfulness or *Redlichkeit*: this is a European event [Ereignis], and Nietzsche's claim is about the last consequence or convulsion of European (Christian-Platonic) morality. As such:

2. *Redlichkeit* is subject to the same critique as all our moral values, or as Nietzsche himself puts it:

> *My claim*: that the moral values themselves must be subjected to a critique. That the impulse of moral feeling must be made to halt before the question: why? That the demand for a 'Why?', for a critique of morality is precisely our *present form of morality* itself, as a sublime sense of probity [Redlichkeit]. That our probity, our will not to deceive ourselves, must prove its worth: 'why *not?*'—Before which forum? (NL 2[191] KSA 12.161)

Nietzsche's call for a 'critique of morality' in this text coincides with the self-same demand made in the preface to GM (GM Preface 6; KSA 5.253): to confront our self-evident values, our moral sentiments or intuitions, with the normative question of their value, or as he puts it here, with the question 'Why?'[11] or indeed—'Why *not?*' This *Nachlass* note makes explicit what remains implicit in GM, namely, that to question the value or 'why (not)?' of our moral values necessarily raises the fundamental question of normativity· By what standard do we measure the value of our values? Before which forum must our values prove their worth?

This note also points to the peculiar self-referential structure of the con-cept of *Redlichkeit* at the limits of morality, where it becomes *Redlichkeit gegen sich*. What Nietzsche initially presents as *his* claim or demand for a critique of morality, as a function of *his Redlichkeit*, soon turns out to be a consequence of morality itself—'*our present form of morality*'. So much was clear from GS 370, where Schopenhauer's honesty or *Redlichkeit* was in-serted in the history of nihilism, as the consequence of Christian morality itself.[12] But in this note, *Redlichkeit* is not just the source of critique but also its object, not just that which demands a critique of morality and questions its value but also the very value whose value is under interrogation. In a sense, this is obvious: if *Redlichkeit* is the final form of morality and if *Redlichkeit* turns against and questions morality, then it must in the end question its own value. But if its very value is in question, then the questioning itself becomes questionable or unstable, and one can ask what the value of this questioning is: as both the source and object of critique, *Redlichkeit* or 'our will not to deceive ourselves must prove its worth [sich ausweisen]'. But since the value of truth or truthfulness is itself in question, this only throws open the question: By what standard of evaluation must *Redlichkeit* prove its worth?

3. An answer to this question is given in a further *Nachlass* note, which casts more light on the critique of morality through *Redlichkeit gegen sich*. Nietzsche begins the note by rehearsing the opening line of thought from GS 107: that *Redlichkeit*, in revealing the pervasiveness of untruth, leads to practical life-negation or suicide:

> If we place ourselves on the most stringent standpoint of morality, e.g. honesty [Ehrlichkeit], then our intercourse with things, all articles of faith in our everyday actions is immoral (e.g. that there are bodies).
> Equally that human = human is to be believed in place of the atomism of individuals.
> Everything becomes in this way *dishonesty [Unredlichkeit]*. And supposing we acknowledge life is dishonesty [Unredlichkeit], that is immorality—*then life is to be negated.*
> Just so unconditional justice leads to the insight that life is essentially unjust.
> Consequence of the most extreme morality of knowledge: demand for destruction. (NL 1[28] KSA 10.16)

If *Redlichkeit* is the highest value, and life (or the belief-system that enables us to interact with things and act, i.e., to live) is *Unredlichkeit*, then life ought to be negated. The stringency of this line of thought is, however, broken by the critique of morality:

> *But* now the critique of morality and moralism comes to redeem us: *it* [morality] *kills itself [bringt sich selber um]*.
> So: life is not to be negated, since morality does stand above it, it is dead. The excess of morality has proved its own opposite, evil, to be *necessary and useful*, and as the source of the good. (NL 1[28] KSA 10.15)

Unpacking the whole argument, we can say: *Redlichkeit* comes to the realisation that (1) *Redlichkeit*, when pursued with full stringency, issues in the demand to negate life (theoretically) for its *Unredlichkeit* and (practically) to destroy it. But (2) *Redlichkeit* as a practice depends upon a form of life to maintain it: life is 'necessary and useful' for *Redlichkeit* to maintain itself and develop; indeed, it is 'the source' of *Redlichkeit*. Therefore (3) *Redlichkeit*, when pursued with full stringency, destroys or kills itself [bringt sich um, ist todt]. But (4) since life is *Unredlichkeit* and *Redlichkeit* is 'the highest standpoint of morality' or 'the good', this means that (5) evil (qua *Unredlichkeit*) proves to be 'necessary and useful' for the good (qua *Redlichkeit*), and to be 'the source of the good'. Or as Nietzsche puts it in another note, the critique of morality results in '*the insight of morality that it can only main-*

tain itself in existence and development by virtue of its opposite' (NL 1[42] KSA 10.20).[13]

From this reconstruction, we can see how exactly *Redlichkeit*, as the source of the critique of morality, comes to question its own value, as the object of critique: by way of a reflection on its necessary conditions in life, where life is taken to be *Unredlichkeit*. As the necessary condition for *Redlichkeit*, life[14] becomes the forum or standard of evaluation before which *Redlichkeit* must prove itself [sich ausweisen]—*or not*. . . . For what is *Redlichkeit* worth if it can only maintain itself by virtue of (life qua) *Unredlichkeit*? Does this spell the end of morality and the renunciation of knowledge? Or, in Nietzsche's words:

> Do we thereby have to *give up* the good? No, *precisely not*! For our probity [Redlichkeit] *need not be so stringent any longer*. It is actually *not* the good ones [who are good]. (NL 1[28] KSA 10.16)

The relaxation of the demands of *Redlichkeit* described in these lines is also thematized in the context of Nietzsche's alternation model in GS 107, when he writes:

> It would be a *relapse* for us, with our irritable probity [*Redlichkeit*], to get completely caught up in morality and, for the sake of the overly severe demands that we there make on ourselves, to become virtuous monsters and scarecrows. We have also *to be able to* stand above morality—. (GS 107)

Here Nietzsche suggests that our *Redlichkeit*, in becoming aware of itself as morality, can help us to break with the unconditional demands of truth. In the light of the *Nachlass* texts we have examined, we can now say: it is the self-destructive dynamic of *Redlichkeit gegen sich*, in which *Redlichkeit* must prove its worth [sich ausweisen] before the forum of life, that results in a relaxation of the demands of *Redlichkeit*. This means that the transition from the perspective of knowledge to that of laughter and art in Nietzsche's alternation model does not require the disruptive force of laughter, but is made possible by the self-destructive logic internal to *Redlichkeit*. Laughter figures, not as *means* needed to break from the perspective of knowledge, but as an alternative perspective altogether, to which we are led by the reflective self-overcoming of *Redlichkeit*—the self-destruction of *Redlichkeit* as the unconditional pursuit of truth, in favour of a more relaxed *Redlichkeit* that acknowledges its dependency on *Unredlichkeit* in order to sustain itself: a *living Redlichkeit*. If the first kind of *Redlichkeit* must place itself outside or 'above life' in order to negate life's *Unredlichkeit* (1[28] KSA 10.15), the second is able to 'stand above morality' (GS 107) precisely because it acknowledges its *immanence* to life, that is, its *inner* dependency on *Unredlichkeit* if it is to be a living *Redlichkeit*. In this regard, *Redlichkeit* offers a privileged or exemplary pathway to the self-overcoming of morality: the insight into the *inner* dependency of *Redlichkeit* on its 'opposite', *Unredlichkeit,* instantiates the broader insight that 'good' is not somehow opposed to 'evil', but that *our highest values are sustained or constituted by an inner dependency on their 'opposites'.* This is the first step towards '*being able to* stand above morality' (GS 107)—towards a standpoint 'beyond good and evil'.

There is, however, a crucial difference between the *Nachlass* and the published text. In GS 107, the perspective of laughter and art, as the privileged perspective *for* life, is presented as the other of *Redlichkeit* and knowledge; it is a temporary, intermittent respite from knowledge that makes a life of knowledge possible. The *Nachlass,* by contrast, points to an alternative form of knowledge. In note 1[28], as we have seen, the relaxation of the demands of *Redlichkeit* is proposed as the way to *sustain* a living *Redlichkeit* in the light of its dependence on *Unredlichkeit. Redlichkeit* is practised, not by the uncompromising pursuit of *Redlichkeit* ['die Guten'], but by those who relax the demands of *Redlichkeit* in the knowledge of its dependence on life in its *Unredlichkeit.* But what kind of perspective is this—a *Redlichkeit* that demands a relaxation of the demands of *Redlichkeit*? If, as Nietzsche claims, knowledge is 'moral' to the extent that it takes the value of truth, truthfulness or *Redlichkeit* as unconditionally binding [maaßgebend],[15] this cannot be a perspective of knowledge—unless, as Nietzsche points out, the will to know can have another source radically different from the will to truth or truthfulness [Wahrhaftigkeit]:

> *the will to know would have to have an entirely different root from truthfulness.* (NL 35[5] KSA 11.510)

It is our contention that in Nietzsche's 'gay science', the other source of knowledge is laughter or the art of laughing.

IV. LAUGHTER, SELF-KNOWLEDGE AND THE PERSPECTIVE OF THE SPECIES (GS 1)

The *Nachlass* notes on *Redlichkeit* point towards laughter as an alternative source of knowledge that would enable the knower to sustain a living form of *Redlichkeit* beyond good and evil. Yet laughter is curiously absent from these notes, which give us no clues as to what knowledge-as-laughter might be. For that we must return to GS, where Nietzsche's practice of knowledge-as-laughter extends further the meaning of *Redlichkeit gegen sich* as a new form of self-critique: one, as we shall see, that enables us to achieve a form of self-overcoming and is constructive, not just self-destructive. Of course, Nietzsche does not present this in any systematic form, but we can see from the very beginning of GS that laughter (and more specifically the ability to laugh at oneself) is meant to play a crucial role in Nietzsche's overall project. In fact, one could say that taking the motto of GS[16] *seriously* means that *the ability to laugh at oneself* is the absolute prerequisite for understanding and reading Nietzsche properly. Likewise, in GS 1—*The teachers of the purpose of existence*—, Nietzsche announces his gay science [fröhliche Wissenschaft] as a future form of science in which 'laughter will have formed an alliance with wisdom' (KSA 3.370).

Although Nietzsche's use of laughter (i.e., the meanings he gives to it and the role it plays in his writings) is by no means univocal throughout his works, there are certain motifs that recur from *Dawn* onwards,[17] and they do so with the greatest intensity in GS and *Thus Spoke Zarathustra*. It is, in effect, as if Nietzsche were trying to define and cultivate a specific type of laughter, one that will constitute an essential element of his thought:

> To laugh at oneself as one would have to laugh in order to laugh *from the whole truth* [um *aus der ganzen Wahrheit heraus* zu lachen]—for that, not even the best have had enough sense of truth, and the most gifted have had far too little genius! (GS 1; KSA 3.370)

As we can see from this quotation, this special type of laughter is one that involves: (1) a process of learning: to laugh properly is something that we have to learn,[18] but also (2) having some form of 'genius', special talent or attitude towards things. It also involves: (3) laughing at oneself and (4) occupying a perspective marked by an acute sensitivity or a privileged relation of kinds to truth and knowledge. Of particular importance for us now is the way in which Nietzsche connects laughter and the ability or will 'to laugh at oneself' (3) with a special ability to appreciate, know, accept and even express the truth (4)—'*the whole truth*'. Indeed, in this rather mysterious passage[19] Nietzsche seems to suggest that the perspective attained through or from within laughter gives us access to certain forms of truth to which we remain blind if we are not able to laugh at ourselves.

Thus, in spite of the many questions that remain open concerning the nature of laughter, it is already clear that it would be wrong to consider that the reason for Nietzsche to introduce 'laughter' into the process of knowledge and science is merely for the sake of the knower—as in GS 107. In other words: if 'laughter' comes into the picture, *it is not for the sake of the knower, but for the sake of knowledge itself—that is to say: a higher form of knowledge*. 'Laughter' figures not simply as an alternative to *Redlichkeit* and knowledge, a temporary, intermittent respite that allows us to return to the unconditional, life-threatening pursuit of truth undamaged. On the contrary, as we have just seen: laughter as such (or rather: a very specific form of laughter) is presented from the very beginning of GS as what enables us to attain a different perspective from which to search, find, understand and also express 'truth'. 'Laughter' represents a different form of knowledge and a different form of truth. Indeed, if it were not because laughter offers us a new perspective from which to search and produce knowledge, if it were not because Nietzsche had 'good reasons' for introducing 'laughter' into the process of science itself: how else could he ever convince us to overcome what he calls 'the prejudice' of science that in order 'to take things *seriously*' and think well, we need to be in a bad mood, a state of irremediable seriousness (cf. GS 327)?[20] However, why and how this is supposed to work still needs to be elucidated.

In GS 333—*What is knowing*—apparently directed against Spinoza, Nietzsche makes the point of introducing what he calls the 'drive to laugh at something [Trieb des Verlachens]' (KSA 3.558) into the overall process of knowing [erkennen]. Likewise, in GS 311—*Refracted light*—Nietzsche talks about 'the law and the nature of things that makes faults and mistakes into something funny [freude machen]!' and invites us to laugh at him for *his* 'faults and mistakes', his 'delusion', 'bad taste', 'confusion', and 'contradictions' (KSA 3.547).[21] For Nietzsche it is clear that laughter is a 'natural' response when errors and contradictions have been exposed, and most importantly: self-contradictions.[22] But of interest in this passage is not only the way in which laughter is presented as something 'natural' and somehow inseparable from knowledge, but the way in which it seems to play a pivotal role in the most fundamental part of the process of knowledge, namely critique and its intensification in self-critique. As a form of critique, laughter is not per se less virulent or destructive than other forms of critique (see *Z* I Reading and Writing; KSA 4.49); nor does Nietzsche deny that laughter can be expression of ignorance or meanness, rather than insight (e.g. GS 125; KSA 3.480). But perhaps in the case of laughing-at-oneself, when *we* become the object of our own laughter, the situation is different; for it cannot be the case that one laughs at oneself, at one's own mistakes or contradictions, unless these are recognized as such from a position that is in some sense *truly* superior and insightful, and, at the same time, benevolent and understanding. The point of view we attain when laughing at ourselves is not one that mistakes or misunderstands us (like a bad joke might or like those who laugh at Zarathustra, cf. *Z* Preface 5; KSA 4.21), but one that enables us to see through ourselves from a distance in a way that gives us not only pain, but also the pleasure of laughter and the chance to overcome ourselves.

In GS 1 Nietzsche describes the perspective we (knowers) attain by laughing at ourselves as the perspective in which the 'comedy of existence' will have become 'aware of itself', and he contrasts this with our present perspective, as one of 'tragedy, moralities and religions' (KSA 3.370). Here laughter is valued not only for its self-reflective and self-critical potential (essential for the process of self-overcoming), but for its radicality: laughter has the power to relativize everything; it is beyond morality, beyond what is 'useful and harmful, good and evil' (KSA 3.370). Nietzsche's promise is that by laughing at ourselves 'as we would have to', we will be able to overcome the most personal and fundamental aspects of our identity as individuals, namely our 'tragedies' (or pessimism), our moral values and our beliefs.[23]

This promise is tied to the curious and puzzling parallel Nietzsche draws in GS 1 between the ability to laugh at ourselves and the ability to think about ourselves from the point of view of the 'human species' [menschliche Gattung].[24] A clue to this parallelism is given when he goes on to define the perspective of morality itself as that perspective from which 'an individual is always an individual, something first and last and tremendous' (GS 1; KSA 3.371). If laughing at ourselves holds the promise of freeing us from morality, from our personal values and beliefs, then this cannot be achieved by the individual *qua* individual, however self-critical; rather, we need to break from the standpoint of the individual altogether—by laughing at ourselves from the perspective of the species. Nietzsche makes this clear when he writes that 'you will never find someone [i.e., any single individual's point of view] who would know how to mock you, the singular individual, even in your best qualities' (KSA 3.370).[25] But once the perspective of laughter is explained through the perspective of the species, the meaning and the art of 'laughing at oneself' becomes even more puzzling, since we cannot avoid asking ourselves: Who is laughing at us, once we take the point of view of the species? Where exactly does this type of laughter have its source, if not in the self-reflective individual?

Nietzsche does not answer this question explicitly, but he does give us some hints. From his description of the future gay science as the only remaining ['nur noch'] form of knowledge, once humanity ['[die] Menschheit'] will have incorporated the proposition that '[t]he species [Art] is everything, a single individual is always no-one' (KSA 3.370), it is clear that the perspective of laughter he is describing is the perspective of an anticipated future knowledge. So we could say that it is 'we' who are laughing at us from the perspective of the species, but only once we have attained a future form of knowledge. We may, with Nietzsche, be somehow able to anticipate this knowledge in the present, but only in a virtual way, since our present is, as Nietzsche reminds us, still one of individual 'tragedy, moralities and religions' (KSA 3.370).

An anticipation of this future knowledge and the laughter that accompanies it is offered by Nietzsche in his account of the process and progress of knowledge thus far. At issue in GS 1 is first and foremost the kind of knowledge propounded by 'the teachers of the purpose of existence'. Just like those for whom thinking is the labour of a 'plodding, somber and grinding machine' (GS 327; KSA 3.555), these teachers have always decreed an absolute prohibition on laughter: neither the teachings themselves nor those to whom they have given meaning could be laughed at.[26] From the perspective of the species, however, this exclusion of laughter is precisely what makes them ridiculous; what is laughable is the fact that for the individual there must be something that cannot be laughed at, something that cannot be relativized: 'And from time to time the human race will always decree: "there is something about which it is absolutely no longer permitted to laugh!"' (KSA 3.373). From the perspective of the species, on the other hand, '[t]here is no denying that *in the long run* each of these great teachers of a purpose was vanquished by laughter, reason and nature', and 'in the end' the great tragedy of existence must be drowned in '"the waves of uncountable laughter"' (KSA 3.373). What the tragic actors in the historical drama of knowledge cannot see, that laughter in league with reason and nature is what moves the plot forward, remains forbidden—until the disclosive laughter from the standpoint of the species. But how could we occupy this decidedly futural, impossible standpoint, and in what sense can it still be seen as 'laughing-at-oneself'?

The movement, whereby laughter embodies a future knowledge, is not only critical (to the point of being absolutely devastating for the point of view of the individual knower) but also constructive, embodying a new way of searching, understanding and expressing 'truth'. What this laughter shows in very abstract terms in GS 1 concerning the process and progress of human knowledge, is described more concretely in GS 246, which we quote in full:

> *Mathematics.*—We want to introduce the precision and rigour of mathematics into all sciences to the extent to which that is at all possible; not in the belief that we will come to know things this way, but in order to *ascertain [festzustellen]* our human relation to things. Mathematics is only the means to general and final knowledge of the human. (KSA 3.514f.)

We can distinguish three moments here: (1) Nietzsche begins the aphorism by describing what we *want* when we take mathematics as an ideal form of knowledge: we want its rigour and precision. But then (2) he exposes the limitation of this form of knowledge by explaining that when we take mathematics as a model of knowledge we do not know things 'as they really are', but '*ascertain* our human relation' to them instead. The word Nietzsche uses is *feststellen*, which can be understood in different ways: finding out, discovering or ascertaining something, but also fixing or determining a certain state of affairs. Thus, in its most critical sense, Nietzsche is saying that when we use mathematics to gain knowledge about the world, we are determining and fixing the way in which we relate to things and thereby limiting the ways these can affect us. The (theoretical) will to truth is unmasked as the (practical) will to dominate, the will to control and determine things around us. There is no such thing as pure knowledge.

Of course, from the perspective of the knower naïvely idealizing mathematics and his or her pristine will to truth, this insight would have shattering consequences, which one might pity or laugh at from a more cynical point of view. But in the last sentence (3), Nietzsche invites us to see things differently: 'Mathematics is only the means to general and final knowledge of the human'.[27] This sentence, which at first sight might seem a mere follow-up to the previous one, is in fact an invitation to see things anew in a more affirmative light. For, although it dismantles the idealization of mathematics and knowledge driven by the will to truth, it does not draw the conclusion that knowledge is therefore impossible. On the contrary, what the last sentence shows us is that there is always a point of view from which *we* (i.e., all of us as humans, including the individual knower who still believes in mathematics and the cynic who does not believe in knowledge) can learn something about ourselves, about the complicity of the business of knowledge in our species interest in self-preservation.

From this perspective, we can only laugh at our single-minded will to truth as individual knowers. But it is a very different type of laughter from the cynic's, who simply dismisses the knower in laughing at his naïvety and folly. In this third moment, we laugh *at ourselves*. As in GS 1, we are invited to occupy the standpoint of 'the human' or 'human species' where we can laugh at our folly as individual knowers, because from this standpoint we are able to break and break with our first-person values and value-oppositions as knowers (truth-error, seriousness-laughter, good-evil). On the other hand, it is also an *inclusive* kind of laughter, one that is both constructive and generous: we laugh *at ourselves*, and in so doing we gain knowledge of ourselves as members of the human species and are able to give value to our failure as knowers. More importantly, when we return from this standpoint to the individual pursuit of knowledge, as we must, we will return transformed and enriched by the knowledge we have gained, as members of the human species, of ourselves, of our values and beliefs as individuals, by the distance it affords—however fleeting or virtual.

CONCLUSION

These considerations can now be brought to bear on our earlier analyses of gay science as a life-experiment of the knower and the liberating thought that life could be '*a means to knowledge*' (GS 324). In the light of GS 1, neither the ability to 'stand above morality' by laughing at ourselves in GS 107, nor the living *Redlichkeit* beyond good and evil described in the *Nachlass* are attainable by us as individual knowers, however self-reflective and self-critical we may be. If the self-destruction of our *Redlichkeit* as the unconditional pursuit of truth is to offer passage to a more relaxed *Redlichkeit* that is really beyond good and evil and oppositional thinking, we must pass through the standpoint of the species. According to GS 1, this is the only way to break and break with our irremediably moral perspective as individuals—our trage- dies, values and beliefs— and the only source of self-knowledge that is responsive to 'the whole truth' that our highest values (truth, *Redlichkeit*, seriousness . . .) are bound up with their 'opposites' (error, *Unredlichkeit*, laughter . . .) in complex, multifarious ways. Similarly, if the perspective of art described in GS 107 really enables us to rise above morality and 'from an artistic distance, laugh *about* us or cry *about* us', it can only do so as an art that breaks and breaks with 'the *hero* and also the *fool* that hides in our passion for knowledge' and anticipates the kind of self-knowledge gained when we can laugh at ourselves from the perspective of the species. And yet, as Nietzsche reminds us time and again, this perspective and the gay wisdom it affords lie in the future; at present we can enjoy this type of laughter only for a moment here and there. This is our new ebb and flow:

'Not only laughter and gay wisdom but also the tragic, with all its sublime unreason, belongs to the means and necessities of the preservation of the species.' And therefore! Therefore! Therefore! Oh, do you understand me, my brothers? Do you understand this new law of ebb and flood? We, too, have our time! (KSA 3.372)

In GS 107, Nietzsche describes the necessity of an alternation between life- threatening *Redlichkeit* and laughter so that the individual free spirit can pursue knowledge under the sign of unconditional *Redlichkeit*; what we can see now is the necessity of an alternation between laughter and tragedy, that is, between occupying the life-affirming perspective of the species that is beyond good and evil and the irremediably moral perspective of the individu- al knower. But in this case: it is for the sake of the species, for the sake of self-knowledge—one is tempted to say, for the sake of laughter!

NOTES

1. References to Nietzsche's published texts follow standard English abbreviations, fol- lowed by volume and page references (volume then page) in KSA (*Kritische Studienausgabe*, ed. G. Colli and M. Montinari, Munich and Berlin: dtv and de Gruyter, 1980). References to the *Nachlass* follow the notation in KSA, preceded by NL and followed by volume and page references in KSA, e.g., NL 1[42] KSA 9.42 = note 1[42] in KSA volume 9, page 42. Nietzs- che's emphases are rendered in *italics*; Nietzsche's double-underlinings in the *Nachlass* in ***bold italics***. Square brackets [. . .] are used for interventions, interpolations, etc., of ours in Nietzsche citations. Translations are ours, although we have leaned on various English translations: *The Gay Science*, ed. Bernard Williams, trans. Josephine Nauckhoff (Cambridge: Cambridge Uni- versity Press, 2001); *On the Genealogy of Morality*, ed. Keith Ansell-Pearson, trans. Carol Diethe (Cambridge: Cambridge University Press, 2006); and *Thus Spoke Zarathustra. A Book for All and None*, ed. Adrian Del Caro and Robert Pippin, trans. Adrian Del Caro (Cambridge: Cambridge University Press, 2006).

2. Cf. *Thus Spoke Zarathustra*, where Nietzsche writes: 'Free from what? What does Zarathustra care! But your sparkling eye should announce to me: free *for what?*' (KSA 4.81).

3. See also TI Morality as Anti-Nature 3: 'The price of *fertility* is to be rich in contradictions; people stay young only if their souls do not stretch out languidly and long for peace . . . Nothing is more foreign to us than that one-time desideratum of 'peacefulness of the soul', the Christian desideratum' (KSA 6.84).

4. 'I doubt that such pain makes us 'better'—but I know that it makes us deeper' (KSA 3.350).

5. The concept of *Redlichkeit* plays a crucial role in Nietzsche's understanding of knowledge, especially in the period from GS to BGE, as we will argue in this chapter. It has a wide range of meanings, connotations and associations: it is sometimes synonymous with truthfulness [Wahrhaftigkeit] or the will the truth [Wille zur Wahrheit], but often carries strong moral connotations, akin to integrity [Rechtschaffenheit], honesty [Ehrlichkeit] or probity and is sometimes linked with conscience [Gewissen], as a kind of intellectual conscience, even cleanliness [Sauberkeit]. A thorough study of Nietzsche's usage has yet to be made, but essays worth mentioning are Jean-Luc Nancy, '"Our Probity": On Truth in the Moral Sense in Nietzsche', in *Looking After Nietzsche*, ed. Laurens Rickels, (Albany: SUNY Press, 1990), 67–87 and Melissa Lane, 'Honesty as the Best Policy?: Nietzsche on Redlichkeit and the Contrast between Stoic and Epicurean Strategies of the Self', in *Histories of Postmodernism: The Precursors, The Heyday, The Legacy*, ed. Mark Bevir, Jill Hargis and Sara Rushing (New York: Routledge, 2007), 25–51. In the present essay, it is used mainly to signify an unconditional and stringent orientation towards truth as the highest value; it will either be left in German or translated as 'probity'.

6. 'But why shouldn't we laugh, when Schopenhauer tries to explain our aversion to toads metaphysically' (KSA 8. 421).

7. See GM Preface 8 where Nietzsche writes: 'With regard to my *Zarathustra*, for example, I do not acknowledge anyone as an expert on it if he has not, at some time, been both profoundly wounded and profoundly delighted by it' (KSA 5.255).

8. 'I make songs and sing them, I laugh and cry when I make my songs' (NL 4[167] KSA 10.161).

9. NL 6[5] KSA 9.195 [*Wahrheitstrieb*]; NL 6[65] KSA 9.210; NL 6[67] KSA 9.211; NL 6[127] KSA 9.228; NL 6[234] KSA 9.259; see also NL 6[236] KSA 9.260.

10. '—I am mistrustful towards the contemplative ones, those at peace and pleased with themselves among philosophers:—they lack form-giving force and the refinement of probity [Feinheit der Redlichkeit], which acknowledges lack as a force' (NL 1[67] KSA 12.28).

11. The question 'why?' is raised in GS 335 in order to question the normative validity of our conscience: '—Aber warum hörst du auf die Sprache deines Gewissens? Und inwiefern hast du ein Recht, ein solches Urtheil als wahr und untrüglich anzusehen? Für diesen Glauben—giebt es da kein Gewissen mehr? Weisst du Nichts von einem intellectuellen Gewissen? Einem Gewissen hinter deinem "Gewissen"?' (GS 357 KSA 3.561)—a clear reference to *Redlichkeit*, to which Nietzsche returns at the end of the aphorism.

12. In this regard, see also: NL 25[447] KSA 11.132 and NL 5[72] KSA 12.217.

13. In this fascinating note on *Freigeisterei* as 'letzte Consequenz der bisherigen Moralität', Nietzsche gives a special place to *Redlichkeit*, and specifically to *Redlichkeit gegen sich*: 'Redlichkeit, selbst als Gegnerin des Idealismus und der Frömmigkeit, ja der Leidenschaft, sogar in Bezug auf die Redlichkeit selber' (NL 1[42] KSA 10.20). The consequence of *Redlichkeit* 'with regard to *Redlichkeit*' is then described at the end of the note as '*die Einsicht der Moralität, nur vermöge ihres Gegentheils sich in der Existenz und Entwicklung zu erhalten*' (NL 1[42] KSA 10.21).

14. That life (as will to power) is the forum before which our values must prove their worth is clear from note 2[190] KSA 12.161.

15. See NL 35[5] KSA 11.510 above.

16. 'This house is my own and here I dwell, / I've never aped anything from anyone / and— laugh at each master, mark me well, / who at himself has not poked fun [ausgelacht]' (KSA 3.343).

17. Such as 'laughing at oneself', laughter in relation to knowledge, laughter in relation to the process of self-overcoming.

18. 'Learn to laugh at yourselves, as man ought to laugh! You higher men, oh how much is still possible!' (Z IV Higher Man; KSA 4.364). 'Learning to laugh' is a recurrent theme in Nietzsche's Z, which he recalls in his 'Attempt to Self-Criticism' in *the Birth of Tragedy* as the key to this-worldly (anti-metaphysical) consolation (KSA 1.21f.).

19. It is unclear what exactly Nietzsche means by the highly idiosyncratic expression: '*aus der ganzen Wahrheit heraus* zu lachen'. It seems that what is required is that we 'laugh' with that special form of laughter which results from having discovered the truth, from having attained some special insight into things. On the other hand, the use of 'heraus' suggests perhaps not only that we laugh *from* the truth or true insight [*aus der Wahrheit heraus*], but are also somehow propelled by this laughter *beyond* truth.

20. 'The delightful human beast seems to lose its good mood when it thinks well; it becomes "serious"! And "where laughter and gaiety are found, thinking is good for nothing"—that is the prejudice of this serious beast against all "gay science". Well then, let us show that it is a prejudice!' (KSA 3.555).

21. See also HH I 213 entitled *Joy from Nonsense* [*Freude am Unsinn*] KSA 2.174.

22. Cf. 'Brahma laughs at himself because he acknowledges the mistake [Täuschung] about himself' (NL 13 [1] KSA 8.271).

23. Note here the similarity with the process of liberation from preface to GS examined at the beginning of this essay.

24. Although it is beyond the scope of our analysis, it is important to note that the similarities in GS between Spinoza and Nietzsche are much stronger than they appear. Indeed, Spinoza's ideal of knowledge as one that is able to 'see things from the perspective of eternity' has many things in common with Nietzsche's idealization of the 'perspective of the species', (distance from the individual, naturalization and de-moralization via the study of the passions in Spinoza or physiology in Nietzsche)—except perhaps for 'laughter'.

25. This sentence immediately precedes the passage about 'laughing at ourselves *from the whole truth*' (see above, p. 127).

26. 'Indeed, he [the teacher of the purpose of existence] absolutely does not want that we *laugh* about existence, nor about us—nor about himself; for him an individual is always an individual, something first and last and tremendous' (KSA 3.371).

27. We find a very similar idea in Spinoza's *Ethics* when he writes about the imagination: 'We see, therefore, that all the notions by which ordinary people are accustomed to explain nature are only modes of imagining, and do not indicate the nature of anything, only the constitution of the imagination'. (*Ethics*, trans. G. H. R. Parkinson [Oxford: Oxford University Press, 2000], I, Appendix).

BIBLIOGRAPHY

Colli, Giorgio. and M. Montinari, eds. *Friedrich Nietzsche: Sämtliche Werke. Kritische Studienausgabe*. Munich and Berlin: dtv and de Gruyter, 1980.

Lane, Melissa. 'Honesty as the Best Policy?: Nietzsche on Redlichkeit and the Contrast between Stoic and Epicurean Strategies of the Self', In *Histories of Postmodernism: The Precursors, The Heyday, The Legacy*, edited by Mark Bevir, Jill Hargis and Sara Rushing, 25–51. New York: Routledge, 2007.

Nancy, Jean-Luc. '"Our Probity": On Truth in the Moral Sense in Nietzsche'. In *Looking After Nietzsche*, edited by Laurens Rickels, 67–87. Albany: SUNY, 1990.

Nietzsche, Friedrich. *The Gay Science*. Edited by Bernard Williams. Translated by J. Nauckhoff. Cambridge: Cambridge University Press, 2001.

Nietzsche, Friedrich. *On the Genealogy of Morality*. Edited by Keith Ansell-Pearson. Translated by Carol Diethe. Cambridge: Cambridge University Press, 2006.

Nietzsche, Friedrich. *Thus Spoke Zarathustra. A Book for All and None*. Edited by A. Del Caro and R. Pippin. Translated by A. Del Caro. Cambridge: Cambridge University Press, 2006.

Spinoza, Benedictus de. *Ethics*. Translated by G. H. R. Parkinson. Oxford: Oxford University Press, 2000.

II

Developments, Applications and Extensions

Chapter Seven

The Experiment of Incorporating Unbounded Truth

Katrina Mitcheson

In *The Gay Science*, the third book of what is sometimes referred to as his 'free spirit trilogy',[1] Nietzsche poses the question: 'To what extent can truth stand to be incorporated?—that is the question; that is the experiment' (GS 110).[2] My claim is that it is the figure of the free spirit who takes up the challenge of the incorporation of truth and that to understand the significance and development of this figure, we have to address the problem of what the incorporation of truth involves. I will argue that the particular challenge of the free spirit is the incorporation of a truth without any *fixed* presuppositions—or immovable boundaries and horizons operating as limits to enquiry. This open-ended truth practice, which the free spirit makes part of their very being, stands in contrast to a truth practice where the possible lines of enquiry are already demarcated and certain regions of investigation lie out of bounds. The free spirit undertakes an open investigation that could lead anywhere—setting off into infinite horizons. What it means, however, to incorporate truth in general, and unbounded truth in particular, is far from obvious. What could it mean to make the questioning of all presuppositions part of who we are?

Having first presented evidence that Nietzsche associates the free spirit with this task of the incorporation of truth, I will go on to try and clarify what this task involves. Nietzsche poses the task as an experimental one. It is not, therefore, given that such incorporation will be possible. I will address two particular problems that the task of the incorporation of an unbounded truth involves. First, Nietzsche claims that some horizons of meaning, and related boundaries to our sense of self, are necessary for life. Thus the pursuit of truth without any fixed horizons or boundaries has to be reconciled with this need. Further, in his late work, Nietzsche is acutely aware that there is no investigation without presuppositions. In particular, to devote oneself to truth involves the presupposition that truth is itself valuable. So the question arises of how a free-spirited investigation with flexible presuppositions can be distinguished from limited investigations with fixed presuppositions, and whether this flexibility can be extended to even the value of truth. Before considering whether these two problems can be overcome, the nature of the free spirit's valuation of truth must first be addressed.

THE FREE SPIRIT'S CONNECTION TO TRUTH

The first point to establish is that the figure of the spirit is associated with truth. This connection has been noted before; both Peter Berkowitz and Amy Mullin have drawn attention to the association between the free spirit and a strong intellectual conscience, though Berkowitz sees this as in tension with Nietzsche's statements on truth elsewhere, and Mullin takes it as evidence that the free spirit is not Nietzsche's highest ideal and argues that a free spirited commitment to truth will be surpassed.[3] The assumption, however, of an irresolvable tension between Nietzsche's criticism of truth and praise of free spirits, arises because neither Berkowitz nor Mullin take sufficient account of the different conceptions of truth at play in Nietzsche's work. They thus fail to recognize that the free spirit is associated with a different kind of truth, or different way of pursuing truth, to those who remain fettered by particular 'truths' or by faith in *the* true or real world as a transcendent, or otherworldly ideal. This is not to suggest that Nietzsche considers the free spirit's relationship to truth to be unproblematic or without cost, but I will argue that it is crucial to an understanding of the free spirit that we recognize that they have a different relationship to truth from that of the 'last idealists of knowledge [Erkenntnis]' (GM III 24).

The association between the free spirit and a new kind of truth is present in both the middle and late works. In the middle works, Nietzsche self-consciously moves away from his association with the person of Wagner and the philosophy of Schopenhauer, an association he will look back on as a dangerous liaison with romanticism (HH II Preface 2).[4] Characteristic of this new phase is Nietzsche's critical attack on the value of metaphysical truth and celebration of the more modest and sceptical truths of scientific spirit: 'And the pathos of possessing the truth does now in fact count for very little in comparison with that other, admittedly gentler and less noisy pathos of seeking truth that never wearies of learning and examining anew'. (HH I 633) Seeking the truth in the right way emerges as a central task in Nietzsche's free spirit trilogy. He comes to formulate this challenge as the question of how we can incorporate the truth (GS 110; KSA 9, 11[141]).[5] In GS, the third of the free spirit trilogy, whether or not the truth can be incorporated is posed as a pressing question. This implies that there is an important sense in which, despite our valuation of the ideal of truth, truth, or the right kind of truth, has not yet been incorporated.

Subsequently to the free spirit trilogy, Nietzsche has Zarathustra declare that, 'It is always in deserts that the truthful [Wahrhaftigen] have dwelt, the free spirits, as the desert's masters' (Z II Famous Wise Men). In the later work, we find that the free spirits of *Beyond Good and Evil* are 'investigators to the point of cruelty, with rash fingers for the ungraspable, with teeth and stomach for the most indigestible', hence they are those with the spirit to pursue truth into the darkest reaches of the history of the human animal (BGE 44).

Thus, while Nietzsche's characterization of free spirits is not static, their association with the project of truth is a continuous theme. Indeed, I will suggest below that if the later free spirit marks a difference from the free spirit of 1876 to 1882, it concerns, at least in part, a change in Nietzsche's estimation of what is necessary for the incorporation of an unbounded truth. What is continuous is that this is their task—and the free spirit is both the figure with the necessary characteristics to take on this experiment, and the figure who will be further emancipated from existing dogma through the process of an incorporation of this method of truth seeking.

THE INCORPORATION OF TRUTH

What then could the incorporation [Einverleibung] of truth mean? That we incorporate the truth means that we in some way take it into ourselves, make it part of us. This is easiest to comprehend in relation to the incorporation of particular beliefs, which are taken to be true. Such so-called truths are incorporated into a way of life and form a precondition for the existence and maintenance of this way of life. This is apparent in Nietzsche's discussion of the origins of truth in *On Truth and Lying in a Non-Moral Sense*. Here 'truth' is inherently fixed: 'For that which is to count as 'truth' from this point onwards now becomes fixed, i.e. a way of designating things is invented which has the same validity and force everywhere'. It is that which is established as a common standard, or convention, as a prerequisite for language and society. Man as the tame social animal, the animal, as it is elaborated in *On the Genealogy of Morality,* who can promise (GM II 1), depends on truth as fixity to communicate, for instance in the making of promises. In this sense, particular truths are incorporated as a condition of our modern existence. The particular truths that were established and agreed upon provided the shared horizons that we needed to live a social life, and allowed us to carve out a definite shape or boundary to our existence. Nietzsche observes,

'How arbitrarily these boundaries are drawn [Abgrenzungen], how one sided the preference for this or that property of a thing!' (TL I, 144).[6] What mattered, then, is that we had agreed terms and concepts, not that they corresponded to the way things were. Nietzsche takes the horizons of these established truths to be fundamental to our existence, suggesting if man 'could escape for just a moment from the prison walls of this faith, it would mean the end of his "consciousness of self" [Selbstbewusstsein]' (or his self-confidence) (TL I, 148). To establish the boundaries of our sense of self there must first be a fixed point in the landscape, a horizon of truth, around which we take our bearings.

Clearly, however, this incorporation of conventions which we take as 'truths', is not the truth that Nietzsche is referring to when he asks in GS whether or not truth can stand, or be tolerated, to be incorporated. Indeed if we understood incorporation of truth according to the portrayal of truth in TL, it would be the incorporation of errors. Nietzsche's discussion in GS of the incorporation of errors, including the error of identical things, resonates with his discussion of the establishment of truth in TL, which he argues requires overlooking what is individual (TL I, 145). Nietzsche now suggests that:

> erroneous articles of faith, which were passed on by inheritance further and further, and finally almost became part of the basic endowment of the species, are for example: that there are enduring things; that there are identical things; that there are things, kinds of material, bodies; that a thing is what it appears to be; that our will is free; that what is good for me is also good in and of itself. (GS 110)

These articles of faith are 'the basic errors that have been incorporated since time immemorial' (GS 110). While, however, in TL 'truth' for Nietzsche is reducible to the establishment and incorporation of such errors, here there is the notion of a truth that emerges in contrast to such errors: 'Only very late did the deniers and doubters of such propositions emerge; only very late did truth emerge as the weakest form of knowledge' (GS 110). Nietzsche suggests that a 'subtler honesty and scepticism arose where two conflicting propositions seemed to be *applicable*' such that in time 'not only faith and conviction, but also scrutiny, denial, suspicion and contradiction were a *power*' (GS 110). So a new form of truth that questions that which was previously taken as 'true' becomes a concern for us. Indeed, the question of the incorporation of truth, in the sense of questioning the 'errors' of our articles of faith, is one that presents itself as an urgency because a drive towards truth in this sense is to some extent already part of us. What could it mean, however, to fully incorporate a truth that serves to question the errors that we have previously incorporated as part of our existence?

As Keith Ansell-Pearson has suggested, we can understand the experiment of the incorporation of truth either in terms of the incorporation of a set of practices, or ways of pursuing truth, or in terms of the incorporation of new and challenging insights which undermine our existing certainties and sense of self.[7] It is the former that I am focusing on here, in terms of the incorporation of the practice of pursuing an unbounded truth that does not take anything to be sacred or beyond question. Though of course, these two ways of viewing incorporation are not unrelated to each other; to pursue truth without limits will allow the cornerstones of our belief system to be challenged and, thus new insights into our history and nature, which do not respect these sacred cows, to be incorporated. But the incorporation of new and challenging truths first depends on the incorporation of a new approach to truth. What then are the practices that must be taken up in the incorporation of unbounded truth? First, we need to cultivate the habits of scepticism and the suspicion of anything that smacks of dogma. This will require learning to do without the need for certainties. Further, it will involve actively engaging in exploration and experiments in knowledge that do not have any set limits. Horizons will come to be seen as mutable—open to being rubbed out and redrawn. Thus, while life, as I will discuss further below, depends on establishing some boundaries around itself and relies on some horizons of meaning to incorporate an unbounded truth, one must loosen one's attachments to any particular horizon of meaning, and with this to any fixed boundary to one's sense of self. The free spirit makes this their way of life, establishing these new habits and values as part of themselves, where previously the errors or fixed 'truths' have been the basis for our existence.[8]

OPEN HORIZONS

The concerns for a freedom from convictions and certainties and a love of open horizons, which are the free-spirited requirements of the incorporation of unbounded truth, are reflected in the language of all the free spirit books. In the first of these, *Human, All Too Human*, Nietzsche is seeking examples of methodology that show the way for free-spirited inquiry. He finds inspiration in both science and art. Artistic presentation allows us to appreciate uncompleted thoughts in comparison to a brute statement of facts, and hence 'one must not torment a poet with subtle exegesis but content oneself with the uncertainty of his horizon as though the way to many thoughts still lay open' (HH I 207).

The art of Nietzsche's own writing itself contributes to the exploration of a new method of truth.[9] The aphoristic style, which he introduces to his work in HH, is one that supports the openness of thoughts that Nietzsche attributes to the poet.[10] Unlike the closed structure of the essay, which introduces and elaborates a thesis, coming to a firm conclusion, aphorisms encourage the ongoing exploration of different perspectives, without working to the horizon of a fully determined conclusion according to the expected essayistic form. The experimentation with style continues in GS with Nietzsche's attempts at poetry. Rohit Sharma has argued that poetry, and the movement that its rhythms can evoke, is employed by Nietzsche precisely in order to work against the tendency of language to fix concepts. Sharma argues further that this tendency is not one that poetry, also confined to operate within language, can ever fully escape, and this tension is expressed in the tone of irony and parody that Nietzsche often employs. [11]

Regarding science, in the broad sense of Wissenschaft, we can see that Nietzsche associates it with the capacity to endure doubt claiming that 'science [Wissenschaft] needs doubt and distrust for its closest allies' (HH I 22), and 'the scientific spirit [wissenschaftlichen Geist] will bring to maturity that virtue of *cautious reserve*' (HH I 631). Nietzsche considers this caution and modesty exemplified by science as an advance over the need for absolute truth that is exhibited by metaphysics and claims that: 'It is the mark of a higher culture to value the little unpretentious truths which have been discovered by means of rigorous method more highly than the errors handed down by metaphysical and artistic ages and men' (HH I 3). Thus, the spirit of scientific enquiry is admired for its capacity to keep open horizons and to be contented with fewer beliefs, in contrast to the religious or metaphysical spirit. This is expressed in Nietzsche's discussion of influential books.

> All influential books try to leave behind this kind of impression: the impression that the widest spiritual and physical horizon has here been circumscribed and that every star visible now or in the future will have to revolve around the sun that shines here.—Must it therefore not be the case that the causes which make such books influential will render every *purely scientific [wissenschaftliche]* book poor in influence? (HH II AOM 98)

Science, as Nietzsche understands it here, questions the horizons which religion has enclosed us in, but it does not attempt to re-establish fixed and absolute horizons of a metaphysical or religious nature. Thus, it refuses to fulfil a long established need for these horizons.

In the aphorism '*Where Indifference Is Needed*', Nietzsche warns against thinking we can cling to our moral and religious certainties, without confronting their character as all too human projections. We are not entitled to think that science, having put into question our religious way of thinking, will replace it and is working away to establish the certainty of our origins and destiny. Rather these 'first and last things' concern what can never be known and are always, therefore, fantasies and fabrications when we attempt to give them any content:

Nothing could be more wrongheaded than to want to wait and see what science [Wissenschaft] will one day determine once and for all concerning the first and last things and until then to continue to think (and especially to believe!) in the *customary* fashion as we are so often advised to do. The impulse to desire in this domain *nothing but certainties* is a *religious after-shoot*, no more—a hidden and only apparently sceptical species of the 'metaphysical need', coupled with the consideration that there is no prospect of these ultimate certainties being to hand for a long time to come and that until then the 'believer' is right not to trouble his head about anything in this domain. We have absolutely no *need* of these certainties regarding the furthest horizon to live a full and excellent human life . . . what is needed now in regard to these last things is not knowledge against faith but *indifference against faith and supposed knowledge* in those domains! (HH II WS 16) [12]

There is, then, an established habit to cling to beliefs in the domains of religion and morality, where we can have no absolute knowledge—habits that would have to be broken if we were to incorporate an unbounded truth which refused to respect any beliefs as sacrosanct, or to establish new idols as unquestionable. Free spirits will be those who have a strong enough will to truth and taste for freedom to break the habits of metaphysical need and who will become freer spirits through this process of emancipation from fixed truths. In place of the incorporation of these customary ways of thinking there is an incorporation of an awareness that our horizon is not closed, that we could live differently, without recourse to any certainties, and thus even the boundaries that define us could shift.

The theme of an ability to separate oneself from one's prior convictions and customary believes continues in *Dawn*. Nietzsche describes the free spirit as someone who has the 'rare and preeminent distinction, especially if continued into old age, of *being able* to alter his opinions!' (D 56). He also suggests a free spirit is someone who breaks the hearts of others because 'Sorrow breaks the heart of those who live to see the one they love the most turn their back on their opinion, their faith—this belongs to the tragedy which free spirits *create*—of which they are sometimes aware' (D 562). This later description comes in the aphorism of '*the settled and the free*' and takes the wandering of Odysseus to be not just his travels but to involve being unsettled in opinion. So free spiritedness lies in contrast to remaining fixed within the horizon of a faith and involves the ability to alter one's convictions and thus to redraw the boundaries of belief that give us our identity.

There is also a strong theme of open horizons, in GS the last of the trilogy. Here Nietzsche engages the metaphor of explorers. In '*In the Horizon of the Infinite*' he declares: 'We have forsaken the land and gone to sea! We have destroyed the bridge behind us—more so, we have destroyed the land behind us!' (GS 124) When the madman tells us that we have killed God, he asks,

'Who gave us the sponge to wipe away the entire horizon?' and 'Aren't we straying through an infinite nothing?' (GS 125). Thus, having destroyed our certainty in the first and last things, in God and morality, we have rubbed out the horizons that demarcated our existence for us, and we are confronted with the dizziness of an open existence. Despite the threatening tenor of this notion of voyaging into the open, it is clear from GS 110, discussed above, that this is a voyage there is no turning back from. We have, after all, destroyed the land behind us. Further, Nietzsche considers holding fast to fixed beliefs to show a lack of 'intellectual conscience', which is a failure to ask ourselves why we take certain things to be right or true. Nietzsche urges on the knowledge seekers who rub out our existing horizons and venture into the horizon of the infinite, not knowing where knowledge will lead them and not circumventing it within a field that is compatible with accepted morality and certainties. The motivation to incorporate unbounded truth is bound up with the need for transformation in response to his critical insights into the problems of contemporary morality, so-called culture and the modern human being.

The theme of open horizons is revisited in 1887 with the fifth book of GS. The opening aphorism makes a clear reference to our being at sea without the land of firm beliefs and to the scrubbing out of horizons implied by the death of God, which appear earlier in aphorisms 124 and 125 respectively. In book 5, the sense of danger is again invoked but the tone is more explicitly cele-bratory:

> Indeed, at hearing the news that 'the old god is dead', we philosophers and 'free spirits' feel illuminated by a new dawn; our heart overflows with grati-tude, amazement, forebodings, expectation—finally the horizon seems, clear again, even if not bright; finally our ships may set out again, set out to face any danger; every daring of the lover of knowledge is allowed again; the sea, *our* sea, lies open again; maybe there has never been such an 'open sea'. (GS 343)

Nietzsche's positive valuation of being able to embrace such open horizons and its association with the free spirit is now evident:

> . . . one could conceive of a delight and power of self-determination, a *freedom* of the will, in which the spirit takes leave of all faith and every wish for certainty, practised as it is in maintaining itself on tight ropes and possibilities and dancing even beside abysses. Such a spirit would be the *free spirit* par excellence. (GS 347)

Here it is clear that this kind of free spiritedness is not to be found in Nietzsche's contemporaries but is something yet to come. Not all will be capable of it. The notion that the task of such investigation requires a particular, strong kind of spirit, the potential free spirit, is apparent in the *Antichrist*, where

Nietzsche writes:

> One should not let oneself be misled: great spirits [Geister] are sceptics. Zara-
> thustra is a sceptic. The vigour of a spirit [Geist], its *freedom* through strength
> and superior strength, is *proved* by scepticism. . . . Freedom from convictions
> of any kind, the *capacity* for an unconstrained view *pertains* to strength. (AC
> 54)

Thus, both in the free spirit trilogy and in later discussions of what it is for a
spirit to be free, we find the notion of freedom from convictions. It is this
freedom that allows the free spirit to incorporate into their way of living an
attitude to the pursuit of truth that is not constrained by any boundaries or
horizons that are taken as unquestionable and fixed. This incorporation will
however require a great deal of strength and health, to begin with, even if it
also serves as a form of recuperation and convalescence.

There are, however, serious, perhaps insurmountable, obstacles that the
free spirit faces, in the attempt to incorporate an unbounded truth.

LIFE'S NEED FOR BOUNDARIES AND HORIZONS

The first problem I want to consider is that it is the very condition of a form of
life that it have some boundary to its sense of self, which relies upon an established horizon of meaning: 'A living thing can be healthy, strong and fruitful
only within a horizon' (UM II 1).[13] This is what underscores Nietzsche's concern in the second of his UM, 'On the Uses and Disadvantages of History for
Life', that critical history be balanced by antiquarian and monumental history,
the latter respectively providing us with a sense of having roots and offering
inspiring models for us to emulate. The antiquarian and monumental both operate at the cost of a great deal of falsification. 'A certain excess of history',
however, by 'continually shifting horizons' deprives youth of a protective
atmosphere, cutting them off from roots and instinctual life, and preventing their
flourishing (UM II 9). Neither the 'infinite horizon' nor the 'smallest egoistic
enclosure' are deemed healthy at this point in Nietzsche's thinking. Where later
he will embrace the dangerous experiment of clearing our horizons to allow us
to redraw even the boundaries of what defines us as human, in the UM he is
seeking to navigate between this Charybdis and Scylla of closed horizons and
narrowness of self, on the one hand, and the loss of any horizon of meaning and
sense of self, on the other. Here the need for boundaries is keenly felt: 'With the
word "unhistorical": I designate the art and power of forgetting and of enclosing
oneself within a bounded *horizon* [begrenzten *Horizont*]' (UM II 10). Nietzsche
expresses his concerns regarding the danger of the scientific attitude which
'hates forgetting, which is the death of knowledge, and seeks to abolish all
limitations of horizon and launch mankind on an infinite and unbounded sea of

light whose light is knowledge of all becoming'. Of this prospect Nietzsche declares: 'If only man could live in it!' (UM II 10). Hence, the scientific spirit that we find in critical history, which exposes the illusions of antiquarian and monumental history for falsifications, has to be countered by the capacity to create new horizons and boundaries. Survival and flourishing requires the ability to draw boundaries around ourselves and make evaluations. Critical history shows the transitory and arbitrary nature of any such boundaries or horizons and the injustice of asserting any value, or position. Hence, Nietzsche considered that, in excess, it deprives us of the conditions in which life can flourish.

The cautious tone of UM II which keeps a tight rein on critical history, allowing it to serve the limited function of creating the space for new growth and keeping the other forms of history in check, gives way in the free spirit trilogy to a stronger emphasis on the need to let go of our entrenched beliefs and let truth destroy the illusions which we have previously relied on. The same metaphors of open seas, which eulogize this dangerous but glorious task, were already present in UM. Here, however, the metaphor of the sea journey is employed with more emphasis on our need for land: 'At last a coast appears in sight: we must land on it whatever it may be like, and the worst of harbours is better than to go reeling back into a hopeless sea of scepticism' (UM II 10). By GS, we hear only of the destruction of the land and the openness of the future voyage, not of the necessity to find a dock, and by its fifth book, the tone is increasingly joyous in response to this openness of the seas and absence of any land filling our horizons.

Despite the change in emphasis and tone, however, that life needs horizons of meanings and boundaries of self cannot be dismissed as Nietzsche's early position. In *Twilight of the Idols* we find Nietzsche claiming that Goethe, a figure who is often presented as exemplary, 'surrounded himself with nothing but closed horizons; he did not sever himself from life' (TI Expeditions 49). Also, in Z, the figure who claims to have 'feared no prohibition' and 'overthrew all boundary stones and images', suffers from being a homeless shadow (Z IV The Shadow). As Zarathustra's shadow, this figure represents the danger Zarathustra has faced in his journey of self-transformation.

Nietzsche does not think that we can ultimately do without horizons to our world and boundaries to our sense of self. If we rub out our horizons, we will have to redraw them; if we step beyond our boundaries, we will have to reform them. This does mean that Nietzsche does not advocate the incorporation of unbounded truth. First, this imperative is in the context of a need for transformation. The incorporation of unbounded truth involves the destruction of the horizons that modern man operates within, and thus the boundaries of what it means to be human, and clears the way to going beyond modern man. So unbounded truth is a prerequisite to the formation of new horizons and with them new boundaries to our sense of self; it brings about the going under of modern humanity to allow the going over to something else. Second, these new horizons and boundaries need not be taken as absolute and immutable; we need not, having opened up our vista, be tied to the idea of one fixed horizon or one idea of what we can be. Rather, if we incorporate unbounded truth, we learn to treat horizons as movable and boundaries as mutable, something that we need to act and live, but something which can be expanded as life demands.

The pursuit of unbounded truth keeps alive the possibility of shifting horizons and thus avoids the 'premature stagnation' of the absolute horizon that is established by monotheism. Nietzsche suggests that:

> In polytheism the free-spiritedness and many-spiritedness of humanity received preliminary form—the power to create for ourselves our own new eyes and ever again new eyes that are ever more our own—so that for humans alone among the animals there are no eternal horizons and perspectives. (GS 143)

Here Nietzsche is reminding us that while we need horizons, they are not fixed, and we are able to question them and re-create them, and with them the boundaries of a life form that has depended on them. Faith tries to solidify our horizons, to trap us within one outlook:

> *Holiness*—perhaps the last, higher value that the people or woman still encounter, the horizon of the ideal for all those who are naturally short-sighted. With philosophers, however, as with every horizon, it is a mere misunderstanding, a kind of slamming of the door, where their world begins,—their danger, their ideal, their desirability. (CW 3)

The desire for uncertainty, infinite horizons, and new boundaries of definition, carries with it its own dangers; it is a desire that has developed only after our immediate physical existence has become less dangerous (KSA 11, 26[280]). Venturing into an 'undiscovered land the boundaries [Grenzen] of which no one has yet survived' (GS 382), will require strength, health and a taste for adventure. The free spirit who undertakes this experimental journey is one who has '*great* health, that superfluity which grants the free spirit the dangerous privilege of living *experimentally* and of being allowed to offer itself to adventure: the master's privilege of the free spirit!' (HH I Preface 4).

So the free spirit takes the risk of destroying its own horizons and boundaries so that it might create new ones. Such a free spirit is not tied down by any faith and is ready to once again break through the horizons it has established for itself, and the boundaries that have defined it. Thus, this spirit pursues a truth without any limit in the form of fixed horizons or in the conditions that form the boundaries of their being. Everything can be questioned and reshaped.

THE NEED FOR PRESUPPOSITIONS

There is a further problem in the notion of an unbounded truth, however, and this is the methodological concern that any enquiry or investigation must operate with some hypothesis. For example, in his late work, Nietzsche's investigations into the origins of morality operate according to the hypothesis of the will to power. In appealing to the will to power of the priests, he provides an explanation of the development of the ascetic ideal but also supports the hypothesis of the will to power (GM III 11). That enquiry operates with hypothetical assumptions, however, is unproblematic if we remember the status of any such hypothesis as a principle that allows investigation into our experiences. What is important is that it is not turned into an unquestionable foundation that cannot be revised.

It is not, though, only a question of what preliminary theoretical assumptions are in operation before being put to the test in investigation; there is also a value commitment to the very pursuit of investigation. This is a problem Nietzsche seems increasingly aware of in his later work. Now he draws attention to the fact that science still rests on the presupposition of the value of truth, in GM, he states that:

> Strictly speaking, there is no presuppositionless science [Wissenschaft], the thought of such a thing is unthinkable, paralogical: a philosophy, a 'faith', always has to be there first, for science [Wissenschaft] to win from it a direction, a sense, a boundary [Grenze], a method, a *right* to exist. (GM III 24)[14]

Again in the additional GS book, he raises the problem of the need for an underlying commitment to truth that is itself a presupposition:

> Wouldn't the cultivation of the scientific spirit [wissenschaftlichen Geist] begin when one permitted oneself no more convictions? That is probably the case; only we need still ask: *in order that the cultivation begin*, must there not be some prior conviction—and indeed one so authoritative and unconditional that is sacrifices all other convictions to itself? We see that science [Wissenschaft], too, rests on a faith; there is simply no presuppositionless science [Wissenschaft]. The question whether truth is necessary must get an answer in advance, the answer 'yes'. (GS 344)

Indeed, we might read this section as a rejection of the possibility of the free spirited, unbounded truth that Nietzsche seemed to hope for in the earlier free spirit trilogy. I take it, however, to signal rather a deepening of Nietzsche's understanding of the extent of this challenge.[15] This corresponds to his insistence that he was wrong to think there were as yet any free spirits (HH I Preface). Looking back, while science exhibits the important virtue of a capacity for doubt, it does not, as it seemed to in HH, offer a model of unbounded truth because, as Nietzsche warns, scientific men 'still believe in truth' (GM III 24). That is, for them truth has become an ideal; it is taken to have a particular value and function and its pursuit is framed in these terms.

Thus, we see a development in Nietzsche's understanding of what a free-spirited truth practice requires. While Mullin and Paul Franco are correct that, in the late work, the free spirit is not Nietzsche's highest ideal,[16] it is also the case that the free spirit remains crucial to the transformation of modern man that any higher ideal, such as the Übermensch, depends on. Nietzsche is therefore still concerned that free spirits should emerge, as the emergence of yet higher types depends on them. Franco suggests that while Nietzsche continues to value intellectual honesty, part of the move beyond the free spirit in Z and BGE is his realization that a quest for knowledge is not sufficient to overcome the crisis of nihilism.[17] Despite this, however, the quest for knowledge remains essential to this overcoming by driving the transformation of modern man. Further, the role of truth can only be understood if we recognize that Nietzsche's understanding of what is required for the pursuit of truth to be free spirited also undergoes development. It is not just that Nietzsche recognizes limits to what the practice of truth can achieve, it is also that he recognizes limits in how truth has been practiced. He, therefore, now questions whether there have ever really been free spirits in the sense of those who pursue a genuinely open truth that is not restricted by its own presuppositions. The ideal of the free spirit trilogy, to pursue an unbounded truth, remains central, but the exemplars he earlier turned to are now seen to fall short of this ideal.

When Nietzsche describes those with an unconditional will to truth as 'free, very free spirits', he places this description in quotation marks and goes on to say they are very far from being free spirits. An unconditional attitude to truth is, therefore, contrasted to what it is to be a *genuine* free spirit. We may need the conviction in the value of truth to begin the process of overturning our other convictions, but in this process Nietzsche still hopes that we can incorporate a truth that will be prepared to question everything, even the value of truth. Thus, for a truly free spirit, even the horizon of the value of truth is one that could be rubbed out, and a self defined by its drive to truth is one that may yet be overcome.

What Nietzsche realizes to be impossible is the pursuit of truth without the involvement of some evaluative perspective or motivating drive. So the question is, does this initial commitment to, or drive towards, truth have to imply that this truth practice will be limited? All that we can do is learn to recognize the presence of all our perspectives, including our will to truth, and to realize that they serve to distort our horizons. The liberated spirit: 'shall learn to grasp the sense of perspective in every value judgement—the displacement, distortion and merely apparent teleology of horizons and whatever else pertains to perspectivism' (HH I Preface 6). Hence, central to pursuing truth without fixed horizons is first establishing an understanding of our horizons of meaning and how they relate to our boundaries of self. To pursue unbounded truth requires that we understand that there could be other horizons and even other delineations of life forms. This practice of truth has to, however, still be pursued from the perspective of our existing boundaries and horizons. The art the free spirit achieves is to not feel permanently constrained by its existing boundaries or dependent on one horizon, allowing it to explore and expose their very contingency.

This awareness of contingency is exactly what Nietzsche is cultivating in his discussion of the presupposition of truth's value involved in scientific endeavour. We need to become aware of our horizons and our boundaries, to understand what forces operate to form and sustain them, and explore how they work to limit enquiry and present themselves as absolute, if we are to recognize them as contingent and unstable, and thus open to question. In particular, we need to become aware of why we pursue truth and why we take it to be valuable, if we are not to find ourselves respecting limits, which we have not even acknowledged the presence of, in our pursuit of truth. For instance, if truth is meant to serve or redeem mankind, then we already set a limit on our investigation, shying away from directions that will lead us to question the value and permanence of mankind. Thus, to pursue unbounded truth, we must also ask where this desire for truth as uncertainty, in contrast to the old truth as certainty, has come from and allow the possibility that our investigation will untether the practice of a truth that doubts and questions all presuppositions from our original motivation for undertaking it.

CONCLUSION

Given, therefore, that we cannot operate with no boundaries or horizons, such as belief in the value of truth, and we will, therefore, always pursue truth with some such presuppositions, the task of the incorporation of unbounded truth does not involve the removal of all horizons and boundaries, but rather an awareness of them and the cultivation of the capacity for detachment from them that allows for their revision. Thus, it involves a particular kind of scepticism. As Andreas Urs Sommer has detailed, there is more than one sense of scepticism at play in Nietzsche's work.[18] I am concerned only to differentiate the scepticism of a free-spirited pursuit of unbounded truth from the kind of scepticism Nietzsche criticizes in BGE when he writes: 'skepticism is the most spiritual expression of a certain complex physiological condition called in ordinary language nervous debility and sickliness' (BGE 208). I would suggest that the kind of skepticism Nietzsche is rejecting here is one that is incapable of any strength of conviction, which refuses to make evaluations and retreats into passivity out of weakness. What Nietzsche is suggesting in his mature works through the figure of the free spirit is that out of a strong commitment to truth, and not an inability to commit, we learn to question even this commitment. He wants the free spirit to fully and completely occupy a variety of different evaluative perspectives such that they learn of the multiplicity of potential boundaries that could be drawn and are not constrained by any one of them. The free spirit does not refuse to engage with perspectives, nor are they held fast by any of them; rather they learn to dance between them. They are not like Zarathustra's thin shadow, but embodied and in touch with their drives. Genuine free spirits will possess that quality that Nietzsche declares his contemporary Germans lack: 'the ability to dance with the feet, with concepts with words' (TI Germans 7). Neither do they give in to the temptation of the 'prison' of fixed beliefs that Zarathustra warns is the free spirit's danger: 'Beware that some narrow belief, a harsh severe illusion does not catch you in the end! For you are now seduced and tempted by anything that is narrow and firm' (Z IV The Shadow). Thus, to pursue truth without any limits requires *actively* learning about the limits that we create for ourselves such that they cease to be absolute and eternal. The free spirit can thereby '*maintain* the drives as the foundation of all knowing', and yet still have the capacity 'to know at what point they become the enemies of knowing' (KSA 9, 9[41]). They live in the drives in order to understand them, and this understanding allows them to better resist the tendency of these drives to try and establish themselves as dominant and absolute, at the cost of more open horizons. The free spirit explores horizons, boundaries, values and perspectives by simultaneously engaging with them and being able to do without the belief that any are absolute and certain. Thus, the free spirit is the figure who both embraces the adventure of open seas and loves the discovery of new lands. They are neither endlessly adrift in an open sea nor marooned on a fixed island. Rather, they can embrace new horizons and boundaries, understanding and incorporating into their way of life the truth of their mutability, in order to once again rub them out and redraw them.

NOTES

1. For example, Paul Franco's *Nietzsche's Enlightenment; The Free-Spirit Trilogy of the Middle Period* (Chicago and London: University of Chicago Press, 2011). Like Franco, I am using 'free spirit trilogy' to refer to *Human, All Too Human, Dawn* and the first three books of *The Gay Science*. It should be noted, however, that *Human, All Too Human* was originally published in three parts and that Nietzsche returns to the theme of the free spirit in later writings.

2. I have referred to the following translations: *The Birth of Tragedy and Other Writings*, trans. Ronald Speirs, ed. Raymond Geuss and Ronald Speirs (Cambridge: Cambridge University Press, 1999); *Untimely Meditations*, trans. Reginald J. Hollingdale, ed. Daniel Breazeale (Cambridge and New York: Cambridge University Press, 1997); *Human, All Too Human*, trans. Reginald J. Hollingdale (Cambridge: Cambridge University Press, 1996); *Dawn:*

Thoughts on the Presumptions of Morality, trans. Brittain Smith (Stanford: Stanford University Press, 2011); *The Gay Science*, trans. Josefine Nauckhoff, ed. Bernard Williams (Cambridge: Cambridge University Press, 2001); *Thus Spoke Zarathustra: A Book for Everyone and Nobody*, trans. Graham Parkes (Oxford: Oxford University Press, 2005); *Beyond Good and Evil*, trans. Reginald J. Hollingdale (London: Penguin, 2003), *On the Genealogy of Morality*, trans. Carol Diethe, ed. Keith Ansell-Pearson (New York: Cambridge University Press, 2007); *Twilight of the Idols* and *The Anti-Christ*, trans. Reginald J. Hollingdale (London: Penguin, 2003).

3. Amy Mullin, 'Nietzsche's Free Spirit', *Journal of the History of Philosophy* 38 (2000): 383–405, 385; Peter Berkowitz, *The Ethics of an Immoralist* (Cambridge, MA and London: Harvard University Press, 1995), esp. 6, 17, 152.

4. This shift is emphasized by Richard Schacht, introduction to *Human, All Too Human*, by Friedrich Nietzsche (Cambridge: Cambridge University Press, 1996), xvii, and by Paul Franco, *Nietzsche's Enlightenment*, 16, 38.

5. The importance of this question to Nietzsche's philosophy is emphasized in Keith Ansell-Pearson and Duncan Large's *Nietzsche Reader* (Malden, MA; Oxford: Blackwell Publishing, 2006) xl, 158.

6. Translation modified.

7. Keith Ansell-Pearson, 'The Incorporation of Truth: Towards the Overhuman', in *A Companion to Nietzsche*, ed. Keith Ansell-Pearson (Malden, MA, and Oxford: Carlton Blackwell Publishing, 2006), 237; 'The Eternal Return of the Overhuman: The Weightiest Knowledge and the Abyss of Light', *Journal of Nietzsche Studies* 30(2005): 1–21, 7.

8. Other practices can operate to support the practice of an unbounded truth. For example, the practice of solitude, emphasized by Horst Hutter, which is also clearly associated with the free spirit, aids the process of detachment from fixed beliefs by cultivating a distance from the shared convictions that have formed our horizon. See Hutter, *Shaping the Future: Nietzsche's Regime of the Soul and Its Ascetic Practices* (Lanham, MD, and Oxford: Lexington Books, 2006). In my *Nietzsche, Truth and Transformation*, I discuss how solitude, a particular kind of scepticism or capacity to do without certainty, and a sensualism or awareness of the body, are practices which mutually reinforce each other as part of a practice of truth (Basingstoke: Palgrave Macmillan, 2013).

9. I would like to thank Duncan Large for his suggestions in this direction.

10. Of course, Nietzsche was also influenced in his choice of the aphorism by his reading of the French moralists, but his selection of the form can be seen to be more than a reflection of his affinity with their ideas. As Alexander Nehamas argues, Nietzsche's employment of the aphorism contributes to his attempt to criticize metaphysics without erecting a new system in its place. See Nehamas, *Nietzsche: Life as Literature* (Cambridge, MA: Harvard University Press, 1985), 34.

11. Rohit Sharma, *On the Seventh Solitude; Endless Becoming and the Eternal Return in the Poetry of Friedrich Nietzsche* (Bern: Peter Lang, 2006), 87, 97–98.

12. As Paul Franco has pointed out, this challenge to the idea of a universal metaphysical need involves an attack on Schopenhauer's philosophy, in which he wrote of such a need (*Nietzsche's Enlightenment*, 19).

13. Translation modified.

14. Translation modified.

15. Bernard Reginster, who has rightly emphasized the importance in the middle period of the opposition of free spirits to the fanatic's need for certainty, argues that Nietzsche originally defines the free spirit through their genuine unconditional will to truth. After the realization that this commitment is itself a form of fanaticism, however, it cannot be taken as definitive of the free spirit. Reginster claims that in the later work, the commitment to truth is merely an indicator of the real definition of free spiritedness—which is strength ('What is a Free Spirit? Nietzsche on Fanaticism', *Archive fur Geschichte Der Philosophie* 85, 1 (2003): 51–85). I maintain, however, that Nietzsche consistently understands free spiritedness in terms of a *distinctive* way of pursuing the truth, or taking up a set of truth practices, and not just as a commitment to it. Hence, GM III 24 is an indication of his growing awareness of the problem that a commitment to truth poses for this free-spirited truth practice. This does not lead Nietzsche to abandon his belief in the importance of attempting this unbounded practice, not just as an

expression of strength but also, more importantly, as the means of transformation which allows a response to Nietzsche's critical concerns and thus serves life. Rather, he explores how potential free spirits might respond to his now more nuanced understanding of the difficulty of incorporating this practice, which is still what characterizes free spiritedness.

16. Mullin, 'Nietzsche's Free Spirit', 383–405, 385; Franco, *Nietzsche's Enlightenment*, 169.

17. Franco, *Nietzsche's Enlightenment*, 162–63.

18. Andreas Urs Sommer, 'Nihilism and Skepticism in Nietzsche', in *A Companion to Nietzsche*, ed. Keith Ansell-Pearson (Malden, MA; Oxford; Carlton: Blackwell Publishing, 2006).

BIBLIOGRAPHY

Ansell-Pearson, Keith. 'The Eternal Return of the Overhuman: The Weightiest Knowledge and the Abyss of Light'. *Journal of Nietzsche Studies* 30 (2005): 1–21.

Ansell-Pearson, Keith. 'The Incorporation of Truth: Towards the Overhuman'. In *A Companion to Nietzsche*, edited by Keith Ansell-Pearson. 230–49. Malden, MA; Oxford; Carlton: Blackwell Publishing, 2006.

Ansell-Pearson, Keith, and Duncan Large. *A Nietzsche Reader*. Malden, MA; Oxford: Blackwell Publishing, 2006.

Berkowitz, Peter. *The Ethics of an Immoralist*. Cambridge, MA; London: Harvard University Press, 1995.

Franco, Paul. *Nietzsche's Enlightenment; The Free-Spirit Trilogy of the Middle Period*. Chicago and London: University of Chicago Press, 2011.

Hutter, Horst. *Shaping the Future; Nietzsche's Regime of the Soul and Its Ascetic Practices*. Lanham, MD and Oxford: Lexington Books, 2006.

Mitcheson, Katrina. *Nietzsche, Truth and Transformation*. Basingstoke: Palgrave Macmillan, 2013.

Mullin, Amy. 'Nietzsche's Free Spirit'. *Journal of the History of Philosophy* 38 (2000): 383–405.

Nehamas, Alexander. *Nietzsche: Life as Literature*. Cambridge, MA: Harvard University Press, 1985.

Nietzsche, Friedrich. *Beyond Good and Evil*. Translated by Reginald J. Hollingdale. London: Penguin, 2003.

Nietzsche, Friedrich. *The Birth of Tragedy and Other Writings*. Translated by Ronald Speirs. Edited by Raymond Geuss and Ronald Speirs. Cambridge: Cambridge University Press, 1999.

Nietzsche, Friedrich. *Dawn: Thoughts on the Presumptions of Morality*. Translated by Brittain Smith. Stanford: Stanford University Press, 2011.

Nietzsche, Friedrich. *The Gay Science*. Translated by Josefine Nauckhoff. Edited by Bernard Williams. Cambridge: Cambridge University Press, 2001.

Nietzsche, Friedrich. *Human, All Too Human*. Translated by Reginald J. Hollingdale. Cambridge: Cambridge University Press, 1996.

Nietzsche, Friedrich. *Thus Spoke Zarathustra: A Book for Everyone and Nobody*. Translated by Graham Parkes. Oxford: Oxford University Press, 2005.

Nietzsche, Friedrich. *On the Genealogy of Morality*. Translated by Carol Diethe. Edited by Keith Ansell-Pearson. New York: Cambridge University Press, 2007.

Nietzsche, Friedrich. *Twilight of the Idols and The Anti-Christ*. Translated by Reginald J. Hollingdale. London: Penguin, 2003.

Nietzsche, Friedrich. *Untimely Meditations*. Translated by Reginald J. Hollingdale. Edited by Daniel Breazeale. Cambridge and New York: Cambridge University Press, 1997.

Reginster, Bernard. 'What Is a Free Spirit? Nietzsche on Fanaticism'. *Archive für Geschichte Der Philosophie* 85(1) (2003): 51–85.

Schacht, Richard. Introduction to *Human, All Too Human*, by Friedrich Nietzsche. vii–xxiii. Cambridge: Cambridge University Press, 1996.

Sharma, Rohit. *On the Seventh Solitude; Endless Becoming and the Eternal Return in the Poetry of Friedrich Nietzsche*. Bern: Peter Lang, 2006.

Sommer, Andreas Urs. 'Nihilism and Skepticism in Nietzsche'. In *A Companion to Nietzsche*, edited by Keith Ansell-Pearson. 250–70. Malden, MA; Oxford; Carlton: Blackwell Publishing, 2006.

Chapter Eight

Perspectives on a Philosophy of the Future in Nietzsche's *Beyond Good and Evil*

Marcus Andreas Born

—Hypocrite lecteur, mon semblable,—mon frère! —Charles Baudelaire: *Les Fleurs du Mal*

'You! hypocrite lecteur!—mon semblable,—mon frère!' —T. S. Eliot: *The Waste Land*

This chapter addresses the significance of the presence and presentation of philosophical perspectives for an interpretation of Nietzsche's *Beyond Good and Evil*. For this purpose the chapter commences with general questions on the rhetoric of the book (section 1) and on the manner in which perspectives are presented in it (section 2). It concludes by focusing the relation of free spirits and philosophers of the future in BGE's second part 'The Free Spirit' (section 3). The crucial changes that some of the aphorisms of this part went through before their publication confirm that those two figures' relation in Nietzsche's book expresses an elaborate reflection on the communication of philosophical knowledge.

1. QUESTIONABLE QUESTIONS ON THE RHETORICS OF A THINKING BEYOND GOOD AND EVIL[1]

Thus Spoke Zarathustra is often considered Nietzsche's chief work and its 'teachings' of the will to power and the eternal recurrence have been as influential as the figure of the Overman, which was given a prominent position in the book. Nietzsche's praise of this work ranges from his letters to his last texts (cf. EH Preface and EH Books). But the stylistic peculiarities of Z (and his other works) have often been the reason for excluding its author from the ranks of the serious philosophers or to place him in the no man's land between literature and philosophy. Its figurative language, its very present metaphors and its proximity to biblical parables were—and still are—a difficulty for its readers. One way of dealing with the difficulty of Nietzsche's books has been to interpret them based on his biography. It has already been pointed out convincingly that, not only is the identification of the author with the book's protagonist rather disputable, but that these 'teachings' are more than just a means to spread Zarathustra's gospel. Instead, it has been proven to be a fruitful access point to understand those teachings as 'anti-teachings',[2] to turn towards the 'aesthetic calculus' ['ästhetisches Kalkül'] with which they are parodied and undermined.[3] Furthermore, it is possible to ask to what extent the teachings are brought forward to provoke objections in terms of a love for enemies.[4] These approaches demonstrate what results can be achieved by an interpretation that takes the characteristics of Nietzsche's way of writing into account.

The statement that those characteristics should be taken into account exceeds the proposition that the author aimed at presenting his thoughts in a peculiar form. The rhetoric and the style of Nietzsche's books, which find their expression in self-referentiality, aphoristic writing and irony, have a value for the presented thoughts that cannot be overestimated. Although these aspects do not impose themselves on the reader as intensively as in Z, they are highly visible in BGE and should not be ignored.[5]

The whole book orchestrates a dynamics of thinking that goes far beyond a 'simple' presentation of assertions and does not shy away from undermining theses that appeared to be valid shortly before. BGE's structure, with its nine parts, might suggest that its author intended to be more 'comprehensible' than in Z, but attempts to determine a definite structure of the book reach their limits quickly. Thus Leo Strauss proposed to separate the first three parts from the other parts by focusing on the peculiarity of the fourth part 'Epigrams and entr'actes'. This approach proves to be problematic if the latter are granted a lower philosophical value compared to the precedent.[6] Though the first part offers an extensive critique of philosophical positions, it offers an insight into the inconscient entanglement of a thinking into its own morality, which is taken into account for the perspectives that are presented in BGE as well. This is underlined by the second part, which carries the famous 'free spirit' in its title and which points out that the free spirit itself is still struggling against his own restrictions. And even if the critique of the 'religious character' in the third part can be identified as one of Nietzsche's 'main' topics, the other parts turn out to be at least as relevant for philosophical questions as the others.[7]

But, nevertheless, the book's entrance with 'On the prejudices of the philosophers' is anything but arbitrary.[8] The starting point of BGE (after its preface) is a reflection and critique of preceding philosophies. The thinker that expresses himself in the first part knows very well that he stands in a tradition that is not yet overcome. While other philosophers are accused of not reflecting their own morals and taking them for granted, BGE invites being scrutinized for, and questioned about, its own moral basis as well.[9]

Nietzsche's process of writing, and working on, BGE is insightful for the question of its possible structure. This process can be comprehended by a reading of BGE's manuscript, which consists of pages that have been edited intensely.[10] It shows that, not only have single aphorisms been displaced several times, but also that even the numbers of the parts changed not long before the publication of the book. This has been demonstrated convincingly by Beat Röllin by means of reconstructing a precedent 'version' of BGE based on the manuscript, which contained an additional part with the title 'Masken' [Masks] that Nietzsche has disassembled and distributed to the other parts.[11] Röllin concludes that BGE would consist of ten parts today if Nietzsche had found an editor earlier.[12]

The arrangement of the aphorisms in BGE shows that the book is not aimed at providing linear arguments. Instead, it addresses themes by discussing them in aphorisms that are sometimes put directly one after the other, and which are sometimes picked up later on.[13] Werner Stegmaier has conceptualized this peculiarity of Nietzsche's writing aptly with 'Aphorismenkette' (chain of aphorisms) and 'Aphorismengeflecht' (netting of aphorisms).[14] This aspect is an important characteristic of BGE, whose aphorisms create a tension for readers: They cannot ultimately decide if the 'uncovered' connections between aphorisms have been found or created in the process of reading.

The numerous interpretations of BGE illustrate that the text seems to allow manifold approaches which differ from each other concerning their focus, which can reach from a single aphorism[15] or its first part[16] to the whole book.[17] In addition, the results of the interpretations differ in a way that can hardly be reduced to a common denominator. BGE has been considered to be Nietzsche's most comprehensible book,[18] on the one hand, while on the other, it has been the starting point of 'esoteric' interpretations which enqueue it to the philosophical tradition by means of presenting it as a deliberate successor to Kant's thinking.[19] The striking differences between the interpretations don't have to be perceived as an expression of their author's flaws but find an explanation in BGE and its textual characteristics, which seem to invite even contradicting approaches.

Against this background some 'questionable questions' (BGE 1) emerge: What significance should be given to 'aesthetic' characteristics of BGE? Do those characteristics allow an approach to the book that—similar to the reception of Z—does not prematurely identify the perspective(s) which the book presents with its author? Closely connected to these questions, another question arises: To what extent does BGE claim to be a philosophy of the future?[20]

2. THE MULTIPLICITY OF *BEYOND GOOD AND EVIL'S* PERSPECTIVES

BGE does not give an explicit answer to the question of how far it is possible to exceed a criticized morality if the philosopher who tries to do so stands in this moral tradition himself. Quite the contrary seems to be the case: the text seems to irritate its readers in an almost programmatic way. In this regard, Nietzsche's 'perspectivism' has become a very popular aspect of his thinking that is relevant not only for the thesis that knowledge is bound to a certain perspective. Particularly in Nietzsche's later works, perspectivism is expressed in his ways of writing.[21] For this reason, my remarks in what follows do not aim to disclose a theory or teaching of Nietzsche's perspectivism, but rather focus on the presence of perspectives throughout BGE. Thus, the perspectives not only provide examples for the entanglement of writing and thinking in Nietzsche's book but also allow an approach to the question of whether the book aims at being understood as a philosophy of the future or if it is 'just' the prelude of such a philosophy (as the book's subtitle and many of its aphorisms suggest).

Several metaphors in BGE express the demand to change the angle of view and to leave the familiar (moral) horizon to evade getting stuck with a thinking that is just an elaborate version of general prejudices. Consequently, the first part asks: 'Is it any wonder if we finally become suspicious, lose patience, turn impatiently away?' (BGE 1), and the second part starts with pointing out the insight into the 'simplification and falsification' that results from having 'put in the eyes for this wonder' (BGE 24).[22] In the third part, BGE presents a playful shift of perspectives. In its beginning, the need for a 'few hundred hunting aides and well-trained bloodhounds' is expressed (thus demanding a perspective close to earth), to which a distant perspective is then added: 'Such a person would still need that vaulting sky of bright, malicious spirituality from whose heights this throng of dangerous and painful experiences could be surveyed, ordered, and forced into formulas.—' (BGE 45). These and numerous other aphorisms show how the book makes use of imagery that demands a shift or transformation of one's own perspective.

Such passages that present metaphors dealing with perspectives have received far less attention from Nietzsche scholarship than aphorisms that treat perspectives in an explicit way and which have been used as a basis of 'theories' of Nietzsche's perspectivism. The preface refers to 'perspectivism, which is the fundamental condition of all life' (BGE Preface), and later on we find: 'Let us admit this much: that life could not exist except on the basis of perspectival valuations and appearances' (BGE 34). By claiming that the 'nature' in morality 'teaches a narrowing of perspective and so, in a certain sense, stupidity as a condition for life and growth' (BGE 188), life is granted the capacity of taking perspectives, and thus makes it possible to arrange the world according to its own needs.[23] The first part of BGE points out that those perspectives are not taken deliberately because the philosopher's history, the grammar of his language and his body (cf. BGE 20) are a basis for prejudices that are inscrutable even to himself.[24] BGE criticizes other philosophers for pretending to have overcome those prejudices and declaring that their drives are ineffective and do not influence their thinking. The book points out that though it does not seem possible to dispose of one's own drives, it is necessary for a philosopher to take their existence and their potential influence into account.

The hypothesis of the will to power can be named as a prime example for a thesis for the book's elaborate way of dealing with perspectives because this will is not depicted as the last ground that knowledge can reach but instead is bound to the perspective of the one presenting it. The reference to 'a world whose essence is will to power' (BGE 186) and the use of 'will to power' in BGE 211 and 259 may remind readers of metaphysical concepts. But the elaboration of the will to power in the first part shows that the 'concept' is accompanied by a hypothetical framing in which it is called '*my* claim' and is bound to the (finite) knowledge of the perspective which presents it: 'The world seen from inside, the world determined and described with respect to its 'intelligible character'—would be just this 'will to power' and nothing else—' (BGE 36).[25] The will to power is not the only element of BGE whose depiction points back to the perspective that presents it. The aphorisms in BGE 231–239 offer a broad spectrum of statements on man and woman and the *Seven little maxims about women* in BGE 237 consist of very pointed aphorisms such as, 'Black gowns and a silent guise make any woman look quite—wise' or 'In youth: a flower-covered lair. In age: a dragon stirs in there'. A frequently quoted passage from BGE 231 seems to underline this devaluation of woman: 'In any cardinal problem, an immutable "that is me" speaks up. When it comes to man and woman, for instance, a thinker cannot change his views but only reinforce them, only finish discovering what, to his mind, "is established"' (BGE 231).[26] These passages, which have been often read as a proof of Nietzsche's misogyny, allow a different interpretation if the continuation of BGE 231 is included: 'In time, certain solutions are found to problems that inspire *our* strong beliefs in particular. . . . Later— they come to be seen as only footsteps to self-knowledge, signposts to the problem that we *are*,—or more accurately, to the great stupidity that we are, to our spiritual *fatum*, to that thing "at the very bottom" that *will not learn*'.[27]

Thus, the quoted passages do not offer final truths on man and woman but allow insights into the idiosyncrasies of the perspective to which they are bound and which refers to itself explicitly: '—On account of the abundant civility that I have just extended to myself, I will perhaps be more readily allowed to pronounce a few truths about the "woman an sich": assuming that people now know from the outset the extent to which these are only—*my* truths.—' By admitting its own blind spots and emphasizing them, the text counteracts its own generalizations.[28] BGE promotes its 'truths' straightforwardly, and they are often presented as the result of a long and intense occupation with philosophical problems. But binding an interpretation to a perspective does not necessarily mean that it refutes itself—this is a task that has be performed by a reader if he or she disagrees with it and is able to provide a stronger interpretation.

The previously quoted passages can be connected to the first part's statement on 'every great philosophy so far' to be 'a confession of faith on the part of its author [Urheber], and a type of involuntary and unself-conscious memoir' (BGE 6)—a statement that is again brought forward by an 'I' that is not specified. The self-referentiality of BGE is highly visible and it plays an important role here: Though the risk to be still caught in prejudices cannot be nullified, the text can invite its readers to consider the presented thoughts as perspectival, thus allowing a reflection on the 'truths' offered. Hereby, readers are confronted with the challenge of figuring out whether those truths are true for them as well.[29] This request for a critical reading can lead to the result that the reader contradicts the perspective presented in the text, in order to overcome the interpretation offered in it.

3. THE FREE SPIRIT'S PRELUDE
TO A PHILOSOPHY OF THE FUTURE

Does BGE claim to have suspended the criticized prejudices of the philosophers and to hold a standpoint outside of the morality that it attacks aggressively? The question of whether the perspectives that are presented throughout the text are themselves beyond good and evil leads back to the book's subtitle, in which it is marked as a 'Prelude to a Philosophy of the Future'. It is not surprising that answers to the question differ in crucial respects: Jakob Dellinger has pointed out that the word 'prelude' [Vorspiel] can be understood in an 'erotic-sexual way' as well as in the mode of a 'simulating, feigning, pretending or fooling'.[30] In the first case, the prelude is something that precedes the play; in the second, it would be possible to see through the 'as-if' of the pretence of what is not the real play. While this interpretation evades determining the definite status of the 'prelude', Leo Strauss asserts that, 'the book is meant to be a specimen of the philosophy of the future'.[31]

Alexander Nehamas develops a position related to that of Strauss, but far more elaborate, when he asserts that BGE's ostensible claims not to be the philosophy of the future that it propagates should lead its readers to the conclusion that the text indeed is such a philosophy because it contains 'the major motifs of one philosophy of that kind'.[32]

The following shows that, given the second part of BGE and the corresponding notebook material [Nachlass], it is not unreasonable to understand the subtitle's 'prelude' in the sense that the book does *not* contain the philosophy of the future. The last aphorisms of the second part shed light on the philosophers of the future as well as on the free spirits. In BGE 42, a 'new breed of philosophers' is christened with the name 'Versucher' [tempter]. But the one performing the christening rite does not seem to be certain that this name is applicable: 'From what I can guess about them, from what they allow to be guessed (since it is typical of them to want to remain riddles in some respect), these philosophers of the future might have the right (and perhaps also the wrong) to be described as those *who attempt*'.[33]

The 'I' that announces the new philosophers is not able—or willing—to determine them. Instead there are speculations that are marked as such. An earlier 'version' of BGE 42 shows crucial transformations before its publication: 'As I know them, as I know myself—because I am one of these upcoming ones—those philosophers of the future will . . . be content, to be called *tempters*'.[34] As in BGE 42, this passage from the notebook is bound to the perspective of an undisclosed 'I'. But in contrast to the notebook, the immodest self-attribution as a philosopher of the future is dropped in BGE 42. The same can be pointed out for BGE 43: 'Are they new friends of "truth", these upcoming philosophers? Probably, since all philosophers so far have loved their truths. But they certainly will not be dogmatists'. In the notebook, we read: 'We as well love 'the truth': so far all philosophers loved their truths— nonetheless we are no dogmatists'.[35] Once again, the published text shifts from the first to the third person; once again the text is cautious with its determinations concerning the upcoming philosophers, although it is said that they will be no dogmatists.

With the turn against dogmatism, the motif of the free spirit is re-introduced, and the subsequent aphorism BGE 44, which concludes the book's second part, addresses the free spirit at length. Here the preceding concern is continued, and the philosophers of the future are distinguished from the free spirits, although some similarities are implied. They shall 'be free, very free spirits, these philosophers of the future—and . . . not just . . . free spirits, but rather something more, higher, greater, and fundamentally different'. Could someone prove himself as a free spirit by being able to endure solitude and loosen their ties? The philosophers of the future seem to be able to overcome the free spirits in these aspects. The free spirits do not stand outside of moral boundaries but 'at the *other* end of all modern ideology and herd desires:

perhaps as their antipodes? Is it any wonder that we "free spirits" are not exactly the most communicative spirits? That we do not want to fully reveal what a spirit might free himself *from* and what he will then perhaps be driven *towards*?' (BGE 44). Even in the liberation from his bonds, the free spirit is still in a relationship to them; as an antipode, the free spirit still appears to be entangled with them.

After pointing out the distinct difference between 'free thinkers' [Frei-denker] and free spirits, BGE 44 aims at providing a multifaceted approxima-tion to the latter. Those who are portrayed as free spirits are, inter alias, 'inventive in schemata, sometimes proud of tables of categories, sometimes pedants, sometimes night owls at work, even in bright daylight; yes, even scarecrows when the need arises—and today the need has arisen'. This list and the second part conclude with a question that is of eminent importance for the relation of free spirit and philosopher of the future: 'This is the type of people we are, we free spirits! and perhaps you are something of this your-selves, *you* who are approaching? you *new* philosophers?—' (BGE 44). This direct address *to* the philosophers of the future is astonishing if it is taken into account that the beginning of BGE 44 writes *about* them ('these philosophers of the future'). While distinguishing the philosophers of the future from the free spirits, the 'I' of the text joined the ranks of the latter ('who are their heralds and precursors, we free spirits!'). Readers could feel themselves included in those ranks and the 'we' of the text invites them to do so. This effect has been strengthened by the contrast of free spirits and free thinkers who 'will be a fully shut window and bolted door with respect to these approaching *new* philosophers'. But at the end of BGE 44, the 'you' of the text allows a stronger identification than the 'we'. It is not surprising that the reader is apostrophised directly—this stylistic device is used in other aphor-isms as well—but it is noteworthy that the apostrophe refers to the philoso-phers of the future as well. It is not by accident that readers might feel flattered and consider themselves possible philosophers of the future: The perspective that expresses itself in the text as a free spirit demands its own overcoming. Thus the address to readers can be understood as an excessive demand to turn towards the challenge of aiming at a philosophy of the fu-ture—and not to see it as already achieved by BGE (or its author).

BGE exposes the narrowness of the particular perspective that is ex-pressed in the text and underlines the existence of blind spots in its knowl-edge. The book not only demands its readers to scrutinize the thesis brought forward in it but can inspire them to reflect the finiteness of their own knowledge. Furthermore, BGE counteracts the possible impression that the text already contains a philosophical knowledge that is passed on to readers to be absorbed passively.[36] It is the reader who is challenged to generate their own—perspectival—truths by struggling with the text's perspectives. The reader is invited to occupy himself with the book's theses and—if necessary—to disband them with the same resoluteness with which they are brought forward.

NOTES

1. This chapter is a revised translation of the author's essay 'Perspektiven auf eine Philosophie der Zukunft in Jenseits von Gut und Böse', in *Klassiker Auslegen: Friedrich Nietzsche, Jenseits von Gut und Böse*, edited by M. A. Born (Berlin: De Gruyter, 2014), 1–16. I would like to thank Rebecca Bamford for her aid with the translation of this paper.
2. Cf. Werner Stegmaier, 'Anti-Lehren. Szene und Lehre in Nietzsches *Also sprach Zarathustra*', in *Klassiker Auslegen: Also sprach Zarathustra*, edited by Volker Gerhardt (Berlin: Akademie Verlag, 2000 [2nd edition 2012]), 143–67.
3. Cf. Claus Zittel, *Das ästhetische Kalkül von Friedrich Nietzsches* Also sprach Zarathustra (Würzburg: Königshausen & Neumann, 2000 [2nd edition 2011]).
4. Cf. Marcus Andreas Born, 'Liebet eure Feinde! Also Sprach Zarathustra', *Nietzscheforschung* 18 (2011): 167–77.
5. The same can be stated for Nietzsche's other works whose rhetorical and polemical aspects culminate into his latest texts such as AC and EH, in which the playful way of communicating philosophical problems to the reader by means of language is taken to extremes. Axel Pichler addresses these (and further) aspects on the basis of detailed interpretations of parts of TI (cf. Axel Pichler, *Philosophie als Text—Zur Darstellungsform der 'Götzen-Dämmerung'* [Berlin/Boston: De Gruyter, 2014]). The question, in how far Nietzsche's ways of writing are inseparably interwoven with his thinking in BGE has been addressed in Marcus Andreas Born and Axel Pichler, ed. *Texturen des Denkens. Nietzsches Inszenierung der Philosophie in 'Jenseits von Gut und Böse'* (Berlin/Boston: De Gruyter, 2013).
6. 'The book as a whole consists of two main parts, which are separated from one another by about 123 'Sayings and Interludes'; the first of the two parts is devoted chiefly to philosophy and religion and the second chiefly to morals and politics'. Strauss, 'Note on the Plan of Nietzsche's *Beyond Good and Evil*', in *Studies in Platonic Political Philosophy*, ed. Leo Strauss (Chicago: University of Chicago Press, 1983), 176. At first glance, this proposition seems to be trivial, but BGE makes clear that philosophy cannot be detached from morals and politics and that, instead, those (and other) elements underlie and motivate philosophy in a profound way.
7. Cf. the interpretations of the respective parts of BGE in Born, ed., *Klassiker Auslegen: Friedrich Nietzsche,* Jenseits von Gut und Böse (Berlin/Boston: De Gruyter, 2014).
8. Throughout, I refer to Judith Norman's translation, noting modifications I have made: Friedrich Nietzsche, *Beyond Good and Evil*, ed. Rolf-Peter Horstmann and Judith Norman, trans. Judith Norman (Cambridge: Cambridge University Press, 2002).
9. The question of how far BGE expresses its own morality has been elaborated in Paul van Tongeren, *Die Moral von Nietzsches Moralkritik. Studie zu* Jenseits von Gut und Böse (Bonn: Bouvier, 1989).
10. The manuscript is kept in the 'Goethe- und Schiller Archiv' in Weimar/Germany (signature GSA 71/26).
11. Cf. Beat Röllin, 'Ein Fädchen um's Druckmanuskript und fertig? Zur Werkgenese von Jenseits von Gut und Böse', in *Texturen des Denkens*, ed. M. A. Born and A. Pichler (Berlin/Boston: De Gruyter, 2013), 47–67.
12. Röllin, 'Ein Fädchen um's Druckmanuskript und fertig?', 55.
13. Cf. Alexander Nehamas 'Who Are 'The Philosophers of the Future'?: A Reading of *Beyond Good and Evil*', in *Reading Nietzsche*, ed. Robert C. Solomon and Kathleen M. Higgins (New York: Oxford University Press, 1988), 51. Here Nehamas also addresses the question of BGE's aphoristic 'logic'.
14. Werner Stegmaier, *Nietzsches Befreiung der Philosophie. Kontextuelle Interpretation des V. Buchs der* Fröhlichen Wissenschaft, (Berlin/Boston De Gruyter, 2012), 466.

15. Nikolaos Loukidelis, 'Es denkt'. Ein Kommentar zum Aphorismus 17 aus *Jenseits von Gut und Böse* (Würzburg: Königshausen & Neumann, 2013).
16. Maudemarie Clark and David Dudrick, *The Soul of Nietzsche's Beyond Good and Evil* (Cambridge: Cambridge University Press, 2012).
17. For example, Laurence Lampert, *Nietzsche's Task: An Interpretation of* Beyond Good and Evil (New Haven/London: Yale University Press, 2001); Douglas Burnham, *Reading Nietzsche: An Analysis of* Beyond Good and Evil (Stocksfield: Acumen, 2007).
18. Cf. Burnham, *Reading Nietzsche*, ix.
19. Cf. Clark and Dudrick, *The Soul of Nietzsche's* Beyond Good and Evil.
20. This question has already been addressed elaborately by Alexander Nehamas in 'Who Are "The Philosophers of the Future"?', 46–67. Cf. note 32 in this chapter.
21. Cf. Bernd Bräutigam, 'Verwegene Kunststücke. Nietzsches ironischer Perspektivismus als schriftstellerisches Verfahren'. *Nietzsche-Studien* 6 (1977), 45–63.
22. My translation of 'sich die Augen für dies Wunder eingesetzt hat'. Judith Norman's translation 'those who devote their eyes to such wondering' does not grasp the drastic picture Nietzsche chose to describe this change of view—and the possible reference to E. T. A. Hoffmann's *Der Sandmann*.
23. Other passages concerning perspectives/perspectivity in the book include BGE 2, 32, 114, 129, 201.
24. Contrary to that, we also find aphorisms like GM III 12 that seems to suggest that the one striving for knowledge should be able to take a perspective or leave it willingly.
25. For a more detailed account, see van Tongeren, *Reinterpreting Modern Culture: An Introduction to Friedrich Nietzsche's Philosophy*. West Lafayette, IN: Purdue University Press, 2000, 155f, and Jakob Dellinger, 'Vorspiel, Subversion und Schleife. Nietzsches Inszenierung des "Willens zur Macht"' in *Jenseits von Gut und Böse*, in *Texturen des Denkens*, edited by M. A. Born and A. Pichler (Berlin/Boston: De Gruyter, 2013), 165–87.
26. Judith Norman's translation of 'Mann und Weib' with 'men and women' had to be emended because it weakens the aphorism's 'general' claim to refer to man and woman 'an sich'.
27. Translation modified (plural 'problems' changed to singular 'problem').
28. Based on BGE 231, Paul van Tongeren has pointed out that '[t]rue knowledge has, according to Nietzsche, both characteristics at the same time: it is absolute and apodictic on the one hand and it relativizes itself as only an interpretation on the other' (van Tongeren, *Reinterpreting Modern Culture*, 167). This aspect of BGE has been illustrated in relation to BGE 231–239 and has already been addressed with regard to BGE 250 and 251 (Born and Pichler, 'Text, Autor, Perspektive', 30–43). See also van Tongeren, 'Nietzsches "Redlichkeit." Das siebte Hauptstück: "unsere Tugenden"', in *Klassiker Auslegen: Friedrich Nietzsche, Jenseits von Gut und Böse*, ed. M .A. Born (Berlin: De Gruyter, 2014), 147–65, and Nehamas, 'Who are "The Philosophers of the Future"?', 62ff.
29. Cf. Nehamas, 'Who Are "The Philosophers of the Future"?', 63.
30. Dellinger, 'Vorspiel, Subversion und Schleife'.
31. Strauss, 'Note on the Plan of Nietzsche's *Beyond Good and Evil*', 175.
32. Nehamas 'Who Are "The Philosophers of the Future"?', 59. Nehamas's reading of BGE as a 'coherent' monologue is still one of the strongest interpretations of BGE so far. He not only points out the complexity of Nietzsche's book, its self-referentiality and the importance of 'perspectivism', but gives good reasons why the so called narrator of BGE should not be identified with its author immediately. Although the chapter in hand confirms many of Nehamas' interpretations, it differs from them in one crucial point: Nehamas weakens the distinction between the narrator of the text and its author and points out that the indirect communication of BGE aims at suggesting that the readers find out that '*Beyond Good and Evil* itself is a philosophy of the future; its narrator (and its author as well) is a genuine philosopher' (Nehamas, 'Who Are "The Philosophers of the Future"?', 59). Nehamas comes to this conclusion because he finds parallels between the description of the philosophers of the future in BGE and the book's own theses. But the description of knowledge as finite and the philosopher's inability to comprehend his own perspectival entanglement completely that is present throughout BGE can be taken more seriously. Therefore, it is possible to object that the perspectives of

BGE prove themselves to be involved in a struggle for knowledge and demand for objection not to lure the reader to the truths the text (or even: author) already possesses but to provoke unforeseeable new truths.

33. For more on the topic of 'Versuch' [attempt] and 'Versucher' [tempter], cf. Bernhard Greiner, *Friedrich Nietzsche: Versuch und Versuchung in seinen Aphorismen* (München: Wilhelm Fink Verlag, 1972), 30ff. Judith Norman's translation '*those who attempt*' leaves one important facet of 'Versucher' untouched. The word already contains the semantic field of 'Versuchung', which alludes to the devil and underlines the ironic circularity of this passage: It suggests that the one attempting to christen the new philosophers himself is a 'Versucher', thus showing a familiarity with them. On this background, the fact that someone is *christened* to the name 'Versucher' bears an irony in itself.

34. KGW IX 4; W I 6, 3. For the late Nachlass, I use the KGW IX (Kritische Gesamtausgabe. Neunte Abteilung) by referring to the number of the volume that is followed by the sigil of Nietzsche's notebook.

35. KGW IX 4; W I 6, 3.

36. Cf. Greiner, *Friedrich Nietzsche*, 12 and 271f.

BIBLIOGRAPHY

Born, Marcus Andreas, ed. *Klassiker Auslegen: Friedrich Nietzsche, Jenseits von Gut und Böse*. Berlin/Boston: De Gruyter, 2014.

Born, Marcus Andreas. 'Liebet eure Feinde! Also sprach Zarathustra'. *Nietzscheforschung* 18 (2011): 167–77.

Born, Marcus Andreas, and Axel Pichler. 'Text, Autor, Perspektive. Zur philosophischen Bedeutung von Textualität und literarischen Inszenierungen in *Jenseits von Gut und Böse*'. In *Texturen des Denkens*, edited by M. A. Born and A. Pichler, 15–46. Berlin/Boston: De Gruyter, 2013.

Born, Marcus Andreas, and Axel Pichler, ed. *Texturen des Denkens. Nietzsches Inszenierung der Philosophie in 'Jenseits von Gut und Böse'*. Berlin/Boston: De Gruyter, 2013.

Bräutigam, Bernd. 'Verwegene Kunststücke. Nietzsches ironischer Perspektivismus als schriftstellerisches Verfahren'. *Nietzsche-Studien* 6 (1977): 45–63.

Burnham, Douglas. *Reading Nietzsche: An Analysis of Beyond Good and Evil*. Stocksfield: Acumen, 2007.

Clark, Maudemarie, and David Dudrick. *The Soul of Nietzsche's Beyond Good and Evil*. Cambridge: Cambridge University Press, 2012.

Dellinger, Jakob. 'Vorspiel, Subversion und Schleife. Nietzsches Inszenierung des "Willens zur Macht"' in *Jenseits von Gut und Böse*. In *Texturen des Denkens*, edited by M. A. Born and A. Pichler, 165–87. Berlin/Boston: De Gruyter, 2013.

Greiner, Bernhard. *Friedrich Nietzsche: Versuch und Versuchung in seinen Aphorismen*. München: Wilhelm Fink Verlag, 1972.

Lampert, Laurence. *Nietzsche's Task: An Interpretation of Beyond Good and Evil*. New Haven/London: Yale University Press, 2001.

Loukidelis, Nikolaos, 'Es denkt'. Ein Kommentar zum Aphorismus 17 aus *Jenseits von Gut und Böse*. Würzburg: Königshausen & Neumann, 2013.

Nehamas, Alexander. 'Who Are "The Philosophers of the Future"?: A Reading of *Beyond Good and Evil*'. In *Reading Nietzsche*, edited by Robert C. Solomon and Kathleen M. Higgins, 46–67. New York: Oxford University Press, 1988.

Nietzsche, Friedrich. *Beyond Good and Evil*. Edited by Rolf-Peter Horstmann and Judith Norman. Translated by Judith Norman. Cambridge: Cambridge University Press, 2002.

Röllin, Beat. 'Ein Fädchen um's Druckmanuskript und fertig? Zur Werkgenese von *Jenseits von Gut und Böse*'. In *Texturen des Denkens*, edited by M. A. Born and A. Pichler, 47–67. Berlin/Boston: De Gruyter, 2013.

Sommer, Andreas Urs. '"Glossarium", "Commentar" oder "Dynamit"? Zu Charakter, Konzeption und Kontext von *Jenseits von Gut und Böse*'. In *Texturen des Denkens*, edited by M. A. Born and A. Pichler, 69–86. Berlin/Boston: De Gruyter, 2013.

Stegmaier, Werner. 'Anti-Lehren. Szene und Lehre in Nietzsches *Also sprach Zarathustra*'. In *Klassiker Auslegen: Also sprach Zarathustra*, edited by Volker Gerhardt, 143–67. Berlin: Akademie Verlag, 2000 (2nd edition, 2012).

Stegmaier, Werner. *Nietzsches Befreiung der Philosophie. Kontextuelle Interpretation des V. Buchs der* Fröhlichen Wissenschaft. Berlin/Boston De Gruyter, 2012.

Strauss, Leo. 'Note on the Plan of Nietzsche's *Beyond Good and Evil*'. In *Studies in Platonic Political Philosophy*, edited by Leo Strauss, 174–91. Chicago: University of Chicago Press, 1983.

van Tongeren, Paul. *Die Moral von Nietzsches Moralkritik. Studie zu* Jenseits von Gut und Böse. Bonn: Bouvier, 1989.

van Tongeren, Paul. 'Nietzsches "Redlichkeit". Das siebte Hauptstück: "unsere Tugenden"'. In *Klassiker Auslegen: Friedrich Nietzsche, Jenseits von Gut und Böse*, edited by M. A. Born, 147–65. Berlin: De Gruyter, 2014.

van Tongeren, Paul. *Reinterpreting Modern Culture: An Introduction to Friedrich Nietzsche's Philosophy*. West Lafayette, IN: Purdue University Press, 2000.

Zittel, Claus. *Das ästhetische Kalkül von Friedrich Nietzsches* Also sprach Zarathustra. Würzburg: Königshausen & Neumann, 2000 (2nd edition, 2011).

Chapter Nine

Nietzsche's "Free Spirit"

Richard Schacht

Nietzsche often characterizes himself as a "free spirit," in *Beyond Good and Evil* and elsewhere. Yet he also contends in BGE that, to the extent that he and we are not *more than* free-spirited thinkers, we are only "heralds and precursors" of the "new species of philosophers" he envisions. He writes that they "also will be free, *very* free spirits, these philosophers of the future—though just as certainly they will not merely be free spirits [nicht bloss frei Geister sein werden] but something more, higher, greater, and fundamentally different [etwas Mehreres, Höheres, Grösseres und Gründlich-Anderes]" (BGE 44). It therefore is important that we consider what his kind of "free spirit" is and what it is not, in relation to his conception of what—or *what else*, that he deems "more, higher, greater, and different"—this envisioned kind of philosopher is (also) to be. That is my topic.

> The truly free in spirit will also think freely regarding the spirit itself and will not dissemble over various dreadful elements pertaining to its source and tendency. [Der wahrhaft Freie im Geiste wird auch über den Geist selber frei denken und sich einiges Furchtbare in Hinsicht auf Quelle und Richtung desselben nicht verhelen.] (HH II AOM 11)[1]

Nietzsche latched onto the idea of being "free in spirit" [freie im Geiste] and the expressions "freie Geister" and "der freie Geist" quite early, even giving *Human, All Too Human*—his first self-consciously philosophical book—the subtitle "A Book for Free Spirits." He subsequently used essentially the same expression—"Freigeist"—to characterize the "common goal" of the whole series of his pre-*Zarathustra* writings from HH onward, in the striking statement he made on the back cover of the first edition of *The Gay Science*: "This book marks the conclusion of a series of writings by Friedrich Nietzsche, whose common goal is to set forth *a new image and ideal of the free spirit* [deren gemeinsames Ziel ist, *ein neues Bild und Ideal des Frei-geistes* aufzustellen]."[2]

This language continued to figure explicitly and prominently in Nietzsche's writings and thought at least as late as BGE, with which his final three-year burst of productive activity began. Indeed, "der freie Geist" is the title he gave to the important second part of that nine-part book, in which he discusses the kind of philosophy he considers his own, at least in large part, to be (throughout the book he speaks repeatedly of "we free spirits"), and to contrast markedly with those of which he is so critical in the preface and the first part, "On the Preju-dices of Philosophers." (Indeed, he employed it significantly yet again, in con-nection with his own philosophical development and thinking, in his 1886 pref-ace to his republication of what then became the first of the two volumes of HH.)

It seems clear, therefore, that for Nietzsche there is a significant connec-tion between what he is talking about when he uses this language and what he is trying to do and say, both in his pre-*Zarathustra* "free spirit" series and in the kind of philosophy he is advocating and pursuing in BGE. Yet it is not obvious that "free-spirited thinking" for him is simply another name for his kind of philosophizing, either pre- or post-*Zarathustra*. So, for example, HH is said in its subtitle to be *"for"* those who are or have it in them to become such "spirits," rather than to be simply a volume of "Reflections *of* a Free Spirit"—even though they certainly may be so described. This may or may not be a distinction without a difference.

But more unambiguously and importantly: while Nietzsche repeatedly characterizes himself as a "free spirit" in BGE, he also makes it quite explicit that, to the extent that he and we are not *more than* free-spirited thinkers, we are only "heralds and precursors" of the "new species of philosophers" he envisions. So he writes: they *"also* will be free, *very* free spirits, these philos-ophers of the future—though just as certainly they will not be merely free spirits [nicht bloss frei Geister sein werden] but something more, higher, greater, and fundamentally different [etwas Mehreres, Höheres, Grösseres und Gründlich-Anderes]" (BGE 44, first emphasis mine). This makes it all the more important that we consider both what his kind of "free spirit" is and what it is not, in relation to his conception of what this kind of philosopher is to be.

It should go without saying (but is worth reminding ourselves) that in taking up this question we must aside whatever might come to mind when we English-speaking readers see the words "free spirit" in English translations of Nietzsche's writings—or even when we German-speaking readers see the words "der freie Geist" in his German texts, drawing upon common usage or our linguistic intuitions in either language. The question is what *Nietzsche* has in mind when he uses this and related expressions; and for that our primary guides must be how *he* uses them and what he says about them. So he insists (in BGE) that "we 'free spirits' . . . are something different from *'libres-penseurs,' 'liberi pensatori,' 'Freidenker'*" and the like (BGE 44), and contends (in *Ecce Homo*) that even before HH, in the essays he subsequently published together as *Untimely Meditations,* "an altogether new type of free spirit thus gained its first expression: to this day nothing is more foreign and less related to me than the whole European and American species of *libres penseurs*" (EH Books UM 2).

1. AUTOBIOGRAPHICAL TEXTS

There are two autobiographical texts that are of particular relevance and interest in this connection. One, mentioned above, is Nietzsche's reflection on the matter in the preface he wrote to the first installment of HH (initially published in 1878), on the occasion of his republication of it (with its two sequels) in 1886. The other is his revisitation of it two years later in EH, in his more abbreviated comments on HH and the other volumes in his "free spirit" series. I shall begin by taking note of the latter, and then the former, before turning to what he does with the "free spirit" idea in BGE.

HH, Nietzsche's "Book for Free Spirits" (as its subtitle proclaims it to be), not only was published in the centenary year of the death of his Enlightenment hero Voltaire (1878) but was dedicated to his memory. It was now Voltaire, rather than Schopenhauer or Wagner, whom Nietzsche considered to be his inspiration and kindred spirit. Looking back upon the book ten years later, he saw it as something more: "the monument of a crisis." In writing it, he tells us, he was struggling to free himself from many things that stood in the way of his (as he later liked to put it) "becoming who he was"—perhaps as a person, but more particularly as a thinker: "here I liberated myself from what in my nature did not belong to me." (EH Books HH 1). In elaborating upon this point, he makes it clear that in HH it was the "freedom" of *his own* spirit that was most immediately at issue, and for the sake of which the book was above all needed.

Nietzsche also emphasizes that by "free spirit" he meant the spirit of a person and thinker who has "become free"—which is to say, has come to be liberated or emancipated. This expression, as he used it here, "wants to be understood" (as he later retrospectively put it) "in no other sense: [it is] a spirit that has *become free [freigewordener* Geist], that has taken possession of itself again [der von sich selber wieder Besitz ergriffen hat]" (EH Books HH 1). It was thus an important part of the sense of the expression for him at that point that it is a contrast concept, and that the "freedom" in question is a freedom the meaning of which is in part a function of the fact that it had to be *attained*, through rebellion against and escape from influences that had previously held sway over him.

In the first instance, Nietzsche says, the influences from which he had to free himself were of a cultural nature, and related to "ideals" associated with his earlier preoccupations and attractions. Thus he refers to HH as a "monument of rigorous self-discipline with which I put a sudden end to all my infections with 'lofty fraudulence [höheren Schwindel],' 'idealism,' 'beautiful feelings'" and the like—presumably meaning Romanticism in general and Wagner in particular.

But the freedom he was seeking—and, in the perspective of 1888, believes himself largely to have attained during the years of his "free spirit" series—was a liberation from other "ideals" as well. He associated them with a broad range of attachments, professional (academic and philological) and philosophical (Schopenhauer) as well as cultural (art and music), with the aid of perspectives upon them developed by way of his avid pursuit of "physiology, medicine, and natural sciences." (EH Books HH 3) Thus he characterizes HH as the work of "a merciless spirit that knows all the hideouts in which the ideal is at home"; and he describes his cleansing strategy as one designed to deprive seductive ideals of their appeal: "This is war, but war without powder and smoke. . . . One error after another is coolly placed on ice; the ideal is not refuted—it *freezes* to death" (EH Books HH 1).

Nietzsche followed the first installment of HH with two supplements he subsequently incorporated into it, and then with another volume of aphorisms he called *Daybreak* or *Dawn* [*Morgenröthe*], presumably to signify the dawning of a new (free-spirited) day, with respect to morality in particular. In that book, he observes in EH, he expanded his "war" to "the prejudices of morality," in the words of its subtitle, launching what he calls "my campaign against morality"— and in particular, "against the morality of self-erradication [*die Entselbstungs-Moral*]." The aim of this "fight" is said to have been "a liberation from all moral values" opening the way to "saying Yes to and having confidence in all that hitherto had been forbidden, despised and damned." (EH Books D 1, 2) And he remarks that, by the end of GS (Nietzsche's next book), that liberation has become so much a part of the new freedom of the "free spirit" that in the "Songs of Prince Free-as-a-Bird [*Vogelfrei*]" appended to it, "one dances right over morality," leaving it altogether behind. (EH Books GS) This "free spirit" is thus above all "beyond" the moralism of "good and evil" thinking, in the language of the title of BGE, its prose sequel.

Two years earlier, in the 1886 preface to the first installment of HH, Nietzsche had taken a much closer and considerably more penetrating look at the kind of liberation process that was for him fundamental to the "freed spirituality" of the "free spirit" for whom the book was purportedly intended. He admits at the outset that "'free spirits' of this kind do not exist, did not exist," and that he had *"invented* for myself the 'free spirits' to whom this melancholy-valiant book . . . is dedicated," because "I had need of them at that time." He needed kindred spirits of that kind—the kind of "free spirit" he himself was still in the process of trying to become; and he felt that he was having to do so entirely alone, on his own.

It was only in retrospect, however, that he felt he understood what it was that he had been striving to attain—and at that point was still far from having attained.

> From the desert of these years of temptation and experimentation [Versuchs-jahren], it is still a long road . . . to that *mature [reifen]* freedom of spirit [Freiheit des Geistes] which is equally self-mastery and discipline of the heart and permits access to many and contradictory modes of thought . . . , to that overabundance of formative, curative, molding and restorative forces which is precisely the sign of *great* health—an over-abundance that grants to the free spirit the dangerous privilege of living *experimentally* and of being allowed to offer itself to adventure: the master-prerogative [Meisterschafts-Vorrecht] of the free spirit! (HH I Preface 4)[3]

Nietzsche's "long road" to this "mature free spirituality" thus began but did not end with the form of it of which he here considers the first installment of HH to have been both the expression and the means of its own attainment, as it boot-strapped its way into existence. It began, he says, "like the shock of an earthquake," with "a sudden terror and suspicion of what it loved, a light-ning-bolt of contempt for what it called 'duty,' a rebellious, arbitrary, volcan-ically erupting desire for travel [and] strange places," resulting in what he calls "a great unshackling [Loslösung]" of a spirit that had previously been "bound [gebundener]" (HH I Preface 3). A "decisive occurrence" of that sort may well produce a powerful reaction; but its initial expressions are likely to be more reactive and exploratory than well considered, as one attempts to find new footing. Or at any rate, that is what he is here surmising to have been the case with himself then. And finding that new footing was itself a process, requiring a multistage period of what he calls "convalescence [Genesung]."

So Nietzsche goes on to identify three *intermediary* stages in the progress of the developing "free spirit"—or at any rate in the history of the origins [Entstehungsgeschichte] of his own "free spirituality." They follow what (in the imagery of Zarathustra's parable of "The Three Metamorphoses") might be characterized as its initial explosively rebellious "lion" stage, and also precede the much later "mature" stage of unfraught spirituality that by contrast (and somewhat ironically) has something innocently childlike and "playful" about it. All are "free-spirited"; but for the Nietzsche of this pref-ace, all leave a good deal to be desired. (Indeed, as shall be seen, it turns out for him that even the culminating mature form does so as well, at least

philosophically speaking, in relation to his conception of the "new philosophers" of whom he speaks in BGE.)

The first of the intermediary stages Nietzsche mentions, beyond the leo-
nine rebellious one, is a "midway condition" he employs a different zoologi-
cal image to characterize: "a feeling of bird-like freedom [Vogel-Freiheit],
bird-like attitude, bird-like exuberance. . . . One lives no longer in the fetters
of love and hatred, without yes, without no." (HH I Preface 4) Here one's
liberation has been carried farther: one has learned how to attain a height
from which one no longer feels moved or obligated to take everything in
such an intensely personal manner.

The next stage or form of free-spiritedness involves liberation from that
very detachment and disengagement: "A step further in convalescence: and
the free spirit again draws near to life," enabled to come back down to earth
and engage in the same undriven but attracted manner with things on a
human scale in the world of human life and experience. "It seems to him as if
his eyes are only now open to what is *close at hand*. . . . What bloom and
magic they have acquired!" (HH I Preface 5) One's liberation has now been
extended to emancipation from the sense that one is under some sort of
obligation to disdain and denigrate mundane human reality and the things of
this life and world.

And then, at the threshold of "mature freedom of spirit" but not yet well
across it, the recovering and developing "free, ever freer spirit begins to
unveil the riddle of that great liberation" itself, and grasps what it is all about:
namely, *self-mastery*, and its philosophical and human employment. So,
strikingly employing language that he used again a year later in an important
digression in the third essay of *On the Genealogy of Morals*, Nietzsche
writes:

> If he has for long hardly dared to ask himself: "why so apart? So alone?
> Renouncing everything I once reverenced? Renouncing reverence itself?" . . . ,
> he [now] hears in reply something like an answer: "You shall become master
> over yourself, master also over your virtues. Formerly *they* were your masters;
> but they must be only your instruments beside other instruments. You shall get
> control over your For and Against and learn how to display first one and then
> the other in accordance with your higher goal." (HH I Preface 6)

In the counterpart passage in GM III 12, the phrase "in accordance with your
higher goal" is replaced by "useful for knowledge [für die Erkenntniss nutz-
bar]," because he there is addressing his remarks to his readers precisely
insofar as he supposes them to share his specific "higher goal" of knowledge
("Let us be grateful, precisely as knowers [Seien wir zuletzt, gerade als
Erkennende]"). What he is discussing there is the possibility and appropriate
manner of pursuing knowledge—notwithstanding his insistence in both pas-

sages on what he here calls "the sense of perspective in every value judgment" (HH I Preface 6).

That concern with knowledge is also central to Nietzsche's earlier conception of the "free spirit." Liberation from the many burdens and inhibitions he associates with the "Christian-moral" tradition certainly was something to which he aspired, not only for himself but for all who would be capable of dispensing with the controls and consolations it has long afforded. So, for example, in the noteworthy concluding aphorism of *The Wanderer and His Shadow* [WS, 1880, incorporated into HH as the second part of its second volume] he writes:

> Many chains have been laid upon man so that he should no longer behave like an animal. . . . Now, however, he suffers from having worn his chains for so long . . .—those heavy and pregnant errors contained in moral, religious and metaphysical representations [Vorstellungen]. . . . Only when this *sickness from one's chains* has also been overcome will the first great goal have truly been attained: the separation of man from the animals.—We stand now in the midst of our work of removing these chains, and we need to proceed with the greatest caution. Only *the ennobled man may be given freedom of spirit* [Nur *dem veredelten Menschen* darf *die Freiheit des Geistes gegeben werden*]. (HH II WS 350)

This, for Nietzsche, is an important point. The "free-spiritedness" he associates with liberation from the "chains" of various sorts of inhibitions (including those he elsewhere associates with what he calls the "ethicality of custom [Sittlichkeit der Sitte]" is to be practical as well as intellectual. But he considers it desirable only in the cases of those who have outgrown the need for such "chains," in their lives as well as in their thought—and that need, he surmises, is still very much the human rule.

For the most part, however, when Nietzsche speaks of the "free spirit," it is the emergence and character of what he takes as a distinctive new and important type of *thinker and thinking* that he more specifically has in mind. That is his focus in the part of BGE that bears "the free spirit [der freie Geist]" as its title; and that is also what is most centrally on display—as a kind of "work in progress"—in the "free spirit" series. What is so important about all of the liberations that make the "free spirit" a progressively more completely "freed" spirit, for him, is—at least in the first instance—that they make possible a more radically *uninhibited* kind of thinking than he finds in philosophers previously, or even in such paragons of "enlightenment" as the Voltaire to whom he paid homage in his dedication of HH.

Thus, in EH after doing Voltaire the honor of characterizing him as, "above all, in contrast to all who wrote after him, a nobleman [*grandseigneur*] of the spirit—like me," Nietzsche then says—with the immodesty so characteristic of him in that late book—that that dedication was intended to indicate that Voltaire "really meant progress—*toward me*"! And he goes on to style the kind of "free spirit" we find in HH a "merciless spirit" that goes after all philosophical prejudices and "the ideal" in all of its guises with gloves off and no holds barred, in alliance with the various scientific and historical disciplines that are capable of shedding light upon and into the all-too-human "*underworld*" of the ideal" (EH Books HH 1).

Indeed, as the passage from HH cited at the outset indicates, Nietzsche goes further (as he was to do again, at greater length—notably in the 1887 fifth book of GS and in the contemporaneous third essay of GM). If it is "truly free," a "free spirit" of his sort "will also *think* freely"—that is, in a completely uninhibited and candid fashion—with respect to the "origin and tendency" of *its own spirituality*, eschewing all "dissembling" (such as that of taking refuge in euphemism and steering clear of hard truths) and pulling no punches (HH II AOM 11, my emphasis).

In short, Nietzsche's "free spirit" is no "blithe spirit" (even if, at least by the time of GS, it has acquired a sense of humor and a dancing style, has learned to enjoy and employ puns and wit, and loves to laugh). The "gaiety [Fröhlichkeit]" of his free-spirited philosophical thinker [Wissenschaftler] is no stranger to dark thoughts, seriousness, and even bloody-mindedness. If this was already the case in his "free spirit" series, it is even more so in BGE, in which the banner of the "free spirit" is again unfurled, and of which he observes in EH that in it "psychology is practiced with admitted hardness and cruelty" (EH Books BGE).

In short, and more generally put, I suggest that pre-*Zarathustra* Nietzsche conceives of the "free spirit" first and foremost as one who engages in radically "dis-illusioned" inquiry aspiring to an unsparing comprehension of all things human, drawing upon all available disciplinary perspectives and resources, and animated by an unflinching "intellectual conscience" of a severity that he complains is all too rare (GS 2). And this for him is done more specifically—and most importantly—in league with the project of a "de-deified" and "naturalizing" reinterpretation of human reality that he announces at the outset of book 3 of GS (109), and the associated project of what he came to call a "revaluation of all values" (EH Books D 1).

It may seem that Nietzsche's commitment to these fundamentally naturalistic projects sits oddly with his profession of the "free spirit's" complete "unfetteredness"; for a commitment to "naturalizing" reinterpretation (GS 109) where both human reality and value are concerned would seem to be a striking and problematic exception to his determination to avoid all philosophical "prejudices," particularly of the sort that he cites and criticizes in the first part of BGE. This would indeed be a problem for him if the "naturalizing" to which he is committed were a substantive physicalist naturalism, and if his commitment to it were a dogmatic one. On my understanding of him, however, neither is the case. For as I conceive of *his* kind of naturalism, it is quite open-ended substantively; and the naturalistic "guiding idea" to which it is committed is only that—a "guiding idea" that remains tentative, experimental, and in principle open to challenge, counter-argument and proffered counter-example.[4]

2. BGE'S "THE FREE SPIRIT" (BGE 24–41)

BGE, to which I now turn, and in which the idea of "the free spirit" looms large (its second part bears that title), was published in 1886, as was Nietzsche's added preface to the first volume of HH. The completion of BGE (its preface is dated "June 1885") antedates the writing of the latter (which is dated "spring 1886"), but by no more than a year. When Nietzsche availed himself of this idea once again in that HH preface, the "mature freedom of spirit" that is the culmination of the development he discusses in it may thus be presumed to be at least akin to what he is talking about in that second part of BGE. So, for example, the positioning of that part—and so of himself, following his critique of "The Prejudices of Philosophers" in its opening part—clearly suggests that, on Nietzsche's view of the matter, those "prejudices" are among the things from which his sort of "mature free spirit" has freed itself.

There are a number of other things Nietzsche says about the "free spirit [freie Geist]" in that HH preface that also echo (and thereby underscore as well as amplify) points made in this connection in BGE. As the philosophical "free, ever freer spirit begins to unveil the riddle of that great liberation," he writes in the former, something more than the importance of "self-mastery" and the "perspectival" character of "every value judgment" comes into view: namely, what he calls "the problem of *order of rank*" (HH I Preface 6). So he continues: "Given that it is *the problem of order of rank* of which we may say that it is *our* problem, we free spirits: it is only now, at the midday of our life, that we understand what preparations, bypaths, experiments, temptations, disguises the problem had need of before it was *allowed* to rise up before us (HH I Preface 7). It is in part that "problem"—and more generally the problem and task of a "revaluation of values," along with a (Nietzschean-naturalistic) rethinking of the very nature of value—for which Nietzsche begins to set the stage in BGE.

Nietzsche's discussion of the "free spirit" in its second part is more generally quite evidently—and explicitly—intended to flesh out his portrait of what he calls "the image of the free-spirited philosopher," by means of the indication of various "traits" he associates with it (BGE 39). One of them, of course, is indicated by the very title of the book itself: such a philosopher is to be "beyond good and evil"—that is, beyond thinking moralistically, in ways influenced by the norms and values of the morality he uses that duality to characterize. Another, as has been observed, is freedom from the various other "prejudices of philosophers" that he discusses in the previous (first) part of the book—as well as from the dogmatic tendencies and Platonistic errors with respect to human spirituality and value that he excoriates in the preface to it. But what else? Let us consider what points Nietzsche chooses to make in each of the twenty-one sections of "The Free Spirit."

The first further or more specific trait in the portrait Nietzsche here sketches recalls the "virtue of modesty" that he had added to his call for "historical philosophizing" at the outset of *Menschliches* (HH I 2). It is the ability to recognize, admit, and take in stride the idea that human life in general—including the human endeavor of cognitive inquiry [Wissenschaft] and the free-spirited inquirer's own pursuit of knowledge [Erkenntniss]— inescapably involves (and even requires) forms of strategic "simplification" and "falsification," and thus at least a measure of "will to ignorance" and "love of error" (BGE 24).

Next (BGE 25), Nietzsche's "free-spirited philosophers" will certainly be "friends of Erkenntniss"; but they are not to be fanatics or martyrs for whom nothing else matters or is more important, and no sacrifice is too great. Further (BGE 26), as would-be knowers [Erkennender], seeking to compre- hend human reality, they must concern themselves not just with exceptional and admirable human beings and possibilities, but also with the human rule and the all-too-human—learning from the observations of cynics with re- spect to them, but without becoming mere cynics themselves. They will be sensitive to how much depends on the contingencies and differences of lan- guages (BGE 28). They of course will need to be independently minded and daring in their interpretive experiments, which requires strength of spirit (BGE 29); and they should be prepared to be misunderstood (BGE 27 and 30). They will know better than to "venerate and despise" too quickly and superficially, and will also understand the importance of "the art of nuances" (BGE 31).

This brief summary of the upshot of what Nietzsche is saying about the "free spirit" here does not do justice to his prose; but these are the things he is talking about in these sections—and it is nothing to take one's breath away, to this point at any rate. These are all good traits for a philosopher to have; but the portrait so far has nothing particularly distinctive or startling about it, at least to contemporary eyes. That, however, is nothing against it. And it is notable that Nietzsche's point of departure would seem to be such a sensible and solid one. The same is true, I might observe, of much of what one finds in Nietzsche's pre-BGE philosophical writings, particularly (and not surpris- ingly) in the "free spirit" series.

At this point, Nietzsche shifts gears for a half dozen sections, mentioning a number of topics and tasks in which he himself is very much interested and engaged, and interpretations he seems prepared to advance with respect to them. One might well wonder what they are doing here, in a part of the book on what it is to be his kind of "free-spirited philosopher"; for thinking about what he does and as he does on these matters obviously cannot be part and parcel of the very nature of "free-spirited" philosophical thinking. My way of making sense of their inclusion here is to suppose that they are intended to serve as *examples* of such thinking (while also taking advantage of the opportunity to put some of his own cards on the table).

The first (BGE 32) concerns the understanding and assessment of human action, and the need for "a fundamental shift in values" and associated "overcoming of morality," the stage for which has been set by "another self-examination of man" and "deepening [Vertiefung]" of our comprehension of ourselves that he anticipates—presumably as we proceed with the task of "de-deifying" our thinking and reinterpreting human reality naturalistically. Nietzsche refers to this "overcoming of morality" as a task that "has been saved up for the finest and most redlich consciences of today"—thereby naming what he subsequently (in part 7 of BGE, "Our Virtues,") identifies as the cardinal virtue of the "free spirit": "Redlichkeit," commonly translated as "honesty," but better understood as "intellectual integrity" (BGE 227). And as he indicates in the next section (BGE 33), the "morality" that is to be "overcome" is "the whole morality of self-relinquishment [Selbstentäusserungs-Moral]—as is "the aesthetics of 'disinterested contemplation.'"

The next example concerns what appears to be an epistemological point, for it pertains to what Nietzsche calls "the *erroneousness* of the world in which we think we live." In fact, however, it has to do fundamentally with the importance of learning to think about such things free of the "moral prejudice that truth is worth more than appearance"—which is a prime example of what he means by associating the "free spirit" with liberation from the morality of "good and evil." The basic matters at hand pertain to the understanding of the basic (perspective-dependent and interdependent) character of "life" and of *value*: "Let at least this much be admitted: there would be no life at all if not on the basis of perspectival valuations and appearances" (BGE 34).

At this point, Nietzsche pauses (in BGE 35) to suggest that the free-spirited philosopher will not be "too human"—that is, too earnest, demanding, dogmatic, all-or-nothing-minded—about and in the "search for truth." He then proceeds (in BGE 36) to provide a striking and important example of an issue such a philosopher might legitimately try to tackle, and of the sort of interpretation such a philosopher might appropriately venture with respect to it. The issue is the basic character of all that transpires in life and the world; and the interpretation is his idea and hypothesis—which he terms "my Satz [proposition or proposal]"—that this basic character may aptly be construed in terms of the fundamental disposition he calls "will to power."

Elsewhere in BGE, on a number of occasions (e.g., BGE 13, 23, 186, 259), as he does again in GM, Nietzsche makes assertions to this effect—which, as the preceding section and the hypothetical framing of this one make clear, are to be taken tentatively and provisionally rather than dogmatically. Here he provides an indication of the kind of case that he suggests a free-spirited philosopher might try (and be able) to make for this hypothesis and interpretation, and might reasonably consider persuasive. My answer to the question "What is this section doing here?" is that it is intended to make clear that Nietzsche's "free-spirited" philosopher is to be understood as *no mere critic*, but also as an interpreter—and a bold and ambitious (if also experimental and tentative) one at that; and to show how such a philosopher might proceed.

After pausing again in the next section (BGE 37) to observe that the free-spirited philosopher will not be deterred by the ready availability of "vulgar" quips and paraphrases to those who might wish to avoid taking such ideas seriously, Nietzsche returns (in BGE 38) to the characterization of such a philosopher. The trait he mentions next is of particular importance for one who (like Nietzsche from HH onward) recognizes that "everything has become" and that this calls for "historical philosophizing" (HH I 2). It is alertness to the temptation people have to interpret things historical "according to their own indignations and enthusiasms," in order to make the past "tolerable to look at"—but at the cost of so "misunderstanding" it that "the text disappears beneath the interpretation." This is something the intellectual integrity [Redlichkeit] of the free-spirited philosopher will not countenance, and so against which such philosophers may be expected to be on guard. They will be as suspicious and wary of this all-too-human tendency to self-indulgent interpreting as they are to the equally common and all-too-human tendency to wishful thinking.

The next trait Nietzsche mentions (in BGE 39) is "strength." Observing that "something might be true while being harmful and dangerous in the highest degree," and that "existence" might be such that "those who would know it completely would perish," he then suggests that "the strength of a spirit should be measured according to how much of the 'truth' one could still barely endure." The free-spirited philosopher would need such strength, and would seek to develop as much of it as is humanly possible. And to this Nietzsche adds (also in BGE 39) "a final trait for the image of the free-spirited philosopher," citing Stendhal's observation that "To be a good philosopher, one must be dry, clear, without illusion"—not least with respect to "seeing clearly into what ['making discoveries in philosophy'] is."

And what is that? Nietzsche has already given his answer to this question. "Discoveries in philosophy," he has been saying and emphasizing all along (e.g., BGE 22, 23, 36), have the character of *interpretations*, and proceed by way of the human activity of *interpreting*. It by no means follows, however, that they therefore are one and all mere fictions and fables, devoid of cognitive significance and yielding no genuine comprehension. There are interpretations and interpretations—and as Nietzsche goes on in the next section (BGE 40) to suggest, those of a philosophical spirit whose freedom has been translated into the more penetrating thinking of a "deep spirit [*tiefe Geist*]" compare favorably to those of more superficial thinkers.

It may be noted in passing that Nietzsche makes the same sorts of claims elsewhere in BGE itself on a number of occasions, both for some of his interpretive conclusions (for example, BGE 13 and 259) and for some of his reinterpretive projects (for example, BGE 23 and 230). It takes a "deep spirit" to get to the bottom of things and to grasp what is there to be found—as he suggests in his preface to *Genealogie*, a year later, when he writes that his "ideas on the origin of our moral prejudices" sprang from a "*fundamental will* of knowledge [*Grundwillen* der Erkenntnis], commanding onward into the depths [in der Tiefe gebietenden], speaking ever more precisely, demanding ever greater precision. For this alone is fitting for a philosopher" (GM Preface 2). It is precisely his free-spirited sort of philosopher that he is talking about here.

In BGE 40 Nietzsche thus associates free-spirited inquiry with the attainment of comprehension that surpasses alternative ways of thinking—most importantly, in "depth." But he also reiterates his thought that a free-spirited philosopher of real "depth" not only must expect to be misunderstood, but will even *want* to be misunderstood, and therefore will "need" and "love masks"—not because they comprehend nothing, but rather precisely because what they comprehend is liable to be only superficially and therefore badly understood—and in any event is often not for everyone to know.

In the following section (BGE 41), Nietzsche returns to the theme of the "independence" that is the heart of the "freedom" of the "free spirit." In it he emphasizes the *attained* character of that independence and elaborates in a rhetorically powerful way upon the point that its attainment comes at a cost. It is said to require detaching oneself from various things to which one very probably and humanly will have previously been attached—and perhaps *needs* first to have been attached, for developmental reasons, and for one's independence from them to be meaningful. In the full text the phrase, "Not to remain attached to [hängen blieben an]" is repeated again and again; and the repetition of the idea of *letting go of* everything of the sort Nietzsche mentions to which one has been attached—and may even have been "hanging onto" for dear life—is part of the power of the passage. In the interest of brevity, however, I will compress it: Not to remain attached [hängen blieben] to a person . . . , to a fatherland . . . , to some pity . . . , to a cognitive discipline [Wissenschaft]—even if it should lure us with the most precious discoveries [Funden] . . . , to one's own detachment . . . , to our own [personal] virtues (BGE 41).

It is quite a list; and these are only examples. I would observe, however, that Nietzsche is not saying that the independence of the "free spirit" involves and requires the *rejection* of everything of the sort, turning away from all such previously near and dear things altogether. Rather, his point is that a "free spirit" is one who is no longer in their sway, and to whom they have become problematic—but to whom they nonetheless remain available, even philosophically, as resources and grist for one's mill.

3. FROM "FREE SPIRITS" TO "NEW PHILOSOPHERS"

And with that, Nietzsche in effect concludes his discussion of "the free spirit" and turns, in the remaining three sections of this part (BGE 42–44), to the idea that "a new species of philosophers is coming up," of whom he says that "we free spirits" are the "heralds and precursors." As was noted at the outset, he suggests that these "new philosophers" will be "something more, higher, greater, and fundamentally different [Gründlich-Anderes]" than the philosophical "free spirits" he has been talking about, even though they "also will be free, *very* free spirits" themselves (BGE 44).

There would appear to be considerable overlap in Nietzsche's conceptions of them. So, for example, he begins by suggesting that the "new philosophers" will have similar "intentions and instincts" to those of the kind of "free spirit" he has been discussing. And he further observes that there is much else that may be said and needs to be understood about "us collectively [uns gemeinsam]"—"free-spirited" and "new" philosophers alike. For example, he writes:

> At home, or at least having been guests, in many countries of the spirit; having escaped again and again from the musty agreeable nooks into which preference and prejudice, youth, origin, the accidents of people and books . . . have banished us; full of malice against the lures of dependence . . . ; curious to a vice, investigators to the point of cruelty . . . , ready for every venture, thanks to an excess of "free will" . . . ; inventive in [interpretive] schemes . . . ; friends of *solitude*: that is the type of Menschen that we are, we free spirits! And perhaps you have something of this, too, you that are coming, you *new* philosophers? (BGE 44)

Further, like the free-spirited philosophers he has been discussing, Nietzsche considers it is "probable enough" that "these coming philosophers" will be "new friends of 'truth'"—but that they too "certainly will not be dogmatists," and will not even want "their truth" to be "supposed to be a truth for everyman." (It is worth observing that by "truths" here Nietzsche means "judgments"; and his point is that, as he puts it, they are likely to be the sort of thinker who would say: "'My judgment is *my* judgment'; no one else is easily entitled to it" [BGE 43]).

Yet another thing Nietzsche's "new philosophers" are to have in common with his type of "free spirit" is that, very differently from those who long for and promote "the universal green-pasture happiness of the herd," considering nothing to be more desirable, "We opposite men, having opened our eyes and conscience to the question of where and how the plant 'Mensch' has so far grown most vigorously to a height—we think that this has happened every time under the opposite conditions" (BGE 44). This commonality suggests that the commitment to "historical philosophizing" in partnership with the other cognitive disciplines [Wissenschaften] (HH I 1, 2) and the "naturalizing turn" in the reinterpretation of human reality (GS 109) that Nietzsche calls for in the "free spirit" series—and calls for again later in this book (for example, in BGE 230)—will be characteristic of these "new philosophers" as well.

What then is the difference? This is an interesting and important question—particularly since Nietzsche here (both in this part of the book and in the book more generally) styles himself to be at least for the most part a philosopher of the "free-spirit" sort. He hints at the difference when he first announces that "a new species of philosophers is coming up" and goes on to say that "these philosophers of the future may have a right . . . to be called Versucher"—by which he may mean experimenters, attempters, tempters, or all three at once (BGE 42). But it has already been seen that he conceives of free-spirited philosophers as having something of the "Versucher" about them as well, in the inventiveness and experimental adventuresomeness with which they approach and pursue the tasks of reinterpretation and revaluation. And the final section of this part of the book (BGE 44) ends on a chord of continuity, with only a suggestion that there is to be a difference nonetheless.

It is only later in BGE that Nietzsche reveals more fully what he has in mind. He hints at it again a little more clearly in the next part of the book, "Religiousness," when he envisions philosophers not only free-spirited enough to be liberated from religious modes of interpretation and scruples, and "noble enough to see the abysmally different order of rank, chasm of rank, between man and man," but also "high and hard enough to have the right to try to shape *man* as artists [um *am Menschen* als Künstler gestalten zu dürfen]" (BGE 62). But this is said without elaboration, at the end of the part's concluding section, seeming quite possibly to be little more than a rhetorical flourish. It actually is a promissory note.

It is in part 6 that Nietzsche puts his cards on the table, and redeems this note. This part follows an indication (in part 5, "On the Natural History of Morality [Zur Naturgeschichte der Moral]") of the kind of treatment of the morality of "good and evil" that he considers to be both necessary and sufficient to dispose of it once and for all as an obstacle and open the way to

a "philosophy of the future" that is "beyond" it. Part 6's title is "Wir Gelehr-
ter," commonly but misleadingly translated as "We Scholars," and more
appropriately translated as something like "We Sophisticated Ones."
The topic of this part is what it takes to become and be not just a good
free-spirited philosopher, but the kind of thinker and force Nietzsche now
envisions as a philosopher of the highest sort. "Toward *new philosophers*,"
he writes, addressing himself to "you free spirits"—new philosophers who
would be "spirits strong and original enough to provide the stimuli for opposite valuations" to those that currently prevail, and who thus would be not
only interpreters but also *leaders*: "It is the image of such leaders that *we*
envision," he writes, who would "teach man the future of man as his *will*, as
dependent on a human will," and "prepare great ventures and collective
attempts of cultivation and breeding [Zucht und Züchtung]," and who would
be "hard" and "strong" enough to "endure the weight of such responsibility"
(BGE 203).[5]
    Nietzsche elaborates upon the relation of this type of philosopher in rela-
tion not only to "philosophical laborers" and "wissenschaftlich Menschen
generally," but also other types of thinker including that of the "free spirit,"
when he writes:

> It may be necessary for the education of a genuine philosopher that he himself
> has also once stood on all these steps. . . . Perhaps he himself must have been
> critic and skeptic and dogmatist and historian and also poet and collector and
> traveler and solver of riddles and moralist and visionary and "free spirit" . . . ,
> and must be *able* to see with many different eyes and consciences, from and
> height and into every distance. . . . But all these are merely preconditions of his
> task: this task itself wants something different—it requires [verlangt] that he
> *create values* [*Werthe schaffe*]. (BGE 211)

One might think that we now have the full answer—with respect to the
difference—in hand, even if it may be puzzling what to make of it: Nietzsche's
"new philosophers," above and beyond being "free spirits," are to be "value-
creators." But even this is not yet to say enough. For what he says here is not that
the "task" of the "genuine [new] philosopher" *is* "value-creation," but that that
their task is something further, which "requires" that values be "created." The
nature of the "task" itself is made clearer in the following section, in which he
writes that the genuine philosopher is "*of necessity* a man of tomorrow and the
day after tomorrow," whose "secret" is "to know of a *new* greatness of man
[Grösse des Menschen]," and to be capable of envisioning some "new untrodden
way to his enhancement [Vergrösserung]" (BGE 212). The genuine philosopher's task and responsibility, for Nietzsche, is nothing less than this actual
"enhancement [Vergrösserung]." It is not just to *talk about* the "enhancement of
life" but to *do something about it*—that is: to do something that will actually
contribute to it. (As Marx put it in his Eleventh Thesis on Feuerbach: "Philoso-

phers hitherto have *only interpreted* the world. The point, however, is to *change* it.") And "value-creation" is required of such philosophers because that is what this enhancing creative transformation of human reality involves and requires. Why should this be up to any sort of philosopher at all? Because the ability to "know of a new greatness of man," envision "a new untrodden way to his enhancement [Vergrösserung]," and contribute to its realization through a "value creation" that brings new value to life, is something Nietzsche thinks a kind of creative philosopher is best positioned and equipped to undertake. The future of humanity is at stake; and this undertaking, for Nietzsche, is its best hope—in a world in which humanity is on its own, and is beset by the multitude of dangers and perils that he so vividly describes, not only in these very passages in BGE but also in previous and subsequent writings, from Z to GM to *Antichrist*. In the aftermath of "the death of God" and with "the advent of nihilism," the situation is getting very serious; and if the field is left to the likes of the proselytizers of new forms of asceticism, providers of new forms of narcosis, and proponents of new forms of idolatry (such as the demonic "New Idol" of the state that Zarathustra excoriates) to do the only "value-creating" that gets done to fill the nihilistic void, the outlook for humanity will be grim.

In GM, Nietzsche envisions a "man of the future" who would be both "Antichrist und Antinihilist," a "creative spirit [schöpferische Geist]" who would take the lead in "redeeming us not only from the hitherto reigning ideal but also from that which was bound to grow out of it, the great nausea, the will to nothingness, nihilism" (GM II 24). That "redemption" is to be by way of the "compelling strength" of that "creativity" that enables it to dispense with the need for anything above and beyond the "reality" of this life in this world to anchor it, and so to express itself in—and content itself with—this-worldly value creation. In BGE we see that his prime candidate for this "man of the future" is his heralded "philosopher of the future," who is to show and lead the way in that very manner. One might well want anyone endeavoring to undertake such "leadership" to have all the qualities and virtues of Nietzsche's "free-spirited" philosopher, to keep that activity from going off the rails; but they by themselves would not suffice for it, for they are no recipe for or guarantee of *the kind of creativity* that is required for it—where both the substance and the cultural realization of the values in question are concerned.

I find it far more difficult to share Nietzsche's hopes than I do to share his worries; but I do at least think that some sense can be made of them—and of the idea of what would set his "new philosopher" apart from his (merely) "free-spirited philosopher." I also think that sense can be made of his conception of human "greatness"—in terms of what he calls "wholeness in manifoldness" or "being capable of being as manifold as whole, as ample as full" (BGE 212)—as well as of his idea that its enhancement involves the emergence of new forms of human cultural life (previously "untrodden ways"), which in turn both requires and results in "value creation." And I also will say that I consider the key to understanding them to be the ideas of "sensibilities" and "sensibility formation and transformation," which I believe to be central to Nietzsche's thinking with respect to all of them.[6]

I would further observe that, with uncharacteristic modesty here (even if not in EH), Nietzsche is content in BGE to refer to himself as being among the free-spirited "heralds and precursors" of this "new" type of philosopher, making no mention of the fact that he had spent the previous three years trying his hand at what might well be considered at least an instance and example of the very sort of thing he is talking about in this discussion of what more the "new philosopher" would do than the free-spirited philosopher does.

I refer, of course, to his conception and creation of *Zarathustra*, which he describes in EH as a work that "stands altogether apart," not only from his other writings but also from just about everything else ever written: "My concept of the 'Dionysian' here becomes a *supreme deed* [*höchste That*]; measured against that, all the rest of human activity seems poor and relative." How so? Because he believes it to be the case that, in the figure and account of his Zarathustra—as "one who first *creates* truth, a *world-governing* spirit, a destiny." (EH Books Z 6)—he has given us an example *par excellence* of the kind of value-creative "deed" he is talking about. It is his own attempt to take a crucial, liberating and sensibility-transforming step in the direction of making the new human greatness he envisions *come true*.

Be that as it may: if sense is to be made of what Nietzsche is proposing, it would seem to me that it will involve taking seriously the idea that in the long run the pen at least can be mightier than the sword, or the vicissitudes of what we ordinarily mean by politics. (I might add, however, that, in the larger conception of politics I believe to have been Nietzsche's, the contest of old and new sensibilities and values always has been and always will be ultimately a kind of political one.)[7]

CONCLUSION

Much of what most of us admire and value in Nietzsche's thought and work seems to me to be encompassed in his conception of the kind of "free-spirited" philosophy we find not only in his "free-spirit" series but also resumed in his post-Z writings (BGE, GM and the fifth book of GS in particular). The "philosophy of the future," to which BGE is proclaimed to be a "Prelude," is not something *altogether* different, but rather is that kind of philosophy continued and developed—*and then some*. There may well be a version of the "then some" that is much more modestly conceived than

Nietzsche conceives of it there, and yet in the spirit of what he is talking about, that is humanly and even philosophically coherent enough and important enough to be worth aspiring to. And I am inclined to think that one reason why I and perhaps many of us think he matters as much as he does, as a philosopher and philosophical conscience, is that he not only was as good a free-spirited philosopher as he was but also aspired to that "something more."

NOTES

1. My translation. In my citations I generally follow the Kaufmann, Hollingdale, or Kaufmann and Hollingdale translations, but occasionally modify them when I consider this to be warranted by Nietzsche's German.
2. See Walter Kaufmann's translation of this work, published under the now-standard English-language title *The Gay Science* (New York: Vintage, 1974), 28–30. I have modified Kaufmann's translation slightly.
3. This description anticipates the penultimate section of the new fifth book of GS that he was to publish the next year, entitled "The great health." It reads (in part): "Another ideal runs ahead of us . . . : the ideal of a spirit who plays naively—that is, not deliberately but from overflowing power and abundance—with all that was hitherto called holy, good, untouchable, divine . . . ; the idea of a human-superhuman [menschlich-übermenschlichen] well-being and well-willing [Wohlwollens] that will often appear *inhuman*—for example, when it confronts all earthly seriousness so far . . .—and despite this, it is perhaps only with [this spirit] that *great seriousness* really begins." (GS 382).
4. I develop this interpretation of his naturalism in a companion essay. See Richard Schacht, "Nietzsche's Naturalism," *Journal of Nietzsche Studies* 43(2) (2012): 185–212.
5. The word Nietzsche naturally enough uses here that is translated as "leaders," never imagining what use would come to be made of it, is "Führer." That simply is the German word for "leader" and "leaders," and carried no more baggage in his time than these words carry in English. When we (Germans today included) see "Führer," we think Hitler—and Hitler was indeed a kind of "leader." But the kind of leader he was is a monstrous travesty of the kind of leader Nietzsche is talking about—even if it were to happen to be the case that Hitler imagined otherwise. Indeed, I believe it would be fair to say that Nietzsche would have regarded Hitler as one of the very types of horrendous human possibilities nihilism can spawn, that his type of new philosopher-leader is so desperately needed to try to preclude or oppose, in the "great politics" of cultural contest that he saw coming. Both may be thought of as "value-creators"—which is precisely why it is so important not to leave Hitler's kind unopposed. The point is not that it takes a Hitler to counter a Hitler, but rather that it takes a value-creating "leader" to be able effectively to counter a value-creating "leader" in the arena of cultural contest. One may think Nietzsche was wrong about this; but one should not reject his idea of a kind of "new philosopher" different from the (merely) free-spirited one by assimilating it to a different one that would have appalled him. (It also is of interest in this connection that, later in the same discussion of these "new philosophers" in BGE 203, Nietzsche writes that his "*real* worry," in view of "the necessity of such leaders," is "the frightening danger that they might fail to appear or that they might turn out badly or degenerate.")
6. Again, see my "Nietzsche's Naturalism," 185–212.
7. See my "Nietzschean Politics," in *The Philosopher in the Public Sphere: Essays for Yirmiahu Yovel*, ed. Pini Ifergan (Jerusalem: The Van Leer Jerusalem Institute, Hakibbutz Hameuhad Publishing House, 2011), 53–65.

BIBLIOGRAPHY

Nietzsche, Friedrich. *Beyond Good and Evil.* Translated by Reginald J. Hollingdale. London: Penguin, 2003.

Nietzsche, Friedrich. *Daybreak: Thoughts on the Prejudices of Morality.* Translated by Reginald J. Hollingdale. Edited by Maudemarie Clark and Brian Leiter. Cambridge: Cambridge University Press, 1997.

Nietzsche, Friedrich. *The Gay Science.* Translated by Walter Kaufmann. New York: Vintage, 1974.

Nietzsche, Friedrich. *Human, All Too Human.* Translated by Reginald J. Hollingdale. Cambridge: Cambridge University Press, 1996.

Nietzsche, Friedrich. *On the Genealogy of Morals.* Translated by Walter Kaufmann and R. J. Hollingdale. New York: Vintage Books, 1969.

Nietzsche, Friedrich. *Thus Spoke Zarathustra: A Book for Everyone and Nobody.* Translated by R. J. Hollingdale. Harmondsworth: Penguin, 1969.

Nietzsche, Friedrich. *Untimely Meditations.* Translated by R. J. Hollingdale. Edited by Daniel Breazeale. Cambridge: Cambridge University Press, 1997.

Schacht, Richard. "Nietzschean Politics." In *The Philosopher in the Public Sphere: Essays for Yirmiahu Yovel,* edited by Pini Ifergan. 53–65. Jerusalem: The Van Leer Jerusalem Institute, Hakibbutz Hameuhad Publishing House, 2011.

Schacht, Richard. "Nietzsche's Naturalism." *Journal of Nietzsche Studies* 43(2) (2012): 185–212.

Chapter Ten

Being Unattached

Freedom and Nietzsche's Free Spirits[1]

Christa Davis Acampora

Unsurprisingly, one finds multiple senses of freedom associated with the *freedom* of the free spirit in Nietzsche's texts. Nietzsche attributes both positive and negative senses of freedom to the free spirits in his works. That is, when describing how free spirits are *free*, Nietzsche sometimes characterizes this as *freedom to* do something (positive), and sometimes as *freedom from* certain kinds of constraints (negative). This chapter surveys a few of these senses and suggests how they add dimensions to Nietzsche's broader views about freedom and agency. One, in particular, revolves around the nature of the lack of attachment [Unabhängigkeit] that characterizes free spirits. As Nietzsche appears to develop the idea, being unattached is not simply being *free from* others. It is not a matter of being radically unbound. Ideally, it includes being *enabled* in a certain way, that is, to be *free to* form significant relations with others. Put another way, the kind of relative lack of attachment that Nietzsche links with free spirits allows one to maximize attachments. Again, this sense is not the only one Nietzsche associates with the kind of freedom free spirits enjoy, but it is an important one and somewhat neglected in the current literature on Nietzsche. Developing this idea, we can see that an available strand of Nietzsche's thinking includes a vision of free spirits as more than rugged individuals or members of an exclusive community of likeminded fellows. Nietzsche's ideal—if it is appropriate to refer to the notion in such terms—entails a certain capacity that he thinks is psychically and socially enabling. Thus, this sense of freedom is critically important in his positive philosophy.

I. WHAT ARE FREE SPIRITS *FREE FROM?* — NEGATIVE FREEDOM

One of the most obvious senses of freedom of the free spirit—which is perhaps the one that at least some people think of as the primary (or even exclusive) sense in which free spirits are free—is cast in terms of being *free from* certain claims of society, particularly those regarded as customary and binding (e.g., HH 225, 230; D 9, 29). As Nietzsche begins to develop the notion of the free spirit in those works designated as part of a series on the free spirit, he carefully works through how customs claim—as well as make possible—individuals (e.g., HH 261). This binding force is exploited by morality, which has a variety of tactics for shaping and molding both the psychic and physical forms of human existence (cf. HH 231). In this respect, morality makes a particular kind of common life possible while it establishes terms for distinction that make one recognizable as an individual, either through exceptional realization of the positively esteemed way of life or by virtue of one standing out from it.

At times, the freedom of the free spirit appears to be at least partially constituted by his or her ability to loosen, if not escape, these bonds. (From the start, I would like to point out that free spirits need not be actual persons or even a type of person. It is also possible to conceive them as spiritual forms that can be realized at various times and to various degrees, a point I shall emphasize and elaborate later in the chapter.) Nietzsche sometimes talks about this feature as a step, sometimes as an initial or at least early stage in a developmental process of becoming a free spirit,[2] and later he designates some as free, very free spirits. Free spirits are contrasted in Nietzsche's texts and in the scholarly literature with various kinds of so-called fettered spirits (e.g., HH 226–228).[3] The free spirits are envisioned by Nietzsche as not *bound* to the morality of custom, convention, superstition, or even morality itself and the habits of thinking (or not thinking) and valuing that characterize such views. Free spirits are, minimally, free of *this*. In short, they have a certain kind of independence that fettered spirits lack.

One form of such independence that Nietzsche repeatedly emphasizes is independence or freedom from association: solitude, being able to withstand a lack of human companionship. Time and again, solitude is described in a sense that suggests that at least one of the ways Nietzsche conceives it is in terms of being free *from* the demands of others, being free from obligations, associations, and their influences. So, it would seem that we have in this notion yet another negative sense of freedom.[4]

This is particularly evident in *Beyond Good and Evil* in the final section of part 2, titled "The Free Spirit [Der Freie Geist]":

> At home, or at least having been guests, in many countries of the spirit; having
> escaped again and again from the musty agreeable nooks into which prefer-

ence and prejudice, youth, origin, the accidents of people and books or even exhaustion from wandering seemed to have banished us; full of malice against the lures of dependence that lie hidden in honors, or money, or offices, or enthusiasms of the senses; . . . we are born, sworn, jealous friends of *solitude*, of our own most profound, most midnightly, most middaily solitude: that is the type of man we are, we free spirits! (BGE 44)

And further, in *GM* I 7, where Nietzsche writes:

Every philosopher would speak as Buddha did when he was told of the birth of a son: "Rahula has been born to me, a fetter has been forged for me" (Rahula here means "a little demon"); every "free spirit" would experience a thoughtful moment, supposing he had previously experienced a thoughtless one, of the kind that once came to the same Buddha—"narrow and oppressive," he thought to himself, "is life in a house, a place of impurity; freedom lies in leaving the house": "thinking thus, he left the house."[5]

This is obviously not the only purpose or benefit of solitude as Nietzsche sees it, and it is a topic that warrants its own discussion, but it is clearly an evident strand in Nietzsche's thinking about the respect in which the free spirit is free. Free spirits to some extent appear to be negatively free of others, communally and individually.

If we look at how Nietzsche compares and contrasts free spirits with fettered ones, as Bernard Reginster does in his article on Nietzsche and fanaticism,[6] then we see that the free spirits are also free from a certain kind of relationship to truth. To be sure, they care very much about the truth, and this motivates what they question and how. But they have a somewhat differ ent relation to truth. This suggests, if the analysis holds, that free spirits are free in ways that might differ from their free-thinking Enlightenment counterparts. For they, too, certainly prized truth and also might be thought to value "thinking for oneself" in ways that, on the face of it, would appear congenial to Nietzsche's views, but Nietzsche is quite clear that his free spirits are distinctive. We see this very clearly in BGE 25, where Nietzsche points to Bruno, and by implication to Nietzsche's own contemporary free thinkers who idealize him as their forefather.

The example is puzzling and instructive. Bruno (1548–1600) is the sort of figure who we might imagine would have appealed to Nietzsche. Bruno was martyred for his support of the ideas of Copernicus. He was shunned from nearly every academic community on account of his opposition to Aristotle; he advanced the view that the world was eternal and ever changing, and he anticipated a theory of relativity in his arguments against Aristotle's notions of opposites: "There is no absolute up or down, as Aristotle taught; no abso-lute position in space; but the position of a body is relative to that of other bodies. Everywhere there is incessant relative change in position throughout the universe, and the observer is always at the center of things."[7] In a play he wrote, which evokes themes of satyr plays, Bruno features the "ass of Cyllene," which skewers superstition. The "ass" is everywhere, not only in the church at the time of the ass festival (and at other times) but also in all other public institutions, including the courts and the schools.[8] Bruno was a skeptic, particularly about theological matters where scientific reasoning offered evidence that contradicts matters of faith, and he was an advocate of free thought.

Bruno achieves freedom *from* many things, even at a great cost, and he would be a good model for a free spirit. Indeed, he was—but *not* the sort that Nietzsche appears to advocate. Bruno was an icon for the "free thinkers" [Freiedenken] movement, with which Nietzsche explicitly contrasts his free spirits in BGE 44.[9] At least part of Nietzsche's opposition to his contemporary free thinkers, particularly those who take Bruno as an icon, focuses on the fact that martyrs to truth evince a kind of unconditionality that ultimately imprisons, fetters—perhaps with even more grave consequences than those who otherwise shirk Enlightenment ideals. Truth at any price—even when used to oppose superstition and the Christianized worldview—might be thought to replace one god with another. It seems clear that Nietzsche thinks his own free spirits are also free from this, or they at least strive to be such— they are oriented toward a kind of *freedom from unconditionality*, including—perhaps especially—with respect to their valuation of truth.

There are two features of this idea of freedom-from-unconditionality that I wish to underscore in characterizing the freedom of the free spirit. Negatively, the free spirit is detached from a particular commitment to truth—in advance of and even in the face of some reasons to believe otherwise. The free spirit is free from *compromising* commitment. But there is still more to be done in order to clarify just what it is that might be compromised in the absence of such independence, something to which I return below when examining some of the positive senses in which free spirits are free. In addition to being free from such commitment, Nietzsche's free spirit is free from a certain kind of accompanying feeling—namely, one linked with a need to produce the feeling of power in this unusual way, even to the point of extinction as those who are martyred for it. Reginster argues for this view: figures Nietzsche regards as fettered spirits (particularly the so-called free spirits Nietzsche anticipates replacing) draw a sense of their own power from their subjection to the immensely binding force of unconditional commitment. By tying themselves to the unconditional valuation of truth, they gather a sense of themselves as joining or being a part of such manifestations of power. Yet another characterization of a negative sense of freedom for the free spirits is that they are *free from* this particular need, to produce the feeling of power (which Nietzsche thinks all beings seek) in this particular way (compare HH 635 and D 542).

At the same time that this condition might be thought of as liberating, it presents us as readers of Nietzsche with an interpretative challenge. Since all beings strive for and take pleasure in the feeling of power, it remains to be seen how Nietzsche's free spirits actually pursue and experience this feeling if not through binding themselves to unconditional commitments. Moreover, we should consider whether the alternative bears any structural resemblance to that associated with the fettered or 'so-called' free spirits. Put more simply, and Reginster does not explore this, we can inquire whether the relation between freedom and unfreedom that characterizes the experience of power for the so-called free spirit is structurally similar in the case of Nietzsche's free spirit. The particular kind of fettered spirit we are considering in this case unconditionally binds himself to truth, and in so doing (by becoming bound) he realizes and finds his freedom, or at least an indicator of his freedom. Is Nietzsche's free spirit simply unbound in a way that the so-called free spirit is not? All of these ways in which the free spirit is *free from*—the ways in which the free spirit has freedom in a negative sense—might appear to suggest as much, but there are positive senses of freedom that the free spirit realizes or to which it aspires. After introducing them, I will suggest that these perhaps similarly require certain kinds of binding as well.

II. POSITIVE SENSES OF FREEDOM FOR FREE SPIRITS

In the discussion of negative freedom of free spirits, I underscored their independence, a feature Nietzsche repeatedly emphasizes, and I explored some of the things in relation to which the free spirit is independent. I now wish to look more closely at a key passage in which Nietzsche describes this feature of free spirits to inquire precisely about just what it is from which the free spirits are free. Looking for this source negatively also provides some clues about the positive sense. Here too, Nietzsche's conception of independence gains some complexity and subtlety that require more reflection than what is sometimes found in the secondary literature. The passage is BGE 41, still in part 2, "The Free Spirit," where Nietzsche writes:

> One has to test oneself to see that one is destined for independence and command—and do it at the right time. One should not dodge one's tests, though they may be the most dangerous game one could play and are tests that are taken in the end before no witness or judge but ourselves.

There are many questions that arise here, but I want to focus on the term translated as "independence": Unabhängigkeit.[10] Literally, this is a state or condition of being unattached. But simply *unattached* might suggest something a bit too casual. I think a stronger translation in the English is warranted, and this stronger sense facilitates a somewhat different understanding of the *kind* of independence Nietzsche is talking about here. Auf Deutsch, Abhängigkeit is the term used for dependence so it is clear how Unabhängigkeit yields an appropriate translation as 'independence.' The 'un' negates the 'dependence'. Unabhängigkeit is a negative condition: to be *not* in a state of dependence. While Abhängigkeit can be used to talk about dependence in a positive sense of cooperation, is it also used to describe another specific kind of dependence that was becoming an object of increasingly intense scrutiny both culturally and biologically in Nietzsche's day, namely, the kind of dependence found in contexts of *addiction*. I think a stronger sense akin (if not a direct reference) to the connotations associated with the immensely powerful pull that addiction commands is appropriate to the context of Nietzsche's concern. The fettered spirits are addicted to what binds them.

In BGE, Nietzsche links independence, when attempted by those who are unprepared for it, with the story of Theseus and the Minotaur, a theme that is echoed at the end of the book.[11] In BGE 29, Nietzsche writes:

> Independence is for the very few; it is a privilege of the strong. And whoever attempts it even with the best right but without inner constraint proves that it is probably not only strong, but also daring to the point of recklessness. He enters a labyrinth, he multiplies a thousandfold the dangers which life brings with it in any case, not the least of which is that no one can see how and where he loses his way, becomes lonely, and is torn piecemeal by some minotaur of conscience. Supposing one like that comes to grief, this happens so far from the comprehension of men that they neither feel it nor sympathize. And he cannot go back any longer. Nor can he go back to the pity of men.—

The German in this case is "Unabhängig zu sein," to be unattached. And this passage is also related to the earlier concern about solitude, only here Nietzsche underscores just how difficult it can be to tolerate such detachment. Clearly, he has in mind something more extreme than simply nonreliance or lack of cooperation in using this term. This condition is dissociative, but it is dissociative from a state of reliance or addiction on substances that themselves induce states of dissociation. Furthermore, insofar as the root "abhang" means hang below, "unabhang" could playfully suggest a certain sort of defiance of gravity. This is an image invoked by Nietzsche in his emphasis on dancing as well as flying like a bird as in "The Songs of Prince Vogelfrei," the appendix to *The Gay Science*, and it is at the core of Nietzsche's therapy for combatting what he calls "the spirit of gravity" in GS (especially sections 380 and 382) and *Thus Spoke Zarathustra*, as mentioned below.[12] All told, independence, for Nietzsche, appears to be much more complex and potentially more significant than it might appear at first glance.

Nietzsche provides greater focus and specificity about his intended meaning when he returns to some related ideas later in the final section (44) of

"The Free Spirit" in BGE. In this case, Nietzsche associates free, *very free* spirits with the philosophers of the future. That is, it would appear that the philosophers of the future are free spirits, but not all free spirits are philosophers of the future. Put another way, philosophers of the future partake of a kind of free spirituality, a kind that differs from the religious existence he describes in the part that follows "The Free Spirit."

In the section linking free spirituality with the philosophers of the future, Nietzsche directly states that he wants to be as clear as possible about the nature of the free spirits so as to avoid misunderstanding and confusing them with other varieties of free spirit advocated by those free thinkers [Freidenker] and the like, mentioned above, those whom Nietzsche describes as "*levelers*"; they are:

> all human beings without solitude [Einsamkeit], without their own solitude [eigne Einsamkeit], clumsy good fellows whom one should not deny either courage or respectable decency—only they are unfree [unfrei] and ridiculously superficial [zum Lachen oberflächlich sind], above all in their basic inclination to find in the forms of the old society as it has existed so far just about the cause of *all* human misery and failure—which is a way of standing truth happily upon her head! What they would like to strive for with all their powers is the universal green-pasture happiness of the herd, with security, lack of danger, comfort, and an easier life for everyone; the two songs and doctrines which they repeat most often are "equality of rights" and "sympathy for all that suffers"—and suffering itself they take for something that must be *abolished*. (BGE 44)

By contrast, those whom Nietzsche sees as truly *free* regard that which opposes the goals of the free thinker [Freidenker], the opposite conditions of security, safety, comfort, and ease, as conditions for growth, even flourishing: "prolonged pressure and constraint" facilitate growth, development, and the gathering of strength and vigor. Famously—and *infamously*—Nietzsche claims certain forms of *unfreedom* condition the opposite spirit: "We think that hardness, forcefulness, slavery, danger in the alley and the heart, life in hiding, stoicism, the art of experiment and devilry of every kind, that everything evil, terrible, tyrannical in man, everything in him that is kin to beasts of prey and serpents serves the enhancement of the species 'man' as much as its opposite does" (BGE 44). I will suggest below how we can see this as potentially contributing to the positive sense of freedom Nietzsche's free spirits realize and how this is related to what the free spirits are ultimately, *possibly*, able to do, but before I get to that point, I wish to take notice of a few things.

Nietzsche is *not* saying that "hardness, forcefulness, slavery," and the like are *more* life-enhancing than their opposite—rather, he claims they are enhancing *at least as much* as their opposites. This is to some extent an acknowledgment and justification (in the sense of recognition of what Nietzsche elsewhere affirms as the *innocence of becoming*) of the fullness of life, an affirmation or love of all that is, rather than just the particular aspects we especially esteem or to which we aspire at any particular moment. This, I suggest later on in the chapter, is an important affective orientation for the free spirit to take. It will play a crucial role in making it possible for Nietzsche's free spirits' detachment to not ultimately undermine them.[13]

Returning to the matter of how unfreedom, more specifically, might be necessary for or potentially in the service of freedom, we should certainly try to gain greater clarity about the matter of *whose unfreedom* serves freedom and in what respect.[14] A possible interpretation, one not unfamiliar in the critical literature on Nietzsche and not without justification, is that Nietzsche might regard it as necessary for *some* to be unfree in order for *others* to be free. In such a case, the unfree are sacrificed for the benefit or advantage of the freedom of those (presumably few) others who will reap the greatest benefits of the forced labor and limited opportunities of those who are enslaved. Others are simply the means to serve the end of the production of rare type who achieves unprecedented freedom. There are a good number of other passages where Nietzsche makes reference to conditions of servitude and subjection of this sort, supporting an interpretation of just this sort (e.g., philosophers are described as exercising a "selective and cultivating influence" placing others "under their spell" [BGE 61]), so I am not categorically denying that such features are apparent in Nietzsche's complicated views on freedom. But it is also the case that part of what Nietzsche seems to think is that *unfreedom conditions a certain kind of freedom* in the very same individuals—it is somehow important that those who would be free, perhaps especially those who would be very free, must somehow first (or perhaps in some respects simultaneously) be unfree, that, minimally, as suggested in BGE 29, cited above, they have an *inner constraint*. To round off discussion of this dimension of Nietzsche's views, I wish to focus on precisely this relation between freedom and unfreedom, which will bring us back to further exploration of what constitutes dependence [Abhängigkeit], of the sort from which the free spirits are free. Section 41 of BGE continues and concludes with the following:

Not to remain stuck to a person—not even the most loved—every person is a prison, also a nook. Not to remain stuck to a fatherland—not even when it suffers most and needs help most—it is less difficult to sever one's heart from a victorious fatherland. Not to remain stuck to some pity—not even for higher men into whose rare torture and helplessness some accident allowed us to look. Not to remain stuck to a science—even if it should lure us with the most precious finds that seem to have been saved up precisely for us. Not to remain stuck to one's own detachment, to that voluptuous remoteness and strangeness of the bird who flees ever higher to see ever more below him—the danger of the flier. Not to remain stuck to our own virtues and become as a whole the victim of some detail in us, such as our hospitality, which is the danger of dangers for superior and rich souls who spend themselves lavishly, almost indifferently, and exaggerate the virtue of generosity into a vice. One must know how *to conserve oneself:* the hardest test of independence.

In this case, dependence is defined not merely in terms of consorting with others, and so on, but rather in terms of "remaining stuck," becoming *dependent*: "Not to remain stuck to a person—not even the most loved"; "Not to remain stuck to a fatherland." Nietzsche does not say, "Don't love, don't bother thinking about or becoming involved with a fatherland." Instead, he says that one who is independent in the way that free spirits are described just a few sections further on in BGE 44, avoids the lures of dependence.

Is it any wonder that we "free spirits" are not exactly the most communicative spirits? that we do not want to betray in every particular *from what* a spirit can liberate himself and *to what* he may then be driven? And as for the meaning of the dangerous formula "beyond good and evil," with which we at least guard against being mistaken for others: we *are* something different from *"libres-penseurs," "liberi pensatori," "Freidenker,"* and whatever else all these good-ly advocates of "modern ideas" like to call themselves.

At home, or at least having been guests, in many countries of the spirit; having escaped again and again from the musty agreeable nooks into which preference and prejudice, youth, origin, the accidents of people and books or even exhaustion from wandering seemed to have banished us; full of malice against the lures of dependence that lie hidden in honors, or money, or offices, or enthusiasms of the senses.

Free of those sorts of attachments, one can then cultivate attachments for other things to the point of gratitude:

grateful even to need and vacillating sickness because they always rid us from some rule and its "prejudice," grateful to god, devil, sheep, and worm in us.

Detached from the lures and preoccupations described above, one can form interests in other things, explore them:

curious to a vice, investigators to the point of cruelty, with uninhibited fingers for the unfathomable, with teeth and stomachs for the most indigestible, ready for every feat that requires a sense of acuteness and acute senses, ready for every venture.

Free spirits are not simply negatively free; they do not lack forms of attachment. Rather, the key point is that *they avoid remaining stuck* to such bonds—even, as Nietzsche writes, *to their notion of themselves as being detached*. So, it is critically important to understand this key distinction and the advantage Nietzsche thinks it affords. Attachments in themselves are not the problem; remaining stuck in any one or particular set of attachments is what Nietzsche finds so limiting. And the reason for this is that once stuck, one misses opportunities for further growth and development; one's capacities are diminished. I have derived this from analysis of Nietzsche's relatively later work, BGE, but the ideas are also evident, though they are somewhat less developed in a sustained way, in earlier writings (see, for example, *Dawn* 205–207).

We can now more fully examine the advantages of being *unstuck*. Nietzsche's reasoning here focuses on the opportunities for development that this affords: being unstuck does not mean being disconnected and isolated. In a condition, awkwardly described here in English for the purposes of this closer analysis as "being *unstuck*"—*Unabhängigkeit*—one is able to form other attachments so that *one is enabled* to expand the range of possible associations rather than limit it. Moreover, because of the way in which they hold their attachments, in contrast with the fettered spirits who are addicted to their attachments, free spirits, at least as described here, appear to be able to *love* in ways that a more narrow partiality might not allow. They enjoy "the greatest experience of human society" (D 205), avoid "inertia of spirit" (HH 637), and are better prepared for a new *form* of love, namely, what Nietzsche associates with a love of life (GS Preface to the Second Edition 3). If we recognize these considerations as related (being unstuck makes one available for, being open for, even more attachments of a different sort), then this provides opportunities to appreciate a distinctively affirmative dimension of Nietzsche's sense of independence and how it potentially positively, rather than negatively, impacts our relations with others.

Frequently in Nietzsche's texts, free spirits are described in terms of being great travelers: they associate with many different and *many different kinds of* people. This appears to be one of the ways in which they negatively avoid remaining stuck, but I think this same characteristic also positively contributes to who and what they are and what they are able to do. Nietzsche thinks they are "restlessly alive" through this "continual change" (HH 637). In these very same associations, part of what the free spirit is able to do by loosening himself from just one or several chains, is form many more associations, develop more and more of his own resources, "spiritual resources" (D 205). In being free from the limitations of the fettered spirit, free spirits are *free to become something more*. But, obviously, it is not sheer multiplicity that Nietzsche admires. Rather, he appears to think of this capacity in terms of a kind of fullness and amplitude, a bounty. I shall return to this topic below, but before doing so, I note that one of the ways in which the free spirit *cannot* be free—because no one can be—is in the sense of having a free will, realizing the classic notion of free will.

Of course, there is no single "classic notion of free will," rather there are classical notions of free will, virtually all of which Nietzsche appears to reject. Nietzsche repeatedly and consistently rails against this view, offering as an alternative a drive psychology that explains the *experience* and *feeling of willing* as a particular perspective of a drive or set of drives in relation to the others, that is, the perspective of the commanding drive or drives that constitute us. Part of the reason why free will in this sense is not possible, Nietzsche thinks, is that he does not think there is any such thing as a will that somehow is in a relationship with other parts of the soul such that it can command. There is no separate ego or *I* behind our actions, willing or directing in the background. We are organizations of drives, and there are varieties of ways in which such organizations take shape and are maintained.[15]

Free spirits, by virtue of the extraordinary associations that their independence facilitates, have a greater, more expansive set of resources enlivened, activated, and ready for recruitment in the organizations they are. If this is a reasonable interpretation, then we might reconsider the various ways in which free spirits, so conceived, are enabled to become and can be said to be *free* (or not). In this respect, the freedom of the free spirit is realized in the relationship of its own constitutive parts or features rather than strictly with respect to other organizations or its political or social situation.

III. CHALLENGING FREEDOM:
THE DIFFICULTY OF FREEDOM FOR THE FREE SPIRITS

Of course, the interpretation offered here does not resolve all troubling and vexing features of Nietzsche's philosophy; moreover, it opens new problems and challenges. For example, how does loosening attachment and amplifying available drives lead to strength rather than disintegration and chaos? That free spirits, so conceived, would be at risk for precisely this condition appears to be anticipated in Nietzsche's association of independence with the Minotaur in the passage from BGE cited above. And it raises the question of how free spirits capitalize on the variety they acquire through their increased associations so that they can be said to be *enabled* by these resources rather than overwhelmed and ruined by them.

One of the dangers associated with enlivening more of the drives and expanding their capacities by virtue of amplifying or increasing one's associations is that it may result in a situation more likely to produce conflict. Homogeneity would seem more conducive to psychic harmony, and such stability would seem to be important for the organization of drives and their recruitment for action, a recurrent theme in the history of moral psychology. The fettered soul has a dominant drive that whips into submission all of the others: the drive for unconditional truth maintains its rule in the fettered spirit by subjugating the other drives. In this situation, as the Platonic Socrates so keenly observes of the tyrant in the *Republic*, the ruling power must always guard against losing its dominance; indeed the project of maintaining power must take precedence over any other. Such a situation is ultimately disabling because one quickly becomes unable to organize for any purpose other than this. It is hard to describe such persons as actually free, even if they have the semblance of tremendous power over others. Such powers might have a certain kind of order, but there is very much in them that would seem to be unfree.

The free spirit, on the other hand, becomes an expansive multiplicity of drives,[16] and this potentially creates and nourishes more contenders for dominance in the soul. The free spirit, perhaps more than any type among Nietzsche's figures, faces certain risks, including a lack of order that would diminish rather than strengthen it. The challenge of the free spirit is to actively recruit the drives and their cooperation so that it can be free in another respect, namely, *free from* certain kinds of disabling conflicts among the drives as well as *freely enabled* and fit enough to realize the kind of activity described above. Although Nietzsche clearly articulates the need for unity in the form of "giving style to one's character" (GS 290) and even suggests how one might "combat the intensity of drives" (D 109), he does not provide us with a sufficiently robust account of how such unification might come about, or how it might work out the way he envisions for those who are not only free but also orderly, given style, strong.

Nietzsche himself at times appears to wonder how such unification, another kind of binding, is possible. In GS, in a passage titled "The Wanderer Speaks," which refers back to a figure featured in the title to one of the parts of *Human, All Too Human*, Nietzsche writes:

> That one *wants* to go precisely out there, up there, may be a minor madness, a peculiar and unreasonable "you must"—for we seekers for knowledge also have our idiosyncrasies of "unfree will"—the question is whether one really *can* get up there. This may depend on manifold conditions. In the main the question is how light or heavy we are—the problem of our "specific gravity." One must have liberated oneself [Man muss sich von Vielem losgebunden haben] from many things that oppress, inhibit, hold down, and make heavy precisely us Europeans today. (GS 380)

Whether it is possible to achieve the kind of loosening of attachment, the *levity* that would be required to achieve the perspective he anticipates, is surely not guaranteed, and there are certain cultural conditions and inheritances, leaving us with opposing tendencies, that would seem to be in tension with this, rendering modern Europeans more susceptible to the forces of (psychic) gravity, so to speak. About this, Nietzsche continues:

The human being of such a beyond who wants to behold the supreme measures of value of his time must first of all "overcome" this time in himself—this is the test of his strength—and consequently not only his time but also his prior aversion and contradiction *against* this time, his suffering from this time, his untimeliness, his *romanticism*. (GS 380)

In this, I think we see ideas similar to the subtle distinctions Nietzsche makes between those free spirits who try to measure their freedom by their relation to the conventional views of their own time and thereby distinguish themselves reactively, and those who also loosen their attachment to their own opposition, those who hold even the oppositional stance *lightly*.

While accounts of Nietzsche that emphasize the cultivation of the self are attractive[17]—both in terms of their anticipated shapely products as well as how they tidy up some philosophical problems—I am not fully satisfied with this response to the puzzle of how one might achieve unity from out of the incredible diversity that Nietzsche anticipates, which he speculates is both the *problem* and the *solution* to modern existence.[18] Neither am I comfortable with going along with solving the problems another way by elaborating the transcendental conditions of agency and the "non-formal, 'qualititative' or substantive commitments necessary for freedom," in large part because I think there is simply insurmountable evidence that Nietzsche does not have a normative ideal for what *we* (rather than *he*) might call "full personhood."[19] Nietzsche's views about the self, setting aside his artful references to spirit and soul, suggest that there is no core subject, no *one* capable of the cultivation, no entity with sufficient independence to be the "artist" of our lives, and certainly no one distinct from the organization one already is.[20]

Yet another solution might be sought in the role that education, self-education, and the cultivation of taste might play in shaping, organizing, and coordinating the multifarious drives that we are.[21] And there are certainly passages to be found in Nietzsche's works that demonstrate he gave serious consideration to such views (e.g., HH II AOM Preface: 2; TI Skirmishes 47), and this seems evident in Nietzsche's own account of himself and how he overcame the influence of Wagner in his life and thought. But, ultimately, I think Nietzsche rather doubted that this was the definite and secure path to achieving psychic well-being. His ambivalence is expressed in D 119, in which he begins with the idea that self-knowledge about our constitutive elements or drives and their "nutrition," how they themselves are fed and the ways in which they nourish, is really unknown, and seemingly unknowable:

Experience and make-believe.—No matter how hard a person struggles for self-knowledge, nothing can be more incomplete than the image of all the drives taken together that constitute his being. Scarcely can he call the cruder ones by name: their number and strength, their ebb and flow, their play and counterplay, and, above all, the laws of their *alimentation* [*Ernährung*] remain completely unknown to him.[22]

The overall nutrition of the entity itself that they constitute appears to be the result of chance rather than deliberate cultivation. Nietzsche continues:

> This alimentation thus becomes the work of chance [Zufalls]: our daily experiences toss willy-nilly to this drive or that drive some prey or other that it seizes greedily, but the whole coming and going of these events exists completely apart from any meaningful connection to the alimentary needs of the sum drives: so that the result will always be twofold: the starving and stunting of some drives and the overstuffing of others. With every moment of our lives some of the polyp-arms of our being grow and others dry up, depending on the nourishment that the moment does or does not supply.[23]

Associations, indeed, shape us; they affect the intensity of drives and their relations to others (see HH II AOM Preface: 5). But any choosing of associations will be done by and in accordance with the preferences of the drives that happen to be on top. In short, while human growth, change, and development are surely possible, planning it (much less *orchestrating* it) appears to be difficult if not impossible. It would seem there can be no micromanaging one's soul in this way because all "management" of this kind will always and only be the work of whatever drive or set of drives happen to be dominant from the start.

In understanding Nietzsche's conception of the independence of the free spirit, discussed above, I think we have some suggestions for how some forms of direction *might* be possible. I underscore *might* because, whatever may be the case, it is certainly true that there are no guarantees here, no recipes or blueprints to follow in becoming what one is. However, loosening the self for attachments, cultivating the variety of resources available would seem to make it at least *possible* that a different political or social structure for the soul might be in the offing. This much is suggested in the added preface to HH II AOM Preface 5,[24] where Nietzsche writes:

> Just as a physician places his patient in a wholly strange environment so that he may be removed from his entire "hitherto", from his cares, friends, letters, duties, stupidities and torments of memory and learn to reach out his hands and senses to new nourishment, a new sun, a new future, so I, as physician and patient in one, compelled myself to an opposite and unexplored *clime of the soul*, and especially to a curative journey into strange parts, into *strangeness* itself, to an inquisitiveness regarding every kind of strange thing. . . . A protracted wandering around, seeking, changing followed from this, a repugnance towards all staying still, towards every blunt affirmation and denial; likewise a dietetic and discipline designed to make it as easy as possible for the spirit to run long distances, to fly to great heights, above all again and again to fly away. A *minimum* of life, in fact, and unchaining from all coarser desires,

an independence in the midst of all kinds of unfavorable outward circumstances together with pride in being *able* to live surrounded by these unfavorable circumstances; a certain amount of cynicism, perhaps, a certain amount of "barrel", but just as surely a great deal of capricious happiness, capricious cheerfulness, a great deal of stillness, light, subtler folly, concealed enthusiasm—all this finally resulted in a great spiritual strengthening, an increasing joy and abundance of health.

This suggests that change: it suggests one is more than a token of a type, weak or strong. But, of course, the outcome here is uncertain, and there are many possibilities that emerge, including tyranny, chaos, and perhaps virtually anything in between.[25] Such risk might be inevitable and unavoidable; it might be what is required, what must be tolerated in, perhaps even loved about, the kind of experimentalism that the free spirits are supposed to exercise, the dancing they are supposed to engage in. (And not only dancing but also "rising, climbing, flying [steigen, klettern, fliegen]," all of which aim to overcome or not be subject to the pull of gravity, to hang below [abhang].) Experiments can be planned to greater and lesser degrees, and they are virtually always guided by what we already know and already value, or at least they are not wholly independent of such. Moreover, it is possible to lose ourselves within them.[26] I am uncertain how one plans to manage the inherent riskiness of this responsibly. Nietzsche provides no definite plan or direction, perhaps because any such guidance might amount to little more than wishful thinking: much as it might be desired, it might not be available. But such risk might nevertheless be *necessary*, and the resultant splendor that such risk taking potentially yields might be better described as product of chance rather than deliberate calculation or determined cultivation. If this is so, then we might say that the free spirit is free in yet one more sense—cosmically free, a piece of fate and chance, care free, and a "free throw" of the dice.[27]

NOTES

1. An earlier version of this material was published as "Senses of Freedom of the Free Spirit" in *Pli: Warwick Journal of Philosophy* 25 (2014): 13–33. I am grateful to audiences who provided suggestions and critical feedback as I developed these ideas. I especially thank those at Warwick University, Stony Brook University, and the Nietzsche Assos conference.
2. For a developmental account of the free spirit, particularly in relation to Nietzsche's views about science and culture, see Jonathan Cohen, *Science, Culture, and Free Spirits: A Study of Nietzsche's "Human, All Too Human"* (New York: Humanity Books, 2009). Amy Mullin also argues for a process of development that admits of various degrees of realization of the ideal she thinks Nietzsche advocates. See her "Nietzsche's Free Spirit," *Journal of the History of Philosophy* 38(3) (July 2000): 383–405.
3. I cite the following translations of Nietzsche's works: *Human, All Too Human: A Book for Free Spirits*, trans. R. J. Hollingdale (Cambridge: Cambridge University Press, 1986); *Daybreak*, trans. R. J. Hollingdale (Cambridge: Cambridge University Press, 1982); *Dawn: Thoughts on the Presumptions of Morality*, trans. Brittain Smith (Stanford: Stanford University

Press, 2011); *The Gay Science*, trans. Walter Kaufmann (New York: Vintage Books, 1974); *Beyond Good and Evil*, trans. Walter Kaufmann (New York: Vintage Books, 1966); *On the Genealogy of Morals*, in *On the Genealogy of Morals/Ecce Homo*, trans. Walter Kaufmann and R. J. Hollingdale (New York: Vintage Books, 1967).

4. Mullin emphasizes the solitude of the free spirit in her "Nietzsche's Free Spirit," 396f, without further recognizing the kinds of relationships Nietzsche also imagines for free spirits (and why).

5. It is not hard to find other passages in which it appears that Nietzsche is keen to emphasize that freedom for free spirits entails freedom from domestic obligations of various sorts. See, for example, HH 426, 429, and 433, although anyone interested in this particular feature of Nietzsche's philosophy should review such passages in their broader context. In the case of the examples just cited, the epigraphs appear in a section (7) with the title "Woman and Child." Both their style and content resemble a group of epigraphs that appear in part 7 of BGE, beginning with the heading "Seven Epigrams on Woman."

6. Bernard Reginster, "What Is a Free Spirit? Nietzsche on Fanaticism" in *Archiv für Geschichte der Philosophie* 85(1) (2003): 51–85.

7. Cited in Jennifer Michael Hecht, *Doubt: A History* (New York: HarperCollins, 2003), 294.

8. For a more extended discussion of the "ass" figure in Nietzsche and as it relates to these themes, see Kathleen Marie Higgins, "Nietzsche and the Mystery of the Ass," in *A Nietzschean Bestiary: Becoming Animal Beyond Docile and Brutal*, ed. Christa Davis Acampora and Ralph R. Acampora (New York: Rowman & Littlefield, 2004), 100–119.

9. Some context related to the composition of the text is helpful. Nietzsche finished *Beyond Good and Evil* in early summer 1885. During the period when he was writing the text, he spent time in Venice, a home of Bruno. While Nietzsche was in Venice, a group of notable figures formed an international committee to erect a monument to Bruno on the site of his execution in Rome. The committee included Victor Hugo (cf. TI Skirmishes 1), Herbert Spencer, Ernest Renan (cf. TI "Skirmishes" 2), Ernst Haeckel, Henrik Ibsen, and Ferdinand Gregorovius. So if we want to know who it is that Nietzsche targets when he talks about the wrong kind of free spirits, we might explore these. The statue of Bruno was eventually erected in 1889.

10. This passage is discussed in its context, elaborating some of the same points below, in *Nietzsche's Beyond Good and Evil: A Reader's Guide*, which I coauthored with Keith Ansell-Pearson (New York: Continuum, 2011).

11. Some notable discussions of Ariadne include Gilles Deleuze, "The Mystery of Ariadne According to Nietzsche," in *Essays Critical and Clinical*, translated by Daniel W. Smith (University of Minnesota Press, 1997); and Gary Shapiro, *Nietzschean Narratives* (Bloomington: Indiana University Press, 1989).

12. I am grateful to Duncan Large for pointing out this connection.

13. For a different, but interesting, account of the significance of the affective orientation toward truth in Nietzsche with respect to its bearing on freedom, see Peter Poellner, "Nietzschean Freedom," in *Nietzsche on Freedom and Autonomy*, edited by Ken Gemes and Simon May (Oxford: Oxford University Press, 2009), 170–77.

14. Mullin helpfully observes that Nietzsche thinks the illusion of free will leads to some of the worst intellectual habits (391f). This remains focused on the free spirits' *beliefs* about freedom, specifically freedom of the will. Nietzsche is also concerned with *conditions* of relative freedom and unfreedom as related to the development of a free spirit.

15. I elaborate these ideas in various publications, most recently my "Beholding Nietzsche: *Ecce Homo*, Fate, and Freedom," in *Oxford Handbook on Nietzsche*, edited by Ken Gemes and John Richardson (Oxford: Oxford University Press, 2013), and in a broader context of Nietzsche's assessments of morality and moral philosophy in my *Contesting Nietzsche* (Chicago: University of Chicago Press, 2013).

16. Nietzsche expresses admiration for this type, not necessarily linked with free spirits, in BGE 212. Compare GS 290 and TI "Skirmishes" 49. See also discussion by Poellner, "Nietzschean Freedom," 153ff.

17. See, for example Keith Ansell-Pearson, "On Nietzsche's Moral Therapy in *Dawn*," *Continental Philosophy Review* 44(2) (2011): 179–204; and Michael Ure, *Nietzsche's Therapy:*

Self-Cultivation in the Middle Works (Lanham, MD: Lexington Books, 2008). See also the essay by Rebecca Bamford in this volume.

18. Nietzsche elaborates this problem (and anticipates the solution) in part 8 of BGE. For discussion, see Acampora and Ansell-Pearson, 2011.

19. See Poellner, "Nietzschean Freedom," 154.

20. For a possible "third way" between artist and no one, see Graham Parkes, *Composing the Soul: Reaches of Nietzsche's Psychology* (Chicago: University of Chicago Press, 1994).

21. See the chapter by Duncan Large in this volume.

22. Citation of Nietzsche's *Dawn* is drawn from Brittain Smith's translation, *Dawn*; I have also consulted Hollingdale's translation.

23. Illuminating discussion of this image of the polyp as it relates to Nietzsche's drive psychology can be found in Brian Domino, "Polyp Man," in *A Nietzschean Bestiary*, 42–49.

24. Hollingdale's translation.

25. If we take the free spirit not as an individual but rather more like the spirit of an age or a spiritual capacity that might be realized by or characteristic of groups, peoples, then we might make more headway on thinking about how such organizations and reorganizations might work by looking at how Nietzsche thinks about the current independence of Europe, its resultant *disintegration* and its simultaneous desire to become one. Being "a good European" might be one way of realizing free spirituality in such a case.

26. But experimentalism is not necessarily inherently good. See GS 356, where Nietzsche writes about contemporary Europeans who are increasingly becoming like superficial actors (rather than real human beings): "The individual becomes convinced that he can do just about everything and *can manage almost any role*, and everybody experiments with himself, improvises, makes new experiments, enjoys his experiments; and all nature ceases and becomes art." Kaufmann's translation.

27. See GS 277.

BIBLIOGRAPHY

Acampora, Christa Davis. "Beholding Nietzsche: *Ecce Homo*, Fate, and Freedom." In *Oxford Handbook on Nietzsche*, edited by Ken Gemes and John Richardson, 363–85. Oxford: Oxford University Press, 2013.

Acampora, Christa Davis. *Contesting Nietzsche*. Chicago: University of Chicago Press, 2013.

Acampora, Christa Davis. "Senses of Freedom of the Free Spirit." *Pli: Warwick Journal of Philosophy* 25 (2014): 13–33.

Acampora, Christa Davis and Keith Ansell-Pearson. *Nietzsche's Beyond Good and Evil: A Reader's Guide*. New York: Continuum, 2011.

Ansell-Pearson, Keith. "On Nietzsche's Moral Therapy in *Dawn*." *Continental Philosophy Review* 44(2) (2011): 179–204

Cohen, Jonathan. *Science, Culture, and Free Spirits: A Study of Nietzsche's Human, All Too Human*. New York: Humanity Books, 2009.

Deleuze, Gilles. "The Mystery of Ariadne According to Nietzsche." In *Essays Critical and Clinical* Translated by Daniel W. Smith. University of Minnesota Press, 1997.

Domino, Brian. "Polyp Man." In *A Nietzschean Bestiary: Becoming Animal Beyond Docile and Brutal*, edited by Christa Davis Acampora and Ralph R. Acampora, 42–49. New York: Rowman & Littlefield, 2004.

Hecht, Jennifer Michael. *Doubt: A History*. New York: HarperCollins, 2003.

Higgins, Kathleen Marie. "Nietzsche and the Mystery of the Ass." In *A Nietzschean Bestiary: Becoming Animal Beyond Docile and Brutal*, edited by Christa Davis Acampora and Ralph R. Acampora, 100–119. New York: Rowman & Littlefield, 2004.

Mullin, Amy. "Nietzsche's Free Spirit." *Journal of the History of Philosophy* 38(3) (2000): 383–405.

Nietzsche, Friedrich. *Beyond Good and Evil*. Translated by Walter Kaufmann. New York: Vintage Books, 1966.

Nietzsche, Friedrich. *Dawn: Thoughts on the Presumptions of Morality.* Translated by Brittain Smith. Stanford: Stanford University Press, 2011.

Nietzsche, Friedrich. *Daybreak.* Translated by R. J. Hollingdale. Cambridge: Cambridge University Press, 1982.

Nietzsche, Friedrich. *The Gay Science.* Translated by Walter Kaufmann. New York: Vintage Books, 1974.

Nietzsche, Friedrich. *Human, All Too Human: A Book for Free Spirits.* Translated by R. J. Hollingdale. Cambridge: Cambridge University Press, 1986.

Nietzsche, Friedrich. *On the Genealogy of Morals* and *Ecce Homo.* Translated by Walter Kaufmann and R. J. Hollingdale. New York: Vintage Books, 1967.

Parkes, Graham. *Composing the Soul: Reaches of Nietzsche's Psychology.* Chicago: University of Chicago Press, 1994.

Poellner, Peter. "Nietzschean Freedom." In *Nietzsche on Freedom and Autonomy*, edited by Ken Gemes and Simon May, 170–77. Oxford: Oxford University Press, 2009.

Reginster, Bernard. "What Is a Free Spirit? Nietzsche on Fanaticism" in *Archiv für Geschichte der Philosophie* 85(1) (2003): 51–85.

Shapiro, Gary. *Nietzschean Narratives.* Bloomington: Indiana University Press, 1989.

Ure, Michael. *Nietzsche's Therapy: Self-Cultivation in the Middle Works.* Lanham, MD: Lexington Books, 2008.

Chapter Eleven

Free the Spirit!

Kantian, Jungian and Neoplatonic Resonances in Nietzsche

Paul Bishop

Dear God, grant that we may be *free in spirit*, everything else you can keep for yourself. [Lieber Himmel, gieb das wir *freien Geistes* seien, alles andere kannst du für dich behalten.] —Nietzsche, letter to Carl Fuchs, 11 August 1875; KSB 5, 103)[1]

In recent years, the role of free spirit in Nietzsche's thought has become a widely debated question, following the publication a decade or so ago of a collection of papers edited by Paolo D'Iorio and Olivier Ponton under the title *Nietzsche, Philosophie de l'esprit libre*,[2] and a recent study by Paolo D'Orio that links Nietzsche's visit to Sorrento in the winter of 1876 to 1877 with the genesis of his philosophy of free spirit.[3] Similarly, Patrick Wotling chooses to entitle his introduction to Nietzsche's thought, *La philosophie de l'esprit libre*, and Paul Franco has devoted a major study to the so-called free spirit trilogy (*Human, All Too Human, Dawn* and *The Gay Science*).[4] The issue of how to understand the concept of free spirit is, then, very much in the air.

As these (and other) authors suggest, the notion of free spirit is associated with the stage of Nietzsche's philosophical development that began in Sorrento and first came to expression in *Human, All Too Human*. This new phase in Nietzsche's thought can be identified, as Sandro Barbera has argued, with a change in the function it accords to art, a change reflected in Nietzsche's progressive shift *away* from Wagner (and Schopenhauer) and *towards* Goethe.[5] For the figure of the 'free spirit' is based—at least in part—on Goethe's description of the writer Laurence Sterne, which serves as one of the originating impulses

behind this motif in Nietzsche's thought. This becomes clear in HH II AOM
113, when Nietzsche alludes to Goethe's remark to the effect that Sterne should
be celebrated as 'the freest spirit of his century'. In fact, Nietzsche explicitly
extends the force of Goethe's encomium:

> How, in a book for free spirits, should there be no mention of Laurence Sterne,
> whom Goethe honoured as the most liberated spirit of his century! Let us
> content ourselves here simply with calling him the most liberated spirit of all
> time.[6]

And the rest of this passage might be considered to constitute a portrait of
free spirit: mastery of ambiguity, knotting together profundity and farce, and
the union of 'an antipathy to seriousness' with 'a tendency to be unable to
regard anything merely superficially' (HH II AOM 113; *KSA* 2, 425).[7] To be
true to the 'spirit' of free spirit means liberating oneself from existing interpretations of this concept, and in this chapter I shall draw on Kant and on
Jung to suggest a different approach to understanding what, with free spirit,
Nietzsche is trying to articulate. But first, let us examine some of his earliest
remarks about free spirit.

FREE SPIRITEDNESS IN *HUMAN, ALL TOO HUMAN*

While Nietzsche discusses the figure of the free spirit [der Freigeist] extensively in his unpublished writings, it is in HH I 30 that it was first mentioned
in a published text.[8] Here Nietzsche presents the free spirit [der Freigeist] as
'acquainted' with the 'erroneousness' of a certain kind of reasoning that
confuses beneficence or utility with logical validity, and as subsequently
'tempted' to the 'opposite' (but equally 'erroneous') conclusion, namely, that
'a thing cannot prevail, therefore it is good; an opinion causes pain and
distress, therefore it is true' (HH I 30; cf. HH I 131, 153). Then, in a series of
aphorisms, Nietzsche explicitly examines what it means to be a free spirit
[Freigeist]: it involves 'think[ing] differently from what, on the basis of
origin, environment, class and profession, or on the basis of the dominant
views of the age, would be expected', and thus being precisely the opposite
of a 'fettered spirit' [gebundener Geist] (HH I 225; cf. HH I 227, 229). (In the
preface added to HH in 1886, Nietzsche playfully and poetically develops
this image, in a wonderfully evocative passage describing how 'the great
liberation' takes place [HH Preface 3; KSA 2, 15–17].)[9] In aphorism 230,
Nietzsche wonders how to turn the free spirit [der Freigeist] into a freethinker [*esprit fort*] (HH I 230; KSA 2, 193), suggesting in this section and in
aphorism 231 that 'the perfect free spirit' [der vollkommene Freigeist] is a
specific type of genius (HH I 231; KSA 2, 198; cf. HH I 232).

In an unpublished fragment from 1876, Nietzsche interrogates further the relation between the free spirit [der Freigeist] and the freethinker [*esprit fort*], suggesting—in the context of the observation that 'the appreciation of the contemplative life has diminished'—that 'previously they were opposites, the priest and the *esprit fort*: a kind of rebirth of both in one person is now possible' (KSA 8, 16[51], 295; cf. KSA 8, 17[41], 304). Later, in 1884–1885, Nietzsche will envisage for a future, and never written, part of *Thus Spoke Zarathustra* a further synthesis, that of 'the creator, the lover, the destroyer' (KSA 11, 31[3], 360), and in his *Nachlass*, Nietzsche repeatedly refers to the theme of unifying all our faculties.

In a further series of aphorisms in HH I, Nietzsche wonders whether the free spirit [der Freigeist] will live with women—the answer is: no (HH I 426, cf. 427, 428, 429, 431, 432, 435, 437); he discusses the political implications of 'free-spiritedness' (HH I 464, 472); and finally he presents the free spirit [der Freigeist] as almost a kind of martyr:

> The free spirit too, and likewise the believer, desire power in order to please through it; when they are threatened by an ill fate, persecution, imprisonment, execution on account of their teaching they rejoice in the thought that in this way their teaching will be cut and burned into mankind; they accept it as a painful but vigorous, if late-acting means of nonetheless attaining to power. (HH I 595; KSA 2, 340)

Given his reference in the context of the earliest published mention of free-thinking [Freigeisterei] to Voltaire (UM I 10; KSA 1, 217), its complex relation of opposition to and affinity with the freethinker [*esprit fort*] (HH I 230), and its association in the second volume of HH, with Voltaire's remark, 'Believe me, my friend, error also has merit' [Croyez-moi, mon ami, l'erreur aussi a son mérite] (HH II AOM 4),[10] and with Sterne and Diderot (HH II AOM 113), is there something specifically French about the free spirit [der Freigeist]?[11] That there may well be, is clearly suggested in *Dawn* 192, where Nietzsche tells us that the French free spirit [der französische Freigeist] 'struggled inwardly against great human beings, and not merely against dogmas and sublime abortions', as did the free spirits [die Freigeister] of other nations (D 192; KSA 3, 166);[12] and in the section entitled '*Esprit* and morality', in which Nietzsche wittily observes that the Germans know 'the secret of how to make spirit [Geist], knowledge [Wissen], and heart [Gemüth] boring' and have become accustomed to feeling that 'boredom is moral', adding that consequently they have a fear that French spirit [*esprit*] might 'put out the eyes of morality', albeit a fear of the fascinated kind that the little bird has in front of the rattlesnake (D 193; KSA 3, 166). Surprisingly, Nietzsche adds the remark that, 'of the celebrated Germans, none perhaps possessed more *esprit* than Hegel', while more characteristically adding that Hegel 'also possessed so great a German fear of it that this fear was responsible for creating the bad style peculiar to him' (D 193; KSA 3, 167). Later, in aphorism 524, Nietzsche comments on the 'jealousy' of the solitary individual, 'the jealousy which all solitary thinkers and passionate dreamers feel towards *esprit*' (D 524).

What, then, is the relationship between the free spirit [der Freigeist] and spirit [*esprit*]? According to *Le Petit Robert*, there are at least six groups of words that serve as synonyms for spirit [*esprit*],[13] from which it emerges that spirit [*esprit*] is, to be sure, something intellectual, but much more than that—it is also something emotional, something affective, something *more than simply* rational. And these synonyms reveal an important aspect of Nietzsche's approach to philosophy: it is ludic, parodic, it is full of spirit [*esprit*]. Hence a significant motif in Nietzsche's thinking, the contrast between spirit [*esprit*] and *Geist*—or, to put it another way, between free spirit [Freigeist] and spirit [Geist]. This motif of *esprit* comes to the fore in *The Gay Science*, when Nietzsche even tells us in GS 82 that *esprit* is 'un-Greek'. 'In good society one must never wish to be solely and entirely right, which is what all pure logic aims at; hence the small dose of unreason in all French *esprit*', Nietzsche writes, and he adds: 'The sociability of the Greeks was far less developed than that of the French has been and still is', and 'that is why we find so little *esprit* even in their most spirited men, so little wit even in their wittiest men' (GS 82; KSA 3, 438).

In GS 103, recapitulating his earlier critique in D, Nietzsche writes that 'in all German music we hear a profound bourgeois envy of nobility, especially of *esprit* and *élégance* as expressions of a courtly, knightly, old, self-assured society', a critique tellingly articulated with a reference to Goethe's ballad, *The Singer* [*Der Sänger*] (GS 103). And more generally, in a passage that seems astonishingly prophetic in the age of e-mail, Internet, Facebook, and Twitter, Nietzsche laments the absence from modern life of leisure and idleness: 'One no longer has time or energy', he writes, 'for ceremonies, for being obliging in an indirect way, for *esprit* in conversation, and for any *otium* at all', since 'living in a constant chase after gain compels people to expend their spirit to the point of exhaustion' (GS 329). In the face of all this activity, Nietzsche calls for a return to the *vita contemplativa*.

This emphasis on contemplation stands in stark contrast to the blind and hectic activism with which, for polemical reasons, Nietzsche's critics sometimes seek to associate him. It is sometimes forgotten that, as Zarathustra reminds us, 'It is the quietest words which bring the storm, thoughts that come on doves' feet guide the world' (Z II Stillest Hour; KSA 4, 189). Later, in *Beyond Good and Evil* 209, Nietzsche wrote—in one of those anecdotal-historical passages whose significance is, for us, sometimes difficult to grasp—the following about Friedrich Wilhelm I and his scepticism regarding his son, Friedrich the Great. In his son, Friedrich Wilhelm saw someone who had 'surrender[ed] to atheism, to *esprit*, to the hedonistic frivolity of clever

Frenchmen', to what Michelet called '*cet esprit fataliste, ironique, méphis-
tophélique*' (and hence an *esprit* by no means uncongenial to Nietzsche himself) (BGE 209). If *esprit* could be 'fatalistic', 'ironical', and 'Mephistophe-
lian', it could also be 'vast' or 'comprehensive'—an '*esprit vaste*', thus
Saint-Évremond's critique of Homer (BGE 224).[14] A few sections later,
Nietzsche brings a sardonic lyric to a conclusion with a line in French, '*Sans
génie et sans esprit*' (BGE 228), and while, on the one hand, this use of a
German cliché is part of the joke, on the other, it raises for us the question
about the relation between genius, *Geist* and *esprit*.

KANT ON *GEIST* AND *SEELE* IN THE THIRD *CRITIQUE*

As Kant tells us in the preface to the second edition of the first *Critique*, he
had found it necessary 'to deny *knowledge* in order to make room for *faith*', a
move that, in Nietzsche's eyes, had allowed Kant to rescue Christianity and
to preserve its 'metaphysics of the gallows' (TI Errors 7).[15] Yet in his third
Critique, in his analytic of the sublime in his critique of aesthetic judgement,
we find a passage in which Kant discourses at length about 'spirit' and about
'soul', about *Geist* and about *Seele*, in a way that can help us understand
what is at stake in Nietzsche's concept of free spirit.[16]

Earlier in his *Critique of Judgement*, Kant had argued for a link between
art and genius, declaring that '*genius* is the talent (natural endowment) which
gives the rule to art' or, more precisely, that '*genius* is the innate mental
aptitude (*ingenium*) *through which* nature gives the rule to art'.[17] (Noting the
etymological root of the word *genius*, Kant observes that 'our word *Genie* is
derived from *genius*, as the peculiar guardian and guiding spirit given to a
man at his birth, by the inspiration of which those original ideas were ob-
tained'.[18]) In this sense, the genius is *not* free: as Kant admits, 'where an
author owes a product to his genius, he does not himself know how the *ideas*
for it have entered into his head, nor has he it in his power to invent the like
at pleasure, or methodically, and communicate the same to others in such
percepts as would put them in a position to produce similar products'.[19] Or,
as Nietzsche later puts it in his account of the composition of Z, 'One hears,
one does not seek; one takes, one does not ask who gives; a thought flashes
up like lightning, with necessity, unfalteringly formed—I have never had any
choice' (EH Z 3).

And yet, as Kant had already set out, art is also in a preeminent sense
about freedom: as he puts it, 'aesthetic finality is the conformity to law of
judgement in its *freedom*'.[20] For art involves free play: as Kant explains, 'the
aesthetic judgement in its estimate of the beautiful refers the imagination in
its free play to the *understanding*',[21] and hence the judgement of beauty is, as
Kant sets out at some length, universal.[22] A dialectic of freedom and neces-

sity thus lies at the heart of Kant's understanding of aesthetics in the third *Critique*.

Now, underpinning Kant's account of beauty is the distinction between two kinds of beauty, one called 'dependent beauty' [*pulchritudo adhaerans*] and the other 'free beauty' [*pulchritudo vaga*]. This second kind is a beauty that 'presupposes no concept of what the object should be',[23] and in the estimation of free beauty, we find 'the pure judgement of taste'.[24] This Kantian concept of free beauty [freie Schönheit] is central to subsequent developments in aesthetic theory in German classicism and Romanticism alike; in Schiller, for example, we find the definition of beauty as 'freedom in appearance' [Freiheit in der Erscheinung].[25] Indeed, it is no exaggeration to say that, in his *Letters on the Aesthetic Education of Humankind*, Schiller endows beauty with a developmental, even salvific power: and precisely this power is later recognized by Nietzsche, too, in his embrace of the world— more, his claim that the world is *justified*—as an 'aesthetic phenomenon'. One might even say that not since the thought of Plotinus has the soteriological role imputed to beauty been so strong. . . .

Returning to the third *Critique* and to its section 49, we find Kant reflecting on the role of *Geist*, of 'spirit' or indeed *esprit*, in art—in a poem, in a narrative, in a speech, in a conversation, or even (!) in a woman. And he offers the following definition of *Geist*, in an aesthetic sense:

> *Spirit*, in an aesthetic sense, signifies the animating principle in the mind. But that whereby this principle animates the soul, the material which it employs for that purpose, is that which sets the mental powers purposefully into motion, i.e., into a play which is self-maintaining and which strengthens those powers for such activity.[26]

Yet what exactly is this animating principle, what is this *Geist*? It is, Kant tells us, nothing other than 'the faculty of presenting *aesthetic ideas*'.[27] So what, in turn, is, for Kant, an idea? In section 29, Kant tells us that 'ideas cannot be represented'—at least, 'in a literal sense and considered logically', they cannot.[28] Nevertheless, as Kant readily admits, 'reason inevitably steps forward . . . and calls forth the effort of the mind, unavailing though it be, to make the representation of senses adequate to this totality [i.e., of reason]'.[29] And so it is, he argues, in section 49, in the case of aesthetic ideas, which he defines as follows: as 'that representation of the imagination which induces much thought, yet without the possibility of any definite thought whatever, i.e., *concept*, being adequate to it'—that is, as non-conceptual—and 'which language, consequently, can never get quite on level terms or render completely intelligible'.[30]

(Aesthetic) ideas, then, are 'representations of the imagination', and as such, for Kant, they constitute what is essential about art in two respects.

First, art takes us beyond the bounds of our experience: '[Aesthetic ideas] at least strain after something lying out beyond the confines of experience, and so seek to approximate to a representation of rational concepts (i.e., intellectual ideas), thus giving to these concepts the semblance of an objective reality'.[31] And second, in so doing, we transcend the boundaries of reason: 'On the other hand, there is this most important reason, that no concept can be wholly adequate to [aesthetic ideas] as internal intuitions'.[32] Thus, Kant says, the poet tries to represent the 'rational ideas' of invisible beings, the kingdom of the blessed, hell, eternity, creation, or such momentous experiential events as death, envy, love, or fame. The poet attempts, 'transgressing the limits of experience' and 'with the aid of an imagination which emulates the display of reason in its attainment of a maximum', to 'body them forth to sense', that is, to make sensual [sinnlich zu machen], 'with a completeness of which nature affords no parallel'.[33]

In other words, the genius deploys to the highest possible degree the 'mental powers' of the imagination and understanding, and in aesthetic production he does so in such a way that the imagination is free.[34] For Kant, this expression of (aesthetic ideas) constitutes nothing less than the task of beauty itself: 'Beauty (whether it be of nature or of art) may in general be termed the *expression* of aesthetic ideas'.[35] Hence, we find in Kant the paradox that the idea, which cannot be depicted, nevertheless offers the experience of freedom—in fact, the experience of the greatest possible freedom that can be attained.

This link between art and freedom may be summed up in his scintillating concept of *pulchritudo vaga*, or 'free beauty' [freie Schönheit]. For the aesthetic experience of beauty reveals the 'enlivening principle' that 'enlivens the soul', or in other words: *Geist*. As we experience beauty, Kant is arguing, so our soul is enlivened by the enlivening effect of *Geist*; in short, it is art that truly makes us alive. . . . Hence, it should come as no surprise that Nietzsche, for all his avowed anti-Kantianism, aligns himself with this conclusion when he chooses to present, as an icon of life itself, an artist: none other than Goethe. In a famous passage from TI, Goethe attains the iconic status of an exemplar of the free spirit, or of the 'spirit-that-has-become-free' [ein freigewordner Geist]:

A spirit thus *emancipated* stands in the midst of the universe with a joyful and trusting fatalism, in the *faith* that only what is separate and individual may be rejected, that in the totality everything is redeemed and affirmed—*he no longer denies*. (TI Expeditions 49)

Thus Nietzsche's philosophy develops its own doctrine of redemption (*Erlösung*), based on a sense of *the whole* (see TI Errors 8).

Is life itself, then, a sort of free spirit [Frei-Geist]? And if so, does this make Nietzsche a closet Kantian? Or Kant a prospective Nietzschean? At any rate, examining anew the concept of the free spirit might allow for a fundamental re-evaluation of Nietzsche's position in relation to Kantianism, and beyond to the Western Idealist tradition as a whole.

JUNG ON SPIRIT IN HIS *ZARATHUSTRA* SEMINAR

We can examine this crucial relation between genius, *Geist, der Freigeist*, and soul [Seele] from another angle, if we consider the approach taken by C. G. Jung in his seminars on Z. Held in Zurich over a number of years between 1934 and 1939, these seminars constitute a remarkable, if sometimes problematic, commentary on Nietzsche's text, revealing the psychological dynamic at work in Nietzsche's work, and his remarks about the function of spirit [Geist] in it are especially pertinent to our discussion of free spirit.

For instance, in relation to the section in the prologue to Z where the Persian prophet declares,

> But he who is wisest among you, he is only a discord and hybrid of plant and of ghost [nur ein Zwiespalt und Zwitter von Pflanze und von Gespenst].
> But do I bid you become ghosts or plants?
> Behold, I teach you the superman [den Übermenschen] (Z Preface 3)[36]

Jung shrewdly observed how Nietzsche's 'whole philosophy' can 'often be seen in the smallest detail of his metaphors', and he went on to elaborate his reading of this passage:

> Nietzsche will speak later on of the blond beast; that is his idea, the Superman in contradistinction to the plant and ghost-wisdom. But I should like to know why just plant and ghost. You see, he says even the wisest is only a discord, or disharmony, and discord is *Entzweiung* in German, which means something that does not fit exactly. A hybrid is a united discord, so it is an objectionable sort of union of opposites. The plant is completely unconscious and the ghost has no flesh, no body, so it is an absolutely metaphysical ghost connected with a plant and forming a unit, something utterly unconscious and close to matter. . . . So that hybrid consists in a natural growth on one side, perfectly sound, yet something died in between, the animal man: the flesh died, and only the ghost remains. The original natural spirit, *anima naturaliter Christiana*,[37] that flesh in which this natural Christian soul once lived, then vanished; and what remains is this hybrid of plant, a sound beginning, and a ghost, a sad end of human life. . . . Nietzsche inserts the middle part, he preaches the flesh again. In other words, the blond beast comes to fill the gap there, so that the plant and the ghost are united once more, and he then concentrates upon the middle part which was lacking before.[38]

As the allusion to Tertullian makes clear, Jung reads Nietzsche in the context, and as an expression, of the post-Christian worldview. For Jung, Nietzsche's philosophy constitutes in a very precise sense a return to the body, and in the course of his seminar, Jung inevitably also turns his attention to those passages where Zarathustra explicitly addresses the theme of spirit or *Geist*.

In 'Of the Despisers of the Body', for instance, Zarathustra offers a famous parable:

> 'I am body and soul'—so speaks the child. And why should one not speak like children?
> But the awakened, the enlightened man says: I am body entirely, and nothing beside; and soul is only a word for something in the body. (Z I Despisers)

And in 'Of the Famous Philosophers', he offers the following, dramatic definition of spirit [Geist]: 'Spirit is the life that itself strikes into life: through its own torment it increases its own knowledge—did you know that before?' [Geist ist das Leben, das selber ins Leben schneidet; an der eignen Qual mehrt sich das eigne Wissen,—wußtet ihr das schon?] (Z II Philosophers; cf. Z IV Leech).[39]

Correspondingly, and in response to these passages, Jung defines *Geist* in the following terms as 'originally a most effervescent thing, like the opening of a champagne bottle . . . , most emotional, really a culmination of life', an interpretation supported by the etymology of the German word.[40] For Jung, the overlap between *esprit* and *spiritus* revealed the original meaning of *Geist*, one that had to be rediscovered in our contemporary use of the word:

> Mind and spirit are nowadays so confused that the words are used interchangeably, as in German you use the word *Geist* for simply anything. It also has the connotation of *esprit*, for instance, and one speaks of *esprit de vin*, *Weingeist*, the 'spirit of alcohol.' Of course, alcohol was called *spiritus* because it is a volatile substance detached from a liquid by distillation, it is the volatile substance which goes over into the alembic. *Geist* is also an expression for a psychological concept, but we have to separate these terms, otherwise, we get entangled in all the nonsense which is happening now. For example, Klages thinks the spirit is the destroyer of life, which is *contradictio in adjecto*, the spirit has always been the creator of life.[41] The orgiastic madness of antiquity is *prana*, the breath of life. A god fills you with his *prana*, or his *pneuma* or wind, and you become an air-being, . . . a ghost or soul; even body becomes breath. That was the original concept.[42]

Yet, as Jung is at pains to point out, this understanding of *Geist* is in no way opposed to materialism or Nietzsche's emphasis on the body:

That we should emphasize the body is Nietzsche's message, and it is also the message of materialism. . . . We should emphasize the body, for thus we give body to concepts, to words. And we should insist on the fact that they are nothing but words since the spirit is gone, that there is no life in them—they are dead things, outside life. We should return to the body in order to create spirit again; without body there is no spirit because spirit is a volatile substance of the body. The body is the alembic, the retort, in which materials are cooked, and out of that process develops the spirit, the effervescent thing that rises.[43]

The position espoused by Jung here could, if one wanted to find a formula for it, perhaps best be summarized in terms of a *vitalist materialism*.

In one of the *Dithyrambs of Dionysos*, 'Amid Birds of Prey', Jung finds evidence of this developmental process at work in Nietzsche, an experience Jung assimilates to the Nietzschean concept (or rather experience) of the Dionysian:

Nietzsche returned to himself, isolated himself from the whole world, crept into his own retort and underwent this process. Then suddenly he discovered that he was filled with a new orgiastic enthusiasm which he called his experience of Dionysos, the god of wine. You see, that is the spirit. Dionysos is the god of prophecy, of prophetic dreams, and he is the god of the body. In the latter part of *Zarathustra* there is a beautiful poem where Nietzsche describes how he was digging down into himself, working into his own shaft; there you can see how intensely he experienced the going-into-himself, till he suddenly produced the explosion of the most original form of spirit, the Dionysian.[44]

As it happens, this image of digging down into the self is exactly one that Nietzsche himself had used earlier, in his fourth *Untimely Meditation* on 'Schopenhauer as Educator'. Here he had written, in the context of the fraught undertaking of gaining self-knowledge, as follows: 'It is an agonizing, dangerous enterprise to dig down into yourself, to descend forcibly by the shortest route the shaft of your own being. A man can easily do himself such damage that no doctor can cure him' (UM III 1).[45] This passage anticipates precisely those images, subsequently found in 'Amid Birds of Prey' in DD, of sinking into one's 'own depths', of becoming 'self-excavated/digging into yourself' (KSA 6, 391).

In this text from DD, Jung discerned, as he would explain in *Symbols of Transformation* (1952), a remarkable expression of the psychological process he termed 'introversion'. In this process, the libido sinks into itself, where it discovers—as Nietzsche says, 'amidst a hundred memories' (DD 43; KSA 6, 390)—what Jung calls 'the world of the child, the paradisal state of early infancy, from which we are driven out by the relentless law of time'.[46] (In the image of Zarathustra as, in Jung's words, 'sunk in his own depths' and 'like one buried in the earth', akin to the image of 'a dead man who has crawled back into the mother', one finds something reminiscent to Jung's mind of Caeneus,[47] Mithras,[48] or Christ.)

In a footnote, Jung compared Nietzsche's images of self-penetration—'thyself pierced through', 'working in thine own pit'—with two ancient intertexts: first, the fifty-second Orphic hymn, in which Bacchus is invoked by the name of *upokholpie* (equal to 'lying in the lap' or 'he who is in the vagina or womb'), suggesting that 'the god entered his devotees as if through the female genitals';[49] and second, a prayer to Hermes, invoking the god as follows: 'Come to me, O Hermes, as children come into the womb of women!'[50] Whatever one makes of Jung's amplificatory style of reading, it can help explain the curious power of these enigmatic texts. For Jung's working principle is that 'what seems like a poetic figure of speech in Nietzsche is really an age-old myth', and that 'it is as if the poet could still sense, beneath the words of contemporary speech and in the images that crowd in upon his imagination, the ghostly presence of bygone spiritual words'—and, above all—'possessed the capacity to make them come alive again'.[51]

Hence, in Jung's view, the epochal significance of Nietzsche's project (and, by implication, Jung's own project of analytical psychology):

> We are now in the age where there is nothing but words, footprints—but we can do nothing with them, they are dead. Therefore, we must turn away from them and go back to the source where the whole thing began originally. And here is a message: Zarathustra says to go back to the body, go into the body, and then everything will be right, for there the greatest intelligence is hidden. Out of that living body everything originally has come.[52]

Elsewhere in his seminar, Jung draws his audience's attention to another remarkable passage in UM IV 6, in which Nietzsche declares that 'if a single spark from the flame of justice falls into the scholar's soul, it is enough to set his life and aspirations afire, purifying them by consuming them, so that he can no longer find peace and is forever expelled from that icy or lukewarm state in which ordinary scholars do their daily work'. In this sentence, Jung claims, Nietzsche 'expresses very clearly the descent of the Holy Ghost: that is a fiery spark of the eternal fires, and this most holy ghost is able to devour the whole of a human life', something that is 'beautiful'—but 'all this beauty and grandeur can also produce the most horrible destruction'.[53]

Later in his seminar, Jung returned to this passage from UM in the context of commenting on a passage from 'Of the Way of the Creator', where Zarathustra declares: 'You must be ready to burn yourself in your own flame: how could you become new, if you had not first become ashes?' (Z I Creator). For Jung, this passage reminds us that 'when man is on the way to himself, he will see his other side, and there will be a tremendous conflict; it will be a conflagration, a flame in which he is burned up'.[54] Referring back to UM IV, Jung pointed to three intertexts. First, the Gnostic myth of the soul, according to which the soul is the spark [spinther] that falls from the pleroma or the empyrean into matter. Second, the New Testament apocrypha, which attributes to Christ the following saying: 'He who is near me is near the fire; he who is far from me is far from the kingdom',[55] suggesting that 'the kingdom is a kingdom of fire' and that 'Christ himself is the flame'.[56] And third, a *logion* of Heraclitus, 'A dry soul is wisest and best'.[57] On the basis of these intertexts, Jung glossed Zarathustra's saying as meaning that 'it is inevitable that anyone who seeks the self is forced into that fight with the shadow, with the other side of himself, his own negation; and that will be a catastrophe in which the ordinary man is as if destroyed: he becomes ashes'.[58]

Over and above these specific intertexts, Jung saw Zarathustra's question as lending itself to interpretation within two further (for Jung, entirely typical) contexts: first, alchemy (in the sense that 'this conflagration is necessary; otherwise the self as the living unit cannot appear, otherwise it would be obliterated by the continuous fight of the Yea and the Nay');[59] and second, the tradition of Neoplatonism. For Jung assimilates Zarathustra's image to the mythological figure of the Phoenix, something that 'burns itself, together with its nest, the soul and the body, and arises from the ashes anew'. Yet such a 'total transformation', Jung warns, is 'hardly possible', for it is not the myth of the ordinary man, but of 'the god in man', of 'the primordial man' or *anthropos*.[60]

At the intersection of early Christian, Gnostic and Neoplatonic thought, we find the figure of *anthropos*, signifying the primordial Man or Adam.[61] Elsewhere, Jung suggests that Zarathustra 'is like the speck of light of the Gnostics, the eternal spirit that falls down into matter and is caught in it', describing Zarathustra as 'something like the first man, the Adam Cadmon of the Kabbalists or the Primus Adam of medieval philosophers' or 'the *anthropos* that has been caught in Nietzsche and shares to a certain extent Nietzsche's experience'.[62] Without pursuing at this juncture the significance or otherwise of the figure of the *anthropos* in Nietzsche's thinking, I should like to follow up Jung's point about a possible Neoplatonic context to it.

NIETZSCHE AND THE (NEO)PLATONIC TRADITION

Nietzsche's apparent hostility to Plato is well-known,[63] and of the many objections he raises against Plato, one is primarily *stylistic*. In TI Ancients 2, for instance, Nietzsche writes: 'It seems to me that Plato mixes together all forms of style; he is therewith in the matter of style a *first décadent*: he has on his conscience something similar to the Cynics who devised the *Satura Menippea*' (KSA 6, 155).[64] Only if one has 'never . . . read any good French writers—Fontenelle, for example', says Nietzsche, can one find in 'the Platonic dialogue, that frightfully self-satisfied and childish kind of "dialectics", any kind of "stimulus'" (TI Ancients 2). High praise, then, for the French *beau esprit* and *philosophe*, Bernard le Bovier de Fontenelle (1657–1757), as opposed to Plato, who is dismissed simply as being 'boring'![65]

Yet it is interesting to note that Nietzsche himself, in 1887, envisaged writing a 'satura menippea' entitled *Dionysos philosophos* (KSA 12, 5[93], 224), and while Nietzsche's anti-Platonism is well documented, reflected in the underlying thematic equation Platonism = Christianity = Idealism, Nietzsche was not shy elsewhere of being complimentary about Plato. Nor was Nietzsche entirely immune to the fascination of Idealism, as we can see from his enthusiastic reception of the American philosopher, essayist, and poet, Ralph Waldo Emerson (1803–1882).[66]

For instance, not simply the title of GS,[67] but its quotation on the very title page of the first edition—'To the poet, to the philosopher, to the saint, all things are friendly and sacred, all events profitable, all days holy, all men divine'[68]—and arguably its entire ethos, demonstrate Nietzsche's indebtedness to Emerson.[69] A note from his *Nachlass* of autumn 1881 testifies to Nietzsche's rereading of Emerson's *Essays* at this time, and to his sense of proximity with the American philosopher: 'Never has a book made me feel so much at home and in my own home—it is not proper for me to praise it, it is too close to me' (KSA 9, 12[68], 588). Among other things, an admiration for Goethe was common to both.[70] And one of the sources for the figure of Zarathustra is Emerson who, in his essay 'Character', refers to Zoroaster in a passage marked in Nietzsche's edition (KSA 14, 279).[71] Equally, the celebrated phrase, which features in the title of Nietzsche's work and with which most chapters conclude, may also have its source in Emerson, whose essay entitled 'Prospects' includes the following words: 'Thus my Orphic poet sang'.[72]

What did it mean, for Emerson, to be an Idealist? In his famous essay, 'Nature', we find a remarkable passage that shows the kind of experience in which Emerson believed the Ideal was experienced:

> Crossing a bare common, in snow puddles, at twilight, under a clouded sky, without having in my thoughts any occurrence of special good fortune, I have enjoyed a perfect exhilaration. I am glad to the brink of fear. In the woods too, a man casts off his years, as the snake his slough, and at what period soever of life, is always a child. In the woods, is perpetual youth. Within these plantations of God, a decorum and sanctity reign, a perennial festival is dressed, and the guest sees not how he should tire of them in a thousand years. In the woods, we return to reason and faith. There I feel nothing can befall me in life,—no disgrace, no calamity, (leaving me my eyes), which nature cannot repair. Standing on the bare ground,—my head bathed by the blithe air, and uplifted into infinite space,—all mean egotism vanishes. I am become a trans-

parent eye-ball; I am nothing; I see all; the currents of the Universal Being circulate through me; I am part or particle of God.[73]

Precisely this kind of transcendental, or even ecstatic, experience was not unknown to Nietzsche, as his account in EH of the composition of Z (and confirmed in his correspondence from this time) suggests. In this account of 'inspiration', Nietzsche claims to have acceded to an apprehension of the world as something *symbolic*, inasmuch as 'things themselves approached and offered themselves as metaphors' (EH Z 3), much as Zarathustra himself tells us they did (Z III Return and Z III Convalescent 2).

Surely it is this aspect of the genesis of Z that Jung had in mind when, in his Seminar, he tries to read Z II Dance Song—particularly its line in the conclusion, 'And again I seemed to sink into the unfathomable'—and Z II Grave Song from the perspective of a kind of double optics:

> From the standpoint of Nietzsche it [i.e., the experience behind *Zarathustra*] is an ordinary human experience—. . . he is first identical with the spirit, uplifted and exalted, and then he sinks down and suddenly discovers an entirely differ-ent aspect of things. . . . Now from the standpoint of Zarathustra . . . things are naturally different. Zarathustra, being the archetype of the spirit[,] is of course not a human being belonging to three-dimensional space and consisting of matter. Well, a spirit has an incorporeal existence. It is in no space; it is four-dimensional. But if that thing enters matter, it comes into space, and then the eternal myth of the descent of the spirit is repeated once more. . . . And now Nietzsche undergoes a certain change: namely, he becomes aware of the other aspect of things, his sun sets, his consciousness goes into the underworld—and through Nietzsche the eternal spirit has that same experience. . . . Zarathustra is really the *anthropos* that has been caught in Nietzsche and shares to a certain extent Nietzsche's experience.[74]

And if this is the case, then a certain limitation is imposed on our own understanding of the work:

> We can imagine ourselves, or we can feel into Zarathustra's mind, and we are to a certain extent able to see things from his point of view. But it is very conjectural because we are not archetypes and cannot feel into archetypes enough to know exactly what has happened to Zarathustra. We can feel prop-erly only what happens to the man Nietzsche. We can put ourselves into his situation and we can also understand what he says about Zarathustra, but what Zarathustra feels about it is divine and beyond us.[75]

The presence of a transcendent, or Neoplatonic, or even mystical resonance in, of all philosophers, Nietzsche's writings prompts one (somewhat hesitant-ly, or perhaps even somewhat mischievously) to pose the question: Was Nietzsche wrong about Neoplatonism? After all, surely Neoplatonism and Nietzsche ultimately have in common an important goal: the search for—and the belief that, in experiential terms, they have, in fact, actually found—a mode of thought that is nondiscursive, a form of reasoning that is *beyond reason*.

FREE YOUR MIND? NIETZSCHE AS MYSTIC

In a radio broadcast examining the philosophy of Plotinus, the French philosophical commentator Raphaël Enthoven observed at one point: 'Nietzsche is a Plotinian thinker, because Nietzsche is mystical' ['Nietzsche est un penseur plotinien, parce que Nietzsche est mystique'].[76] In more detail, Herbert Theierl has argued that Zarathustra's demand for a 'going-under' [Untergang], in order that the superman [Übermensch] 'may come into being', opens up the possibility that both terms, 'going-under' and 'superman' [Übermensch]', refer to one and the same thing, namely, to 'a mystical expansion of consciousness, which is experienced as redemption;' correspondingly, the 'superman' [Übermensch] refers, not to an individual, but to 'a state of mystical ecstasy'.[77]

In line with this approach, I should like in conclusion to propose a different way of thinking about *der Freigeist* or *der freie Geist*: instead of thinking of it as a type of individual or person, I should like to suggest that we translate it, not as 'free spirit' but rather as '*free mind*'. There are several reasons in favour of such a translation, above all the way in which Nietzsche, more often than not, actually uses the term *der Freigeist* (or related expressions). Take, for example, GS 297, where Nietzsche defines 'the step of steps of the liberated spirit' [des befreiten Geistes] as 'the ability to contradict, the attainment of a good conscience when one feels hostile to what is accustomed, traditional, and hallowed'—here *der befreite Geist* is defined as a set of faculties or abilities.

Or look again at the famous preface from 1886, written for volume I of *Human, All Too Human* when it was reissued as a two-volume work. Here Nietzsche talks about how 'a spirit in whom the type "free spirit" will one day become ripe and sweet to the point of perfection' will experience 'a *great liberation*' (HH I Preface 3; KSA 2, 15). This 'great liberation' of the *Geist* is further described (among other things) in terms of the soul—'the youthful soul is all at once convulsed, torn loose, torn away'—; of one's metaphysical orientation—'a desecrating blow and glance *backwards*'—; of the will—'this will to *free* will' (HH I Preface 3; KSA 2, 16–17). Is not the great liberation described here in the same way that the Neoplatonic tradition describes a mystical experience?[78]

Time and again, Nietzsche emphasizes the experiential aspect of this 'liberation'. On the one hand, 'the master's privilege of the free spirit' lies in 'a tenacious *will to health*' (HH I Preface 4; KSA 2, 18), and on the other, it consists in:

- a view from above: 'one lives . . . near or far as one wishes, preferably slipping away, evading, fluttering off, gone again, again flying aloft; one is spoiled, as everyone is who has at some time seen a tremendous number of things *beneath* him' (HH I Preface 4);
- a kind of mystical eye-opening: 'the free spirit again draws nearer to life. . . . It seems to him as if his eyes are only now open to what is *close at hand*. . . . These close and closest things: how changed they seem! what bloom and magic they have acquired!' (HH I Preface 5);
- a mystical 'shudder': 'Only now does he see himself—and what surprises he experiences as he does so! What unprecedented shudders [Schauder]![79] What happiness!' (HH I Preface 5; KSA 2, 19);
- and, as in the ancient mysteries, it is important both to recognize the validity of these experiences, but also to remain silent about them: 'my philosophy advises me to keep silent and to ask no more questions; especially as in certain cases, as the saying has it, one *remains* a philosopher only by—keeping silent'. (HH I Preface 8)[80]

In particular, there is (as noted above) an important link between *der Freigeist* and the (absence of the) will. In GS 347, Nietzsche discusses the persistence of the need for 'faith' and 'metaphysics', for 'that famous "proof of strength" of which the Bible speaks',[81] and 'that impetuous *demand for certainty* that today discharges itself among large numbers of people in a scientific-positivistic form' (KSA 3, 581). For Nietzsche, this kind of faith—whether (institutionally) religious or (positivistically) scientific—is a sign of (and arises from) *a lack of will*: 'Faith is always coveted most and needed most urgently where will is lacking. . . . [T]he two world religions, Buddhism and Christianity, may have owed their origin and above all their sudden spread to a tremendous collapse and *disease of the will*' (KSA 3, 582).

By contrast, *der Freigeist* turns its back on faith and the need for certainty alike, entering a new kind of experiential realm: experiencing 'such a pleasure and power of self-determination, such a *freedom* of the will . . . that the spirit would take leave of all faith and every wish for certainty, being practised in maintaining himself on insubstantial ropes and possibilities and dancing even near abysses'—'such a spirit', Nietzsche maintains, 'would be the *free spirit* par excellence' (GS 347; KSA 23, 583). Similarly, in Z II Philosophers, Nietzsche offers the following characterization of *der freie Geist*:

- first of all, 'the free spirit, the enemy of fetters, the non-worshipper, the dweller in forests' is 'hated by the people as a wolf is by the dogs';

- *der freie Geist* is existentially authentic: 'Genuine—this is what I call him who goes into god-forsaken deserts and has broken his venerating heart. / In the yellow sand and burned by the sun, perhaps he blinks thirstily at the islands filled with springs where living creatures rest beneath shady trees. / . . . Hungered, violent, solitary, godless: that is how the lion-will wants to be';
- and it is characterized by isolation and the desert, a traditional location for mystical experiences: 'Free from the happiness of serfs, redeemed from gods and worship, fearless and fearful, great and solitary: that is how the will of the genuine man is. / The genuine men, the free spirits, have always dwelt in the desert, as the lords of the desert.'

What is striking about these passages is that, although *der freie Geist* is described here in a personified way, it is not at all obvious that it is referring to an individual rather than to an attitude or outlook. And such a reading is confirmed by the way in which, in BGE, Nietzsche talks about 'free spirit' as an attitude, that is, as 'the piety of knowledge', and a *type* [Typus]—the 'free spirit' type [(der) Typus "freier Geist"]—in the context of 'a profound lack of understanding for the Church' (BGE 105). And in BGE 44, an aphorism that draws to a close the second section that bears the concept of free spirit as its title, he offers another extensive characterization of *der freie Geist*, assimilating the figure of 'the free spirit' to 'the philosopher of the future' (and note the ambiguity here: these philosophers of the future [diese Philosophen der Zukunft] are both those philosophers who are to come and those philosophers who investigate the future).

Once again, the transformation of the will plays a central role in this passage, where Nietzsche tells us that 'the dangerousness of [the plant "man's"] situation must . . . grow to the point of enormity, his powers of invention and simulation (his "spirit") had to develop under prolonged pressure and constraint into refinement and audacity, his life-will had to be enhanced into an unconditional power-will' (BGE 44). And Nietzsche continues with an explanation of what it means for 'life-will' to be transformed into 'power-will', observing that 'hardness, forcefulness, slavery, danger in the alley and in the heart, life in hiding, stoicism, the art of experiment and devilry of every kind, . . . everything evil, terrible, tyrannical in man, everything in him that is kin to beasts of prey and serpents, serves the enhancement of the species "man" as much as its opposite does' (BGE 44).

In the same aphorism, Nietzsche places great emphasis on the secrecy of the free spirit, asking: 'Is it any wonder that we "free spirits" are not exactly the most communicative spirits? that we do not want to betray in every particular *from what* a spirit can liberate himself and *to what* he may then be driven?' And he brings the aphorism to the following dramatic conclusion which outlines, in a series of extended metaphors, the characteristic of free spirit:

> At home . . . in many countries of the spirit; having escaped again and again from the musty agreeable nooks . . . ; full of malice against the lures of dependence that lie hidden . . . ; grateful even to need and vacillating sickness . . . ; curious to a vice, investigators to the point of cruelty . . . , ready for every venture, thanks to an excess of 'free will', with fore- and back-souls . . . ; concealed under cloaks of light, conquerors . . . occasionally night owls of work even in broad daylight; . . . born, sworn, jealous friends of *solitude*, of our own most profound, most midnightly, most middaily solitude: that is the type of man we are, we free spirits! (BGE 44)

In this passage, we can clearly see that *der freie Geist* is not so much an individual as it is rather a type [Typus], that it is linked to the question of the will, and that it could well be translated, not so much by *free spirit*, as by *free mind*.

What I am proposing, then, could be summarized as follows:

1. that Nietzsche's concept of *der Freigeist* can be read as a variant of Kant's notion of free beauty, and thus as essentially aesthetic;
2. that *der Freigeist* (or *der freie Geist*) can be translated as 'free mind', and read in an Idealist way, perhaps even (following Jung's suggestion) in a Neoplatonic way;
3. that the notion of *der Freigeist* opens up perspectives for a whole new set of questions about how to read Nietzsche and about the implications of his thought (viz., could it be that Nietzsche was wrong about Plato?).[82] Is it possible to be a Nietzschean and nevertheless an Idealist?[83] And finally: could it be that what the free spirit should ultimately seek to free itself from is—Nietzsche himself?

NOTES

1. In this chapter I have drawn on the following translations of R. J. Hollingdale and Walter Kaufmann: *Basic Writings*, ed. and trans. Walter Kaufmann (New York: The Modern Library, 1968); *Untimely Meditations*, trans. R. J. Hollingdale (Cambridge: Cambridge University Press, 1983); *Human, All Too Human*, trans. R. J. Hollindale (Cambridge: Cambridge University Press, 1986); *Daybreak*, trans. R. J. Hollingdale (Cambridge: Cambridge University Press, 1982); *The Gay Science*, trans. Walter Kaufmann (New York: Random House, 1974); *Thus Spoke Zarathustra*, trans. R. J. Hollingdale (Harmondsworth: Penguin, 1969) *Twilight of the Idols/The Anti-Christ*, trans. R. J. Hollingdale. (Harmondsworth: Penguin, 1968); *Dithyrambs of Dionysus*. Bilingual Edition, trans. R. J. Hollingdale (London: Anvil Press, 1984); *Ecce Homo*, trans. R. J. Hollingdale (Harmondsworth: Penguin, 1992); and *The Will to Power*, ed. Walter Kaufmann, trans. R. J. Hollingdale and Walter Kaufmann (New York: Random House, 1967).

2. Paolo D'Iorio and Olivier Ponton, eds, *Nietzsche, Philosophie de l'esprit libre: Etudes sur la genèse de "Choses humaines, trop humaines"* (Paris: Rue d'Ulm, 2004).

3. Paolo D'Iorio, *Le voyage de Nietzsche à Sorrente: Genèse de la philosophie de l'esprit libre* (Paris: CNRS Éditions, 2012).

4. Patrick Wotling, *La philosophie de l'esprit libre: Introduction à Nietzsche* (Paris: Flammarion, 2008). See also Paul Franco, *Nietzsche's Enlightenment: The Free Spirit Trilogy of the Middle Period* (Chicago and London: University of Chicago Press, 2011).

5. Sandro Barbera, 'Goethe *versus* Wagner: Le changement de fonction de l'art dans *Choses humaines, trop humaines*', in *Nietzsche, Philosophie de l'esprit libre*, ed. Paolo D'Iorio and Olivier Ponton, 37–60.

6. HH II AOM 113; KSA 2, 424. In 'From Makarien's Archive', §126, in *Wilhelm Meister's Journeyman Years*, Goethe writes: 'Yorik-Sterne was the most beautiful spirit ever active; anyone who reads him immediately feels free and beautiful; his humour is inimitable, and not all humour frees the soul'; and later, §171, he remarks: 'He is a model in nothing and a guide and stimulator in everything'; translated in Duncan Large, '"Sterne-Bilder": Sterne in the German-Speaking World', in *The Reception of Laurence Sterne in Europe*, ed. Peter de Voogd and John Neubauer (London and New York: Continuum/Thoemmes, 2004), 76.

7. Large points to the ironic overlap between Nietzsche's assessment of Sterne and Hegel's (in his *Lectures on Aesthetics*), and suggests it was due to Nietzsche's influence that, in the winter of 1869–1870, Richard and Cosmia Wagner began reading *Tristram Shandy*—although, or so it seems, with little profit (Large, '"Sterne-Bilder"', 81).

8. But see the earlier use of the adjectives *freigeisterisch* in UM I 10; KSA 1, 217 and *freigeistisch* in *Philosophy in the Tragic Age of the Greeks* 19 (KSA 1, 869), where the term *Freigeister* is associated with the Athenian followers of Anaxagoras in general and with Euripides in particular (KSA 1, 869).

9. On this passage, and its concluding reference to *mater saeva cupidinum*, see C. G. Jung, *Psychology of the Unconscious: A Study of the Transformations and Symbolisms of the Libido: A Contribution to the History of the Evolution of Thought*, trans. Beatrice M. Hinkle (London: Routledge, 1991), §478 to §481. Nietzsche's textual allusion is to 'the cruel mother of the Cupids' or 'the cruel mother of sweet desires' in Horace, *Odes*, book 1, no. 19, and book 4, no. 1 (Horace, *Odes and Epodes*, ed. and trans. Niall Rudd [Cambridge, MA; London: Harvard University Press, 2004], 63 and 219).

10. The final line from Voltaire's philosophical fable in, 'Ce qui plaît aux dames' (1764).

11. For a discussion of Nietzsche's relation to the French *moralistes*, see W. D. Williams, *Nietzsche and the French: A Study of the Influence of Nietzsche's French Reading on his Thought and Writing* (Oxford: Blackwell, 1952); and Claus Zittel, 'Französische Moralistik', in *Nietzsche-Handbuch. Leben—Werk—Wirkung*, ed. Henning Ottmann (Stuttgart and Weimar: Metzler, 2000), 399–401. See also Vivetta Vivarelli, *Nietzsche und die Masken des freien Geistes: Montaigne, Pascal und Sterne* (Würzburg: Königshausen und Neumann, 1998).

12. Another remark in this aphorism is to the effect that, 'in no way superficial, a great Frenchman nonetheless always preserves his surface, a natural skin to cover his content and depths', anticipates his famous observation in GS Preface that the Greeks were 'superficial—out of profundity'.

13. A. Rey and J. Rey-Debove, eds. *Le Petit Robert 1: Dictionnaire alphabétique et analogique de la langue française* (Paris: Le Robert, 1985), 690–91.

14. Cf. Pierre Desmaizeaux, 'La Vie de Monsieur de Saint-Evremond', in Charles de Saint-Evremond, *Œuvres meslées*, vol. 1 (London: Tonson, 1709), lxvii. In fact, Saint-Evremond attributes a *génie vaste* to Homer and Aristotle, and an *esprit vaste* to Pyrrhus, Catiline, Charles V, and Cardinal Richelieu.

15. Kant, 'Preface' to second edition of the first *Critique* (B xxx), in Immanuel Kant, *Critique of Pure Reason*, ed. and trans. Paul Guyer and Allen W. Wood (Cambridge: Cambridge University Press, 1997), 117.

16. Immanuel Kant, *The Critique of Judgement*, trans. James Creed Meredith (Oxford: Clarendon Press, 1952), §49, 175–82. Henceforth cited as *CJ* followed by section and page reference.

17. *CJ*, §46, 168.

18. *CJ*, §46, 169.

19. *CJ*, §46, 169. In §49, 179–91, and in §57, Note 1, 212–13, Kant returns to the figure of the genius (179–81). In short, '*genius* may also be defined as the faculty of *aesthetic ideas*' (*CJ*, §57, Remark 1; 212).

20. *CJ*, §29, 122.

21. *CJ*, §26, 104.

22. *CJ*, §9, 57–60. The dialectic of purposefulness and freedom is evident in Kant's following definition: 'Aesthetic finality is the conformity of the law of judgement in its *freedom*' (*CJ*, §29, 122).

23. *CJ*, §16, 72.

24. *CJ*, §29, 72. For Nietzsche's critique of Kant's assertion that 'what pleases without interest is beautiful' [schön ist, was ohne Interesse gefällt], see *GM* III 6.

25. See Schiller's formulation in his *Kallias* letter (18 February 1773) of beauty as 'freedom in appearance' [Freiheit in der Erscheinung], also referred to in his *Aesthetic Letters* (Letter 23, §7, fn.1); Friedrich Schiller, *On the Aesthetic Education of Man*, ed. and trans. Elizabeth M. Wilkinson and L. A. Willoughby (Oxford: Clarendon Press, 1982), 166–67. Strong evidence also suggests that an association of both 'free' [frei] and 'illusion' [Schein] with the notion of beauty was established in German usage long before Schiller used the term 'freedom in appearance' [Freiheit in der Erscheinung] to cover his own distinctive, finely elaborated concept. According to the Grimms' *Deutsches Wörterbuch*, the collocation goes back to Middle High German, a view that Keith Spalding's *Historical Dictionary of German Figurative Usage* supports.

26. *CJ*, §49, 175. Translation modified.

27. *CJ*, §49, 175.

28. *CJ*, §29, 119. Translation modified.

29. *CJ*, §29, 119. Translation modified.

30. *CJ*, 175–76. As Kant goes on to explain, an 'aesthetic idea' is the counterpart to a 'rational idea', which in turn is a concept to which no intuition, or 'representation of the imagination', can be adequate. See also further in *CJ* §49 (179), and *CJ* §57, Note 1 (209–10).

31. *CJ*, §49, 176.

32. *CJ*, §49, 176.

33. *CJ*, §49, 176–77. For Kant, the faculty of aesthetic ideas, or the imagination, 'can show itself to its full advantage' precisely in the poetic art [die Dichtkunst]. Further on in §49, Kant cites a poem by Frederick the Great. See §51 for Kant's division of fine arts into rhetoric and poetry, formative arts (plastic art and painting), and 'the beautiful play of sensations' (music and 'the art of colour'), a division on which subsequent sections expand (§52–§53).

34. *CJ*, §49, 179.

35. *CJ*, §51, 183. This notion of 'expression' may also be seen to depend on Spinozean monism, especially given Nietzsche's intense interest, if ambiguous attitude, toward Spinoza (as Rebecca Bamford has pointed out to me, private e-mail, 12/02/2015). In a note written in the autumn of 1881, Nietzsche declared: 'When I talk about Plato, Pascal, Spinoza, and Goethe, I know that their blood is mixed with mine' (KSA 9, 12[52], 585; cf. KSA 9, 15[17], 642); and in the spring of 1884, he noted: 'My predecessors: Heraclitus, Empedocles, Spinoza, Goethe' (KSA 11, 25[454], 134). In a letter to Franz Overbeck from the end of July 1881, Nietzsche enumerated various points of doctrine shared with Spinoza, including the denial of free will, of a moral world order and of evil (KSB 6, 111). Yet there are important differences between Spinoza and Nietzsche, as Yirmiyahu Yovel has noted (*Spinoza and Other Heretics: The Adventures of Immanence* [Princeton, NJ: Princeton University Press, 1989], 106), and the entire question of Nietzsche's relation to Spinoza requires further investigation, especially in relation to Nietzsche's reception of Plato; Spinoza's letter to Hugo Boxel of 1674 about the existence of ghosts or spirits constitutes a possible starting point for such a constellation, for here Spinoza writes: 'The authority of Plato, Aristotle, and Socrates, does not carry much weight with me. I should have been astonished, if you had brought forward Epicurus, Democritus, Lucretius, or any of the atomists, or upholders of the atomic theory' (*On the Improvement of the Understanding; The Ethics; Correspondence*, trans. R. H. M. Elwes [New York: Dover, 1955], 388). For further discussion, see William S. Wurzer, *Nietzsche und Spinoza* (Meisenheim am Glan: Hain, 1975); Reiner Wiehl, 'Nietzsches Anti-Platonismus und Spinoza', in

Zeitwelten: Philosophisches Denken an den Rändern von Natur und Geschichte (Frankfurt am Main: Suhrkamp, 1998), 129–49; and Hans-Gerd von Seggern, 'Die Spur von Spinozas Affektenlehre', in *Nietzsche und die Weimarer Klassik* (Tübingen: Francke, 2005), 127–47.

36. Cf. BGE 44, where Nietzsche talks about 'the plant "man"' [der Pflanze "Mensch"].

37. 'The human soul is naturally Christian' (Tertullian, *Apologeticum*, chapter 17; cf. appendix, *De testimonio animae*). For further discussion, see Bardo Weiss, 'Die "anima naturaliter Christiana" im Verständnis Tertullians', *Mitteilungen und Forschungsbeiträge der Cusanus-Gesellschaft*, 13 (1978): 292–304.

38. C. G. Jung, *Nietzsche's 'Zarathustra': Notes of the Seminar Given in 1934–1939*, ed. James L. Jarrett, vol. 1 (London: Routledge, 1989), 62. Henceforth referred to as *SNZ* plus volume number and page reference.

39. In a letter to Freud of 26 June 1910 and subsequently in *Transformations and Symbols of Libido*, Jung transfers this idea into psychoanalytic discourse, talking about how 'libido is opposed to libido, will against will' (*The Freud/Jung Letters: The Correspondence between Sigmund Freud and C.G. Jung*, ed. William McGuire, trans. Ralph Manheim and R. F. C. Hull (Cambridge, MA and London: Harvard University Press, 1988), 336; and *Psychology of the Unconscious*, §398; cf. §249 and §457).

40. Jung, *SNZ*, vol. 1, 365. According to *Wahrig Deutsches Wörterbuch*, the word *Geist* derives from the Indogermanic root *gheis-*, '"aufgebracht, außer Fassung, erregt;" zugrunde liegt wohl die Vorstellung eines (kultisch) erregten Zustands des Menschen'.

41. Jung is referring to Ludwig Klages (1872–1956) and the central thesis of his major work, *Der Geist als Widersacher der Seele*, 3 vols. (1929–1932).

42. Jung, *SNZ*, vol. 1, 368.

43. Jung, *SNZ*, vol. 1, 368.

44. Jung, *SNZ*, vol. 1, 368–69.

45. On the link between Schopenhauer and *die freien Geister*, see UM IV 7 (KSA 1, 407).

46. C. G. Jung, *Symbols of Transformation* [*Collected Works*, vol. 5], trans. R. F. C. Hull (London: Routledge & Kegan Paul, 1967), §448.

47. See Ovid, *Metamorphoses*, book 12, ll. 171–209 and 459–525; Pindar, fragments, no. 166 (147). See Ovid, *Metamorphoses*, trans. A. D. Melville (Oxford and New York: Oxford University Press, 1987), 179–280 and 288–90; and Pindar, *Odes of Pindar, including the Principal Fragments*, trans. John Sandys, London: Heinemann; New York: Putnam, 1927, 602–5.

48. Cf. Nietzsche on 'Mithraswahn', or the insanity of the cult of Mithras (KSA 8, 28[22] and 28[34], 50 / and 508).

49. C. G. Jung, *Symbols of Transformation* (*CW* 5), §530. See Orphic Hymn No. 52, 'To Trietericus', in *Hymns and Initiations*, trans. Thomas Taylor [Thomas Taylor Series, vol. 5] (Frome: The Prometheus Trust, 2003), 112, where *upokholpie* is translated as 'virginlike'.

50. Papyrus no. 122, ll. 2–3; in F. G. Kenyon, *Greek Papyri in the British Museum*, 5 vols (London: British Museum, 1893–1917), vol. 1, 116; cited from Dieterich, *Eine Mithrasliturgie*. 2nd edition (Leipzig and Berlin: Teubner, 1910), 97.

51. Jung, *Symbols of Transformation* (*CW* 5), §460.

52. Jung, *SNZ*, vol. 1, 370. Here resides, for Jung, the importance of his understanding of the unconscious: 'It is a great discovery that below or aside from one's own psyche, or consciousness, or mind, is another intelligence of which one is not the maker, and upon which one depends. . . . There is, prior to unconsciousness, an conscious out of which consciousness once arose, and that is an intelligence which surely exceeds our intelligence in an indefinite way' (*SNZ*, vol. 1, 370–371).

53. Jung, *SNZ*, vol. 1, 171.

54. Jung, *SNZ*, vol. 1, 722.

55. *The Gospel of Thomas*, logion 82, cited by Origen in his *Homilies on Jeremiah*, Homily 27 (on Jeremiah 27: 23–29); *The Original Gospel of Thomas in Translation*, ed. and trans. April D. DeConick (London and New York: Continuum, 1986), 246; cf. Origen, *Homilies on Jeremiah; Homily on 1 Kings 28*, trans. John Clark Smith [The Fathers of the Church, vol. 97] (Washington, DC: Catholic University of America Press, 1998), 254.

56. Jung, *SNZ*, vol. 1, 722. For Jung, the same motif is in evidence in the miracle or mystery of Pentecost, when the Holy Spirit descended in tongues of fire (cf. Acts 2: 1–2) (Jung, *SNZ*, vol. 1, 722).

57. Heraclitus, Diels-Kranz fragment 118; *Die Vorsokratiker*, ed. and trans. Jaap Mansfeld, Vol. 1 (Stuttgart: Reclam, 1983–1986), 270–71.

58. Jung, *SNZ*, vol. 1, 722.

59. Jung, *SNZ*, vol. 1, 723.

60. Jung, *SNZ*, vol. 1, 722.

61. Later, in alchemical writings, *anthropos* represents something whole or complete, and hence it is a symbol of the Self; cf. Jung, *Mysterium Coniunctionis* [*Collected Works*, vol. 14], trans. R. F. C. Hull (London: Routledge & Kegan Paul, 1974), §484–§497. Elsewhere, Jung explains that 'the *Nous* of the Gnosis was attracted by his own reflection in the chaotic waters, and instantly the Physis leapt up and took him in and he dissolved in matter', resulting in 'the creation of man, the ordinary man' from whom the *anthropos* was born (*SNZ*, vol. 2, 1180). For further discussion, see Richard T. Wallis and Jay Bregman (eds), *Neoplatonism and Gnosticism* (Albany: State University of New York Press, 1992).

62. Jung, *SNZ*, vol. 2, 1179–80. The relation between Zarathustra and Nietzsche is a recurring problem for Jung in his seminar; at this point, Jung suggests that 'the man Nietzsche is a sort of tool or vehicle for the eternal four-dimensional spirit of Zarathustra' (*SNZ*, vol. 2, 1180).

63. For further discussion of Nietzsche's relation to Plato, which is a vast topic, see for instance Reiner Wiehl, 'L'antiplatonisme de Nietzsche', in *Contre Platon*, vol. 2, *Le platonisme renversé*, ed. Monique Dixsaut (Paris: Vrin, 1993), 25–45; Monique Dixsaut, 'Nietzsche lecteur de Platon', in *Images de Platon et lectures de ses œuvres: Les interprétations de Platon à travers des siècles*, ed. Ada Neschke-Hentschke (Louvain: Peeters, 1997), 295–313; Thomas H. Brobjer, 'Nietzsche's Wrestling with Plato and Platonism', in *Nietzsche and Antiquity: His Reaction and Response to the Classical Tradition*, ed. Paul Bishop (Rochester, NY: Camden House, 2004), 241–59; John Sallis, *Platonic Legacies* (Albany: State University of New York Press, 2004); Monique Dixsaut, 'Platon, Nietzsche et les images', in *Puissances de l'image*, ed. Jean-Claude Gens and Pierre Rodrigo (Dijon: Editions universitaire de Dijon, 2007), 11–24; Thomas H. Brobjer, *Nietzsche's Philosophical Context: An Intellectual Biography* (Urbana and Chicago: University of Illinois Press, 2008), 25–28; and, most recently, Mark Anderson, *Plato and Nietzsche: Their Philosophical Art* (London: Bloomsbury, 2014).

64. The *Satura Menippea* is 'a medley of prose and verse, treating of all kinds of subjects just as they came to hand in the plebeian style, often with much grossness, but with sparkling point. . . . Menippus of Gadara, the originator of this style of composition, lived about 280 BC; he interspersed jocular and commonplace topics with moral maxims and philosophical doctrines. . . .' (Charles Thomas Cruttwell, *A History of Roman Literature: From the Earliest Period to the Death of Marcus Aurelius* [New York: Scribner, 1906], 144).

65. For a further encomium to Fontenelle (and to the tradition of the French *moralistes* in general), see HH II WS 214; KSA 2, 646–47. In this section, however, the French *philosophes* are not set against, but rather aligned with, the ancient Greeks, and both contrasted with the Germans. For a portrait of Fontenelle, see *Gazette littéraire de Grimm* (Paris: Didier, 1854), 58–63, reprinted in Cioran, *Anthologie du portrait: De Saint-Simon à Tocqueville* (Paris: Gallimard, 1996), 55–60.

66. For further discussion, see George J. Stack, *Nietzsche and Emerson: An Elective Affinity* (Athens, OH: Ohio University Press, 1994); Thomas H. Brobjer, *Nietzsche's Philosophical Context: An Intellectual Biography*, 21–26; Michel Onfray, *La Construction du surhomme* [*Contre-histoire de la philosophie*, vol. 7] (Paris: Grasset, 2011), 30–38; and, most recently, Benedetta Zavatta, 'Historical Sense as Vice and Virtue in Nietzsche's Reading of Emerson', *Journal of Nietzsche Studies* 44(3) (Autumn 2013): 372–97, part of a special section in this issue on Nietzsche and Emerson.

67. In 'The Scholar', Emerson says: 'I think the peculiar office of scholars in a careful and gloomy generation is to be (as the poets were called in the Middle Ages) Professors of the Joyous Science' (Ralph Waldo Emerson, *Lectures and Biographical Sketches* (London: Waverley Book Company, 1883), 249–71, 250.

68. Emerson, 'History', in Ralph Waldo Emerson, *Essays and Lectures*, ed. Joel Porte (New York: Library of America, 1983), 237–56, 242. For Nietzsche's ironic use of this quotation in his correspondence, see his letters to Paul Rée of end of August 1882 and to Erwin Rohde of 25 December 1882 (KSB 6, 247 and 312).

69. Similarly, it has been argued that Emerson's notion of the over-soul (see his essay, 'The Over-Soul', in *Essays and Lectures*, 383–400), could have provided inspiration for Nietzsche's concept of the *Übermensch*.

70. See, for example, the lecture entitled 'Goethe; or, the Writer', in *Representative Men* (1850); Emerson, *Essays and Lectures*, 746–61.

71. See Emerson, 'Character', in Emerson, *Essays and Lectures*, 495–509, 505.

72. See Emerson, 'Prospects', in Emerson, *Essays and Lectures*, 43–49, 46.

73. Emerson, *Nature*, chapter 1, 'Nature', in Emerson, *Essays and Lectures*, 9–11, 10.

74. Jung, *SNZ*, vol. 2, 1178–80.

75. Jung, *SNZ*, vol. 2, 1180. Some may baulk for methodological reasons at Jung's hermeneutic approach, but Jung is trying to take seriously those passages—such as in the poem, 'Sils Maria', and in his account of the composition of Z in EH Z 3—where Nietzsche imputes an absolute autonomy to the figure of Zarathustra. As Nietzsche himself puts it, 'it was on these two walks [i.e., from Rapallo to Zoagli, and from Santa Margherita to Porto Fino] that the whole of the first Zarathustra came to me, above all Zarathustra himself, as a type [als Typus]: more accurately, *he stole up on me*' (EH Z 1).

76. Raphaël Enthoven, remark at 49: 40–42 in *Le Gai savoir*, episode entitled '*Plotin: une terrible beauté*', broadcast on France Culture on 02/12/2012. Enthoven justifies this remark with a reference to Nietzsche's distinction between the ego and the self.

77. Herbert Theierl, *Nietzsche—Mystik als Selbstversuch* (Würzburg: Königshausen & Neumann, 2000), 13–14; cf. 47–48 and 90.

78. In the Eastern philosophical tradition, this experience is investigated in the *Tibetan Book of the Great Liberation*, a text discussed by Jung from an analytical psychological angle in his 'Psychological Commentary on "The Tibetan Book of the Great Liberation"' (1939), in *Psychology and Religion: West and East* [*Collected Works*, vol. 11], trans. R. F. C. Hull (London: Routledge & Kegan Paul, 1969), §759–830.

79. Cf. the Mothers scene in *Faust*, part 2, where one finds the famous line, when Faust tells Mephistopheles:

Yet not in torpor would I comfort find,
Awe is the finest portion of mankind;
However scarce the world may make this sense—
In awe one feels profoundly the immense.

(*Faust II*, ll. 6271–6274; in J. W. von Goethe, *Faust*, ed. Cyrus Hamlin, trans. Walter Arndt, 2nd edition (New York and London: Norton, 2001], 178).

80. Cf. Nietzsche's allusion in GS 82, to Martial, *Est res magna tacere* (it is a big thing to remain silent) (cf. Martial, *Epigrams*, IV, 80.6). For further discussion of the theme of silence in Nietzsche, see Martin Heidegger, 'Tragedy, Satyr-Play, and Telling Silence in Nietzsche's Thought of Eternal Recurrence', trans. David Farrell Krell, *boundary 2* 9-10(3-1) (1981): 25–39; and Claudia Crawford, 'Nietzsche's Dionysian Arts: Dance, Song, and Silence', in *Nietzsche, Philosophy and the Arts*, edited by Salim Kemal, Ivan Gaskell, and Daniel M. Conway (Cambridge: Cambridge University Press, 1998), 318–41.

81. Cf. 1 Corinthians 2: 4: 'in demonstration of the Spirit and of power' (KJV). Cf. *The Anti-Christ* 50; and *The Will to Power* 171 and 452.

82. Compare with Mark Anderson's observations that 'Nietzsche was closer to Plato than he realized or wanted to admit' and that 'Plato as a thinker and artist was closer to [Nietzsche] than he cared to acknowledge'; his designation of Plato's and Nietzsche's philosophies as a form of 'aristocratic radicalism'; and his assessment that, although Nietzsche is 'profound' whereas Plato is 'sublime', we must 'look through the differences between the two to see the one great thing behind them' (*Plato and Nietzsche*, 113, 120, 154, 183).

83. Compare with Michel Onfray's observation that to be Nietzschean means to take Nietzsche as a starting point, not to think like Nietzsche [*être nietzschéen, c'est penser à partir de Nietzsche—pas comme lui*] (*L'Archipel des comètes: Journal hédoniste III* (Paris: Grasset & Fasquelle, 2001), 267–82, 278 and 281).

BIBLIOGRAPHY

Anderson, Mark. *Plato and Nietzsche: Their Philosophical Art*. London: Bloomsbury, 2014.
Barbera, Sandro. 'Goethe *versus* Wagner: Le changement de fonction de l'art dans *Choses humaines, trop humaines*'. In *Nietzsche, Philosophie de l'esprit libre: Etudes sur la genèse de 'Choses humaines, trop humaines'*, edited by Paolo D'Iorio and Olivier Ponton. Paris: Rue d'Ulm, 2004.
Brobjer, Thomas H. *Nietzsche's Philosophical Context: An Intellectual Biography*. Urbana and Chicago: University of Illinois Press, 2008.
Brobjer, Thomas H. 'Nietzsche's Wrestling with Plato and Platonism'. In *Nietzsche and Antiquity: His Reaction and Response to the Classical Tradition*, edited by Paul Bishop, 241–59. Rochester, NY: Camden House, 2004.
Cioran, E. M. *Anthologie du portrait: De Saint-Simon à Tocqueville*. Paris: Gallimard, 1996.
Crawford, Claudia. 'Nietzsche's Dionysian Arts: Dance, Song, and Silence'. In *Nietzsche, Philosophy and the Arts*, edited by Salim Kemal, Ivan Gaskell, and Daniel M. Conway, 318–41. Cambridge: Cambridge University Press, 1998.
Cruttwell, Charles Thomas. *A History of Roman Literature: From the Earliest Period to the Death of Marcus Aurelius*. New York: Scribner, 1906.
Dieterich, Albrecht. *Eine Mithrasliturgie*. 2nd edition. Leipzig and Berlin: Teubner, 1910.
D'Iorio, Paolo. *Le voyage de Nietzsche à Sorrente: Genèse de la philosophie de l'esprit libre*. Paris: CNRS Éditions, 2012.
D'Iorio, Paolo, and Olivier Ponton, eds. *Nietzsche, Philosophie de l'esprit libre: Etudes sur la genèse de "Choses humaines, trop humaines"*. Paris: Rue d'Ulm, 2004.
Dixsaut, Monique. 'Nietzsche lecteur de Platon'. In *Images de Platon et lectures de ses œuvres: Les interprétations de Platon à travers des siècles*, edited by Ada Neschke-Hentschke, 295–313. Louvain: Peeters, 1997.
Dixsaut, Monique. 'Platon, Nietzsche et les images'. In *Puissances de l'image*, edited by Jean-Claude Gens and Pierre Rodrigo, 11–24. Dijon: Editions universitaires de Dijon, 2007.
Emerson, Ralph Waldo. *Essays and Lectures*, edited by Joel Porte. New York: Library of America, 1983.
Emerson, Ralph Waldo. *Lectures and Biographical Sketches*. London: Waverley Book Company, 1883.
Enthoven, Raphaël. Remark at 49: 40–42 in *Le Gai savoir*, episode entitled '*Plotin: une terrible beauté*', broadcast on France Culture on 02/12/2012.
Franco, Paul. *Nietzsche's Enlightenment: The Free Spirit Trilogy of the Middle Period*. Chicago and London: University of Chicago Press, 2011.
Freud, Sigmund, and Jung, C. G. *The Freud/Jung Letters: The Correspondence between Sigmund Freud and C.G. Jung*, edited by William McGuire. Translated by Ralph Manheim and R. F. C. Hull. Cambridge, MA, and London: Harvard University Press, 1988.
Goethe, J. W. von. *Faust*, edited by Cyrus Hamlin. Translated by Walter Arndt. 2nd edition. New York and London: Norton, 2001.
Grimms, Jacob and Wilhelm, *Deutsches Wörterbuch* [1889]. 33 volumes. Munich: Deutscher Taschenbuchverlag, 1984.
Heidegger, Martin. 'Tragedy, Satyr-Play, and Telling Silence in Nietzsche's Thought of Eternal Recurrence'. Translated by David Farrell Krell. *boundary 2* 9-10(3-1) (1981): 25–39.
Horace. *Odes and Epodes*. Niall Rudd, ed. and trans. Cambridge, MA; London: Harvard University Press, 2004.
Jung, C. G. *Mysterium Coniunctionis* [*Collected Works*, vol. 14]. Translated by R. F. C. Hull. London: Routledge & Kegan Paul, 1974.

Jung, C. G. *Nietzsche's 'Zarathustra': Notes of the Seminar Given in 1934–1939*, vol. 1, edited by James L. Jarrett. Vol 1. London: Routledge, 1989.

Jung, C. G. *Psychology and Religion: West and East [Collected Works*, vol. 11]. Translated by R. F. C. Hull. London: Routledge & Kegan Paul, 1969.

Jung, C. G. *Psychology of the Unconscious: A Study of the Transformations and Symbolisms of the Libido: A Contribution to the History of the Evolution of Thought*. Translated by Beatrice M. Hinkle. London: Routledge, 1991.

Jung, C. G. *Symbols of Transformation [Collected Works*, vol. 5]. Translated by R. F. C. Hull. London: Routledge & Kegan Paul, 1967.

Kant, Immanuel. *The Critique of Judgement*. Translated by James Creed Meredith. Oxford: Clarendon Press, 1952.

Kant, Immanuel. *Critique of Pure Reason*, edited and translated by Paul Guyer and Allen W. Wood. Cambridge: Cambridge University Press, 1997.

Klages, Ludwig. *Der Geist als Widersacher der Seele*. 6th edition. Bonn: Bouvier Verlag Herbert Grundmann, 1981.

Large, Duncan. "'Sterne-Bilder": Sterne in the German-Speaking World'. In *The Reception of Laurence Sterne in Europe*, edited by Peter de Voogd and John Neubauer, 68–85. London and New York: Continuum/Thoemmes, 2004.

Mansfeld, Jaap, ed. and trans. *Die Vorsokratiker*, vol. 1. Stuttgart: Reclam, 1983–1986.

Nietzsche, Friedrich. *Basic Writings*, edited and translated by Walter Kaufmann. New York: The Modern Library, 1968.

Nietzsche, Friedrich. *Daybreak*. Translated by R. J. Hollingdale. Cambridge: Cambridge University Press, 1982.

Nietzsche, Friedrich. *Dithyrambs of Dionysus*. Bilingual Edition. Translated by R. J. Hollingdale. London: Anvil Press, 1984.

Nietzsche, Friedrich. *Ecce Homo*. Translated by R. J. Hollingdale. Harmondsworth: Penguin, 1992.

Nietzsche, Friedrich. *The Gay Science*. Translated by Walter Kaufmann. New York: Random House, 1974.

Nietzsche, Friedrich. *Human, All Too Human*. Translated by R. J. Hollindale. Cambridge: Cambridge University Press, 1986.

Nietzsche, Friedrich. *Friedrich Nietzsche: Sämtliche Briefe. Kritische Studienausgabe*. 8 volumes. Edited by Giorgio Colli and Mazzino Montinari. Berlin and New York: de Gruyter, 1986.

Nietzsche, Friedrich. *Friedrich Nietzsche: Sämtliche Werke. Kritische Studienausgabe*. 2nd edition. 15 volumes. Edited by Giorgio Colli and Mazzino Montinari. Berlin and New York: de Gruyter, 1988.

Nietzsche, Friedrich. *Thus Spoke Zarathustra*. Translated by R. J. Hollingdale. Harmondsworth: Penguin, 1969.

Nietzsche, Friedrich. *Twilight of the Idols/The Anti-Christ*. Translated by R. J. Hollingdale. Harmondsworth: Penguin, 1968.

Nietzsche, Friedrich. *Untimely Meditations*, edited by Daniel Breazeale. Translated by R. J. Hollingdale. Cambridge: Cambridge University Press, 1983.

Nietzsche, Friedrich. *The Will to Power*, edited by Walter Kaufmann. Translated by R. J. Hollingdale and Walter Kaufmann. New York: Random House, 1967.

Onfray, Michel. *L'Archipel des comètes: Journal hédoniste III*. Paris: Grasset & Fasquelle, 2001.

Onfray, Michel. *La Construction du surhomme [Contre-histoire de la philosophie*, vol. 7]. Paris: Grasset, 2011.

Origen. *Homilies on Jeremiah*. In *The Original Gospel of Thomas in Translation*. Edited and translated by April D. DeConick. London and New York: Continuum, 1986.

Origen. *Homilies on Jeremiah. Homily on 1 Kings 28*. Translated by John Clark Smith [The Fathers of the Church, vol. 97]. Washington, DC: Catholic University of America Press, 1998.

Ovid, *Metamorphoses*. Translated by A. D. Melville. Oxford and New York: Oxford University Press, 1987.

Pindar, *The Odes of Pindar, including the Principal Fragments*. Translated by John Sandys. London: Heinemann; New York: Putnam, 1927.

Rey, A. and J. Rey-Debove, eds. *Le Petit Robert 1: Dictionnaire alphabétique et analogique de la langue française*. Paris: Le Robert, 1985.

Saint-Evremond, Charles de *Œuvres meslées*, vol. 1. 2nd edition. London: Tonson, 1709: Pierre Desmaizeaux, 'La Vie de Monsieur de Saint-Evremond', iii–lxxiv.

Sallis, John. *Platonic Legacies*. Albany: State University of New York Press, 2004.

Schiller, Friedrich. *On the Aesthetic Education of Man*, edited and translated by Elizabeth M. Wilkinson and L. A. Willoughby. Oxford: Clarendon Press, 1982.

Seggern, Hans-Gerd von. *Nietzsche und die Weimarer Klassik*. Tübingen: Francke, 2005.

Spalding, Keith. *Historical Dictionary of German Figurative Usage*. Oxford: Blackwell, 1952–1958.

Spinoza, Benedict de. *On the Improvement of the Understanding; The Ethics; Correspondence*. Translated by R. H. M. Elwes. New York: Dover, 1955.

Stack, George J. *Nietzsche and Emerson: An Elective Affinity*, Athens, OH: Ohio University Press, 1994.

Taylor, Thomas, trans. Orphic Hymn No. 52, 'To Trietericus'. In *Hymns and Initiations* [Thomas Taylor Series, vol. 5]. Frome: The Prometheus Trust, 2003.

Theierl, Herbert. *Nietzsche—Mystik als Selbstversuch*. Würzburg: Königshausen & Neumann, 2000.

Vivarelli, Vivetta. *Nietzsche und die Masken des freien Geistes: Montaigne, Pascal und Sterne*. Würzburg: Königshausen und Neumann, 1998.

Wahrig, Gerhard. *Deutsches Wörterbuch*, new edition. Munich: Mosaik, 1975.

Wallis, Richard T., and Jay Bregman, eds. *Neoplatonism and Gnosticism*. Albany: State University of New York Press, 1992.

Weiss, Bardo. 'Die "anima naturaliter Christiana" im Verständnis Tertullians', *Mitteilungen und Forschungsbeiträge der Cusanus-Gesellschaft* 13 (1978): 292–304.

Wiehl, Reiner. 'L'antiplatonisme de Nietzsche', In *Contre Platon*, vol. 2, *Le platonisme renversé*, edited by Monique Dixsaut, 25–45. Paris: Vrin, 1993.

Wiehl, Reiner. *Zeitwelten: Philosophisches Denken an den Rändern von Natur und Geschichte*. Frankfurt am Main: Suhrkamp, 1998.

Williams, W. D. *Nietzsche and the French: A Study of the Influence of Nietzsche's French Reading on His Thought and Writing*. Oxford: Blackwell, 1952.

Wotling, Patrick. *La philosophie de l'esprit libre: Introduction à Nietzsche*. Paris: Flammarion, 2008.

Wurzer, William S. *Nietzsche und Spinoza*. Meisenheim am Glan: Hain, 1975.

Yovel, Yirmiyahu. *Spinoza and Other Heretics: The Adventures of Immanence*. Princeton, NJ: Princeton University Press, 1989.

Zavatta, Benedetta. 'Historical Sense as Vice and Virtue in Nietzsche's Reading of Emerson', *Journal of Nietzsche Studies* 44(3) (Autumn 2013): 372–97.

Zittel, Claus. 'Französische Moralistik'. In *Nietzsche-Handbuch: Leben—Werk—Wirkung*, edited by Henning Ottmann, 399–401. Stuttgart and Weimar: Metzler, 2000.

Chapter Twelve

Almost Everything Is Permitted

Nietzsche's Not-So-Free Spirits

Daniel Conway

We immoralists . . . have been spun into a severe yarn and suit of duties and *cannot* get out of that—and in this we are 'men of duty', we, too. Occasionally, that is true, we dance in our 'chains' and between our 'swords'; more often, that is no less true, we gnash our teeth and feel impatient with all the secret hardness of our destiny. —Friedrich Nietzsche, *Beyond Good and Evil* 226

In his 1886 preface to the new edition of *Human, All Too Human*, Nietzsche begins by acknowledging—and, apparently, endorsing—the view that his books are designed to ambush his readers. As he explains, his aim in setting rhetorical snares for his readers is to inure them to the practice of examining their most firmly entrenched prejudices:

> I have been told often enough, and always with an expression of great surprise, that all my writings . . . contain snares and nets for unwary birds and in effect a persistent invitation to the overturning of habitual evaluations and valued habits. (HH I Preface 1)

Nietzsche's confirmation of this familiar sentiment is hardly surprising. Many readers are drawn to his books precisely in response to the 'invitation' he cites. Some of these readers are attracted in particular by the prospect of extricating themselves from morality and other vestiges of what remains 'human, all too human' within them.

As Nietzsche proceeds to disclose, this particular approach to writing is not without its costs. Before he could school his readers in therapeutic mistrust, he first needed to immerse himself in an arduous regimen of self-directed suspicion. While the fruits of this regimen are available for anyone to survey, the toll it exacted from Nietzsche has gone largely unremarked—until now, that is. As he now explains, his mistrust occasionally got the better of him, at which point he was obliged to invent the saving fictions that would permit him to regroup:

> [I]n an effort to recover from myself, as it were to induce a temporary self-forgetting, I have sought shelter in this or that—in some piece of admiration or enmity or scientificality or frivolity or stupidity; and why, where I could not find what I *needed*, I had artificially to enforce, falsify and invent a suitable fiction for myself (—and what else have poets ever done? And to what end does art exist in the world at all?). (HH I Preface 1)

This point too is familiar to Nietzsche's readers: Availing himself of the poet's prerogative, he fed himself the stories and lies that were needed to sustain him as he pursued his regimen of self-directed suspicion. One lie in particular is worth noting here:

> What I again and again needed most for my cure and self-restoration, however, was the belief that I was not thus isolated, not alone in *seeing* as I did. . . . (HH I Preface 1)

On the one hand, this confession is not particularly alarming. We know that Nietzsche had become increasingly isolated in his illness, estranged from friends, family, and the comfortable routines of his academic life. We know, in fact, that his experience of isolation was perhaps the most debilitating of the symptoms he endured. On the other hand, this confession is bound to capture our attention, inasmuch as it confirms the imaginary (or imagined) status of those rare others whom he had reported as sharing his unique way of 'seeing' the world. When we read the following, in fact, our interest is likely to be piqued:

> —Thus when I needed to I once also invented for myself the 'free spirits' to whom this melancholy-valiant book . . . is dedicated: 'free spirits' of this kind do not exist, did not exist—but, as I have said, I had need of them at that time if I was to keep in good spirits while surrounded by ills (sickness, solitude, unfamiliar places, *acedia*, inactivity): as brave companions and familiars with whom one can laugh and chatter when one feels like laughing and chattering, and whom one can send to the Devil when they become tedious—as compensation for the friends I lacked. (HH I Preface 2)

Here we may be inclined to take umbrage: The *free spirits* as imaginary friends? As compensatory constructs of a wearied, fevered mind? But what of the central role the *ideal* of the free spirit is thought to play in Nietzsche's philosophy?[1] And what of those among his faithful readers who aspire to this ideal and even claim to have attained it? Are they, too, but 'unwary birds', ensnared in a sudden rhetorical thicket?

Resisting the deflationary conclusion implied by these questions, Nietzsche adroitly changes the subject. Explaining that his invention of the free spirits has had salutary effects in excess of the intended restoration of his own health, he boasts of his modest success thus far in summoning these 'brave companions' into existence. A genuinely noble lie, he or we might say, makes possible the emergence of that which is fabricated:

> That free spirits of this kind *could* one day exist. . . . *I* should wish to be the last to doubt it. I see them already *coming*, slowly, slowly; and perhaps I shall do something to speed their coming if I describe in advance under what vicissitudes, upon what paths, I *see* them coming?— (HH I Preface 2)

Another fabrication? Another snare? Nietzsche does not say, and we should scarcely believe him if he did. Schooled by him in suspicion, we must sort this out for ourselves. That free spirits are already on their way, we must acknowledge, may be the snare reserved for us, the noble lie meant to persuade us to remain steadfast in our own regimen of self-directed suspicion.

Indeed, here we may detect a larger pattern of evasion and misdirection. That potentially redemptive resources are just around the corner, in the possession or person of a dashingly untimely figure endowed with over-human stores of strength, health, courage, and so on, is a familiar claim in Nietzsche's post-Zarathustran writings. This familiar claim is also the basis of the *hope* to which he occasionally refers his readers, often in situations that appear rather hopeless.[2] This is a matter of no little significance, moreover, for the (faint) hope expressed by Nietzsche is believed by many, perhaps including him, to be all that separates his philosophy from the garden-variety nihilisms to which he opposes it. As we shall see, in fact, he engenders (or fabricates) hope as a consolation prize for those readers whom he calls but does not choose.

Of particular note in this context is the following invocation, which, not coincidentally, accompanies Nietzsche's disclosure to his best readers that he has assigned them to a lesser role in the envisioned redemption of humankind:

> But some day, in a stronger age than this decaying, self-doubting present, he must yet come to us, the *redeeming* man of great love and contempt, . . . who will redeem us not only from the hitherto reigning ideal, but also from that which was bound to grow out of it, the great nausea, the will to nothingness, nihilism. . . . [T]his victor over God and nothingness—*he must come one day.*— (GM II 24)

There as here, Nietzsche conjures a glorious and imminent future as a way of easing his readers into the decidedly less glamorous role he has reserved for them. He does so, as we have seen, to buoy their hopes, thereby preserving the slightest thread of continuity between the future they believe they deserve and the present he needs them to endure. For all we know, of course, he also may believe what he says in such passages. Nevertheless, the fact remains that (some of) his readers, especially those who felt called to become free spirits, are likely to be disappointed by their demotion in rank and status. Whether they will take solace in the consolation prize he has promised them remains to be seen.

Returning to the 1886 preface, we note that Nietzsche continues to evade. He waxes eloquent in his praise of the free spirit type, describing in rich, patently autobiographical detail how one might expect to progress toward the experience of 'a *great liberation*' (HH I Preface 3). Although he does not say so explicitly, moreover, he apparently wishes for his best readers to regard *his* life, as described in the retrospective prefaces of 1886–1887 and *Ecce Homo*, as exemplary of the progress to which they (or their progeny) realistically might aspire. Still, the new, improved free spirits whom he describes here belong exclusively to the future, while his best readers remain rooted, perhaps unhappily, in the constrained freedom of the present. As the writings from the post-Zarathustran period of his career variously assert, in short, the free spirit ideal extolled in his so-called middle period is yesterday's news. A *new* ideal, associated with the 'great health' he glimpses in Zarathustra and the 'new philosophers' (GS 382), now commands his primary allegiance.[3]

To be sure, the timing of the new preface to HH bears noting: Several years have passed,[4] and Nietzsche himself has graduated from illness to convalescence and, perhaps, to resurgent health. In the interim, or so he claims, he has grown in spirit, strength, power, confidence and vitality, becoming in the process tantalizingly similar to those redemptive figures whose approach he claims to spy on the horizon (GS 382). Most notably, he has survived the ordeal of birthing his *Zarathustra* (EH Books Z 5), which has prepared him to witness, pronounce and relish the 'death of God' (GS 343). In short, what was true of him then, as he succumbed to the illness that would drag him to his nadir (EH Wise 1), is no longer the case.[5]

In particular, Nietzsche explains, he no longer needs the free spirits as compensation for the companions he lacks, though he may yet have need of them for other tasks, and one task in particular.[6] Nor does he need any longer the sick and sympathetic readers who cling to the belief that his imaginary friends were (and are) real. As the new preface to HH confirms, in fact, he now needs suspicious readers who, as 'friends' in their own right, are in a position to renounce their attachment to the free spirit ideal. That he has been successful thus far in nudging some of his readers toward the achievement of this ideal is a fortuity that he now aims to exploit.

BEHOLD THE 'LAST IDEALISTS'

Before he can mobilize the not-so-free spirits among his best readers, Nietzsche first must disabuse them of a notion they have taken to heart, a notion that *he* is responsible for encouraging them to embrace. Simply put, those among his readers who identify themselves as free spirits are mistaken about their achievement. As we shall see, they are in fact the 'last idealists' whom Nietzsche describes in essay 3 of *On the Genealogy of Morality*. Through no fault of their own, these 'last idealists' are not, and never will be, the free spirits he has emboldened them to become. They are nevertheless valuable to him, provided he can persuade them to affirm the non-negotiable limitations that attend their rank and station. His bold renunciation of the free spirit ideal in the new preface to HH thus serves as an unsubtle prompt to his best readers that the time has come for them to follow his lead.

Before turning to consider the decisive passages in essay 3 of GM, let us set the context in which they appear. The summary conclusion of essay 3, wherein Nietzsche pronounces the ascetic ideal '*the true calamity* [*das eigentliche Verhängniss*] in the history of European health' (GM III 21), arrives in section 21. The *meaning* [Bedeutung] of ascetic ideals, or so he takes himself to have established, lies in the *meaning* [Sinn] they confer upon those whose lives are otherwise ruined and bereft. Under the savvy direction of the ascetic priest, ascetic ideals have enabled the sick and sicker among human beings to refuse the temptation of 'suicidal nihilism' (GM III 28). These sufferers have secured meaning for their wretched lives, but they have done so only at a prohibitive (and persistently escalating) cost to their health.

If this is the summary conclusion of essay 3, however, what is the point of its remaining sections? As I have argued elsewhere,[7] sections 22–28 stage a complex rhetorical exercise, in which Nietzsche indirectly attempts to acquaint his best readers with their true identity and status.[8] Unbeknownst to them, they are not (yet) opponents of the ascetic ideal, for they continue to partake of the ascetic ideal as they conduct their admittedly bold and daring scholarly investigations. If they are to become genuine (and effective) opponents of the ascetic ideal, they must become apprised of their remaining attachments to it, precisely so that they might capitalize on these attachments in opposing the ascetic ideal. Toward this end, Nietzsche attempts to show them that they are not free spirits after all, but the 'last idealists' whom he describes for them in vivid and intimate terms. So long as they cling to the notion that they are free spirits, a notion he has encouraged in them, they are of no use to him in turning the destructive power of the ascetic ideal against its generative source.

Nietzsche turns in section 24 to consider the 'rare exceptions' he mentioned in section 23.[9] In particular, he wonders if 'the last idealists left among philosophers and scholars' might be the 'desired *opponents* of the ascetic ideal, the counter-idealists' (GM III 24). That *they* believe this to be the case is clear enough from the 'seriousness' and 'passion' with which they profess their opposition to the ascetic ideal.

As we know or suspect by now, however, these 'last idealists' are not yet in a position to offer an objective assessment of their supposed opposition to the ascetic ideal. Although they are not entirely mistaken to regard themselves as 'counter-idealists', they labour under the misconception that the target of their opposition, the ascetic ideal, is external and unrelated to them. As it turns out, or so Nietzsche wishes them to understand, they will become genuine (and effective) opponents of the ascetic ideal only in the event that they resolve to oppose *themselves*, for they are the last remaining champions of the ascetic ideal.

At this point, Nietzsche once again presumes to speak on behalf of his target audience, while also placing himself in their midst. His aim here, as elsewhere in GM, is to call his best readers to attention as a 'we', rousing them from their drowsy self-estrangement, so that he might further their advancement toward the historically unique destiny that awaits them. 'We "knowers"', he asserts, 'have gradually come to mistrust believers of all kinds' (GM III 24),[10] for strong belief typically attests to the likelihood of self-deception on the part of self-avowed believers.[11] Hoping to stimulate the interest of his best readers, he asks them if this is true as well of those 'last idealists' who fancy themselves opponents of the ascetic ideal. Of course, the easy answer to this question is 'no', while the correct answer, toward which Nietzsche hopes to prod his best readers, is 'yes'. As he will proceed to explain, these 'last idealists' are still 'too close' to themselves to understand their actual relationship to the ascetic ideals they claim to oppose.

In order to appreciate the directive thrust of this rhetorical question, let us note that Nietzsche's reference here to *mistrust* recalls the opening sentences of section 20, where he conceded that he and his best readers are probably 'too good' to conduct the honest psychological inquiry that is required of them. At that point, of course, their mistrust was explicitly identified as directed at *themselves*. At this point, their mistrust is once again directed at themselves, even though it is not identified as such, for *they* are the 'last idealists' to whom he refers in this section. Nietzsche and his fellow 'knowers' thus belong *among* those believers whom they have already come with good reason to mistrust. This means, of course, that they should eventually extend their mistrust to themselves, which is precisely what Nietzsche means for them to do. As we shall see, in fact, it is time for them to become '"knowers" with respect to [them]selves' (GM Preface 1).[12]

Hoping to guide his best readers toward the realization that they are the 'last idealists' described in this section, he now embarks upon a strategy of rhetorical indirection.[13] First, he describes these 'last idealists' as if they were a third party (or 'they'), while emphasizing their affinities with himself and his aforementioned 'we'. His ensuing description of these 'last idealists' thus ascribes to them virtues, attributes and accomplishments that he elsewhere assigns to himself and his fellow 'knowers'.[14] In particular, we might note, his best readers are apparently meant to discern the similarity between the 'they' described here and the 'we' described in book 5 of GS.[15]

Despite their many virtues and attributes, however, these 'last idealists' are blind to an essential, non-negotiable feature of their identity. Because 'they are too close to themselves [sie stehen sich zu nahe]', they 'cannot see' that the ascetic ideal, from which they proudly proclaim their independence, 'is precisely *their* ideal, too' (GM III 24). Like Nietzsche's best readers, that is, these 'last idealists' are unknowingly estranged from themselves and, as we shall see, unresponsive to direct disclosures. Like his best readers, moreover, these 'last idealists' are in need of an insight that Nietzsche himself possesses and wishes to share. To wit: 'They are far from being *free* spirits: *for they still have faith in truth*' (GM III 24).

BEHOLD THE ISLAMIC ASSASSINS

In order to illustrate this point, Nietzsche draws a fanciful distinction between the Christian crusaders, whom he proposes as emblematic of European spiritual discipline, and the 'invincible order of Assassins', whom he summons as emblematic of non-Western, or 'Oriental', spiritual discipline (GM III 24). The point of this distinction is to pronounce the Assassins, and not the Christian Crusaders, as the 'order of free spirits *par excellence*', and to do so on the basis of the '*freedom* of spirit' attained by the Assassins (GM III 24). Unlike their occidental counterparts, Nietzsche explains, the Assassins managed to free themselves even from the 'faith in truth itself' (GM III 24). Whereas the Crusaders (and, so, all Western idealists) are bound to seek the truth and act accordingly, the Assassins were (and are) not similarly obliged. For them, he ominously intones, 'Nothing is true, everything is permitted' (GM III 24).[16] This, he reveals, is the guiding *secretum* of the 'highest ranks' within the fearless order of Assassins (GM III 24).

Nietzsche's idealized account of the Assassins warrants further comment. First of all, he presents their *secretum*, versions of which we might expect to hear from village atheists, cynics, or self-styled realists, as an achievement and mark of distinction. Within the order of Assassins, apparently, one must earn the right to the realization that 'nothing is true', and one must prove oneself worthy of its attendant freedoms and responsibilities. Second, one earns this right through the exercise of spiritual disciplines that formally resemble those conducted by Nietzsche and the free spirits. That is, here we encounter the familiar Nietzschean maxim that the highest degree and greatest experience of freedom is reserved for those who first subject themselves to the strictest 'rule of obedience'. Third, Nietzsche identifies the 'rule of obedience' followed by the 'lowest ranks' within the order of Assassins as incomparably more demanding than that of any 'order of [Western] monks' (GM III 24). This difference perhaps explains why the 'Christian crusaders in the Orient' were able to glean only a 'hint' [Wink] of the *secretum* reserved for the 'highest ranks' of the Assassins (GM III 24).

Taken together, these points position us to understand that Nietzsche's admiration for the Assassins does not entail a wish or demand on his part that his readers aspire to a similar achievement of spiritual freedom. Mindful of the enormous investments of time and discipline needed to produce the 'highest ranks' within the order of Assassins, he recommends that his best readers discover and embrace their own *secretum*, which, as we shall see, he indirectly discloses to them in essay 3 of GM. While he urges his best readers to be *like* the Assassins in certain respects, he also needs for them to understand that they fall more squarely within the 'occidental' lineage of the Crusaders. If they are to succeed in what he apparently envisions as the final crusade—viz., against the ascetic ideal itself—they must be made to understand that they are not, and never will be, free spirits on the model of the Islamic Assassins.

With respect to Nietzsche's sketch of a clash between cultures, Gary Shapiro furnishes welcome insight and detail:

> Here we have a bit of geophilosophy in miniature. Nietzsche believes—more or less accurately—that the Assassins, or properly the Nizari Ismailis, a branch of the Shia, had liberated themselves from the morality of truth and developed a culture of self-discipline that set itself goals no longer human, all-too-human.[17]

According to Shapiro, in fact, Nietzsche's sympathies clearly lie with the Assassins, especially inasmuch as their regimen of self-discipline serves as a blueprint of sorts for the development of a post-modern culture that might credibly assert itself beyond good and evil. If 'everything is permitted', after all, 'then what is permitted', according to Shapiro, 'includes grand experiments in overcoming the human. It is the transhuman, the posthuman, or Übermensch, who looms on the horizon'.[18] It is in this context, Shapiro suggests, that we should understand and take very seriously the increasingly truculent vocabulary and martial imagery of Nietzsche's post-Zarathustran writings. With respect to the bellicose conclusion of *The Antichrist(ian)*, for example, Shapiro observes that,

> When Nietzsche declares war on Christianity he does so in a context shaped by admiration for Islam and the Assassins. . . . The last formula, in his text, is not a license for individualism, for arbitrary whim, or vulgar existentialism. It is a formula of military discipline.[19]

As we shall see, however, Nietzsche's admiration for the Assassins does not prevent him from also celebrating the (comparatively modest) liberation of the 'last idealists' among his readers, to whom he assigns a task commensurate with their achievement. These late modern crusaders may be limited in all the ways identified by Nietzsche in this section, including their expectation 'to be paid' for their knightly service, but he is determined nonetheless to turn their 'will to truth' to his (and their) advantage. Indeed, here we see Nietzsche in the familiar position of affirming a necessity of which he initially (or provisionally) disapproved. Rather than dwell on the limitations of the 'last idealists' among his readers, he devises a plan to weaponize their residual will to truth. Not unlike those crafty Popes and Emperors whom he credits with exploiting the uniquely Germanic lust for blood and treasure, Nietzsche plans to unleash these 'last idealists', who are thirsty for the truth, against Christian morality itself.

To be sure, however, his playful characterization of these 'last idealists' as latter-day crusaders also conveys his understanding of them as recruits in his larger 'war' on morality,[20] as conscripts whom he intends to mobilize and exploit. In this respect, Shapiro is certainly right to emphasize Nietzsche's 'unremitting hostility toward the Crusaders',[21] which likely feeds his contempt for the 'last idealists' among his late modern readers. That is, even if we conclude that he genuinely admires them, we should bear in mind that he fully intends to use them and, eventually, to use them up.[22]

It is difficult to know how seriously Nietzsche intended this stylized account of a clash of cultures. In the writings from the post-Zarathustran period of his career, on the one hand, he is generally appreciative of the cultural advancements and spiritual development that he gratefully attributes to Islam. As he rumbles toward the summary 'curse' that marks the conclusion of *The Antchrist(ian)*, for example, he offers the following comparative observation:

> Christianity has cheated us out of the harvest of ancient cultures; later it cheated us again, out of the harvest of *Islam*. The wonderful world of the Moorish culture of Spain, really more closely related to *us*, more congenial to our senses and tastes than Rome and Greece, was *trampled down* (I do not say by what kind of feet). Why? Because it owed its origin to noble, to *male* instincts, because it said Yes to life even with the rare and refined luxuries of Moorish life. (AC 60)

As this passage confirms, on the other hand, Nietzsche's sympathetic depictions of Islam, and especially those found in A, often appear to invite (and justify) the aspersions he proceeds to cast on the comparatively inferior accomplishments of European Christianity. As he sneers in the previous section, for example, 'Islam is a thousand times right in despising Christianity: Islam presupposes *men*' (AC 59). So although Nietzsche often praises the achievements of Islam, he usually does so as a means of highlighting his dissatisfactions with Christianity and the non-men it has produced. Especially in his writings from 1888, in fact, the juxtaposition of Islam and Christianity appears to reproduce in certain respects the conjectured clash between the noble and slave moralities.

In any event, the point of *this* fanciful comparison is not to demean the Christian faith of the 'last idealists' among his best readers, but to apprise them of the advantage they enjoy by virtue of their European (i.e., Christian) lineage. While generally contemptuous of Christianity, to be sure, Nietzsche nevertheless reserves for these 'last idealists' a privileged place in the linage of European Christianity and a distinguished standing among all Christians. According to him, in fact, they are the last of the knights of faith, the final arbiters of Christian morality, and the sole remaining devotees of the ascetic ideal. To these omega Christians falls the vaguely noble task of steering Christian morality toward a fitting and final conclusion. As Christians, that is, they will seek the truth, which, once revealed, will seal the demise of the ascetic ideal and the collapse of Christian morality.[23] Or so Nietzsche means for them to believe.

As this clash of cultures is apparently meant to illustrate, no European (or Christian) free spirit should be considered a genuinely free spirit. Compared to other Europeans, to be sure, the 'last idealists' among Nietzsche's best readers are to be praised for their superlative achievement and expression of freedom. As he confirms in both the 1886 preface to HH and his review of this book in EH, these 'last idealists', and especially those among them who believe themselves to be free spirits, have managed to liberate themselves from tradition, prejudice, superstition, taboo, and ignorance. When measured against the absolute (and idealized) standard of the Islamic Assassins, however, these 'last idealists' cannot be regarded as free spirits. This is the case, as we shall see, not only because any such designation would be undeserved, but also because the source of the limitations of the European free spirits, (viz., their residual faith in truth) is also the source of their most potent opposition to the ascetic ideal. Hoping to encourage the 'last idealists' among his best readers to join him in his campaign against the ascetic ideal, he needs for them to own and affirm their residual idealism.

Thus we see, in fact, that the proffered insight into the limits of their (and his) freedom is meant to serve as an index of their successful convalescence. Although they once needed—and, so, were entitled—to believe in the free spirit ideal, as embodied either by them or by those who inspired them, they now must sever and renounce their attachments to this ideal. In short, Nietzsche wishes to suggest, the 'last idealists' among his best readers have outgrown the ideal of the free spirit and can no longer afford the luxury of clinging to it. For Nietzsche and his best readers, that is, the healing fiction of the free spirit, whether conceived as a sympathetic companion or an ideal of self-cultivation, has exhausted its usefulness. As we have seen, these 'last idealists' are in fact seekers of the truth, and above all else seekers of the truth about *themselves*. As such, they are no longer entitled to consider themselves free spirits. Continuing to do so, Nietzsche wishes them to understand, is now beneath them.

BEHOLD NIETZSCHE

In order to drive home this important point, Nietzsche shifts the focus of his narrative from the 'last idealists', described as a third party, to *himself*. Appealing once again to his own experience, he subtly reminds his best readers that he, too, has travelled the path they currently tread, and that he too once believed himself to be a free spirit. Figuring the *secretum* of the Assassins as a labyrinth unexplored by 'any European, any Christian free spirit', he asks, 'Has [any] one of them ever known the Minotaur of this cave *from experience?*' (GM III 24). Alert to this allusion to Theseus, Nietzsche's best readers might expect him at this point to advert to his own experience with this 'Minotaur' and, perhaps, to commence their initiation into the *secretum* of the Assassins. Instead, however, he draws on his own experience to quash any hope they might have of becoming free spirits on the model of the Assassins. According to him, *no* European, *no* Christian free spirit, has slain this Minotaur or, for that matter, wandered this labyrinth. After initially registering his 'doubt' that anyone has done so, moreover, he subsequently claims to 'know' that 'nothing is more foreign to . . . these *so-called* "free spirits" than freedom and liberation in this sense' (GM III 24). Of this Minotaur and this labyrinth, he assures his readers, the 'last idealists' have no relevant experience despite their claims to the contrary.

Nietzsche could know this about the 'last idealists', of course, only if he were one of them, which is precisely what he means to communicate. Indeed, his attentive readers will note here that he has all but identified himself as one of the 'last idealists'—*primus inter pares*, to be sure—whom he has just described. If these readers are inclined to include themselves within his 'we', moreover, they will understand (or suspect) that he speaks for them as well. In that event, they will (begin to) understand that they are not free spirits *and* that being counted among the 'last idealists' is not such a shabby fate after all.

Nietzsche's sudden transition from the battlefields of the Crusades to the mythic landscape of Greek antiquity communicates his sense, to be confirmed later in the section, that the limitations revealed to the Crusaders in their encounter with the Assassins are far older than Christianity itself. As eager as he is to heap scorn upon Christianity, he is aware that it has prevailed in the West only by exploiting a preexisting condition—namely, the 'metaphysical' faith in truth. (Before there was Christian morality, after all,

there was morality, whose origins Nietzsche traces to the metaphysical opposition posited by Zoroaster [EH Destiny 3], presumably in well-intentioned
response to a deeply felt existential crisis.[24]) Christianity may have steered
Western civilization into the penumbra of European nihilism, perhaps also to
the brink of extinction, but it did not inflict the wound it has so thoroughly
infected.

Indeed, here we find Nietzsche's best attempt at a definitive characterization of Western (or European) civilization: Its dominant feature, he suggests,
is the (redemptive) quest for truth, which is already apparent, or so he observes, in the writings of Plato.[25] But his aim here is not limited to the
academic exercise involved in defining what is uniquely Western (or European) about Western (or European) civilization. In isolating the will to
truth—and, as we shall see, revealing its reliance on an unacknowledged
faith in truth—he has illuminated the frame within which, *ceteris paribus*,
everything is permitted. In doing so, moreover, he has identified the context
of a battle in which the non-negotiable limitations of these 'last idealists'
might be leveraged to their advantage. Unlike the aforementioned Crusaders,
the 'last idealists' need not fear an encounter with a faithless 'Oriental' foe,
for the context Nietzsche has identified is restricted to those who share a
residual faith in the saving power of truth. That is, inasmuch as they fearless-
ly seek the truth, the 'last idealists' among his best readers may become *like*
the Islamic Assassins he has taught them to admire. Their *secretum*, or so he
apparently means to convey, is that *almost* everything is permitted.

Renewing his earlier appeal to personal experience, Nietzsche proceeds to
disclose that he 'know[s] all this from too close up [zu sehr aus der Nähe]
perhaps' (GM III 24), which suggests an intimate, personal acquaintance
with the plight of those reluctant idealists who *claim*, mistakenly, to be free
spirits.[26] Clearly, the inference he wishes his best readers to draw is that their
situation, as described obliquely by him, mirrors his own. Until very recently, he too believed himself to be a free spirit, which meant to him, as it still
does to them, that he saw himself as both liberated from, and unconditionally
opposed to, the ascetic ideal. Having seen (and corrected) the error of his
ways, his present goal is to help his fellow 'knowers' to attain for themselves
the insight, or self-knowledge, that he recently managed to acquire for himself.[27] They are in a position to do so, he believes (or wishes them to believe), inasmuch as they too have progressed in their own efforts at convalescence. Still, he stops just short of ascribing to his readers the residual faith-
fulness of these 'last idealists'. Throughout this section, in fact, he conspicu-
ously refrains from avowing his own allegiance to the ascetic ideal, even
though, as we shall see, he freely does so elsewhere.

These 'last idealists' are not free spirits, he proceeds to explain, because
their 'unconditional will to truth' betrays their 'faith in a *metaphysical* value,
the absolute value of truth' (GM III 24). His argument here is a bit com-

pressed, but he apparently means to claim that: (1) Insofar as idealism informs and motivates the practice of science, it does so on the strength of a *will to truth*; which (2) rests on an unacknowledged *faith in truth*; which in turn (3) takes the value of truth to be *absolute*; which (4) is a *metaphysical* value; which (5) presupposes the validity of the *ascetic ideal*. He thus identifies the 'unconditional will to truth' that constrains these 'last idealists' with a '*faith in the ascetic ideal itself*' (GM III 24).

Having exposed these 'last idealists' as unwitting knights of faith, Nietzsche once again becomes directive with his readers. As if anticipating their likely objection, he warns them not to be 'deceived about' the faith that constrains these 'last idealists', especially inasmuch as it may operate in them as an 'unconscious imperative' (GM III 24). Drawing on his own experience, he cautions his best readers that the 'last idealists' are not likely to be aware of their faith in truth and are not to be trusted in this matter in any event. Were it not for their unacknowledged allegiance to the ascetic ideal, in fact, these 'last idealists' would be indistinguishable from those 'modest and worthy laborers' who pursue scientific research as a means of preventing themselves from 'regaining consciousness' (GM III 23).

In support of his claim that science, too, is guided by unexamined presuppositions, Nietzsche cites at length from GS 344, which bears the eye-opening title, '*How We, Too, Are Still Pious*'. (Here we might note as well that GS 344 follows a section in which Nietzsche confirms the 'death of God' and furthermore claims to be 'cheerful' in the aftermath of this momentous event [GS 343].)[28] Launching a second strategy of indirection, Nietzsche begins to rely on passages imported from GS to convey truths and insights that he is not yet willing to impart directly to the readers of GM. Indeed, whereas the text that is original to GM stops short of identifying Nietzsche and his 'we' with the 'last idealists' described in this section, the text imported from GS 344 leaves no doubt that he and his fellow 'knowers' are inextricably implicated in the faith in truth that is emblematic of these 'last idealists'. This second strategy of indirection is apparently meant to remind his devoted readers of what they already (should) know from GS 344, and to encourage them to apply these recovered insights to their own situation. Having previously encouraged them to 'mistrust' their preferred mode of self-understanding, that is, he now urges them to close the circle of self-reference. He thus writes, and for the second time, that

It is still a *metaphysical faith* that underlies our faith in science—and we knowers[29] of today, we godless ones and anti-metaphysicians, we, too, still derive *our* flame from the fire ignited by a faith millennia old, the Christian faith, which was also Plato's, that God is truth, that truth is *divine*. (GM III 24)

Especially when considered within its original context, which Nietzsche expressly recommends to his readers (viz., GS 344, the whole of GS, book 5, and the 1886 preface to *Dawn*), this extract clearly identifies him and his fellow 'knowers' as the 'last idealists' described in this section.[30]

A NEW TASK EMERGES

Finding it 'necessary to pause and take careful stock', Nietzsche ventures an answer to the question with which the extracted passage concludes. 'If God himself turns out be our *longest lie*', then 'we knowers' must acknowledge the 'lacuna' lurking at the heart of 'every philosophy—namely, that the *will to truth* as yet 'requires justification' (GM III 24). This is not to suggest, of course, that said justification, whether of science itself or of its animating will to truth, is likely to be found. What Nietzsche means here, as he explains, is that no justification (of science or the will to truth) has been sought or even considered necessary; we have taken on faith the value of truth. As we are now in a position to understand, that is, science has rested from its inception on an unscientific foundation, while the will to truth has derived its urgency from an unacknowledged faith in truth. This is the case, he explains, because until very recently 'truth was not *permitted* to be a problem at all' (GM III 24). What has changed for him and his best readers is their awareness of 'the death of God'. Now that belief in the God of Christianity 'is becoming more and more unbelievable [unglaubwürdig]' (GM III 24),[31] it is possible *for the first time* to inquire after the value of truth itself. If we wish to continue the progress marked by our renunciation of belief in the Christian God, that is, we will need to interrogate our allegiance to the successor deity.

Nietzsche's best readers may not be the free spirits they thought they were, but they may yet become historically significant nonetheless, especially if they embrace the residual idealism that secures their membership in the aforementioned 'we'. Their envisioned opposition to the ascetic ideal, as an entity external and unrelated to them, will not come to pass, but they may yet oppose the ascetic ideal as it resides within them and authorizes their quest for truth. Having earlier alerted his readers to the affinities they share with the 'last idealists', Nietzsche here announces the *task* that separates his best readers from all other idealists:

> From the moment faith in the God of the ascetic ideal is denied, *a new problem arises*: that of the *value* of truth. The will to truth requires a critique—let us thus define our own task [Aufgabe]—the value of truth must for once be experimentally [versuchsweise][32] *called into question*. (GM III 24)

Once again, Nietzsche leaves it to his best readers to draw the intended inference. As they may (or soon will) suspect, they may participate in this collective task *only* in the event that they are in fact guided in their inquiries by a potent will to truth. (In this case, they would be tasked to discover the truth about truth itself.)[33] If they find within themselves a potent will to truth, however, they also will find the residual idealism that disqualifies them as free spirits. If they are in a position to affirm their residual idealism, however, they may turn it to the advantage of the 'we' they have been invited to join. In order to accept Nietzsche's invitation, that is, his best readers first must recognize themselves as the 'last idealists' whom he has described in this section.

Hence the strategic advantage that he wishes to disclose to the 'last idealists' among his readers: The Islamic Assassins may be free to trifle with the truth, but the 'last idealists' among his best readers are uniquely positioned to employ their defining faith in truth in the service of the 'new task' that Nietzsche discloses. Although they are not 'free spirits', that is, these 'last idealists' are uniquely positioned to conduct an unprecedented (and experimental) inquiry into the value of truth. Owing precisely to the limitations imposed on them by their non-negotiable faith in truth, these 'last idealists' may endeavour to tell the truth about truth itself and thereby launch an assault on the ascetic ideal. They will do so, according to Nietzsche, tenaciously, indefatigably, and with no regard for their own safety or survival. Guided by their animating will to truth, they may (and perhaps will) perish in the process of conducting their experimental assessments of the true value of truth. In *this* respect, notwithstanding their residual faith in truth, they may yet prove themselves the equals of the faithless Assassins. Within the restricted context of their quest for truth, after all, 'everything is permitted'.

Indeed, their self-directed demise is crucial to Nietzsche's larger plan, for the will to truth, which is all that now remains of the ascetic ideal, currently resides only in them. That is, if they are to succeed in vanquishing the ascetic ideal, they must do so by turning their will to truth against its generative source. So although these 'last idealists' are not the free spirits they take themselves to be, an important and potentially world-historical task awaits them nonetheless—provided, of course, that they are able to disabuse themselves of the notion that they are in fact free spirits.

CONCLUSION: DANCING IN OUR CHAINS?

At this point, Nietzsche's best readers may be reminded of some of his more puzzling remarks about the free spirit in BGE. [34] There, as we recall, he similarly qualified his earlier teaching by drawing attention to a newly emergent order of rank and distinction *among* the free spirits. Those whom he formerly had hailed as free spirits were demoted to the rank of 'free, *very* free spirits', and they were urged to see themselves as secondary figures, as preparatory to the emergence of the 'philosophers of the future' (BGE 44).

As in GM, moreover, Nietzsche placed himself in the company of those merely free spirits who must accustom themselves to a lesser role in the endgame sequence of late modernity. Taking it upon himself to acquaint these merely free spirits with their new task, he offered them a candid, sober, and occasionally unflattering account of themselves as constrained agents. In his inventory of 'Our Virtues', for example, he revealed that *'we immoral-ists'* are also "'men of duty'" (BGE 226), and he proceeded to identify *truthfulness* [Redlichkeit] as the 'virtue from which we cannot get away, we free spirits' (BGE 227). As we have seen, this particular virtue will be useful to Nietzsche's best readers as they take up their new task, for they will attempt to speak the truth about truth itself.[35] That *truthfulness* is a virtue from which these free spirits will not be liberated furthermore confirms the restrictions under which they are obliged to operate. Again, Nietzsche's aim is to translate the non-negotiable constraints of their situation into their signal advantage vis-à-vis the ascetic ideal.[36]

The important point here is that his best readers will contribute to this task *not* as the free spirits they take themselves to be, but as the 'last idealists' to whom they currently oppose themselves. This disclosure accounts not only for the urgency of Nietzsche's campaign to acquaint his best readers with their residual idealism, but also for the indirection with which he conducts this campaign. If they are to join him in making the will to truth conscious of itself as a problem, or so he apparently believes, they must arrive *on their own* at the insight that he only recently acquired for himself. As we have seen, the belief that he was a 'free spirit', in the salutary company of other 'free spirits', may have been decisive for his convalescence, but it was inimi-cal to the resurgence of his health. Having disabused himself of this belief, he now encourages his best readers to do likewise. If they are to succeed in their assault on the ascetic ideal, they will need to avail themselves of the full destructive power of their residual idealism.

NOTES

1. According to Walter Kaufmann in his translation of *The Gay Science* (New York: Random House, 1974), 33, Nietzsche is responsible for the description that appears on the back cover of the original edition of *The Gay Science*, which, we learn, 'marks the conclusion of a series of writings by FRIEDRICH NIETZSCHE whose common goal is to erect *a new image and ideal of the free spirit'*. He lists (the original) *Human, All Too Human, The Wanderer and His Shadow, Dawn* and *The Gay Science* as belonging to the aforementioned 'series of writ-ings'. A similar description of this 'series' appears in Nietzsche's letter to Lou Salomé of 27/28 June 1882 (KSB 6, #251, 213). In addition to Kaufmann's translation of GS, I have drawn on the following translations: *Human, All Too Human*, trans. R. J. Hollingdale (Cambridge: Cam-bridge University Press, 1986); On *the Genealogy of Morals*, trans. Walter Kaufmann and R. J. Hollingdale (New York: Random House/Vintage Books, 1989); *Twilight of the Idols*, in *The*

Portable Nietzsche, ed. and trans. Walter Kaufmann (New York: Viking Penguin, 1982); *The Antichrist(ian)*, in *The Portable Nietzsche*, ed. and trans. Walter Kaufmann (New York: Viking Penguin, 1982); and *Ecce Homo*, trans. Walter Kaufmann (New York: Random House/Vintage Books, 1989).

2. A notable reference to *hope* appears in the otherwise gloomy conclusion to GM III 27, where Nietzsche describes 'the great spectacle in a hundred acts that is reserved for the next two centuries in Europe' as 'the most terrible, most questionable, and perhaps also the most hopeful of all spectacles.—' (GM III 27). See also Aaron Ridley, *Nietzsche's Conscience: Six Character Studies from the* Genealogy (Ithaca, NY: Cornell University Press, 1998), 124–26; and Daniel Conway, 'Nietzsche's Immoralism and the Advent of "Great Politics"', *Nietzsche and Political Thought*, ed. Keith Ansell-Pearson (London: Bloomsbury Academic, 2014), 205–9.

3. I am indebted here to Jonathan R. Cohen, *Science, Culture, and Free Spirits: A Study of Nietzsche's* Human, All-Too-Human (Amherst, NY: Humanity Books, 2010), 218–21; Paul Loeb, *The Death of Nietzsche's Zarathustra* (Cambridge: Cambridge University Press, 2010), 234–32, and chapter 5 more generally; and Paul Franco, *Nietzsche's Enlightenment: The Free-Spirit Trilogy of the Middle Period* (Chicago: University of Chicago Press, 2011), 161–63, and chapter 4 more generally.

4. A full decade, in fact, if one follows Nietzsche in dating the germination of the original HH to 1876 (EH Books HH 6).

5. The book that marks his 'minimum', *The Wanderer and His Shadow*, is incorporated into Volume II of the 1886 edition of *Human, All Too Human* (EH Wise 1).

6. I am indebted here to Jonathan Cohen, 'Nietzsche's Second Turning', *Pli: The Warwick Journal of Philosophy* 25 (2014): 35–36. I am especially sympathetic to Cohen's characterization of this 'second turning' as involving Nietzsche and his readers in 'the battle over culture' (52–53). See also Cohen, *Science, Culture, and Free Spirits*, 213–28; and Franco, *Nietzsche's Enlightenment*, 191–92.

7. See, for example, Daniel Conway, *Nietzsche's* On the Genealogy of Morals*: A Reader's Guide* (London: Continuum Books, 2008), 134–52; Daniel Conway, *'Does That Sound Strange to You?*: Education and Indirection in Essay III of *On the Genealogy of Morals*', *Nietzsche, Nihilism and the Future of Philosophy*, ed. Jeffrey Metzger (London: Continuum Books, 2009), 89–98; and Daniel Conway, 'Heeding the Law of Life: Receptivity, Submission, Hospitality', *Nietzsche and the Becoming of Life*, ed. Vanessa Lemm (New York: Fordham University Press, 2015), 143–53.

8. See also Lawrence J. Hatab, *Nietzsche's Genealogy of Morality: An Introduction* (Cambridge: Cambridge University Press, 2008), 164–68.

9. My interpretation of GM III 24 draws on material that originally appeared in Conway, *Nietzsche's* On the Genealogy of Morals, 137–40. I also make occasional use of, or reference to, material that originally appeared in Conway, *'Does That Sound Strange to You?'*, 89–93.

10. Here I follow Maudemarie Clark and Alan J. Swensen's translation of Friedrich Nietzsche, *On the Genealogy of Morality*, trans. Maudemarie Clark and Alan J, Swensen, (Indianapolis, IN: Hackett, 1998), 108.

11. Cf. GS 375. See also Randall Havas, *Nietzsche's Genealogy: Nihilism and the Will to Knowledge* (Ithaca, NY: Cornell University Press, 1995), 152–64; and Ridley, *Nietzsche's Conscience*, 119–20.

12. Here I follow the translation suggested by Clark and Swensen in their translation of Nietzsche, *On the Genealogy of Morality*, 1.

13. I am indebted here to the interpretation developed by Ken Gemes, '"We Remain of Necessity Strangers to Ourselves": The Key Message of Nietzsche's *Genealogy*, in *Nietzsche's* On the Genealogy of Morals: Critical Essays, ed. Christa Davis Acampora (Lanham, MD: Rowman & Littlefield, 2006), 206.

14. For example, his reference to the 'Nay-sayers and outsiders of today' recalls his description of his 'we' in GS 357, which he imports into the text of GM III 27.

15. See Franco, *Nietzsche's Enlightenment*, 211–13.

16. The freedom attained by the Assassins may be what Nietzsche has in mind when he remarks that 'the crusaders fought something before which they might more properly have

prostrated themselves in the dust—a culture compared to which even our nineteenth century might well feel very poor, very 'late'" (AC 60).

17. Gary Shapiro, 'Assassins and Crusaders: Nietzsche After 9/11', *Reading Nietzsche at the Margins*, S. Hicks and A. Rosenberg, eds. (West Lafayette, IN: Purdue University Press, 2008), 190.

18. Shapiro, 'Assassins and Crusaders', 191.

19. Shapiro, 'Assassins and Crusaders', 197.

20. See May, *Nietzsche's Ethics and his War on 'Morality'* (Oxford: Oxford University Press, 1999), 177–80.

21. Shapiro, 'Assassins and Crusaders', 202.

22. Shapiro, 'Assassins and Crusaders', 200–02. The notion that Nietzsche deliberately aimed to mobilize and exploit his readers is explored by Stanley Rosen, *The Mask of Enlightenment: Nietzsche's Zarathustra* (Cambridge: Cambridge University Press, 1995), 56–60; and Geoff Waite, *Nietzsche's Corps/e: Aesthetics, Politics, Prophecy, or, the Spectacular Techno-culture of Everyday Life* (Durham, NC: Duke University Press, 1996), 275–88.

23. See Havas, *Nietzsche's Genealogy*, 152–66; Aaron Ridley, *Nietzsche's Conscience: Six Character Studies from the Genealogy* (Ithaca, NY: Cornell University Press, 1998), 124–26; David Owen, *Nietzsche's Genealogy of Morality* (Stocksfield: Acumen, 2007), 126–29; Christopher Janaway, *Beyond Selflessness: Reading Nietzsche's Genealogy* (Oxford: Oxford University Press, 2007), 237–39; Hatab, *Nietzsche's On the Genealogy of Morality*, 166–71; Loeb, *The Death of Nietzsche's Zarathustra*, 234–40; and Conway, 'Nietzsche's Immoralism', 205–11.

24. At the conclusion of GM, Nietzsche suggests that the preponderance of ascetic ideals means that 'something was *lacking*, that humankind was surrounded by a fearful *void*—he did not know how to justify, to account for, to affirm himself; he *suffered* from the problem of his meaning [er *litt* am Probleme seines Sinns]' (GM III 28).

25. Nietzsche places Plato in Stage 1 of the progression he outlines in 'How the "True World" Finally Became a Fable' (TI True World). Later in TI, Nietzsche identifies Plato as a 'cowardly' and 'decadent' deviation from the nobler instincts of the Hellenes, and he 'rues the fact that this Athenian received his education from the Egyptians (—or from the Jews in Egypt?)' (TI Ancients 2).

26. He explicitly identifies himself and his 'we' as 'free spirits' at HH I Preface 7.

27. For a careful investigation of the 'unconditional will to truth' (GM III 24; GS 344), see Havas, *Nietzsche's Genealogy*, 157–66. See also Ridley, *Nietzsche's Conscience*, 115–20.

28. On the death of God, see Havas, *Nietzsche's Genealogy*, 173–81; Robert B. Pippin, *Nietzsche, Psychology, and First Philosophy* (Chicago: University of Chicago Press, 2010), 47–59; and Daniel Conway, 'Life after the Death of God: Thus Spoke Nietzsche', *The History of Continental Philosophy*, Volume II: *Nineteenth-Century Philosophy: Revolutionary Responses to the Existing Order*, eds. Alan D. Schrift and Daniel Conway, (Chicago: University of Chicago Press, 2010; London: Acumen Press, 2010), 122–25.

29. Here I follow Clark and Swensen's translation.

30. For an excellent account of the demotion of the free spirit ideal in book 5 of GS, see Franco, *Nietzsche's Enlightenment*, 209–24. See also Cohen, *Science, Culture, and Free Spirits*, 224–28.

31. Nietzsche makes a similar claim in GS 343, where he revisits his teaching of the 'death of God' and pronounces himself 'cheerful' in his initial reception of this event. See Havas, *Nietzsche's Genealogy*, 166–71; and Conway, 'Life after the Death of God', 125–32.

32. Kaufmann and Hollingdale offer 'experimentally' as their translation of the German adverb 'versuchsweise', which is a term of increasing importance in the post-Zarathustran period of Nietzsche's career. A 'Versuch' is an experiment or an attempt, but it also suggests a temptation or enticement. Nietzsche called his 1886 Preface to the new edition of *The Birth of Tragedy* 'An Attempt at a Self-Criticism [Versuch einer Selbstkritik]'. He also suggests '*Versucher*' as a name for the 'new species of philosopher' that he sees 'coming up' (BGE 42).

33. See, for example, May, *Nietzsche's Ethics*, 137–39, 177–82; Ridley, *Nietzsche's Conscience*, 123–26 and Janaway, *Beyond Selflessness*, 229–33.

34. I am indebted here to Franco, *Nietzsche's Enlightenment*, chapter 4.

35. I am indebted here to Alan White, 'The Youngest Virtue', *Nietzsche's Postmoralism: Essays on Nietzsche's Prelude to Philosophy's Future*, ed. Richard Schacht (Cambridge: Cambridge University Press, 2001), 63–66; and Laurence Lampert, *Nietzsche's Task: An Interpretation of Beyond Good and Evil* (New Haven, CT: Yale University Press, 2001), 219–23; and Franco, *Nietzsche's Enlightenment*, 184–87. See also Conway, 'Nietzsche's Immoralism', 207–9.

36. Here it bears noting that Nietzsche assigns the free spirits to the *penultimate* (or fifth) stage of what he describes as 'the history of an error', reserving the *ultimate* (or sixth) stage—and the completion of the 'abolition' attempted by the free spirits—for Zarathustra (TI Real World).

BIBLIOGRAPHY

Cohen, Jonathan R. 'Nietzsche's Second Turning'. *Pli: The Warwick Journal of Philosophy* 25 (2014): 35–54.

Cohen, Jonathan R. *Science, Culture, and Free Spirits: A Study of Nietzsche's Human, All-Too-Human*. Amherst, NY: Humanity Books, 2010.

Conway, Daniel. *'Does That Sound Strange to You?*: Education and Indirection in Essay III of *On the Genealogy of Morals'*. In *Nietzsche, Nihilism and the Future of Philosophy*, edited by Jeffrey Metzger, 79–101, 181–84, 202–3. London: Continuum Books, 2009.

Conway, Daniel. 'Heeding the Law of Life: Receptivity, Submission, Hospitality'. In *Nietzsche and the Becoming of Life*, edited by Vanessa Lemm, 137–58, 338–42. New York: Fordham University Press, 2015.

Conway, Daniel. 'Life after the Death of God: Thus Spoke Nietzsche'. In *The History of Continental Philosophy*, volume 2: *Nineteenth-Century Philosophy: Revolutionary Responses to the Existing Order*, edited by Alan D. Schrift and Daniel Conway, 103–38. Chicago: University of Chicago Press, 2010; London: Acumen Press, 2010.

Conway, Daniel. 'Nietzsche's Immoralism and the Advent of "Great Politics"'. In *Nietzsche and Political Thought*, edited by Keith Ansell-Pearson, 197–217. London: Bloomsbury Academic, 2014.

Conway, Daniel. *Nietzsche's On the Genealogy of Morals: A Reader's Guide*. London: Continuum Books, 2008.

Franco, Paul. *Nietzsche's Enlightenment. The Free-Spirit Trilogy of the Middle Period*. Chicago: University of Chicago Press, 2011.

Gemes, Ken. '"We Remain of Necessity Strangers to Ourselves": The Key Message of Nietzsche's *Genealogy'*. In *Nietzsche's On the Genealogy of Morals: Critical Essays*, edited by Christa Davis Acampora, 191–208. Lanham, MD: Rowman & Littlefield, 2006.

Hatab, Lawrence J. *Nietzsche's On the Genealogy of Morality: An Introduction'*. Cambridge: Cambridge University Press, 2008.

Havas, Randall. *Nietzsche's Genealogy: Nihilism and the Will to Knowledge*. Ithaca, NY: Cornell University Press, 1995.

Janaway, Christopher. *Beyond Selflessness: Reading Nietzsche's Genealogy*. Oxford: Oxford University Press, 2007.

Lampert, Laurence. *Nietzsche's Task: An Interpretation of Beyond Good and Evil*. New Haven, CT: Yale University Press, 2001.

Loeb, Paul S. *The Death of Nietzsche's Zarathustra*. Cambridge: Cambridge University Press, 2010.

May, Simon. *Nietzsche's Ethics and his War on 'Morality'*. Oxford: Oxford University Press, 1999.

Nietzsche, Friedrich. *The Antichrist*, in *The Portable Nietzsche*. Edited and translated by Walter Kaufmann. New York: Viking Penguin, 1982.

Nietzsche, Friedrich. *Ecce Homo*. Translated by Walter Kaufmann. New York: Random House/Vintage Books, 1989.

Nietzsche, Friedrich. *Friedrich Nietzsche: Sämtliche Werke: Kritische Studienausgabe in 15 Bänden*, edited by Giorgio Colli and Mazzino Montinari. Berlin: dtv/de Gruyter, 1980.

Nietzsche, Friedrich. *Friedrich Nietzsche: Sämtliche Briefe. Kritische Studienausgabe.* 8 volumes. Edited by Giorgio Colli and Mazzino Montinari. Berlin and New York: de Gruyter, 1986.

Nietzsche, Friedrich. *The Gay Science.* Translated by Walter Kaufmann. New York: Random House, 1974.

Nietzsche, Friedrich. *Human, All Too Human.* Translated by R. J. Hollingdale. Cambridge: Cambridge University Press, 1986.

Nietzsche, Friedrich. *On the Genealogy of Morals,* Translated by Walter Kaufmann and R. J. Hollingdale. New York: Random House/Vintage Books, 1989.

Nietzsche, Friedrich. *On the Genealogy of Morality.* Translated by Maudemarie Clark and Alan J. Swensen. Indianapolis, IN: Hackett, 1998.

Nietzsche, Friedrich. *Twilight of the Idols,* in *The Portable Nietzsche.* Edited and translated by Walter Kaufmann. New York: Viking Penguin, 1982.

Owen, David. *Nietzsche's* Genealogy of Morality. Stocksfield: Acumen, 2007.

Pippin, Robert B. *Nietzsche, Psychology, and First Philosophy.* Chicago: University of Chicago Press, 2010.

Ridley, Aaron. *Nietzsche's Conscience: Six Character Studies from the* Genealogy. Ithaca, NY: Cornell University Press, 1998.

Rosen, Stanley. *The Mask of Enlightenment: Nietzsche's* Zarathustra. Cambridge: Cambridge University Press, 1995.

Shapiro, Gary. 'Assassins and Crusaders: Nietzsche after 9/11'. In *Reading Nietzsche at the Margins,* edited by S. Hicks and A. Rosenberg, 168–204. West Lafayette, IN: Purdue University Press, 2008.

Waite, Geoff. *Nietzsche's Corps/e: Aesthetics, Politics, Prophecy, or, the Spectacular Technoculture of Everyday Life.* Durham, NC: Duke University Press, 1996.

White, Alan. 'The Youngest Virtue'. In *Nietzsche's Postmoralism: Essays on Nietzsche's Prelude to Philosophy's Future,* edited by Richard Schacht, 63–78. Cambridge: Cambridge University Press, 2001.

Chapter Thirteen

Is There a Free Spirit in Nietzsche's Late Writings?

Andreas Urs Sommer

The chapter explores the role of the free spirit [freier Geist] and the freed spirit [freigewordener Geist] in Nietzsche's last writings. Obviously, this figure so prominent in Nietzsche's middle period does not simply disappear, but it changes its shape. The chapter follows these transformations. Nietzsche's books written in 1888 can be read as a self-empowerment of the free spirit. Nietzsche believed to have passed the free spirit of traditional style, while he understood his own free thought as a radicalization and an overcoming of the old ideal of a free spirit. The new freed spirit should not shrink back from the passions and taboos of this old-fashioned free spirit, namely, from the humanitarian morals and from the scientific truth. Nietzsche tries to unmask particularly these human-itarian morals, based on the doctrines of Enlightenment, as psychological naïvety. Comfortable and cozy free spirit skepticism is not the concern of Nietzsche's free spirit. Therefore, the skeptical listeners desirous of a peace of mind easily attained are frightened when they hear "some evil-threatening sound in the distance, as if a new kind of explosive were being tried somewhere, a dynamite of the spirit" (BGE 208; KSA 5, 137), for the new free spirits want to be dynamite. Finally in 1888, the free spirit poses as a legislator. *Ecce Homo* projects this role of a legislator back on the book *Thus Spoke Zarathustra* and on the figure of Zarathustra.

If we try to take stock of Nietzsche's statements on the subject of the "free spirit" and of "freethought"/"freethinking" [Freigeisterei], we may realize that the quantitative distribution of these statements corresponds widely with the quantitative distribution of another great Nietzsche subject, namely, the subject of laughter.[1] In Nietzsche's early writings, there are only few passages in which laughter or the free spirit plays an eminent role. In *The Birth of Tragedy*, the wise Silenus tells King Midas, giving "a shrill laugh" [endlich unter gellem Lachen], that it would be the best of all things for humans not to be born, and the second-best to die soon (BT 3; KSA 1, 35). Around the same time, Nietzsche reflected—in view of Richard Wagner, who then seemed the prototypical free spirit to him—about a book never written, bearing the title "The tragedy and the free spirits" (NL 1870/71; KSA 7, 5[22], 97).

Laughter and the free spirit gained a greater prominence in the middle of the 1870s, while Nietzsche turned gradually away from Schopenhauer as well as from Wagner. In a letter to Reinhart von Seydlitz, written 24 September 1876, Nietzsche imagined "a kind of monastery for free*r* spirits" (KSB 5, no. 554, 189).[2] In the writings of his so-called free spirit-period, this free spirit is not the sole object of permanent reflection. Laughter is as frequently considered as an excellent instrument for the dissociation from traditional truths and their annihilation. In no other of his works is there as much laughter as in Nietzsche's Z, and in all four parts equally. The free spirit is not explicitly present there, but has a last great appearance, together with laughter, shortly afterwards in *Beyond Good and Evil* (BGE 24–44; KSA 5, 41–63). After this book, it seems as if the free spirit disappears into the lost property room, and the laughter falls silent under the pressure of the eschatologically serious 'transvaluation of all values.' Does Nietzsche no longer need the free spirit, who kills the traditional truths with his laugh? Or is there no longer a necessity for Nietzsche to make the free spirit and his laughter subject of discussion because he has already become self-evident as a type, as an attitude?

If we focus a little bit more, we will soon realize that the free spirit still plays a certain role in Nietzsche's books of 1888. He does not simply disappear, but he changes his shape. I would like to follow these transformations. While the free spirit was difficult to trace in the late writings at first glance, a second, still superficial glance discloses these late writings as a self-empowerment of the free spirit. Nietzsche believed to have passed beyond the free spirit of traditional style—his preferred example is David Friedrich Strauss, attacked already in the first of the *Untimely Meditations*—, while he understood his own freethought as a radicalization and an overcoming of the old ideal of a free spirit. The new freed spirit does not shrink back from the passions and taboos of that old ideal, namely, from the humanitarian morals and from the scientific truth. Particularly these humanitarian morals of the traditional free spirit, based on the doctrines of Enlightenment, are unmasked as psychological naïvety. Comfortable, cozy, free spirit skepticism is not the concern of Nietzsche's freed spirit. Therefore, the skeptical listeners, thirsting for comfort and coziness, are frightened when they hear "some evil-threatening sound in the distance, as if a new kind of explosive were being tried somewhere, a dynamite of the spirit" (BGE 208; KSA 5, 137), for the new free spirits are not mild, irenical skeptics, but wanting to be dynamite.[3] Finally, in 1888, even this is not enough. At this point, the free spirit comes forward as a legislator. EH projects this role of a legislator back on Z and on the figure of Zarathustra.

But first things first—let us therefore take a third, much more detailed look at the late metamorphoses of the free spirit. First, I would like to investigate the strategies by which Nietzsche distances himself in the works of his last creative year from the free spirit of the traditional type. A second section examines how the following type, that is the *freed* spirit, specifically distinguishes itself from the free spirit—from the traditional free spirit of the Enlightenment as well as from the free spirit of Nietzsche's own free spirit period. The third and final section highlights the main feature of the freed spirit, which distinguishes him from most previous free spirits, namely, the function of the legislator.

FAREWELL TO THE FREE SPIRIT

In EH, his auto-genealogy, a review and reshaping of his own becoming, Nietzsche presents his first appearance in the field of direct controversy *ad personam*, namely, the first *Untimely Meditation* against Strauss, as a discussion of a specific form of a free spirit:

> And how I had chosen my opponents! Germany's first free-spirit! . . . In fact, an altogether *new* type of free spirit thus gained his first expression: Nothing is more foreign to me and less related to me than the whole European and American species of 'libres penseurs'. With them as incorrigible flat heads and pantaloons of 'modern ideas', I find myself in an even deeper conflict than with anyone from their opponents. They also want in their own way to 'improve' the human race, according to their own image, they would begin an irreconcilable war against what I am, what I *want* if they understood me—they all still believe in the 'ideal' . . . I am the first *immoralist*. (EH Books 2; KSA 6, 319)

If you now look at UM I with this expectation in mind, you will quickly find that, contrary to Nietzsche's retrospection, the subject of the free spirit was of minor importance. The free spirit appeared explicitly only in a single passage. There, Nietzsche argues that Strauss often wavers as to "whether he should imitate the brave dialectical fury of Lessing, or whether he would to better to behave as a faun, a free-spirited old man in the manner of Voltaire" (UM I 10; KSA 1, 216–217). The alleged indecisiveness of Strauss as to the direction in which to go with his freethinking is precisely what seems to have caused Nietzsche's displeasure. In *Twilight of the Idols*, he also claims that he had intended to show "the degeneration of our first German free spirit" (TI Germans 2; KSA 6, 104, 31) with his polemic against Strauss. When he wrote UM I, Nietzsche was still fond of the freethinking in a general sense, namely, as a departure from the traditional religious and ideological bonds. For the early Nietzsche, a typical free spirit of this kind was the American philosopher Ralph Waldo Emerson, whose works he studied intensively. Also, Richard Wagner appeared as a free spirit—long before Nietzsche developed his own free spirit philosophy. However, to contemporary readers, UM I does not seem to have been planned as a critique of the degeneration of the old-fashioned free spirit in favor of another form of free spirit. Nevertheless, one and a half decades later, Nietzsche tries to persuade the reader of exactly this understanding and to impose a new and authoritative interpretation on his own early work. An earlier version of this review in EH specifies the freethinking Nietzsche claims retrospectively for his early days:

> A new free-thinking came there to express itself, not only an anti-theological one, but something foreign, for which the Germans, but not only the Germans, had been missing the ear, the concept and even the word. Today they have the word, I gave it to them—*immoralist* . . . righteousness, the intellectual conscience revolting against morality. (KSA 14, 488–89)

Without any hesitation, Nietzsche pretends here that the entire free spirit program had already been realized in the Strauss controversy. However, it seems that this retrospective manipulation occurred even to him to be a little too excessive, so that the less ambitious version of the remodeled past, quoted above, was preferred in the printer's final manuscript.

Leaving Wagner behind, Nietzsche wrote *Human, All Too Human*, a book addressed to the "Free Spirits" according to its subtitle (KSA 2, 9). Here, Nietzsche connected with the freethinking tradition of the French Enlightenment, and to make the difference clear from the popular, mediocre *Freigeist* of his contemporaries, he used to replace the compositum *Freigeist* in his self-attribution with *freier Geist*. In his later works, Nietzsche treats the freethinking of his contemporaries with scorn, for example where he laments the subcutaneous Christian and moral contamination of all common philosophy. The free spirits, explicitly represented by Strauss in his later writings, are not radical enough: They give up Christianity, but not the modern morality inspired by Christianity. According to BGE 44, the "concept 'free spirit' has been made opaque. . . . In all the countries of Europe and also in America there is now something that abuses this name, a very narrow, imprisoned, chained kind of spirits who want just about the opposite of what is in our intentions and instincts" (BGE 44; KSA 5, 60–61).

In the aforementioned EH passage on the book against Strauss, Nietzsche defines his own intentions toward the too tame and too civilized "libres penseurs" through negation: immoralism, abandonment of "ideals" and of "modern ideas" are the keywords. In the second part of BGE, which is entitled "The Free Spirit," the "free spirits" confess still to be "friends of solitude" (BGE 44; KSA 5, 63):

> Is it any wonder that we 'free spirits' are not the most communicative spirits? That we do not wish to betray in every respect, *from what* a spirit can free himself from and *where* he may then be driven to? And what it is all about with the dangerous formula 'beyond good and evil' with which we protect ourselves at least to avoid confusion: we are something different from 'libres-penseurs', 'liberi pensatori', 'free thinkers' and whatever else all these honest advocates of 'modern ideas' like to call themselves. (KSA 5, 62)

According to this rather brief declaration, it seems to be characteristic for the "free spirits" to provide only very scanty information. Their strong will to distinguish themselves from everything and everybody with whom they could be confused is structurally evident. The pamphlet against Strauss now has to prove that Nietzsche had already distanced himself from the not sufficiently radical type of freethinking very early in his intellectual life.

Similarly, the collage *Nietzsche contra Wagner* demonstrates that at the end of 1888, Nietzsche had dissociated from Wagner, his freethinking and his art as a substitute religion shortly after BT. The gesture is the same and is intended to state: Nietzsche has at all times been different from all others. In *The Case of Wagner*, written in the first half of 1888, the free spirit theme also occurs, for example where Nietzsche ridicules the "case" of the *Ring des Nibelungen* and where he attests the "old god"—read: Wotan—that he "is saved by a free spirit and immoralist" (CW 3; KSA 6, 17)—read: Siegfried. Nietzsche has described the fate of the old god Wotan in Wagner's tetralogy once before in UM IV, albeit without any polemical connotation. There, he characterizes Wotan as a "tragic hero": "He needs the free fearless man, who, without his advice and assistance, even in a struggle against the divine order, accomplishes by himself the act denied to the god" (UM IV 11; KSA 1, 508). In UM IV on Wagner in Bayreuth, redemption [*Erlösung*] and the need of redemption were still crucial to Nietzsche's understanding of human existence. In 1888, Nietzsche had reread the entire passage on Wotan and on Wotan's redemption in his own work from 1876 when he found it quoted in Ludwig Nohl's biography of Wagner.[4] The reconsideration of the whole issue in CW disguises the fact that the "old god" is not the Christian, but the Germanic god, and thereby suggests an affinity between Wagner and Nietzsche's own atheistic immoralism. This opens up the association to the death of the Christian god, too (cf. GS 125; KSA 3, 480–82). According to Nietzsche, the end of the gods has a liberating effect: "Indeed, we philosophers and free spirits feel at the news that the 'old god is dead' as if we are touched by a new dawn" (GS 343; KSA 3, 574). If we follow CW, then Wagner, however, turned out not to be mature enough for this liberation and kept looking for new securities in Christianity and Christian compassion. For Nietzsche, Christianity has to be overcome as well as the Germanic religion had been overcome. In the course of his struggle with Wagner, Nietzsche positions himself consequentially as a free spirit, when he denounces the once-revered master as "old wizard" and "Klingsor of all Klingsors." He understands this whole artistic wizardry as a declaration of war: "Herewith he makes *us* the war! us, free spirits!" (CW Epilogue; KSA 6, 43).

In EH, Nietzsche also recontextualizes those works that are most commonly associated with the free spirit. There, he writes about *Human, All Too Human I* (1878): "It is called a book for *free* spirits: almost every sentence expresses a victory—with this book, I have cleared my nature from *what does not belong to it*" (EH HH 1; KSA 6, 322). Since 1876, Nietzsche had considered writing a fifth *Untimely Meditation* on the type of the free spirit, a project from which would eventually emerge HH I. The motif of victory and liberation from what does not belong to his own nature, pointed out in EH, is already present in Nietzsche's preface to the first volume (HH I Preface 3; KSA 2, 15–17) and is resumed in the preface to the second volume (1886) under the premise of an "*anti-romantic* self-treatment" (HH AOM Preface 2; KSA 2, 371). Important for the type of free spirit that Nietzsche creates is the active moment: *Acts* of liberation constitute the free spirit, who is explicitly renamed a "freed spirit" in the late works. In his *Ecce Homo* review, Nietzsche highlights that the hundredth anniversary of Voltaire's death "excuses the publication of the book already for the year 1878": "For Voltaire, in contrast to all who wrote after him, was above all, a grandseigneur of the mind: just what I am.—The name of Voltaire on one of my books—that was really a progress—*towards me*" (EH HH 1; KSA 6, 322). In 1878, Nietzsche already stated that he wanted to offer "a personal tribute to one of the greatest liberators of the mind at the right moment" (HH I; KSA 2, 10). In the new edition of 1886, Voltaire is no longer mentioned on the title page (KGW IV 2, 5), although the allegedly aristocratic French philosopher remained a role model for Nietzsche's own understanding of the free spirit. In his later thinking, however, Nietzsche saw a necessity to overcome the Enlightenment tied to the name of Voltaire because this Enlightenment maintained the metaphysical opposition between "good" and "evil" and was therefore trapped within a traditional moral perspective.[5] Thus, the free spirit in its original French version was no longer suitable for Nietzsche in 1888. The spirit becoming free has to liberate himself from the illusions of the enlightened *libres esprits* as much as from all others.

Nevertheless, Nietzsche's reservations about conventional freethinkers in 1888 do not only address the anti-theological and the French representatives (as seen in varying degrees) but also the freethinking of the scientists of his time. In *The Antichrist*, where Nietzsche speaks about the theologians who it was necessary to refute radically, he adds the remark: "The freethinking of our gentlemen naturalists and physiologists is, in my eyes, just a *joke*—they are lacking passion in these things, the *suffering* of them" (A 8; KSA 6, 174). This "suffering," this very personal affection by the fate of philosophy is what propels Nietzsche's "we" to their mercilessness. The scientific free spirits are missing the ultimate—shall I say eschatological?—seriousness in dealing with the theological infection that has corrupted philosophy. According to Nietzsche's late works, the scientific free spirits are as superficial as the uncomprehending audience that does not understand the depth of the "God is dead" diagnosis in GS 125.

Increasingly, when Nietzsche turns to the project of the "transvaluation of all values," he takes the old-school free spirits to be powerless, treating them as merely powerless talkers. Illustrative of this view is, for example, the announcement of A in a draft letter from December 1888 to Georg Brandes: "Since it is a *devastating blow* against *Christianity*, it is obvious that the only international power having an instinct-interest in the extermination of Christianity are the Jews—here there is an instinctive hostility, not something 'imaginary' as in any 'free spirits' or socialists—I do not care about free spirits." (KSB 8 no. 1170, 500–501) Rather, these free spirits belong under the heading "*licentiousness of the modern spirit*" (NL 1887; KSA 12, 9[165], 432 = KGW IX/6, W II 1, 18), to which Nietzsche opposes an "aristocratism of the mind" in TI (TI Reconnaissance Raids 2; KSA 6, 112).

The conventional free spirit is for Nietzsche much too conservative, too dispassionate, too indecisive, and too powerless to qualify as a serious ally in the business of a transvaluation of all values. In the person of Wagner, the conventional free spirit is even suspected of being a pathological figure. However, this explicit demarcation cannot hide the fact that the program of various individuals and groups operating under the name of free spirits often comes dangerously close to Nietzsche's own efforts. Nietzsche has to pretend his complete otherness and incomparability; otherwise some readers could think he is as conservative, as dispassionate, as indecisive, and as powerless as his alleged free-spirited opponents.

FREED SPIRITS

The label under which Nietzsche summarizes the "we" speaking in his writings of 1888 is no longer "free spirits," but "free*d* spirits" [freigewordne Geister]. Already in the late 1870s, his thinking took a radically enlightened, free-spirited character. After the analysis and destruction of the prevalent religious, metaphysical, and moral foundations of present human existence,

Nietzsche was on the lookout for a new, 'positive' doctrine in the early 1880s—a search that coincided with a phase of consolidation with the alleged doctrines of Z. In 1888, Nietzsche vehemently resumed his critical stance especially in TI and in A (after preludes in BGE and *On the Genealogy of Morals*), that he had already held in the books of his free spirit period: The "transvaluation of all values," which according to Nietzsche is accomplished in A in November 1888, is essentially a destructive enterprise that shows only from far what constitutes a new morality that is not detrimental to "life."

However, the "free spirit" does not disappear entirely: "You could, with some tolerance in the expression, call Jesus a 'free spirit'" (A 32; KSA 6, 204). This judgment is surprising only at first glance. At second glance, one realizes that it is part of a liberal Protestant tradition to praise Jesus as the hero of "intellectual freedom."[6] Biblical texts such as the story of the encounter with the Samaritan woman at Jacob's well (John 4, 5–24) are frequently cited by theologians as evidence of freethinking tendencies in Jesus.

But Nietzsche does, of course, not see himself as one who maintains liberal theology. He is primarily interested in snatching Jesus away from his theological interpreters and to re-encode him by applying his *own* conception of the free spirit to him: Nietzsche's Jesus cuts all traditional social, moral, and religious ties. In A 36, Nietzsche managed to connect the passages about the "type of the Redeemer" with the passages about the movement that pretends to follow Jesus, that is, Christianity. A self-reflection of the "we" speaking as "freed spirits" (A 36; KSA 6, 208) serves as a bridge between the two.

But what constitutes these "freed spirits," who is this "we," repelling and including Nietzsche's readers simultaneously? What makes this collective different from the free spirit Jesus, who abandons all contradictions and exercises a "practice" allowing everything, giving up all boundaries? It notably constitutes the group that they have "restored the greatest existing value-contrast," namely, the contrast between the "Christian" and the "noble values" (A 37; KSA 6, 209). Herewith, they interpret the history of the Christian West as a nondialectical history, as the monotonic decline under the regime of a single canon of values. The speakers appear therefore as radical innovators who define themselves as the new measure by which judgment will pass in the future. Now, "neutrality" is no longer asked for as it was asked for in the face of Jesus (A 36; KSA 6, 208), but it is required to take sides in favor of "*noble* values" (KSA 6, 209). From the "*sick barbarism*" (KSA 6, 209) of Christianity, the "freed spirits" dissociated themselves and are now pushing for the restoration of the archaic noblesse. The emphasis lies on the act of liberation.

But the "freed spirits" should not slip into a fanaticism of new values bossiness. On the contrary, Nietzsche understands the "fanatic" not only as a pathological case—he names Savonarola, Luther, Rousseau, Robespierre, and Saint-Simon—but explicitly as the "opposite type of the strong, *freed* spirits" (A 54; KSA 6, 237). Fanaticism seems to be independent from specific beliefs; it is not a particularly Christian decadence symptom. Rather, the need of beliefs is in itself a symptom of weakness which fanatical behavior is obviously supposed to overcompensate for.

However, Nietzsche does not consistently convert his vocabulary from "free spirits" to "freed spirits" in order to also terminologically overcome the vagueness and indecisiveness of the figure of "free spirit" in his middle-period writings. Rather, the desire for decisiveness and for erecting boundaries against that which had been valid is now inscribed into the concept of "free spirit." The "free spirits" come close to the "freed spirits": *"we ourselves, we free spirits, are already a 'transvaluation of all values'"* (A 13; KSA 6, 179).

Passages like this, declaring the "transvaluation of all values" not as a literary work, but as realized in real human existence, help to explain why Nietzsche finally renounced writing, as he had planned, a *Transvaluation of All Values* in four books, but viewed this work as already completed in A. In EH, Nietzsche presents himself as the executive in the transvaluation overcoming decadence. The free or freed spirits are "an *incarnate* [*leibhafte*] war and victory declaration to all the old notions of 'true' and 'untrue'" (A 13; KSA 6, 179). The letter spacing of "incarnate" points first to the rehabilitation of the physical nature, rejecting the hostility toward the body sustained by theology and metaphysics. Second, the "free spirits" identify themselves completely with their determination, just as Christ identified himself with the way, the truth, and the life (John 14, 6). Moreover and third, "incarnate" [leibhaft], is a quality ascribed to the devil the more we have become accustomed to doubt the devil's existence. At the same time, Nietzsche says in the next section of A that "we" "have become modest in all things" (A 14; KSA 6, 180). This modesty is to deprive man of his metaphysical destiny and to degrade him to an animal among animals. The collective identified as "we" is understood as caretaker of a naturalistic disillusionment. While metaphysical conviction honored the human being as an *animal rationale*, this counts now as a symptom of the human being's pathology. This insight should go hand in hand with a "great liberation" from the moral world view—"with this, the *innocence* of becoming is restored " (TI Errors 8; KSA 6, 97). The keyword o f the "innocence of becoming," (is it a key concept?) which Nietzsche already explored intensively in 1883 as a worldview excluding all purposes (NL 1883; KSA 10, 7[21], 245), barely appears in Nietzsche's published works after 1883 and also loses significance in the posthumous notes. Directly relevant to the interpretation of the section TI Errors 8 is the religious and metaphysical context of the note NL 1887, KSA 12, 9[91], 385–86 (corrected to KGW IX 6, W II 1, 72): "As soon as we *imagine* someone who is responsible for the fact that we are so and so and so etc. (God, nature), thus attributing him our existence, our happiness and misery as an *intention*, we are spoiling us the *innocence of becoming*. We then have someone who wants to achieve something through us and with us." While in 1883, under the impression of Kuno Fischer's book on Spinoza,[7] the teleological view of nature is excluded with the help of "the innocence of becoming" and while in NL 1887, 9[91], the invention of an extra-human instance responsible for us spoils "the innocence of becoming," the section in TI combines the criticism of the concept of purpose in philosophy of nature (KSA 6, 96) with the criticism of a first cause of our existence (KSA 6, 97). In the preceding TI section, the innocence of becoming is opposed to the (religious and moral) invention of guilt (TI Errors 7; KSA 6, 96). "Innocence of becoming" can therefore be contextualized differently and does not even condense into a fixed notion within TI. It thus becomes evident that the free spirits have taken up the cause of this "innocence of becoming," with the final meaning of this formula remaining unclear.

The negation of tradition, of the prevailing morality and of its religion congealed in the form of Christianity is certainly not the free spirits' furthest stage of development. TI designs the quasi-eschatological vision of a "freed spirit" who no longer obtains his self-understanding through negation alone:

> Such a *freed* spirit stands with a joyous and trusting fatalism in the middle of the universe, in the *belief* that only the individual is condemnable, that in the whole, everything is redeemed and affirmed—*he does not deny anymore.* . . . But such a belief is the highest of all possible beliefs: I have baptized it with the name of *Dionysus.*" (TI Reconnaisance Raids 49; KSA 6, 152)

The aspect of destruction, that remains a characterizing trait of Dionysus in other parts of TI (TI Ancients 5; KSA 6, 160), is completely disregarded here—as if the affirmation of the world as it is would render it redundant even to mention the negation of those who despise this world: This universal Yes already implies the partial No, while the general moral negation of the world is canceled. It is striking that in connection with Dionysus, Nietzsche does not only hint at affirmation but also at redemption.

THE FREED MIND AS LEGISLATOR

Despite the rhetoric of solitude and loneliness that pervades Nietzsche's writings—and especially his late writings—the freed spirit of 1888 obviously does not want to remain alone. With the abolition of the "real world", that is, the abolition of all metaphysical illusions of a final knowledge of things and morals, a "devil's din from all free spirits" arises (TI Fable 5; KSA 6, 81). With the collapse of old certainties, there seems to occur something like a solidarity effect of free spirits—although Nietzsche emphasizes elsewhere that he himself has found not one peer in this world and must therefore be born posthumously.

The personality profile of the "most minded people," as Nietzsche develops it in reference to his very idiosyncratic interpretation of the Hindu *Manu Law*, foils the criticism of the ascetic ideal of the "priests"—an ideal that appeared, namely in GM III, as a sign of weakness: "The most minded people, as the *strongest*, find their happiness where others would find their destruction: in the labyrinth, in hardness against themselves and others, in the attempt; their lust is self-mastery: asceticism becomes nature in them, need, instinct." (A 57; KSA 6, 243) The will to the "labyrinth" and to "attempt" is in flagrant contradiction of the stated objectives of the *Law of Manu* given at the beginning of the same A section, namely, to prevent for the Present and all Future "the continuation of the liquid state of values, of the testing, selection, criticism of values in infinitum" (A 57; KSA 6, 241). According to the *Law of Manu*, the highest caste is subject to stringent regulations as well as the lowest caste. These regulations should render all mental experiments impossible.

The freed spirits are not only, or primarily, agents of destruction and negation, but rather the creators of something new. They are in the same way experimenters, tempters,[8] and legislators. Thus, the later Nietzsche stylizes his Zarathustra figure and his book Z to the epitome of this new type of man:

> That a Goethe, a Shakespeare would not know to breathe in this tremendous passion and height for a moment, that Dante held against Zarathustra is merely a believer and not someone who first *creates* the truth, a *world-ruling* spirit, a destiny—, that the poets of the Veda are priests and not even worthy to loosen the shoe soles of a Zarathustra, that is all the least, and gives no idea of the distance, of the *azure* loneliness, in which that work lives." (EH Z 6; KSA 6, 343)

The question and the task of legislation is the crucial point saving the freed spirit of the embarrassment to be, in the end, just one who denies: "The psychological problem in the type of Zarathustra is how the one who says No, who *does* No to all what was affirmed so far, can still be the opposite of a denying spirit; how the one who carries the most difficult destiny, a fate of task can nevertheless be the easiest and otherworldliest spirit" (EH Z 6; KSA 6, 344–45). The "problem" of Zarathustra consists essentially in affirming unreservedly and, unlike the nihilists, in accomplishing the feat to let the negation spring from the Yes at the same time. With the suggestion of a legislative competence, a legislative capacity for the whole world, Nietzsche creates for his freed spirit and, namely his Zarathustra, the semblance of productivity, the semblance of affirmation. On the other hand, the laws proclaimed by the late Nietzsche—for example the *Law against Christianity* at the end of A—are only the denial of the laws of the Past. The new positive creation of values in the "transvaluation of all values" remains nebulous. Does Nietzsche fail to prove that the freed spirit is able to decree positives laws for the future? Or does Nietzsche tempt and challenge us to become ourselves the philosophers of the future? Is it *our* task to invent new positive laws?

NOTES

I am very grateful to Julia Maas for having corrected the first draft of this chapter.

1. Natalie Schulte has shown this in *Die Bedeutung des Lachens bei Nietzsche* (BA Thesis, University of Freiburg, 2012).
2. See also NL 1876; KSA 8, 16[45], 294: "Modern monasteries—foundations for such free spirits—something light in our great fortune." [Moderne Klöster—Stiftungen für solche Freigeister—etwas Leichtes bei unsern grossen Vermögen.]
3. See Andreas Urs Sommer, "Nihilism and Skepticism in Nietzsche," in *A Companion to Nietzsche*, ed. Keith Ansell Pearson. (Malden, MA; Oxford; Carlton: Blackwell Publishing, 2006), 250–69.
4. Ludwig Nohl, *Musiker-Biographien. Fünfter Band: Wagner*. (Zweite, vervollständigte Auflage, Leipzig s. d. [ca. 1886]), 95–96.
5. Cf. BGE 35; KSA 5, 54.
6. As one of Nietzsche's sources, see Daniel Schenkel, *Das Charakterbild Jesu. Ein biblischer Versuch*, (Dritte Auflage, Wiesbaden 1864), 22–23: "His [sc. Jesus] inner freedom of mind based on the kingdom of heaven was, however, incompatible with the traditional statutes, the hierarchical institution, the temples, the sacrificial and Sabbath service, and in particular with the future plans of the national Judaism [Sein (sc. Jesu) innerliches, auf Geistesfreiheit begründetes Himmelreich war allerdings mit der überlieferten Satzung, der hierarchischen Anstalt, mit Tempel-, Opfer- und Sabbath-Dienst, insbesondere auch mit den Zukunftsplänen des nationalen Judenthums unverträglich]."
7. Cf. Andreas Urs Sommer, "Nietzsche's Readings on Spinoza. A Contextualist Study, Particularly on the Reception of Kuno Fischer," *Journal of Nietzsche Studies* 43(2) (2012): 156–84.
8. See BGE 42; KSA 5, 59.

BIBLIOGRAPHY

Nietzsche, Friedrich. *Friedrich Nietzsche: Sämtliche Briefe. Kritische Studienausgabe*. Edited by Giorgio Colli and Mazzino Montinari. 8 volumes. Berlin and New York: de Gruyter; 1986.
Nietzsche, Friedrich. *Friedrich Nietzsche: Sämtliche Werke. Kritische Studienausgabe*. Second Edition. 15 volumes. Edited by Giorgio Colli and Mazzino Montinari. Berlin and New York: de Gruyter, 1988.
Nietzsche, Friedrich. *Werke: Kritische Gesamtausgabe*. Edited by Giorgio Colli and Mazzino Montinari. Berlin: Walter de Gruyter, 1967.
Nohl, Ludwig. *Musiker-Biographien. Fünfter Band: Wagner*. Zweite, vervollständigte Auflage, Leipzig s. d. [ca. 1886].
Schenkel, Daniel. *Das Charakterbild Jesu. Ein biblischer Versuch*. Dritte Auflage, Wiesbaden 1864.
Schulte, Natalie. *Die Bedeutung des Lachens bei Nietzsche*. BA Thesis, University of Freiburg, 2012.

Sommer, Andreas Urs. "Nietzsche's Readings on Spinoza. A Contextualist Study, Particularly on the Reception of Kuno Fischer." *Journal of Nietzsche Studies* 43(2) (2012): 156–84.

Sommer, Andreas Urs. "Nihilism and Skepticism in Nietzsche." In *A Companion to Nietzsche.* Edited by Keith Ansell Pearson, 250–69. Malden, MA; Oxford; Carlton: Blackwell Publishing, 2006.

Notes on Contributors

Ruth Abbey is in the Political Science Department and the Kroc Institute for International Peace Studies at the University of Notre Dame. She is the author of *Nietzsche's Middle Period*; *Philosophy Now: Charles Taylor* and *The Return of Feminist Liberalism*. She is the editor of *Contemporary Philosophy in Focus: Charles Taylor* and *Feminist Interpretations of Rawls*. She also has written journal articles and book chapters on issues including contemporary liberalism, conceptions of marriage and animal ethics. She currently is Book Review Editor for *The Review of Politics*.

Christa Davis Acampora is Professor of Philosophy at Hunter College and the Graduate Center of the City University of New York. She is the author of *Contesting Nietzsche* (2013) and co-author and editor of several other books on Nietzsche. Since 2006, she has been the editor of the *Journal of Nietzsche Studies*, and she serves on the board of *Nietzsche-Studien* and several other scholarly organizations.

Keith Ansell-Pearson holds a Personal Chair in Philosophy at the University of Warwick, which he has held since 1998. In 2013–2014 he was Visiting Senior Research Fellow in the Humanities at Rice University. Imminent/ future publications include a co-authored book with Rebecca Bamford entitled *Nietzsche's Dawn* and *Evolution and Ethics: Bergson as Educator*.

Rebecca Bamford is Assistant Professor of Philosophy in the Department of Philosophy and Political Science at Quinnipiac University. Her main research interests lie in nineteenth-century philosophy, ethics, social and political philosophy, and the history and philosophy of science and mind. She is the author of multiple articles and book chapters on Nietzsche's philosophy,

Notes on Contributors

and on problems in contemporary bioethics. Her forthcoming work includes articles on Nietzsche and physician-assisted dying and on Nietzsche's philosophy of science, and a book on Nietzsche's *Dawn* co-authored with Keith Ansell-Pearson.

Paul Bishop is the William Jacks Chair of Modern Languages (German) in the School of Modern Languages and Cultures at the University of Glasgow. His main research interests focus on the history of ideas, especially psychoanalysis and analytical psychology. He has published and edited in these fields, often with reference to Nietzsche. In the future, he plans to work on the German vitalist philosopher, Ludwig Klages, and his school.

Marcus Andreas Born's research focuses on philosophy, literature and questions in their threshold. He published a monograph, editions and several articles on Nietzsche, on whose *Beyond Good and Evil* he researched in the last few years by concentrating on Nietzsche's philosophical writing. His last publications include an edition of stories of Hanns Heinz Ewers ('Lustmord einer Schildkröte und weitere Erzählungen'). In his forthcoming work he addresses the motif of self-referentiality in German post-war radio plays.

Daniel Conway is Professor of Philosophy and Humanities and Affiliate Professor of Religious Studies at Texas A&M University. He has lectured and published widely on topics pertaining to nineteenth-century Philosophy, Social and Political Philosophy, Philosophy and Literature, Philosophy and Film and Philosophy of Religion. He is the author of *Nietzsche's Dangerous Game* (1997), *Nietzsche and the Political* (1997), and *Reader's Guide to Nietzsche's* On the Genealogy of Morals (2008). He is also the editor of the four-volume series *Nietzsche: Critical Assessments of Leading Philosophers* (1998) and the co-editor of *Nietzsche und die antike Philosophie* (1992), *Nietzsche, Philosophy, and the Arts* (1998), and *The History of Continental Philosophy*, Volume II (2010). His current research projects include an interpretation of Kierkegaard's *Fear and Trembling*; a re-appraisal of Nietzsche's teaching of the 'death of God'; an investigation of the conservation of evil; commentaries on Nietzsche's *On the Genealogy of Morality* and *Ecce Homo*; a study of Marx's *18th Brumaire*; a reconsideration of Hannah Arendt's report on the Eichmann trial; and an examination of Rembrandt's depictions of Abraham.

Christine Daigle is Professor of Philosophy and Chancellor's Chair for Research Excellence at Brock University. Her current research focuses on Nietzsche and phenomenology as well as posthumanism and its challenge to subjectivity. She has authored books and articles on various aspects of Nietzsche's, Sartre's and Beauvoir's philosophies. She has also edited and co-edited volumes on existentialist ethics, the question of influence between Beauvoir and Sartre, and Nietzsche and phenomenology. She is authoring the monograph *Nietzsche as Phenomenologist* and is co-editing the book *Posthumanisms Through Deleuze* with Terrance McDonald.

Katia Hay completed a double PhD (*cotutelle*) in Munich (LMU) and Paris (Sorbonne Paris IV) on Schelling and the Tragic in 2008. She is now a postdoc researcher at the University of Lisbon, where she was awarded a six-year grant from the FCT (Fundaçãopara a Ciência e a Tecnologia) for a project on Nietzsche, laughter and language. She has worked mainly on nineteenth-century philosophy, aesthetics and existentialism. She is the author of *Die Notwendigkeit des Scheiterns. Das Tragische als Bestimmung der Philosophie bei Schelling* (2012), and several articles on Schelling and Nietzsche. She is the editor of *Nietzsche, German Idealism and its Critics* (2015).

Duncan Large is Academic Director of the British Centre for Literary Translation at the University of East Anglia. He is the author of *Nietzsche and Proust: A Comparative Study* along with a number of articles on Nietzsche, and has translated editions of Nietzsche's *Twilight of the Idols: How to Philosophize with a Hammer* and *Ecce Homo: How to Become What You Are*. He is also the editor of several volumes: with H. de Berg, *Modern German Thought from Kant to Habermas: An Annotated German-Language Reader*, with Keith Ansell-Pearson, *The Nietzsche Reader*, and with R. Görner, *Ecce Opus: Nietzsche-Revisionen im 20. Jahrhundert*.

Katrina Mitcheson is Senior Lecturer in Philosophy at the University of the West of England. Her main research areas are the history of European philosophy, the ethics of self-cultivation and the philosophy of art. She has published on the philosophy of photography and film, Foucault, and Nietzsche, and is author of *Nietzsche, Truth and Transformation* (2013). She is currently working on the book *Visual Art and Projects of the Self*.

Richard Schacht is Professor of Philosophy and Jubilee Professor of Liberal Arts and Sciences (Emeritus) at the University of Illinois. He has written extensively on Nietzsche and other figures and developments in the post-Kantian interpretive tradition. His interests revolve around the general topic of human reality and issues in social, normative and value theory. His books include *Nietzsche* (1983, in the 'Arguments of the Philosophers' series); *Making Sense of Nietzsche* (1995); *Hegel and After* (1975); *Alienation* (1970); *The Future of Alienation* (1994) and *Finding an Ending: Reflections on Wagner's Ring* (2004, with Philip Kitcher). He is editor of a forthcoming Norton anthology, *After Kant: The Interpretive Tradition* (2015); *Nietzsche:*

Selections (1993); *Nietzsche, Genealogy, Morality* (1994) and *Nietzsche's Postmoralism* (2001).

Herman Siemens is Associate Professor in Modern Philosophy at Leiden University in the Netherlands and is President of the Friedrich Nietzsche Society of Great Britain. He is a chief editor and contributor to the ongoing *Nietzsche Dictionary* project, based at the Radboud University of Nijmegen and Leiden. He has published widely on Nietzsche, including concept-studies and articles on his main areas of interest: art, law, the agon and its political implications. He is co-editor of the 2008 volume *Nietzsche, Power and Politics* and directs a research programme funded by the NWO (Netherlands Organsiation for Scientific Research): *Between Deliberation and Agonism: Rethinking Conflict and Its Relation to Law in Political Philosophy*. Siemens is Adjunct Professor at the Universidad Diego Portales (Chile), and Research Associate of the University of Pretoria (South Africa) and the Universidade de Lisboa (Portugal).

Andreas Urs Sommer is Professor of Philosophy at the University of Freiburg in Germany, and the Headmaster of the 'Nietzsche-Kommentar' at the Heidelberg Academy of Sciences. Among his several books the most recent are: *Kommentar zu Nietzsches 'Der Fall Wagner'. 'Götzen-Dämmerung'* (2012); *Lexikon der imaginären philosophischen Werke* (2012); *Kommentar zu Nietzsches 'Der Antichrist'. 'Ecce homo'. 'Dionysos-Dithyramben'. 'Nietzsche contra Wagner'* (2013) and *Charles-Augustin Sainte-Beuve: Menschen des XVIII. Jahrhunderts* (2014).

Index

Abbey, Ruth, 4, 29n26, 29n27, 30n42, 30n48, 57, 65n35, 65n36, 65n37, 65n38, 70, 80, 81n6, 82n22, 92, 105n17, 105n27, 106n34

Acampora, Christa Davis, 6, 47n32, 47n35, 99, 100, 104n12, 105n26, 106n34, 106n41, 106n46, 106n52, 107n56, 107n57, 107n58, 107n68, 204n8, 249n13

Acampora, Ralph R., 106n46, 204n8, 205n18

aesthetic(s), 4, 5, 7, 24, 50, 69–71, 74, 75, 76, 77, 79, 80, 117, 118, 119, 158, 160, 179, 212–213, 224; judgment, Kant's critique of, 211, 226n22, 226n30; pleasure, 88, 106n44; *der Freigeist* as essentially aesthetic, 224. *See also* art

agonistic, 34, 42, 43, 47n30

alcohol, 215

altruism, 30n44, 54. *See also* selflessness

Ansell-Pearson, Keith, 4, 46n18, 85, 104n7, 105n16, 105n29, 106n50, 107n59, 143, 154n7, 204n17, 205n18

aphorism, 15, 88, 98, 144, 154n10, 157, 159, 161, 164, 166n24

Aristotle, 46n17, 192, 225n14, 226n35

art, 34, 46n21, 69–71, 72, 74, 76, 80, 117, 118, 119, 125, 126, 143, 148, 172, 178, 195, 205n26, 208, 211, 212, 213, 223, 226n33, 234, 258; artist(s), 69, 70, 71, 183, 201, 205n20, 213, 229n82; artistic

wizardry, 258; of the free spirit, 151; of laughter, 119, 126, 129, 132; of living, 50; of psychological observation, 16; of transfiguration, philosophy as, 113. *See also* aesthetic(s)

ascetic ideal, 7, 75, 150, 237–238, 239, 240, 242, 244–245, 246, 247, 248, 263; asceticism, 185, 263

Assassins, 239–241, 242, 243, 244, 247

atheism, 106n38, 122, 211

attachments, 99, 172, 189, 197, 198, 199, 200, 201, 202, 237, 242

bad conscience, 60

Bamford, Rebecca, 64, 106n48, 106n49, 165n1, 204n17, 226n35

beauty, 7, 76, 212, 213, 217, 224, 226n25

becoming, 38, 39, 42, 43, 46n17, 46n20, 81, 103, 116, 117, 148, 171, 190, 196, 202, 243, 255, 258, 262

Berry, Jessica N., 85, 104n1, 104n2, 104n3, 104n4, 104n5

Bible, 222

Bishop, Paul, 7, 64n4, 107n68

Brandes, Georg, 259

Brobjer, Thomas, 29n10, 29n12, 64n6, 64n7, 65n44, 105n33, 228n63, 228n66

Berkowitz, Peter, 140, 154n3

body, 35, 36, 37, 38, 41, 53, 63, 75, 76, 93, 94, 112, 113, 114, 154n8, 161, 192, 213, 214–215, 215, 216, 217, 218, 261